School-Based
Play Therapy

School-Based Play Therapy

Edited by
Athena A. Drewes
Lois J. Carey
Charles E. Schaefer

John Wiley & Sons, Inc.

New York • Chichester • Weinheim • Brisbane • Singapore • Toronto

Library of Congress Cataloging-in-Publication Data:

School-based play therapy / edited by Athena Drewes, Lois Carey, and Charles Schaefer.
    p.   cm.
   Includes bibliographical references.
   ISBN 0-471-39402-5 (cloth : alk. paper)
   1. School psychology—United States.   2. Play therapy—United States.
I. Drewes, Athena A., 1948–   II. Carey, Lois J.   III. Schaefer, Charles E.
LB1027.55 .S34 2001
155.4'18—dc21

                                          00-067455

Printed in the United States of America.

10 9 8 7 6 5 4 3 2 1

"A hundred years from now it will not matter what my bank account was, the sort of house I lived in, or the kind of car I drove, but the world may be different because I was important in the life of a child."

Forest Witcraft

This book is dedicated to all of our families:

To my husband James Richard Bridges and sons
Scott Richard Drewes Bridges and Seth Andrew Bridges

About the Authors

Athena A. Drewes, PsyD, has been the motivating force for this book, which has grown directly out of her past work as a school psychologist and play therapist in special education preschool and public elementary school settings, and currently in a residential treatment center, and as an Adjunct Professor teaching play therapy to undergraduates and graduate education students at Mount St. Mary College. She is also the founder/coordinator of the Play Therapy Institute at Mount St. Mary College in Newburgh, New York. Her credits also include being the founder and past president of the New York branch of the Association for Play Therapy, author of articles and chapters on play therapy, workshop presenter throughout New York and at conferences, and Membership committee sub-chair for the national Association for Play Therapy. As a Registered Play Therapist and Supervisor, she has supervised numerous trainees and professionals, many of whom she has helped to become Registered Play Therapists.

Lois J. Carey, MSW, CSW, was invited to coedit this volume based on her many years of experience training play therapists to use Sandplay, as well as her early experience working as an elementary school secretary. A high percentage of her Sandplay trainees have been employed in schools and have implemented Sandplay in their settings. She has also given workshops at Mount St. Mary's Play Therapy Institute as well as at numerous play therapy conferences throughout the country and abroad. She is a Registered Play Therapist and Supervisor through the Association for Play Therapy and is the current president of the New York branch of APT. She continues to be active in private practice as well. She has authored *Sandplay Therapy with Children and Families* and coedited *Family Play Therapy* with Charles Schaefer, both volumes published by Jason Aronson.

Charles E. Schaefer, PhD, has been a major force behind the growth of play therapy practice in this country. He is cofounder and board member emeritus of the Association for Play Therapy, founder of the Play Therapy Training Institute in New Jersey, director of the Institute of Playology, and author/editor of numerous books in the field, including *Handbook of Play Therapy*, volumes 1 and 2, *Short-Term Play Therapy, The Playing Cure, Game Play,* and *Play Diagnosis and Assessment.* Dr. Schaefer is Professor of Psychology at Fairleigh Dickinson University in New Jersey.

Contributors

W. Barry Chaloner, MEd
Licensed Professional
  Counselor/School Counselor,
  and Pre-K-2 Early Intervention
  Consultant
Barry Chaloner, MEd and
  Associates
Durango, Colorado

David A. Crenshaw, PhD, ABPP
Clinical Director, Residential
  Programs
The Astor Home for Children
Rhinebeck, New York

Athena A. Drewes, PsyD, RPT-S
Senior Psychologist/Clinical
  Coordinator
The Astor Home for Children
Rhinebeck, New York
Adjunct Professor
Mount St. Mary College
Newburgh, New York

James G. Emshoff, PhD
Associate Professor of Psychology
Georgia State University
Atlanta, Georgia

Marijane Fall, EdD
Associate Professor
University of Southern Maine
Gorham, Maryland

Barbara A. Fischetti, DEd, RPT
Coordinator of Psychological
  Services and School
  Psychologist
Westport Public Schools
Bethel, Connecticut

Christine Foreacre, MS
Clinical Coordinator, Residential
  Programs
The Astor Home for Children
Rhinebeck, New York

**Ruthellen Griffin, MEd, MA,
ADTR**
Friends of Hospice, Litchfield and
  New Milford
Visiting Nursing Association, New
  Milford
Visiting Nurses Services of
  Connecticut, Torrington
West Cornwall, Connecticut

Tara M. Hall, MA
School of Psychology
Fairleigh Dickinson
    University
Teaneck, New Jersey

A. Dirk Hightower, PhD
Children's Institute
Rochester, New York

Laura L. Jacobus
Graduate Student in Psychology
    Department
Georgia State University
Atlanta, Georgia

Theresa Kestly, PhD
Director, Program Development
    and Training
Sand Tray Training Institute of
    New Mexico
Corrales, New Mexico

Patti J. Knoblauch, PhD
Warwick, New York

Maxine Lynn, PhD
Director of Academic Affairs
Adelphi University
School of Social Work
Garden City, New York

Doris M. Martin
James Madison University
School of Education
Harrisonburg, Virginia

Danielle Nisivoccia, DSW
Research Associate and Adjunct
    Associate Professor
Fordham University
Graduate School of Social Service
Center for Hispanic Mental Health
    Research
New York, New York

Anthony J. Pabon, CSWR
Rockland Children's Psychiatric
    Center
Orangeburg, New York

Phyllis Post, PhD
University of North Carolina at
    Charlotte
Department of Counseling, Special
    Education, and Child
    Development
Charlotte, North Carolina

Linda A. Reddy, PhD
Assistant Professor and Director of
    the Child and Adolescent
    ADHD Clinic
School of Psychology
Fairleigh Dickinson University
Teaneck, New Jersey

Cynthia Reynolds, PhD
Assistant Professor
University of Akron
Akron, Ohio

Elizabeth Rubel, MA
School of Psychology
Fairleigh Dickinson University
Teaneck, New Jersey

Mary May Schmidt, MS, MA
National Certified Counselor
Registered Play Therapist
School Psychologist
Tri-Valley Elementary School
Graham, New York

Priscilla Spencer, PhD
School of Psychology
Fairleigh Dickinson University
Teaneck, New Jersey

Carol Stanley, MEd
School Counselor
Woodridge Primary School
Cuyahoga Falls, Ohio

Alison Van Dyk, MA, RPT
Private Practice
Greenwich, Connecticut

Donald Wiedis, PhD, ABPP
Private Practice
New York, New York

Nancy Wohl, CSW, RPT-S
North Tonawanda City School
    District
North Tonawanda, New York

Preface

WITH THE growth of play therapy as a respected modality, many school counselors, psychologists, teachers, and social workers have been searching for techniques that could be incorporated into their school settings. They have been avid attendees at play therapy conferences in recent years where they seek the latest information to help them develop their own creative approaches to the very valuable work they perform. This volume is the editors' contribution to help meet their needs. Two of the criteria that we looked for in choosing these authors were that they were actively employed in a school setting and that play therapy was a hallmark of their work.

A wide variety of authors/practitioners use various techniques in their work with children from preschool through elementary school years, the ages that are most conducive to the use of play materials. The authors in this book are found in preschools and public, private, and residential schools and have broad experience with the age groups that they serve. The chapters in Parts One and Two describe child-centered play therapy, Theraplay, and assessment techniques that use play, sandplay, art exercises, and so on. Chapters in Part Three discuss working with individual children, and those in Part Four focus on work with specialized groups, such as children needing crisis intervention, children from alcoholic homes, bereaved children, children needing anger management, and children with ADHD. Part Five is devoted to exploring new uses for play therapy as well as preventive and developmental issues. All chapters are meant to be applicable to the school or classroom setting. There are clear descriptions of each approach with suggestions as to how they might be implemented. Several chapters discuss some of the problems and difficulties in engaging other staff members and administration to accept play therapy as a valid milieu; all of these authors have managed to accomplish this.

ATHENA A. DREWES
LOIS J. CAREY
CHARLES E. SCHAEFER

Contents

PART FOUR GROUP PLAY THERAPY AND
SPECIAL POPULATIONS

PART FIVE ISSUES AND INNOVATIONS

PART ONE

SCHOOL-BASED PLAY ASSESSMENT

CHAPTER 1

Using Play Therapy Assessment in an Elementary and Intermediate School Setting

MARY MAY SCHMIDT

SCHOOL-BASED ASSESSMENT, whether time-limited for a specific purpose or ongoing, is an inescapable feature of education. Assessment occurs daily in the classroom as children work through the curriculum. Teachers monitor growth using multidimensional curriculum tools such as Rubrics to measure acquisition of readiness skills and, then, the academic skills themselves. When learning is not occurring at the rate hoped for, staff teams, often called child study teams, meet to suggest and design individualized remediation models. Sometimes, the interference with learning is related to social-emotional-behavioral problems of the target child, the child in the classroom setting, and/or the child in the family, but the tools of play therapy can be more informative than those of just social-emotional adjustment. The principles and techniques of play assessment are widely applicable and developmentally appropriate to use to observe this child in the elementary classroom or on the playground. Play assessment can assist the child study team in developing recommendations for remediation, or for more formal processes such as developing a functional behavioral assessment and a behavior intervention plan, a school intervention plan (now called Academic Intervention Services), a Section 504 plan, or for developing a Committee on Special Education (CSE) individualized education plan. The focus of this chapter is on using a play assessment process for the CSE because these evaluations are the most comprehensive of the school-based assessments. Later, the chapter addresses some ongoing assessment issues.

EVALUATIONS

An evaluation through the CSE is multifaceted. It includes ability measures, achievement measures, a review of the child's academic history, information about the child's health and physical development, a social history interview with the parents, other evaluations as related to the referring question or expanded evaluations raised by observations during testing, a classroom observation, and an assessment of the child's social and emotional functioning. Play can be used as a primary source of information in two areas of the CSE evaluation: the classroom observation and the social-emotional assessment. Play also can provide insight into how the child applies native abilities from a developmental point of view.

The team approach is important from the play assessor's point of view (this may be a school counselor or school psychologist) because the play assessor can get feedback from and make recommendations to involved staff and parents, which puts these adults in the roles of cotherapists. As a result, these adults feel supported and willing to try something new. For example, a simple system-level intervention might be to reconceptualize the behavior of a child who is "testing the waters." Rather than the behavior's being a challenge to the educator's or parent's authority, the behavior may actually be functioning as a means of finding out what is constant from an object relations point of view. Such a reconceptualization views the child's behavior as trying to connect with what is dependable rather than as trying to challenge and disconnect from what is antagonistic to the child's felt needs.

FORMAL ASSESSMENT

Public schools are obligated to provide a free and appropriate education to all children. When parents and teachers have been steadily communicating about a child's strengths and weaknesses, there should be no surprise when the issue of assessment is raised. Sometimes, there is resistance to assessment, particularly social-emotional assessment, which may make parents feel insecure in their parenting. Assessment, then, needs to be as comprehensive as possible, working to identify the presenting problem, the salient problem, the plan or method, and the measurement criteria. Formal assessment implies a time-limited task. Play therapy itself is process-oriented and assessment within the therapy is ongoing. Both must be developmentally appropriate.

Formal and Informal Observations of Play in Naturalistic Settings

Sometimes I go into a classroom or go out to the playground with no particular agenda but to observe play. This refreshes my skills in distinguishing between normal and at-risk children, and I become a familiar and approachable person in the classroom landscape. At a later time in the school year, I may need to target a child in that classroom. If so, I want all the children to behave within typical patterns and not put on party manners for the unknown adult in the room.

I tend to use a combination of play observations in naturalistic settings (classroom and playground): formal schedules, informal multiple-observer type, and informal single-observer type. For formal observations, I sometimes refer to an exhaustive compilation of play diagnostics titled *Play Diagnosis and Assessment* (Schaefer, Gitlin, & Sandgrund, 1991). When parents deny that their child has social-emotional needs, a formal schedule is used because of its research base and objectivity.

Also highly persuasive is the use of multiple observers who have documented behaviors over a relatively long period of time. Multiple observers might include the classroom teacher, a remedial teacher, a speech therapist, and any other professional staff member who works with the child. The single observation is limited in its usefulness because it tends to be a "slice of life" that may not be representative of the total range of behavior to be observed.

Observations of play in naturalistic settings focus on how the child interacts with the environment and things in the environment, with other children (same age, younger or older; same or different gender), and with adults in the environment. Broad-spectrum questions to keep in mind include the following: How intense is the play? Is there repetition compulsion? Is play focused around a theme or is it random or listless? How much confidence and mastery is exhibited? Is the child tentative and observing? Does the child seek eye contact with any particular person for acknowledgment, approval, or permission? What affect dominates the play? How interactive is the play?

Developmental Factors

The developmental perspective cannot be ignored when observing a child, particularly for the purposes of assessment. The observation should be able to comment on five areas of development: cognitive, language, self-control/regulation, relationships, and self-concept/emotions.

Cognitive Skills

Young school-age children (ages 4 to 6, kindergarten and first grade) lack the cognitive ability to distinguish between thoughts and actions. Repetition of a thought may create a memory or an intention that has no truth but that confuses, even terrifies, the child. To complicate the problem, the child may not be able to express or modulate his or her reactions. The child may not be able to distinguish that personal needs (social, emotional, and physical) are separate from those of the family's or of the play group to which the child temporarily belongs. For example, the observer might note that the child developed a game involving others but only partly explained the rules. As the game proceeds, a second child does something "wrong" and is criticized harshly. The child who invented the game did not distinguish between thoughts and verbal explanation; the child assumed that the other child thought as he or she thought and understood as he or she understood. The resulting confusion and anger may end the game and negatively impact the potential or intention for future play with that other child. These younger children think simplistically and concretely. They are not expected to be able to plan out a whole game, but to get it started. Categorizing toys is likely to be controlled by a single criterion such as size, color, or type. Similarly, linear thinking, hierarchical thinking, and cause and effect will also be simple and concrete.

Older children (ages 7 to 10, grades 2 through 5) will exhibit more complex schemata in their play, and their games are likely to be planned out to some degree of agreed-upon ending. They will use multiple criteria in their thinking and shift their organization consciously when the original game plan isn't working.

Language Skills

The language skills of children ages 4 to 6 or 7 to 10 are closely tied to their cognitive development. Younger children use concrete vocabulary and simple sentence structures and are fascinated with prereading language skills such as rhyming words and rhythmic patterns. Pointing and touch counting can amplify their play intentions when vocabulary isn't developed enough to meet the play's need. Candyland is a popular game with small children because they can master its cognitive and language demands. Older children are able to be more flexible in their use of language. They can understand the concept of multiple meanings, use some of the tools of supralinguistics (inference, irony, and figurative language), and integrate language more fluidly. They might integrate a variety of levels of play such as the physical rhythm of many children chanting rhymes or songs while playing an elimination competition of jump rope, hopscotch, or Mother May I? The play observer should note the language content and structure of the child being observed: Is the language similar to or different from the other children in this play group, or have these children gravitated toward each other because their ability to communicate and get along is equal but their ages or genders are dissimilar? If there are other play groups of the same membership nearby, is the child in the observed group the same as or different from the children in the second group?

Sometimes, a child's language seems to exceed expectations based on age and on what is known about cognitive ability. Such a child may be parroting the prose of adults and appear to have advanced language skills but actually have only masked weak skills. The observer should listen for quality of content, not quantity. Some speech and language therapists call this phenomenon "cocktail chatter."

Self-Control

Another area to be observed in the assessment process is the child's ability to exercise self-control. For younger children, self-control may be achieved by discovering the behaviors that please adults and performing those behaviors. Smiling and using good manners receive adult approval and reinforce behaviors that conform to expectations for self-control. Self-control is not a given for a child with no preschool experience who now enters kindergarten, or for a child with a brittle temperament. Internalized self-control seen in older children requires patience for successive approximations, the ability to tolerate mistakes in oneself and in others, and the ability to detach and observe the self. These complex skills are life-long learning skills that older children are developing but have rarely mastered. Children are aided in acquiring these skills by the structures of the environment: classroom routines, teacher intervention, limited resources in the environment that require sharing and turn taking, and so on. The observer looks for ways that the child demonstrates social problem-solving skills: Does the child share, take turns, negotiate a win-win situation, set personal goals, and act assertively when being bullied? Is the child careful in choosing words? Is the child intrusive, egocentric, and quick to throw a tantrum? Is the child fearful and insecure in his or her abilities to self-regulate? If so, the child may be the bully or may retreat into solitude. Either role would protect the child from being discovered.

Relationships

Related to issues of self-control are the issues of relationships. Children in both elementary and intermediate grades tend to gravitate toward children of the same gender. Children of the same gender are a mirror and a measuring stick for self-concept. Children form friendships and experiment with likes and dislikes. Their personalities expand with a growing sense of humor and wider interests. Younger children may identify a few friends, some absolute likes and dislikes, or a magnanimous love of all living things. Older children identify loyalties to best friends and begin to differentiate among friends based on common interests. Some friendships may be tied to settings or activities such as Little League or Cub Scouts. The observer will need to identify at least the important relationships that a child has. Are the relationships two-way and equally respectful relationships, or is there a greater need/dependency felt by one of the children in the relationship? If so, what is the role of the target child? Does the target child repeat a pattern in other relationships? What if the child gravitates toward relationships with children of the opposite gender or of another age group or of another qualifier? If these differences exclude other relationships, the observer would need to generate a hypothesis about the link. Perhaps the child is attracted to children of similar cognitive or language abilities, similar abilities to self-regulate, or similar levels of self-concept. Precocious attractions to friends of the opposite gender may reflect a familial dynamic for which the friendship is intended to compensate.

During the social history phase of the CSE evaluation, parents can provide information on the social functioning of the child within the family and within the community. If the child's social functioning is deteriorated in one or more of the three primary environments—home, school, or community—the interview needs to discern possible triggers and interventions parents have identified as successful.

Self-Concept and Emotion

Finally, the observer must consider issues of self-concept and of emotion. Self-concept and emotional development for younger and older children are intimately tied to self-control and self-regulation. Younger children depend more on externally imposed controls; older children are learning to internalize those controls and experiment with their own. When a child gains control over strong and frightening impulses, he or she gains in self-esteem. A child with a healthy self-concept is able to risk, to initiate, to have considered opinions, to enjoy the company of others, to take in alternative points of view, to laugh at himself or herself, to expect to be respected, to use appropriate means to express negative emotion, and so on. Such a child is able to identify a self-regulated state as a happy one. Does the child being observed have these qualities?

Observations in naturalistic settings should address all five of these areas for young children and older children. Each of the areas interacts dynamically with the others, and, to complicate the observation for evaluation, the naturalistic setting, whether it is the classroom or the playground, changes rapidly. Different chunks of time during the observation may involve a different constellation of actors within the observation, thus affecting dynamics but enriching the total observation.

USE OF RECORDS

Another source of observations coming out of naturalistic settings is discipline records. Discipline records presuppose that behaviors are negative. Most children do not behave so far from expectations that they have discipline records. But, when such records exist, it is appropriate to include discipline reports as part of the multiple-observer method of gathering information. An analysis of these records hopes to quantify and qualify answers to these questions: What is the behavior? What are the triggers? Are triggers related to the time of day or to the degree of structure and adult supervision? Is behavior recent and time-limited, or is behavior cyclical or over long periods of time? What function does the behavior serve for the child? The benefit of these records is that they broaden the scope of multiple observers. There is also a problem with weighting discipline records. The degree of objectivity in the record is an unknown; often, they are written in the heat of the moment, when the staff member or bus driver expects behavioral conformity (a behavioral product) rather than teaching in a child-centered way to achieve internalized behaviors (a behavior process). On the other hand, discipline records do help to establish a longitudinal scope and clues to possible interventions.

FORMAL AND INFORMAL OBSERVATIONS OF PLAY IN THE PLAYROOM

Observations of play in the playroom are more controlled than in the classroom or on the playground. These sessions are individual as opposed to whole group and combine directive (formal) and nondirective (informal) play. In the playroom, the same developmental considerations apply as in naturalistic settings. When play is nondirective, the therapist can trust that the child will gravitate toward materials that are developmentally appropriate to express the needs of the child. When play is directive, the play therapist must choose developmentally appropriate materials, and the materials themselves are likely to have structure, such as games.

Here, choices as to whether to use both directive and nondirective play or which to choose as a starting point depends on what you already know or hypothesize about the child. Generally, I allow the child to explore the playroom first; there are games, toys, art supplies, and a sand tray with a generous supply of miniatures.

Some children can initiate their own play; others are tentative and seek some direction. Some children invite the play therapist to join in, and some do not. When play is nondirective and the therapist is not invited to join the child, the therapist must be especially careful about arriving at any hypothesis too soon. The relationship between the child and the therapist is just beginning, and trust has not been established. Multiple observations over time increase the probability of accurate assessment, whereas initial play may be guarded and stereotypical or may be testing the therapist and the setting. Drawing any hypothesis based on one nondirective play observation risks too many confounds. But, for CSE evaluations, time is an important factor, as there are established time limits for the CSE process. It may not be possible to use a nondirective approach. Competing with time constraints, it has also been my experience that children with deeper needs who are not willing or able to directly verbalize those needs are drawn to nondirective materials in the playroom, especially the sand tray.

Children do not need much introduction to sandplay. They take to it quite naturally because of its familiarity, and this tool provides projective material at least as rich as projective drawing techniques, which require the directive to draw. (The same child might be somewhat guarded if asked to draw a house, a tree, and a person; the context would seem artificial.)

I recently used the sand tray technique with a 6-year-old girl who was caught between angry parents in a four-year-long custody battle. Both her needs and her distrust were great. Her first attempt in the sand was a single line of animals, domesticated and wild, all facing her from the back of the sand tray. The animals were not perfectly divided by type, but the effort to do so was clear. Something about the lineup did not please her, so she scooped them all up and buried them in a common grave, brushed off her hands, and stomped out. Subsequent sand trays also included burying and unburying, with a general lack of organizing principles and a final common grave. As she became more trusting, she added subvocalizations that indicated her frustration and disgust and, finally, vocalizations of her confusion and distrust. During this period, to test my sincerity with her, she asked me to engage in a guessing game about which animal was buried or where. She always controlled the length of time she was willing to stay in my office and I allowed her that control.

Directive play in assessment often includes the use of games that have rules to follow or the use of projectives with game-like attributes. A popular nontherapeutic game such as Connect Four is useful in assessing a child's ability to plan, anticipate, learn from experience, handle frustration, mediate social anxiety through the practice of game-controlled interaction, and so on. I sometimes end a testing session with a few rounds of Connect Four. The child feels rewarded for good effort, and I get to see how the child applies his or her abilities across the developmental schemata.

Play dovetails very nicely with formal social-emotional assessment tools, especially in poverty of expression versus richness of expression, themes, and developmentally appropriate tasks. The Story Telling Card Game, a game developed by Dr. Richard Gardner (1988), is similar to the Children's Thematic Apperception Test. The game-like qualities include a spinner that lands on a space that asks the child to choose a setting card from a list of three, dice that indicate the number of people that can be chosen for the story, and chips that can be lost or accumulated.

Several years ago, I used this game to assess an 8-year-old boy whom I thought I knew quite well but who often surprised me. By the time of his CSE evaluation, he had alienated every child in his class, had pressured speech with a great deal of interesting content, behaved impulsively and sometimes angrily, but sometimes had satisfying conversations with adults and clearly sought that attention. Self-concept scales did not show at-risk or significant perceptions about himself. Ability and achievement testing showed him to be above average, but formal testing could not have tapped the creativity that I was about to observe. We had played several rounds of the Story Telling Game when he selected a setting card picturing a stage. He rolled a high number on the dice, but he negotiated the chance to use all the people in the game. He put all of the children on the stage and all of the adults in the audience. He said that "this was a National Geographic Special Performance at the famous Ford Theater." Then he spontaneously created and acted out a song and dance number. Not only had he integrated high levels of all the developmental issues, but he also intimated the seriousness of adults failing to pay attention to children. "President Lincoln was shot at the Ford Theater," he said at the end.

For the most part, play therapy observations dovetail very nicely with formal projective tools and self-concept rating scales used as part of the holistic evaluation for the CSE. In the above example, play surpassed those instruments in getting to the heart of this child's need.

ONGOING ASSESSMENT

About eight years ago, I developed a checklist (see Figure 1.1) of desired behaviors (constructs) to help me track the themes that the children within a group were processing at any given time in the school year. The checklist spanned cognitive, behavioral, and emotional constructs. I checked off constructs as they were incorporated into each session. For instance, did we focus on social problem solving? The accompanying notes would address who initiated the topic, what comments were made and by whom. The checklist helped flesh out my notes, enabling me to focus more on dynamics within the group and on individual development than on topics raised spontaneously by the children. At the end of the year, each child was given a blank checklist and asked to check off each topic/behavior that they recalled addressing in counseling during the year, and check each one again if they tried to practice that behavior outside counseling. One year, a highly involved boy reviewed the list and said, "Mrs. Schmidt, you don't have anything about alcohol and drug abuse. We talked about that a lot." From then on, that boy's suggestion has appeared on the checklist, giving him parenthetical credit.

I compiled the student data collected from this checklist for three consecutive years. Granted, a posttest-only design given to children struggling with a host of developmental issues has more confounds than can be counted, but it is important to note that all constructs, measured in percentiles, grew consistently in years two and three as compared to the baseline year and the previous year. In other words, children reported greater and greater awareness of their own self-concept as measured by the cognitive, behavioral, and emotional constructs on the checklist, both in their self-concept in the group and in their efforts to generalize those constructs outside the group. If program success can be measured from the child's point of view, this technique has given me some important insights.

CRITERIA FOR DETERMINING INDIVIDUAL OR GROUP TREATMENT

Once the formal assessment is completed and goals are identified, how will treatment be expressed? Most children have social and emotional needs that are best served in a group setting. The group functions as a microcosm of family and social relationships. As group cohesion increases, children can safely experiment with social skills that they then take back with them into the settings where problems had originated and into new settings, too.

Check all that apply to *you.*

Place a second check next to the skills you tried outside group.

This year, I learned about

- ❏ ❏ Controlling stress.
- ❏ ❏ Taking turns.
- ❏ ❏ Finding someone to help me.
- ❏ ❏ Apologizing.
- ❏ ❏ Being responsible for my words and actions.
- ❏ ❏ Making the best possible choices.
- ❏ ❏ Helping friends do the right thing.
- ❏ ❏ Listening.
- ❏ ❏ Finding more than one way to look at and solve a problem.
- ❏ ❏ Staying out of my parents' problems.
- ❏ ❏ Cooperating.
- ❏ ❏ Not giving up.
- ❏ ❏ Saying comforting things to a sad friend.
- ❏ ❏ Being loyal.
- ❏ ❏ Trying something new.
- ❏ ❏ Good sportsmanship.
- ❏ ❏ Drug and alcohol education (Thor's contribution*).

This year, I feel

- ❏ More trust.
- ❏ Better about myself.
- ❏ Less lonely.
- ❏ Respected by my group members.
- ❏ Less hurt by teasing.
- ❏ More patient.
- ❏ Capable.
- ❏ Less afraid.
- ❏ More tolerant of people I don't like.

I can name _____ different feelings and emotions.

My group was (too big, too small, just right) for me.

---

*Written parental consent received to use this student's name.

Figure 1.1   Student Evaluation of Counseling.

Groups are organized around my philosophy that elementary-age children need to develop friendships with others of the same age and gender. Age and gender are important aspects of self-concept. In addition, from a child's point of view, most problems "feel" about the same: lonely, sad, confusing, and the like. From a feeling perspective, empathy is learned, practiced, and valued as a means of understanding the self and others. Many diverse counseling goals across group members can be reached through such mutual understanding.

The difficult aspects of working with a group are the speed at which children interact and alter their relationships and their beliefs. For each child and for each dyad in the group, the multidimensional developmental model needs to be tracked. The checklist helps make tracking more efficient. For example, in a kindergarten boys group, I have used a game that emphasizes social problem-solving skills. I give the player one chip for each solution to a problem. When that player has exhausted his repertoire, I give other players a chance to make suggestions that have not yet been given, and they too can earn chips. This particular group consisted of a boy with Attention-Deficit/Hyperactivity Disorder (ADHD) and at least average ability and many socioeconomic advantages, a developmentally delayed boy, and an angry boy with probably average ability. The angry boy could generate a single and passive solution: "Tell a grown-up." The boy with ADHD could also generate only simple solutions to social problems. The developmentally delayed boy did an excellent job generating solutions that he could initiate. This example illustrates the need to be sensitive to all developmental factors because all aspects of development are not necessarily evenly developed within a given child. In this case, each boy became aware of a shift in each other's status. An equalizing effect had taken place. Subsequent sessions with this group showed increased camaraderie and increased tolerance for frustration.

When individual counseling is appropriate, it may be a precursor to readying a child to join an established group or to support a child who has needs beyond the scope of the group. A multiply traumatized child would need individual counseling as an adjunct to group counseling or as a sole service. The child always chooses the mode of expression: directive play, nondirective play, with or without talk therapy.

CORRECTIVE EMOTIONAL EXPERIENCES

Corrective emotional experiences are experiences that work to undo wounding and build self-concept. They are immediately recognized by the child, who flushes with pleasure. Because of the immediacy of the experience, the insight need not be overanalyzed, only acknowledged (perhaps by a shared smile) and referenced in the notes. Over the course of a school year, the experiences for that child may require repetition and/or stepwise growth.

Moral development, which depends on emotional development, and emotional competencies, like any other developmental competency, may be delayed due to intrusive and traumatic events or repeated events that distort a child's worldview. If a child's sense of security and attachment are disrupted, the child's ability to trust in the self will be affected and thus, so will his or her ability to trust others, develop social relationships, and so on. In addition, medical problems such as ADHD can interfere with emotional development because the child is unable to tune into the verbal and nonverbal cues of communication. More than any other aspect of a child's educational program, play therapy must be especially sensitive to this developmental need. Assessment and programming for emotional development lay the foundation for moral development.

SUMMARY

Play is tightly tied to developmental theories for assessment and to the projective hypothesis for insight and applied to the uniqueness of the child. It is a very effective modality for time-limited assessment and for ongoing or process-oriented assessment for individuals and groups. It fits very naturally into the school setting. The corrective emotional experiences that are born of the process help children learn to accept and tolerate each other's differences, recognize the universality of their own experiences, develop friendships, manage stress, and prepare for life. These are experiences of guided hope expressed in laughter.

REFERENCES

Gardner, R. (1988). *The story telling card game.* Cresskill, NJ: Creative Therapeutics.
Schaefer, C., Gitlin, K., & Sandgrund, A. (1991). *Play diagnosis and assessment.* New York: Wiley.

GAME SOURCES

Childswork Childsplay, 135 Dupont Street, P. O. Box 760, Plainview, NY 11803-0760, 800-962-1141, www.childswork.com.
WPS Creative Therapy Store, 12031 Wilshire Boulevard, Los Angeles, CA 90025-1251, 800-648-8857.

CHAPTER 2

Sandplay and Assessment Techniques with Preschool-Age Children

ALISON VAN DYK and DONALD WIEDIS

EMOTIONAL PROBLEMS begin early in life and can seriously affect a preschool child's learning and adjustment to school. They can continue to lower a child's performance benefit from and enjoyment of school as long as they remain untreated; thus, an entire school career can be affected. Each child has innate gifts, but if the emotional problems are not treated, the child's potential is at risk.

For many decades, the literature has demonstrated that children's emotional problems can be successfully treated and that this improves the child's ability to learn. It makes sense then that the earlier children receive treatment, the sooner their potential can be applied to the task of learning. Most child therapy takes place in clinical settings. More recently, it has been demonstrated that therapy also can take place in school, providing the additional advantage of the participation of teachers, administrators, parents, and therapists to coordinate a more comprehensive and broad-based approach to treating emotional problems. However, treatment of preschool-age children presents a particular challenge for therapeutic intervention. Because children at this age do not have the ability to express themselves easily in words, very specific techniques need to be used to learn the nature of any problem that is disturbing them. A 3- or 4-year-old is unlikely to be aware of a problem such as "I feel unwanted" or "I feel that I am bad." Nor are these children able to ask for help. The basic survival instinct that young children are born with prevents them from cognitively registering such fears as annihilation or abandonment. Instead, these fears are felt viscerally and are expressed somatically through such behaviors as bed-wetting, stomachaches, and so on. How can we understand the 3- to 4-year-old's difficulties with the means that the child has to communicate?

Sandplay is particularly revealing with this age group. Play is the natural medium of the child. Young children use play for a variety of skill-building purposes. Through play, children practice mastery, express feelings, and learn new ways of doing things; they explore the solutions to various fears and aspirations they have; they use drama and toys to try out new roles and how safe or unsafe they are. In addition, psychological testing is useful in understanding the content of the child's mental processes. By diagnosing the emotional problems and using treatment approaches to help the child overcome his or her psychological difficulties in the school setting, we hope to avert the continued interference of problems later on. This chapter describes the assessment and treatment approaches that have been successful in ameliorating the emotional problems that interfered with children's academic and social adjustment in a parochial preschool program in the South Bronx.

The population of this school is 85% Hispanic, 18% African American, and 2% other. The grades range from prekindergarten to eighth. For the past 10 years, the preschool program has featured a sandplay therapy component, which addresses the emotional needs of 20 to 25 students. This is a mainstream preschool, not a therapeutic nursery school. The preschool teacher selects students that are in the normal range for IQ, developmental level, and emotional difficulties. Thus, students who have more serious issues are referred to special programs in other schools.

In this model, the play therapist spends the first two weeks of school in the classroom observing the children and getting acquainted with them. In this way, the therapist is involved with the children from the first day of school, helps them adjust to the class, and spends time with the ones who are having separation problems. She consults with the teacher on ways to handle individual children and advises the parents as well. Parents fill out a questionnaire about their child and the therapist goes over this material with the parent, who stays with the child in the first week. Thus, she is able to gain a good picture of each child's developmental history, family background, and any problems the child might be having at home.

The teacher and the therapist meet to compare their observations of each child to determine who may need extra help to adjust to school life.

They assess those children who have unusual difficulty in separating, playing with other children, and relating to and trusting adults. Can the child deal with normal frustrations without falling apart? Does he or she fear taking part in circle time or spontaneous play activities? Does the child exhibit depression, aimlessness, inability to concentrate, or excessive crying? Teacher and therapist discuss the developmental history of each child to determine if unusual circumstances, such as divorce, death, illness, parental pathology, alcohol, drugs, or incarceration, have interfered with normal healthy development. Some children are not affected by these events; others can be deeply traumatized. Therapy is provided to correct the emotional damage so that it will not interfere with the child's success in learning.

NONVERBAL TESTING

To better detect and understand these problems, we have developed a battery of nonverbal tests that are useful in giving an accurate picture of the child's inner world, strengths and weaknesses, and problem areas that have delayed or inhibited emotional growth and impeded learning. Permission has been granted by the parents or guardians to test their child and provide therapy if needed. The school's policy is to address the emotional needs of the preschool-age child and help him or her at this early stage of development to move beyond a problem to foster learning success and classroom adjustment.

The first assessment tool, the Levy-Wiedis Animal Drawing Story test (LADS; Hammer, 1980) is given to the children in the classroom to reduce the stress of the child's being taken away from a familiar setting. The therapist asks the children to draw an animal, any animal they wish. The therapist then asks a series of 34 questions about the animal; the questions are chosen to obtain information about the child's self-concept (e.g., a tiger, a lamb, and a pig each has a different connotation). These answers and the drawing give the therapist information on each child's perception of family relationships (Does the child feel liked or not?); fears, concerns, and aspirations; hidden wishes or hopes; competencies (What is the child proud of? What can the child do? etc.); ability to perform in class; ability to empathize, compete; degree of separation and independence; curiosity; how the child deals with anger; degree of security versus level of anxiety; self-confidence; degree of guilt, self-blame, depression, ego strength; mood swings and preoccupations.

The second test, the Lowenfeld Mosaic Test (LMT; Lowenfeld, 1954), is a box of 456 plastic tiles and a shallow tray with paper on which the child is asked to make a picture. The instructions include showing the child each of the five shapes and six colors. As part of the introduction, the therapist shows the child the mathematical relationship of the shapes and the natural progression to larger shapes that can be constructed (large square, large triangle, etc.). The children are timed and asked to tell the therapist when they are done. Then the therapist asks the child to tell a story about the picture. The information obtained from this test includes the child's reaction to a new task; ability to perform versus insecurity; developmental level; degree of pride in accomplishment; level of anger, depression, ego strength; and ability to cooperate. The LMT also gives the therapist a gauge of the child's spatial and mathematical concept skill, two-dimensional representational ability, small motor coordination, and nonverbal as well as verbal skill level.

The third test, the Lowenfeld Kaleidoblock Test (LKT; Lowenfeld, 1976), is given at the same time as the LMT, in a 45-minute session. This test consists of a set of 26 blocks that the child is asked to use to construct something on a piece of paper. The child is timed, and the instructions include showing the child the mathematical relationship of the blocks. The information obtained includes the child's ability to complete a task with familiar objects; to assess pride versus self-doubt; three-dimensional representational ability; developmental level; small motor coordination; concept ability and verbal ability. The last two tests are given after the first three weeks of school, when the child has had a chance to form a good relationship with the therapist. This creates a positive experience of test taking and minimizes unwanted distractions.

In addition to the first three tests, a standardized test known as the Burks' Behavior Rating Scale (Burks, 1977) is used. This test gives the therapist an opportunity to objectively evaluate in-class behavior because the teacher rates the children by answering 105 questions. The therapist processes the test results and interprets them. This test is a helpful gauge of the relative severity of a problem versus a child's reacting to newness. Combined with the nonverbal material from the other three tests, this information gives teacher and therapist the guidelines they need to agree on problem areas and plan an individualized program for each child. Parents are included in these planning meetings so that suggestions for the classroom can also be carried out at home. All four of these tests are readministered at the end of the year to give a measure of changes in the child's mental health. The teacher also administers the Dial-R Test (Mardell-Czuanowski & Goldberg, 1980) at the beginning and end of the year; this test measures premath and prereading skills and is used to assess the child's academic abilities and gains at the end of the year.

SANDPLAY THERAPY

Once a child has been chosen for therapy, a 45-minute meeting is arranged on a weekly basis. The child is taken to the playroom and introduced to the materials by being shown the categories of toys: moving vehicles, houses, ordinary people, fantasy and comic book characters, animals both domestic and wild, army figures, cowboys and Indians, and so on. The child is invited to place the toys in a sandbox and to tell a story. The children begin to play out themes that have a personal meaning for them. They choose certain characters to represent themselves and others in their lives. The therapist records the play themes of the child and analyzes them later to understand the child's innermost fears and wishes. By accessing early childhood memories and processing experiences, the child is able to release his or her concerns, making energy available for learning. By witnessing and verbally reflecting back the child's play process, the therapist is able to encourage the child to explore a new sense of self. Through sandplay, this experience of self-discovery provides a mirror for children to see themselves in the context of their strengths and to try out new ways of doing things, which helps them overcome obstacles to learning. They can explore new solutions; get used to new thoughts, feelings, and impulses; see relationships in new patterns and outcomes; and experience new roles that are uniquely their own.

Heinz Kohut, one of the pioneers of self psychology, defined health in childhood as the result of ways of parenting that supported the "selves" of children and eased them through the healthy stages of development. For instance, "the normal development of healthy narcissism . . . would be reflected in a feeling of internal solidarity and vitality, the ability to harness talents and reach steadily for goals like self-esteem that is reliable and durable in the face of disappointments and that allows for expansive pride and pleasure of success" (Mitchell & Black, 1995, p. 159). When a model for health is seen from this perspective, the serious impact on learning when a child is diagnosed as having disturbances in early development is more obvious. This early detection and remediation of emotional problems is the goal of the clinical component of this program. It takes professional training and practice to learn how to make use of the nonverbal material to determine psychological issues and blocks to normal development.

The role of the therapist is to provide empathy and emotional support for the 3- to 4-year-old students. In self psychology theory, this is known as "mirroring" or a reflection from a parent that is proud and encouraging (Mitchell & Black, 1995, p. 159). Children also need an "involvement with powerful others, to whom the child will look up and with whom he can merge as an image of calmness, infallibility and omnipotence" (p. 159). The therapist provides this by receiving and acknowledging the thoughts of the child in the sandplay medium. Kohut notes that a child needs a parent or other who can be a positive and comforting authority figure, one to be idealized and admired. Both therapist and teacher can help to fulfill that role if parenting has not been sufficient for the child. In this program, work is done with the parents to help them learn how to repair the damage by improving their parenting skills. Therapy is provided for the child to reparent him or her. Let us now look at a case study to illustrate the use of sandplay and the assessment tools with a preschool student.

The Case of Jamie

On the surface, Jamie looked like a needy child who was unable to let his mother go even after months of coming to school. He had a 1½-year-old brother, and the family lived in their own apartment in the father's family's house. The father is Portuguese and the mother African American. Jamie was 3 years 9 months old at the beginning of school. When the decision came to let Jamie's mother leave him for longer periods of the school day, he sobbed uncontrollably for at least two hours and attached himself to the teacher in a desperate attempt for support. Jamie's separation anxieties were extreme.

His mother asked to see me right away and explained that she and Jamie's father were having serious marital problems. She was open about her own depression and feelings of failure in her marriage and in terms of parenting Jamie. She was worried about his dependency, fearfulness, and shy manner, and she was very relieved to hear that her son was identified for therapy. My sense of her was of a well-educated woman who was overwhelmed with marital and financial problems. Both she and her husband had worked for an advertising firm in Manhattan. She quit her job and stayed home to take care of the children, but her husband came home late and was not involved in the children's lives, even on weekends. She was convinced that he had an addiction problem and portrayed him as distant and remote as a parent. She also expressed her own fears of not being a good parent because of her personal history of sexual abuse. I referred her to the social worker at the school for individual counseling and she was very receptive and diligent about her therapy work. She was adamant that if things did not improve between her and her husband, she would move out of the state to be closer to relatives.

Meanwhile, in class Jamie was too preoccupied by his concerns to access the learning environment. The tension between his parents created a difficult home atmosphere. If we apply the theory of self psychology to Jamie, we can see that:

> The Oedipal aggressiveness and incestuous strivings that we see in pa-
> tients are reactions to injury. For example, a small boy will look to his fa-
> ther for help in developing normal assertiveness, and if the father takes
> pride and shows pleasure in his son's healthy assertiveness, the boy will
> not feel conflict. If, however, the father feels threatened by his son's as-
> sertiveness and reacts with anger, disapproval, and contempt, his son will
> feel hurt, angry and humiliated. This tension is the cause of the irrational
> guilt and competitive rage previously thought to be part of normal devel-
> opment. (Shapiro, 1995, p. 22)

Thus, Jamie was suffering from his father's distant attitude and his
mother's stress and depression. His feelings of conflict over his normal
assertive and competitive strivings were evident in his interactions
with his peers and in his clinging behavior with the teacher.

Although Jamie's problems first manifested as intense separation
anxiety, the underlying cause was a serious "fragmentation or enfeeblement of the self" (Shapiro, 1995, p. 23), which is the result of a
lack of adequate parenting. Some of the other children teased him
about crying and acting like a baby, which infuriated him but did not
change his clinging behavior. Instead, he opted for physical closeness
to the teacher. This kept him apart from the group for most of the day
and protected him from having to stand up for himself or compete
with the other children. For the first few months of school, this was
necessary for Jamie's development of a self. Gradually, he was able to
join his peers and overcome his insecurity. As we shall see, Jamie had
strengths that the sandplay sessions helped him to access.

JAMIE'S TEST RESULTS

The battery of tests that Jamie took gave a very coherent picture of his
emotional anxieties and their cause. The Burks Behavior Rating Scale
showed Jamie to rate very high for excessive dependency and slightly
lower for excessive self-blame and excessive anxiety.

In his LADS test, his drawing was very diffuse and formless, revealing
an undefined, fragmented sense of self (Figure 2.1). Developmentally,
Jamie is below the age level appropriate for a sense of self. His animal
choice is a giraffe, a tall, harmless creature and one that doesn't take in
nurturance easily because of its long neck. His first thought was of drawing a lion, a very aggressive animal, but he suppressed this and settled for
a giraffe. His answer to "Is it big or little?" is "Big," but he adds, "It is a
mom, dad, and a baby"; that is, he is still fused with the parental system.
He says that the animal is "one year old," which is, in fact, his developmental age. For gender identity, Jamie says the animal is "a man and a
dad"; that is, he needs his father's powerful identity to feel masculine. In

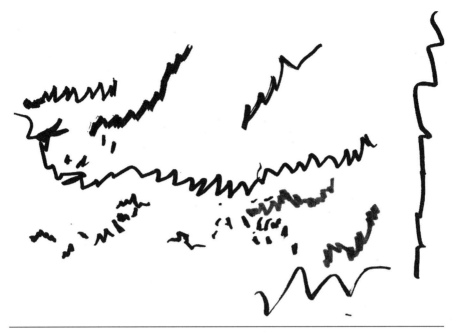

Figure 2.1 Jamie's LADS Drawing #1.

the beginning of the year, he feels liked by his peers. His answer to what makes the animal angry is "not wanting to be hit or beaten." This alerted me to the fact that physical punishment was used at home, and a discussion with Jamie's mother helped her adjust her discipline methods of spanking or just losing control and hitting him to the classroom method of time-out. This was important for Jamie's self-esteem.

The LADS question about competition was answered by Jamie's stating, "I can't talk." In the picture, he stated that the animal is "trying to sleep"; that is, he has escapist wishes. He denies that the animal is afraid of anything. The animal "can't cross the street because of the cars"; that is, he feels vulnerable but no mention of help from his parents is made. Similarly, he denies feelings of sadness at being alone. The answer revealing a child's curiosity shows that Jamie is too fearful to allow himself to explore unknown territory, a requirement for learning. In a question looking for a child's level of compassion, Jamie imagined an attack on a helpless creature, expressing inappropriately the anger he attempts to control. This corresponds to Kohut's theory of aggressiveness as a result of abnormal Oedipal development due to lack of parental acceptance and positive mirroring of his normal masculine assertiveness. The Oedipal stage of psychological development for Jamie was so taboo that behaviorally he regressed to being a baby. It now became clear that because

Jamie was unable to comfort himself or maintain an internal image of his mother, he needed to physically cling to the teacher for support.

Jamie's Mosaic Test (not shown) gives us a revealing glimpse into the dynamic of his emotional blocks to learning. He made two large squares and many two-, four-, and six-piece structures. He is almost able to make a hexagon, an advanced mathematical structure for his age. In the beginning of the test, he messes up his product and says he "can't do it." Then, after making an arrow shape (a phallic symbol), he states, "I don't know how to make these so I don't mess up like before." Here Jamie admits to phallic aggressive anxiety and guilt, which he can handle only by "messing" or behaving at an anal stage of development, that is, below the more advanced phallic level. After completing the test, Jamie explains that the center large squares are cars and to the right is a butterfly. He worries out loud, "I don't want to crash into the butterfly," a perfect example of the impulse to destructive hostility that he experiences and fears within himself. Although Jamie shows an above-average math ability and concept skill, he is not able to feel proud of his product. He is self-conscious and anticipates failure. He fears being unable to control his aggressive, destructive drives. This underlying self-defeating theme was also evident in his earlier answer of not knowing if he could win and insisting, "I can't talk" in the LADS answers. Jamie's innate gift in math is revealed in this test, but so is his inability to feel proud of his product, have confidence in his work, or be able to overcome his self-defeating attitude. In terms of self psychology, Jamie's parents were unable to take delight in his normal assertiveness and increased ability to be affectionate. Instead, Jamie needed to hide these qualities, just as he did not draw the lion first but instead chose the giraffe. Children all have a built-in radar system for maintaining parental love and care. If a child detects that his actions are unacceptable, he will suppress that aspect of himself, and if it appears, it creates a painful conflict for him and causes more inhibition. Thus, Jamie's fearfulness of his own destructive hostility that he might not be able to contain and that he openly worries about controlling is expressed with the cars and butterfly images he has made. It is interesting to note that Jamie rarely ever exhibited aggressiveness in his classroom behavior. Instead, he was terrified at any expression of his unwelcome phallic aggression and was even willing to sacrifice his self-esteem and be called a baby by his peers, rather than developing more mature, masculine ways of interacting. In the words of Irene M. Josselyn:

> To the extent that he can find gratifying channels of expression for his impulses, the child will be psychologically healthier. He will be freer of anxiety, will have more emotional energy. He will develop more completely

his total psychological potential if he does not have to hold in check part of it because in its unmodified form it is destructive rather than constructive. (Josselyn, 1995)

It is the goal of this program to make education a psychologically healthy avenue for the expression of a child's natural impulses.

In the first Kaleidoblock Test (not shown), Jamie makes a tall structure that falls down. He then spreads out the blocks to make a bridge, which is a premathematical use of the blocks. Again his Oedipal anxiety forces him to regress to a younger age level. He redoes the tall structure, which falls, and then redoes it with fewer blocks. Even in these seemingly innocent educational tasks, Jamie is troubled by unwelcome aggressive impulses. He demonstrates how difficult it is for him to allow himself to succeed in an aggressive phallic manner even in a symbolic form. Instead, he reacts to his own anxiety with inhibition, wanting to undo his products or mess them up. This self-defeating attitude makes it impossible for Jamie to feel confident or enjoy a positive self-image, both of which are necessary for learning. As we shall see, this theme is continually expressed in Jamie's sandplay process.

An individualized program was set up for Jamie in the class. It was decided to pair him with other students who were less competitive and more nurturing. Jamie was encouraged to try new materials, and the teacher sometimes walked him through a project from beginning to end to model how to complete tasks. At home, the parents were encouraged to spend quality time with him apart from his sibling. His father was asked to bring him to school in the morning to give them more time together, and in late November his mother reported that she was on medication that helped her be more patient with Jamie. The marital problems now seemed to be less acute because of the therapist's intervention and the help the mother was getting in individual therapy.

JAMIE'S EARLY SANDPLAY PROCESS

In his first sandplay session in October, Jamie demonstrated where he was most concerned: becoming a competitive, masculine individual. He begins with Hercules killing a monster; then a plane lands, falls down and flips over, and then can't move. His phallic drive to fly is blocked or is stuck. Here he again seeks expression of his phallic drives by the hero defeating a monster, but this causes him anxiety and the need to regress. In the next session, he makes a tray in which he continues to use the plane to express his phallic drives in an inanimate form (i.e., a more disguised form of phallic aggression). However, the plane falls apart and "Someone needs an ambulance," he says, perhaps a symbol of feeling castrated and damaged. Then he expresses the phallic drive in a scene where he as Robin (symbolic son) challenges Batman (symbolic father) and is defeated. His fear of competing with his father is dealt with by punishment. Jamie finds it easier to try out his phallic wish with inanimate objects to see if it is safe, but he invariably crashes the planes just as he could not easily maintain a tall structure in the Kaleidoblock Test. Towers, trains, planes, cars, motorcycles, fire trucks, and so on are all phallic objects and therefore symbolize phallic aggressive drives. We can see here how Jamie projects his phallic aggression onto the play scenes and then reacts with anxiety, conflict, and disorganization such as crashing, falling apart, or being punished. We see this in his classroom behavior as well. Sandplay gives him a symbolic outlet for this material that is pushing for expression in spite of Jamie's severe inhibitions.

In this third session, he puts the house in the right rear corner of the sand tray (Figure 2.2). He puts sand on it and then knocks off the roof, symbolizing hostility toward home. A plane tries to fly, but it falls (center). Then a train is set out in the rear, and some cars and trucks have an accident caused by the man on the motorcycle (left center). A fire truck tries to rescue the situation, but in general, the energy is blocked and stuck. The race car can't move. In this same session, he makes a drawing

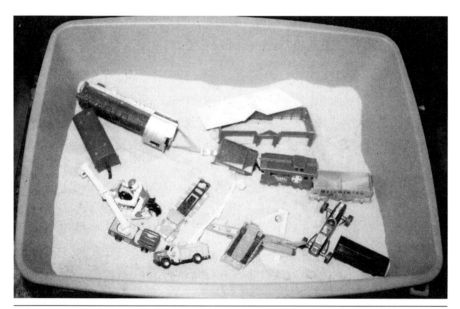

Figure 2.2   Jamie's Third Session Sand Tray.

of a tree whose leaves all fall off (castration). Jamie is trying to find a way for his phallic drives to be expressed, and he experiments with direct challenges and indirect (inanimate object) forays into dealing with his castration feelings. He wishes to challenge a strong father figure (man on motorcycle), but this image symbolically causes his energy to be derailed or blocked in the play theme. Sandplay offers him an opportunity to deal with underlying drives and tensions that he can't deal with in real life. In class, he continues to cling to his mom in the morning or the teacher, whereas in sandplay, he can begin to find the means to express a more mature side of himself. On the surface, he is shy and fearful, his drawings are formless, and his answers to the LADS questions give us the sense that he is uncertain of his individuality or identity. In sandplay he can try out the aggressive little boy aspect of himself who has phallic drives that he is fearful of. He can experiment with issues that make him feel that he can't do it and also themes in which he gains, little by little, the permission and confidence to succeed. We must keep in mind that play gives the child the opportunity to do and undo, to bury and uncover, to take two steps forward and one step back in the slow process of developing a strong, healthy ego.

A Theoretical Framework

The sandplay therapist empathically mirrors back to the child a positive feeling about the growth and development that has occurred all year, thus repatterning the child's selfobject experience. The more the therapist and the teacher plan for the child's success and praise him or her for it, the more the child is able to take chances and try new ways of communicating. Changes from hitting to asking, from withdrawing to participating, whatever the goals, are all encouraged with positive feedback. This affirms the child's self and provides a corrective experience and a conflict-free emotional state, all of which is critical for optimum learning. If a child is experiencing a disintegration of the self, this corrective experience is an intervention at the right time, when it is part of the natural process of a 4-year-old's developmental challenges that begin at this period of working through the Oedipal stage. As Josselyn puts it:

> As the Oedipal conflict becomes more solvable, the child directs much of his energy towards learning without, instead of primarily through, experiencing. His innate curiosity offers him a way to occupy himself, thus diverting him from the more personal problems with which he has been struggling. He is ready and eager for more formal education. (1995, p. 88)

As Jamie began to be able to individuate from the family unit, his socialization skills improved and so did his interest in school activities. Instead of reporting to his mom that he did not miss her today, he would say, "I did this or that all by myself," "I played with a friend," or some other accomplishment he was proud of, that is, showing a growing development of a sense of self.

Jamie's Midyear LADS

Jamie's second LADS test in the middle of the year shows this progress. His drawing consists of oblong, curved shapes that have distinct boundaries and are more defined than his previous squiggle lines (Figure 2.3). Some of the shapes almost resemble actual figures. His animal drawing is a snake, a sly but aggressive animal, which shows progress in allowing some of his aggressive drives to be expressed. His answer reveals that it is separate as opposed to being fused with the family. It is a boy instead of a "boy and a father" (i.e., fused gender identity). It is 12 rather than age 1. At this midyear point, Jamie is aware that his classmates have not yet accepted him, thus the animal is not liked. In answer to the question of something bad happening to the animal he says, "He died. Someone

Figure 2.3   LADS Drawing #2.

killed him." Jamie is still experiencing Oedipal fears of castration and death. His animal now gets angry when others destroy his product in the classroom instead of when he is hit (referring to family dynamics), and his animal wins all the time by "breaking" the competitor. Thus, his aggression is now more conscious, more acceptable, and more available for learning. He has grown from denial of fear to being afraid of monsters, to being able to feel and express his feelings. He acknowledges a need for help from Mom and Dad to cross the street instead of the previous vulnerable and unprotected fear of cars, suggesting that the changes the parents made over the prior few months allowed Jamie to see them as protective. When left alone, he can acknowledge the normal emotion of sadness ("The animal is crying"). His ability to be empathic improved from attacking to a new idea of calling for help. Overall, the midyear LADS test shows that Jamie is gaining in ego strength because he is able to express his feelings. He shows more awareness of himself in relation to his peers and a newfound sense of anger at peers (acceptable aggression) for just causes. He was able to overcome his separation anxiety and clinging behavior after three months of therapy and he was responding very well to his father's involvement in bringing him to school.

JAMIE'S LATER SANDPLAY PROCESS

Let us now look at the expression of the phallic drives and the development of the Oedipal wishes that characterize Jamie's psychosexual development after five months of therapy. In this session in February, a plane flies and crashes into the sand (Figure 2.4). An ambulance comes and "they get hurt" (punishment for phallic drives). He looks for someone to wear Mr. Sinister's cape. Then Green Lantern, a youthful male character, takes Mr. Sinister's wings. Then Luke Skywalker defeats evil aliens. Luke calls Obi-Wan Dad and then takes his cape off and laughs at him in his underwear. Luke has defeated Dad and now puts on Obi-Wan's cape. In fantasy play, Jamie can fulfill the Oedipal wish to take away his father's power and wear the mantle of power, so to speak. Luke looks at Princess Leia and undresses her. Having defeated his father, he can now possess the female sexually, but he feels guilty and puts her clothes back on. Then he defeats another villain, Mr. Punisher (front center in tray). He removes the couple, Luke and Princess Leia, "so no one can see them." In Oedipal competition he can allow himself to win the female and have a secret sexual union. He then lines up the inanimate phallic symbols, cars, wagon, plane, and helicopter, to fortify his Oedipal forces and protect them against being destroyed, as had happened in previous car crash scenes.

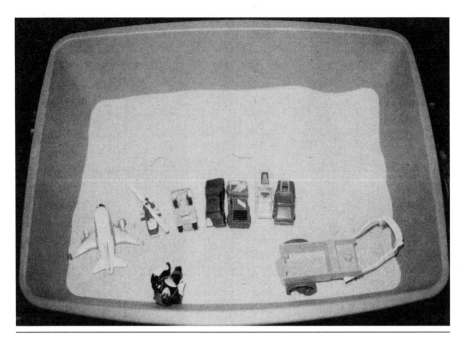

Figure 2.4   Sand Tray at Five Months' Therapy.

Jamie has been able to defeat Dad and use his power; to possess the female and not be punished for it; and to move from the plane-crashing (castrating) first scene to protecting his phallic symbols by lining them up and remaining strong in the last scene. Both the changes in the family dynamic and therapy have impacted Jamie's inner life so that he no longer fears losing the connection with his parents if he acts in a more successful and phallic way. He can even borrow from Dad's strength in the form of Batman's cape, and he no longer fears being successful. One can anticipate now that he is more internally ready to be successful in the academic and social areas of school life.

The Emergence of Core Issues

A month later, Jamie makes this sandplay process (Figure 2.5). Nightcrawler (not shown) puts the Barbie with the pink dress in jail (left rear). He undresses her (dress in front), showing his sexual interest. Then Spiderman wins some Oedipal competitions with male bad guys and is removed. Batman (left edge) puts sexy Black Cat with white hair (right front), Cat Woman (center rear), and Spiderman (left rear in front of Barbie) in the tray, but Jamie says, "They are missing." In this session, the

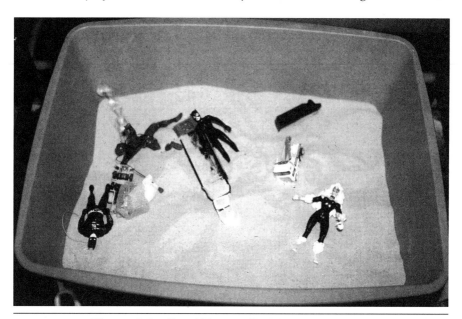

Figure 2.5   Sand Tray at Six Months' Therapy.

Oedipal drives are clearly and openly expressed, but there is still an inhibiting factor. He hides the sexual symbols (Spiderman, Black Cat, and Cat Woman) from view, demonstrating his avoidance of sexuality. In the next session, Jamie states that his interest in girls is strong, but "Mommies take care of boys," implying that therefore mothers cannot be sexual objects. This denial of his Oedipal interests gave me the sense that perhaps Jamie's mother was unconsciously turning to her son as an emotional substitute for her unhappy marriage. In self psychology, such behavior on the part of the mother makes a boy "feel sexually stimulated and conflicted, like a child who is molested" (Shapiro, 1995, p. 23). Jamie's frank sandplay dramas of sexuality seemed to point to this as a possible hypothesis.

In April, Jamie begins more openly to express his conflict with his mother around Oedipal issues. Black Cat kisses Spiderman because "she likes him." The small plane flies on top of the big one; this symbolizes his need for his father's power to protect him from his Oedipal wishes for mother. Hercules attacks April (from the Ninja Turtles) with his sword; phallic aggression is now directed toward females. Then he takes a third plane apart and buries it. In this session, the Oedipal competitive drives emerge and cause him anxiety and the next emotion, hostility, but now it is directed toward the seductive mother. He is having difficulty dealing with the painful truth that Mother is not always the nurturing person he wishes for. He projects onto girls the seductive quality he does not want to admit he feels from mother. He uses Father's identity and power to confront and defeat the female figures in his play. However, this causes him internal anxiety, and his only solution seems to be to dismantle the phallic object (Delta plane) and retreat from being a phallic male.

In this last tray made in May, Jamie acts out this drama of a volcano (Figure 2.6), which is made using the trailer truck (left edge) and bulldozer (removed). A large plane (partially buried center left) crashes into the volcano and he says, "It's gonna crash some ugly thing" (pile of sand in left rear). Then he says, "The volcano is broken." He rebuilds it. Next, Dr. Octopus straddles the volcano and Batman in a Batmobile crashes into the volcano and stays buried there. "It broke," Jamie says. Then another Batman figure (front center, face down) straddles the volcano, and the motorcycle man (a symbol of father; right front edge) crashes into it while Batman calls out, "No, my volcano."

In this last session, Jamie expresses his conflicted feelings for his mother ("some ugly thing": volcano/breast) on a symbolic level. He is also expressing his awareness of his father (motorcycle man, Batmobile) as a competitive hostile force. The volcano is both the positive and negative aspect of the Great Mother (Cirlot, 1962, pp. 341–342). As the volcano image resembles the maternal breast, he is invoking an early childhood memory of both the negative or destructive aspect of the feminine and the nurturing, loving aspect of the feminine. Melanie Klein referred to this image as a "good breast" and a "bad breast." "Klein saw that the breast

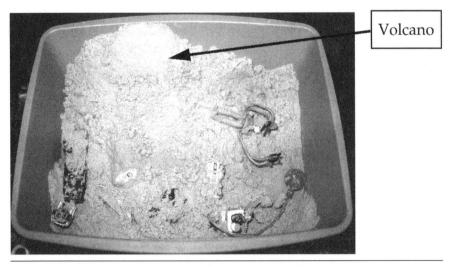

Figure 2.6   Jamie's Last Session Sand Tray.

could be an object of love and attachment and one of hate and rejection (as, for example, when it is needed and not available)" (Clegg, 1984). The volcano/breast image is also archetypal; as such, it also contains within it a possible resolution of both positive and negative aspects. The Batman figure who straddles the volcano is here a new identity figure previously used as a symbol of Father. This Batman verbally mourns the destruction of the breast symbol when he says, "No, my volcano."

Jamie is exhibiting what Kohut considers "the boy's primary Oedipal fears . . . of being confronted by a nonempathic sexually seductive rather than affection-accepting maternal selfobject or by a competitive-hostile rather than pridefully pleased paternal one" (Shapiro, 1995, p. 23). It is helpful to remember Kohut's statement "that pathological sexual driven-ness and destructive hostility arise secondary to experiences of fragmen-tation or enfeeblement of the self" (p. 23). Here again we see the effects of the parental rejection of Jamie's normal healthy development. Jamie has a precocious preoccupation with sexual impulses that are symptomatic of his dysfunctional family system.

> In normal development, a father will take pride in his son's developing sex-uality, but if the father feels competitive with his son, the boy's affection for his mother will make the boy anxious. If the father also withdraws from his son, the boy may feel more isolated and anxious, and forced to rely on erotic feelings for comfort. (p. 23)

In this last tray scene, there are some positive signs of change. Jamie is now confident in using his father's power to help him with his assertive strivings, unlike at the beginning of the year. He tries out new solutions to deal with his Oedipal anxieties and he explores his inner conflict in an archetypal dimension that holds the possibility of resolution and a union of opposites.

FINAL TEST RESULTS

His third LADS animal is a "green dinosaur who is blowing out wind" (Figure 2.7). In contrast to the giraffe and the snake, this animal is large and represents a greater sense of power and the ability to be aggressive—but not too aggressive or he would be blowing fire, not air. He answers the question of size with "big" and therefore individuated from the family system. Likewise, the animal is "a man" and is no longer fused with Dad. It is "20 years old," a sign of aspirations of maturity versus wanting to be a baby or age 1, as in his first LADS. And nothing bad happens to the an-imal, in contrast to its being killed in the midyear LADS.

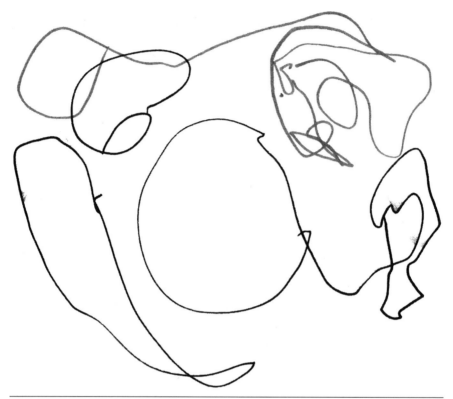

Figure 2.7 Third LADS Animal.

In the drawing, the animal is "blowing the wind out of him," as opposed to sleeping as in the midyear test, showing Jamie's interest in a new assertive role. He also states that he is not afraid of anything and that he can cross the street "alone because he is big" as opposed to needing Mom and Dad (midyear). The dinosaur can win as opposed to not being able to win or talk about it (first), or to winning by breaking his opponent (midyear). He now feels "fine" when left alone, in contrast to the animal's crying (midyear). The answer revealing a child's curiosity shows that at first Jamie was fearful; then in midyear, he could identify what he was afraid of ("Open the box and a monster comes out"); at the end of the year, he says he would open the box, but "if it is not yours, don't open it," showing a more socialized awareness. His sense of compassion also changes from aggression (first), to calling for help (midyear), to helping himself and knowing how to get help at school, again showing a step forward in independence.

In Jamie's second Mosaic Test, he makes a complete hexagon and says, "I told you I can make a circle with these"; he calls it "a wheel." Then he fits four isosceles triangles on the left side between two equilateral triangles by experimenting to make a circle with pieces other than the usual six equilateral sectioned hexagon. He is not able to accomplish this more advanced structure but calls it "a dragon." Now he can accept some limitation of his abilities versus needing to destroy his work. This shows remarkable progress. Jamie is now able to feel proud of his product and to identify with a large, powerful image, the dragon. In his Kaleidoblock Test on the same day, he made a tower and tunnel and then a car crashed into it, knocking it down. He states, "I want a car like a Power Ranger megaship," and he fits the blocks into a mathematically advanced structure that resembles a ship. During the test Jamie complained, "I don't know how" and repeated "Help me." However, he was able to make a successful product by himself. Although residues of destructive tendencies and insecurity still plague Jamie, he is far more confident, assertive, and successful than he was at the beginning of the year. As we would expect, his Burks score showed a marked improvement in excessive dependency. His improvements in excessive self-blame and excessive anxiety were less dramatic.

Jamie's Dial-R scores reflect his overall improvement. The test results are compared with both his classmates and a comparison with other children of the same age using a minority sample to determine his percentile placement. In October his test results were: Motor: 16 raw score and 42nd percentile; Concepts: 12 raw score and 18th percentile; Language: 22 raw score and 74th percentile. This adds up to a total of 48 raw score and 74th percentile in the beginning of the year. In May, his test results were: Motor: 24 raw score and 76th percentile; Concepts: 28 raw score and 87th percentile; Language: 24 raw score and 64th percentile. Thus his raw score total went from 48 to 76 and he went from the 74th percentile to the 84th percentile at years end.

Weekly sandplay therapy gave Jamie the opportunity to present and rehearse many different outcomes of his Oedipal conflict and phallic drives. In nine months his surface behavior changed from a shy, clinging child to one who is more self-confident and self-defined. Jamie's experimenting with these deeper aspects of his drives and wishes in sandplay allows him to leave some of these conflicts in the tray. This frees him to adjust to the real world of school, cooperating with peers, and learning. Sandplay has also helped Jamie find identity symbols that are aggressive without being destructive and to look to school and peers for more support and healthy, age-appropriate activity rather than being blocked by immature and regressive behavior. Therapy gave Jamie the mirroring, empathy, and the opportunity to idealize an adult, all of which he needed for a greater integration of his self. This helped him to move into a new place of self-acceptance and self-confidence. Without help, Jamie would have had serious difficulty being able to learn and develop his innate potential.

CONCLUSION

In this chapter, we have presented the treatment of a 4-year-old child in an innovative preschool program. The in-school approach to therapy with this age group offers many advantages. By using a special test battery, the therapist is able to uncover many of the factors operating in the child's inner world. Identifying and treating conflicts that impede adjustment to school are important parts of this program. Sandplay is used to alleviate these emotional problems and to repattern in a positive and affirming way the child's innate self.

Self psychology as described by Kohut (1971), Mitchel and Black (1995), Shapiro (1995) and others, serves to help us relate our findings in sand-play therapy with child-rearing practices and family dynamics. Emphasis is put on consultations with teachers and interventions with parents to determine a plan for educational and home environments. Parents are helped to change behaviors that impede their child's normal growth and development. Teachers are encouraged to instruct children in emotional and behavioral ways that improve their interest in and capacity to learn. Sandplay, drawing, and storytelling are the main techniques used by the therapist to analyze and theorize about the child's strengths and weaknesses and to remove anxieties that may be the cause of those weaknesses. A child needs both parents to be mature enough to serve as good role models. If both parents cannot be loving, nurturing, and emotionally present, for whatever reason, children suffer emotional insecurities and disruption in their normal emotional development and formation of an integrated self.

In self psychology, children react to inappropriate rejection of their normal developmental achievements by having anxiety about maintaining the love and contact of the parent. They feel they must conform or lose their parents' love; unless Jamie suppressed his aggressive, assertive side, his parents would no longer love or care for him. For some children, meeting the needs of parents can create an enfeebled and fragmented sense of self. Instead, the child represses or inappropriately expresses taboo emotions. In Jamie's case, we have seen how destructive aggressive impulses can impede a child's normal growth. The burden of such anxieties lowers the child's ability to cope and concentrate on educational tasks and social relationships. For this child, therapy gave him the means to feel confident and the energy for a renewed interest in the world around him.

Some of the implications of our findings are that children can be helped to improve academic achievement. Parents are eager to be given insight into their family dynamic so that it can be a healthy one for their child. And a specialized program in the preschool classroom can improve a child's chances for success in learning. Preschool age is the best time to remove blocks to learning and the team approach of teacher and therapist is well suited for this work. The gains that are made at the preschool level make for solid building blocks later on in life. We believe that a new vision of education must include the consideration of the emotional needs of children. And we are certain that early intervention is key to lasting school success.

REFERENCES

Burks, H.F. (1977). *Burks' Behavior Rating Scales.* Los Angeles: Western Psychological Services.

Cirlot, J.E. (1962). *A dictionary of symbols.* New York: Philosophical Library.

Clegg, H.G. (1984). *The reparative motif.* New York: Aronson.

Hammer, E.F. (1980). *The clinical applications of projective drawings.* In S. Levy & R.A. Levy (Eds.), *Symbolism in animal drawings* (pp.311–343). Springfield, IL: Thomas.

Josselyn, I.M. (1995). *The happy child.* New York: Random House.

Lowenfeld, M. (1954). *The Lowenfeld Mosaic Test.* London: Newman Neame.

Mardell-Czuanowski, C., & Goldberg, D.S. (1980). *DIAL-R, Developmental Indicators for the Assessment of Learning–Revised.* Circle Pines, MN: American Guidance Service.

Metraux, R., & Able, T. (1976). *The Lowenfeld Kaleidobloc Test, A nonverbal technique* (Rev. ed.). Available: Dr. Beric Wright, Brudenell House, Quainton, Aylesbury, Bucks HP22 4 AW, United Kingdom.

Mitchell, S.A., & Black, M.J. (1995). *Freud and beyond.* New York: Basic Books.

Shapiro, S. (1995). *Talking with patients: A self psychological view.* Northern Bergen, NJ: Book-Mart Press.

PART TWO

IMPLEMENTING PLAY THERAPY IN THE SCHOOLS

CHAPTER 3

The Possibilities and Challenges in Using Play Therapy in Schools

ATHENA A. DREWES

THE NEED for psychological services within the school system dates back to the turn of the twentieth century, when a societal shift occurred in viewing children as being less of an economic family asset to becoming more of an emotional family investment (Fagan, 2000). Laws came into effect by 1920 making it compulsory in all states for children to attend school, resulting in dramatically increased enrollment. Between 1890 and 1930, there was a 28% increase in the number of average days of the school year, going from 135 to 173. Enrollment went from 12.7 to 25.7 million students in primary (elementary) school, and an even greater jump occurred in the enrollment in secondary school (junior and senior high school), from 203,000 to 4.4 million students (Snyder, Hoffman, & Geddes, 1997). Students were also staying in school for longer periods during the school year, averaging 143 days of attendance as compared to a previous average of 135 days. A classroom size of 65 to 68 students, however, was not uncommon, along with a teacher's evaluation based on the general class average for achievement (Slater, 1980).

Consequently, a great need arose for professionals and school practitioners who had the expertise to address the growing concerns around attendance and children's health issues (specifically, hearing and speech) and to be able to offer psychological and social work services, as well as to help begin the formation of special education classes (Fagan, 2000). Soon school districts were forced to formulate ways to deal with the burgeoning referrals from teachers for help in dealing with their students' behavioral, physical (health), and academic problems. Children were referred by teachers and/or parents into the school system's classification process. Children in the younger grades were often referred for academic failure or suspicion of mental retardation or being gifted. Older children often were referred for being truant, delinquent, and dropping out of school. Boys were referred more often than girls (Fagan, 1995).

Clinics were formed in school districts along with community agencies to address these needs, and by 1910 a classification system evolved, similar to the current state and federal regulations (Fagan, 2000). In the beginning of the twentieth century, schoolchildren evidenced problems with speech, health (notably respiratory diseases), and sensory disorders. Many of the children's academic and behavioral problems, which resulted in referrals by the teachers, may have been exacerbated by or the result of underlying physical health problems. In addition, the society at large was faced with many life-threatening diseases, resulting in many deaths not only of children, but also of parents. As a result there were many single-parent families, which compounded even further many children's adjustment to the demands of school and learning (Safford & Safford, 1996).

Now, 100 years later, in the twenty-first century, school clinicians (which include school psychologists, guidance counselors, school or area counselors, social workers, and even paraprofessionals, called child associates or youth and family workers) are faced with similar issues. Children continue to need psychological services and there continues to be an ever increasing number of referrals from teachers and/or parents of children struggling with emotional issues and disruptive classroom behavior.

Even 100 years later, children of all ages still must cope with challenging problems that affect their growth and achievement. There are more than 15 million American children under the age of 4. Nearly a quarter of the families with children under 3 live in poverty. Most of these (over 50% of Black children) are families headed by a single parent, which usually means the mother, who does not have access to regular health care or other social services. Over 300,000 children live in foster care, tens of thousands have been left motherless by the HIV/AIDS epidemic, at least 7 million live with an alcoholic parent, and 10% to 20% live with a mentally ill parent (Wright & Devine, 1993; Zelman, 1996). More than a third of kindergartners are not ready to learn when they arrive at school (Kantrowitz, 1997).

INFLUENCES AFFECTING EMOTIONAL
AND ACADEMIC DEVELOPMENT

COGNITIVE STYLE

Children have different temperamental styles, which impact on learning ability. Temperament can also have a strong influence on the child's social, emotional, and academic functioning (Shaw & Feldman, 1997a). Chess and Thomas (1986) noted that impulsive children will generally respond quickly and without reflection, resulting in giving a wrong answer. Reflective children, on the other hand, tend to respond slowly and more thoughtfully. The wrong match between a teaching style and pace and a child's cognitive style or temperament can create problems for the child in learning as well as secondary issues around self-esteem.

FAMILY INFLUENCES

Parents who take an active interest in their child's academic achievement are more likely to have children with higher levels of performance. In contrast, families who show indifference to their child's school performance, for whatever reasons, may promote feelings in their child of inadequacy and of not being important, which in turn leads to behavioral and emotional problems (Steiner, 1997).

PEER INFLUENCES

Peer groups can significantly impact a child's academic performance and emotional growth. Those peer groups that devalue academic achievement will undermine both the child's and the school's efforts and may further result in secondary emotional aspects, such as truancy, delinquency, drug use, classroom misbehavior, and conduct disorder (Shaw & Feldman, 1997b).

SCHOOL ATMOSPHERE

Having the right match between a child's learning ability and temperament and the teacher's teaching style and classroom atmosphere can significantly impact students. The teacher's attitude and skill in managing classroom behavior can either result in a classroom atmosphere that emphasizes praise and positive incentives, which nurtures self-esteem and worth, or one that relies on punishment, removal of students, and in turn a lowering of self-esteem (Shaw & Feldman, 1997b). A teacher trained to be an empathic and reflective listener and able to use play therapy techniques for expression of feelings in the classroom is in a much better position to help de-escalate a child's anger and maintain control and thereby create a positive learning atmosphere. An experienced teacher can develop strategies for managing "difficult" behavior. For example, rather than labeling an active, restless child as hyperactive, the teacher can send the child on regular errands as an outlet for motor activity or give opportunities to learn that match the short, energetic bursts of the child's short attention span. For a child to flourish academically and emotionally there needs to be a good match between the child's temperament and environment, including the parenting environment. Parents and schoolteachers need to accommodate the needs of the child, but it is equally important for the child to learn to accommodate the environment, particularly when it comes to impulse control (Shaw & Feldman, 1997a).

CHILD ABUSE AND TRAUMA

Almost 3 million alleged victims of child abuse were reported by the National Center on Child Abuse and Neglect (NCCAN) in 1993, and 1 million of the cases were found to be substantiated. The median age of the child victim was 6 years, with 53% girls and 46% boys. The alleged perpetrators were parents (79%), other relatives (12%), noncaretakers (5%), and foster parents and/or child care workers (2%; NCCAN, 1994). Childhood trauma, in addition to the impact of child abuse, has a profound impact on the emotional, behavioral, cognitive, social, and physical functioning of children. Conservative estimates of the number of children in America exposed to a traumatic event in one year exceed 5 million (Perry, 1996). These experiences may be pervasive and chronic (e.g., incest, physical abuse, witnessing domestic violence or community violence) or time-limited (e.g., natural disaster, drive-by shooting, surviving a serious car accident). All have an impact on the child's development (Osofsky, 1995).

The short-term effects of abuse on children are increased anxiety, depression, low self-esteem, aggressive behaviors, cognitive and developmental delays, school difficulties, and difficulties with attachment and social interaction (Sanders & Dyer-Friedman, 1997). In a long-term study of over 20 years, Maxfield and Widom (1996) found that out of 908 victims of child abuse, a significantly higher percentage of abuse victims were more likely to have been arrested for violent crimes in comparison to a matched control group.

Perry (1997) found that trauma elevates stress hormones, such as cortisol, that wash over an infant's or child's developing brain like acid. As a result, regions in the cortex and limbic system (which are responsible for emotions, including attachment) are 20% to 30% smaller in abused children than in normal children. High cortisol levels during the vulnerable years of birth to 3 increase activity in the brain structure (locus ceruleus) involved in vigilance and arousal. As a result, the brain is wired to be on hair-trigger alert. Regions that were originally activated by the original trauma are immediately reactivated whenever the child dreams of, thinks about, or is reminded of the trauma (even by the presence of the abuser). The slightest stress unleashes a new surge of stress hormones, resulting in hyperactivity, anxiety, and impulsive behavior. Children exposed to chronic and unpredictable stress will suffer deficits in their ability to learn. They have problems in attention regulation and self-control. A piece of the child is lost forever (Perry, 1997).

SCHOOL VIOLENCE

Not all children experience trauma directly, but most are exposed to violence through the media, which include movies, TV shows, cartoons, and news reports (Van Fleet, 1998). In addition, over the past several years the media have increasingly reported on the tragic number of children bringing handguns and rifles to school and shooting and killing peers, teachers, and ultimately themselves. Children exposed to chronic violence are more likely to be violent. In part, this is related to modeling and learning that violent aggression is an acceptable, even a preferable and honorable, solution to problems. Analysis of much of the violent behavior by children and adolescents today reveals a troubling degree of impulsive and reactive violence. A survey conducted by the Centers for Disease Control and Prevention (1998) found that 8.5% of students surveyed (out of 16,262 nationwide) had carried a weapon to school, 7.4 % had been threatened or injured at school, and 14.8% had been in a physical fight at school. Often, these incidents of school violence occur after a student has felt angry over a perceived emotional hurt or incident by a peer or adult and sees violence as the only solution to rage. Along with these tragedies are the numerous stressful life events that may also occur during a school year. Children may be exposed to parental psychopathology, dysfunctional parenting, homelessness, living in severely disrupted or chaotic families, placement in foster care, marital discord, parental divorce or arrests, teen suicide (which is the third leading cause of teen deaths; Surgeon General, 1999), deaths of peers and teachers in car accidents, or the death of school personnel through disease.

EMOTIONAL DISORDERS

School clinicians and teachers also must address the ever growing number of children who are at risk for and/or manifest emotional and behavioral problems. Research shows that approximately 14% to 22% of

school-age American youth manifest emotional disorders, which trans-
lates to approximately 6 to 9 million youngsters who have serious mental
health problems (Brandenburg, Friedman, & Silver, 1990). Children with
Attention-Deficit/Hyperactivity Disorder (ADHD) constitute up to 5%
of all school-age children. ADHD affects boys more than girls at a rate of
4 to 1 (DuPaul & Stoner, 1994). The key features of ADHD include difficulty paying attention, restlessness or difficulty sitting still, and impulsivity. In addition, up to 30% of ADHD children may also have a learning
disability resulting in academic underachievement (Anastopoulos &
Barkley, 1992). The long-term prognosis for ADHD children who go untreated is poor, including dropping out of high school, having a greater
risk for substance abuse, engaging in criminal activity because of increased unemployment and lower earning potential, having emotional
problems, and having difficulties with interpersonal relationships
(Barkley, 1998; Gage, 1990).

In addition, up to 4% of the nation's students may display symptoms of
Oppositional Defiant Disorder and Conduct Disorder, manifested through
aggressive responses. These serious mental health problems are reflected
in antisocial behaviors, including getting into fights, committing petty
crimes, deliberately inflicting cruelty on peers and animals, lack of
empathy, lack of impulse control, and poor social skills (Shaw & Feldman, 1997b).

These symptoms may have underlying physiological and developmental bases (genetic, neurological, in utero or postnatal origins) and/or environmental causes (lack of parental limit-setting, parental drug or
alcohol use, low socioeconomic status, exposure to domestic violence, neglect, physical or sexual abuse/trauma, chaotic home life, etc.). Children
who manifest behavioral problems are not able to attend and learn, which
is further exacerbated by frequent removals from class or school. They
also disrupt their peers and create a negative atmosphere for other students, which is not conducive for their learning.

RATIONALE FOR USING PLAY
THERAPY IN SCHOOLS

Often, these serious mental health problems and behavioral difficulties
go untreated, and even undiagnosed. Up to 25% of schoolchildren experience moderate to severe school adjustment problems. Children who do
not experience success in early schooling are much more at risk of school
failure, dropping out, becoming drug addicted and delinquent, and developing serious emotional disorders. In turn, many of these children become chronic and costly burdens to society as adults (addicts, poorly

skilled workers, welfare cases, etc.). With the continually increasing number of children living in poverty, being abused, having HIV-infected parents, and being exposed to violence, the need for early intervention is increasing as well. When interventions are implemented early in the problem stage, success rates are often high. If the need for early intervention is not met, the incidence of substance abuse, crime, and mental illness in the next generation will increase as well (Zelman, 1996).

There are many reasons why the school system is the ideal setting to be an ongoing coprovider of early intervention and preventive services, as well as being a therapeutic milieu:

1. This type of setting could act as an extension into elementary school for children entering from the milieu of a therapeutic nursery or special education preschool (Zigler & Lang, 1991).
2. More children can be reached than through outside services. Children are often brought to outpatient clinics or private practices because of a crisis situation. Although this may also be the case for psychological service referrals in a school system, the school is in the unique position of being able to additionally offer primary prevention and developmental enhancement through play therapy. Many children are not eligible for play therapy services through the usual school referral process because their behavioral or academic functioning is not yet severe enough; however, they too are experiencing stress and are at potential risk for emotional disorganization and behavioral or learning problems. These children can be significantly helped to work out such stress-inducing problems as the birth of a sibling, death of a parent, parental alcoholism, parental remarriage, or a recent hospitalization or move.
3. Additional staff can be utilized. The use of paraprofessionals, such as child associates or certified teachers with specialized counselor education and training, has been successfully used in school districts to offer primary prevention and intervention services, which in the long run become cost-effective.
4. More families can be reached. Many families of school-age children with emotional and behavioral difficulties do not have the financial or inner emotional resources to pursue outside counseling services. They may not even be aware of the impact their chaotic or disorganized lives are having on their children's emotional and academic life. Consequently, the school becomes the only resource available to help address these issues and to offer service, both on a preventive level and in response to the child's level of dysfunction.

5. Play and, consequently, play therapy is a natural way for children to express their feelings and emotions. "Children's language development often lags behind their cognitive development" (Landreth & Bratton, 1999, p. 1). Consequently, children need alternative methods of expressing their feelings. The symbolic elements of pretend play allow children to express their inner feelings and transfer their negative emotions to objects rather than people (Landreth & Bratton, 1999). The use of toys and various play materials allows for the development of expressive and affective skills as well as the playing out of life situations and traumas. These tools become the central mode of communication between the child and the caring and skilled school clinician or teacher (Kottman, 1995). Play allows the children to progress through their development and work through abnormal behavior (Schaefer, 1993), as well as helps to enhance self-esteem and problem-solving skills. It is an ideal way to help children deal with their frustrations and conflicts (Landreth, 1983).

Further, play encourages social, emotional, and academic development. If a child is not ready to learn, due to the interference of emotional issues, play therapy would then serve as "an adjunct to the learning environment, an experience which assists children in maximizing their opportunities to learn" (Landreth, 1983, p. 201).

6. Because children attend school daily, it is an ideal environment for offering needed mental health services. They are able to form attachments and try out newly learned behavioral management skills with peers and benefit from the consistency and dependability of the caring clinician, be it the school clinician or teacher. The adaptive skills acquired in the playroom can generalize to other life situations and become the basis for improvement in academic and social skill areas.

7. Scheduling issues are easily managed and can be flexible, as the child is in school regularly and for a long period of time. Overburdened parents with limited financial resources do not have to worry about getting their child to sessions or paying for them.

8. In addition, the child is already familiar with the school counselor in the building or the classroom teacher, which helps to more quickly facilitate the initial stage of building a trusting relationship with the clinician.

9. The availability of teachers who can also be utilized to offer play therapy services and/or implement play therapy techniques in the classroom setting could help lessen the shortage of trained clinicians to meet the demand for in-school mental health services.

Kranz (1972) reported positive changes in the children in play therapy with a teacher, as evidenced in the children's being more relaxed, more open to educational experiences, and having more adequate peer relationships.

10. Finally, the interdisciplinary approach to the child in one setting allows for economical use of time in gathering the input of not only the teacher and school clinician but also the speech therapist, social worker, remedial reading teacher, and school nurse who may have contact with the child. Consultation services are readily available to assist in problem solving and individualizing approaches to the child. It is easy to observe the child in the natural school setting and watch interactions in a variety of areas over the course of assessment and treatment. Consequently, the play therapist can receive and offer on a regular basis concrete input and suggestions to those school personnel involved with the child without violating the child's confidentiality. This also allows the school personnel to feel collaborative in the process and supported by the suggestions. Alexander (1964) viewed the play therapist as helping to create an expanding therapeutic attitude throughout the school system, through sharing insights into and understanding of the child's behavior with the teacher. This sharing can in turn help teachers to develop more therapeutic attitudes toward all students.

ADVANTAGES OF USING PLAY THERAPY/TECHNIQUES IN THE SCHOOL

In many schools, children may perceive going to see the school psychologist, counselor, or social worker as a punishment or as evidence that they are in trouble and bad. The use of toys and play materials in the school clinician's office makes it an inviting place and a comfortable one, conveying the notion that talking is not always required or expected. It also establishes that the setting and play therapist are different from the academic environment and allows the child to be less performance-oriented and more relaxed. The child quickly comes to learn that the school clinician is there to truly focus on the child and understand the child's communications through play in a nonjudgmental way. "Since play is the language of the child, play provides a medium for building the essential relationship between counselor and child. The counselor is able to enter into the child's emotional world as it is freely revealed and acted upon by the child" (Landreth, 1983, p. 202). Through the use of play, the school clinician can establish a therapeutic and working relationship with the child to help the child break through defenses and work out emotional issues. The ability of the school clinician to offer the consistency of a reliable and stable therapeutic environment and supportive individual is critical for children coming from chaotic and unpredictable households. The school clinician can offer a consistent space, along with the same toys and materials that each week are in their own special place within the therapy room (or classroom).

In addition, referred children can develop play interests that can be carried throughout their daily life and help strengthen social interaction skills. Play can also be used to assist in the diagnostic understanding of the child and help assess developmental levels. Play as therapy can be directed to address developmental challenges and lags. Through the use of play and play therapy, children can alleviate abnormal behavior and facilitate normal development (Schaefer, 1993). Play therapy can also be used to encourage children to understand that their feelings are important and valid. They can learn to deal constructively with their negative feelings as well as build self-esteem, resiliency, and confidence. By dealing with conflicts and negatively impacting behaviors, children can improve their academic success (Ray & Bratton, 1999).

Play therapy with children with ADHD has been a successful modality, as it involves the child in the process while it teaches him or her life management skills. ADHD impacts a child's emerging personality and cognitive skills. Skill deficits result in negative feedback in various areas of the child's environment, most notably in peer social interactions. Often, children with ADHD have difficulty connecting with their own feelings and expressing them in words. Through play, children are able to enhance their communication and allow issues to evolve in a non-threatening manner. In individual or group sessions with peers, a child with ADHD is able to work on self-control, which is a major deficit; such children act impulsively, without thinking, and beyond their conscious intent and control. In play therapy, the child is able to gain self-control through game play and a variety of other techniques, including behavioral management components.

For children with a variety of emotional disorders, anger management skills can more readily be taught and practiced using play therapy techniques. A variety of materials can be utilized, such as clay, balls, and expressive art materials for anger release, along with child-centered play therapy and/or cognitive-behavioral play therapy modalities. Specific anger management activities along with relaxation training can further help teach needed skills to control physical aggression and impulsivity. By making the time spent with the school clinician more fun, the work of addressing behavioral problems becomes more productive and the child does not see coming to sessions as punishment or evidence that he or she is bad. Rather, the child comes to see the sessions as a collaborative effort to help improve school functioning and peer interactions. It is important that the school clinician offers sessions unconditionally, and not have them tied to a teacher's or administrator's view of whether the student misbehaved or deserves the time with the clinician. The child's attendance in sessions must occur regardless of the behavior.

Play therapy techniques are also very effective when combined with skill building in working with groups of children to address a variety of issues (poor social skills, anger management, death of a loved one, sexual abuse, parental divorce or alcoholism, etc.). Role playing, bibliotherapy, and cooperative activities help to lessen the individual child's feelings of isolation and helps children feel that their situation is not unique or unusual. In addition, having other peers together in a group setting allows for participants to practice their newly learned skills in a safe and supportive environment before trying them out with classroom peers. Play therapy techniques and groups can also be utilized in the classroom setting, led either by the school clinician or teacher or by both working together. Enhanced cooperative peer interactions, social skills, and problem solving can result when working with the full classroom, along with the added benefit of a more cohesive classroom and calmer learning environment.

There is also the benefit of having a full school year to work with a child. The school clinician has the time to work through to completion many emotional and behavioral issues. If further work needs to be done the following school year, the student will more than likely be returning to the same school building again for an additional year. This allows for further sessions or periodic checkins on progress with the student and the next grade teacher, even if the child was discharged from receiving services.

Administrators are often pleased to have school clinicians deal through creative and innovative ways with the many children with behavioral problems. By lessening the number of problem students and by improving their behavioral and academic performance, the school clinician can help convince administrators of the need for play therapy services and financial support for materials, training, and supervision. Play therapy services in the school also have the advantage of assisting numerous children who would not be able to receive psychological services outside of the school due to lack of parental support, involvement, financial ability, or motivation. In addition, by having the teacher join with the school clinician as a coleader in running classroom groups, or by consulting with teachers on how play therapy techniques can be implemented in the classroom, the school clinician helps to increase the supportive inter-actions available. This collaborative effort also helps the school clinician in managing or even increasing the amount of psychological services of-fered in the school.

CHALLENGES OF USING PLAY THERAPY/TECHNIQUES IN THE SCHOOL

CAN WE CALL IT THERAPY?

Therapy is often an emotionally laden term that many parents negatively associate with deep emotional disturbance or a judgment on their parent-ing skills. School administrators may state that therapy is outside the scope of the school, and even beyond the expertise of the school clinician. However, if a child is already classified as eligible for special support and needs psychological services, the school clinician will need to use some type of play therapy framework, theory, and technique to meet that child's mandated service. Although a parent may have already given con-sent to the service, the child and/or parent may still have feelings about the child's needing to see someone for emotional or behavioral problems. In addition, there may be a special group program conducted in the class-room around building self-esteem or positive peer interactions or a spe-cial group formed outside of the classroom for a particular common issue (divorce, death, etc.) that will require consent or notification of the par-ent. Some school clinicians have found that calling their play therapy ses-sions or their use of play therapy techniques by another name helps to lessen the stigma and can get around any potential objections about the term therapy. Alternative descriptive terms include developmental play, play counseling (play counselor), play development, and "play media pro-grams, counseling with toys, emotional growth through play, develop-mental growth through play" (Landreth, 1983, p. 205).

The school clinician must become a vocal and strong advocate of play therapy service. Play therapy needs to be translated into concrete specifics: what it is, how it can help children, and how it fits into the school's educational objectives. School personnel (teachers, principal, ad-ministrators) will better understand what you are offering when you ex-plain it in a way that realistically portrays what play therapy can accomplish and how it is relevant to the state's standards and mandates. Play therapy can readily be explained as the means of offering children the ability to gain self-control and self-direction, and that these goals are similar to those of teachers and administrators. The school clinician will still need to educate the administration, principal, parents, teachers, and support service professionals and even the child that play therapy does not mean "playing around" or "playing" with the child or spending the session nonproductively "fooling around." The school clinician will need to show research on the benefits of play therapy, offer brochures and books explaining what play therapy is, refer to the Web sites available on play therapy and of the national and state branch associations of play therapy, explain the training needed to be a play therapist, and share articles and videotapes about play therapy and the various techniques. By giving a presentation at a staff in-service training and/or at a Parent-Teacher Association meeting, school clinicians can help dispel misconceptions about the field of play therapy and the work they are doing with the children.

The best way of "selling" your work is having a satisfied "customer." Often, there is one teacher who, perhaps at first skeptical about the use of play therapy, has found that a child was dramatically helped by the service. This teacher can often be the best public relations person for you, telling other teachers and staff of his or her student's success and the benefits of the play therapy service. Also, having teachers join with the school clinician in running a special group using play therapy techniques or helping teachers utilize specific play therapy techniques or materials in their classroom will dramatically help to get others to see what you do and the benefits of play therapy in helping children grow intellectually, emotionally, and academically. Further, this collaboration will help dispel the negative feeling that a child who has misbehaved all day does not deserve to be rewarded by going to play therapy and having "fun." Teachers will see that play therapy is work, on the part of both the school clinician and the teacher as well as the child who is trying to work out problems and feelings.

"QUICK FIX" MANDATE

School clinicians have limited time to work with children. The ideal ratio is 1 school clinician for every 250 students, yet often the untenable ratio is 1:1,000 or more, which may include traveling to several schools during the week to provide services. Many school districts have gone from a centralized system (with the school clinician staying in one building full time) to a decentralized system where one person may have four areas or locations to go to, with little congruency among them. There may be no space or materials for seeing children in play therapy at some of the sites, or resistance toward having materials left in a space shared by other school personnel. Teachers may have the expectation that the clinician will return the child to the classroom "all fixed up" or "straightened out." The school clinician can support teachers' efforts to help get children more on task, but teachers need to be helped to understand the underlying premise of the therapeutic process, which is giving children freedom to choose what they work on and how. Therefore, the teachers' agenda may not even be addressed on a particular day.

The downsizing of school staff, cutting school clinician jobs and those of middle management, may result in having a principal or nonpsychologically trained supervisor being responsible for assigning the school clinician's caseload and overseeing problems. Long waiting lists begin to occur, especially as school clinician jobs are lost.

Teachers, feeling the constraints of meeting their state's standards through required curricula and grade performance, often feel impatient waiting for a child to be helped in reducing disruptive behaviors or difficulty in learning. They need to be educated in the process of play therapy and that it requires time for a child to work out issues and learn new behaviors. Teachers can also be helped to utilize techniques in the classroom to address anger management and release of feelings; these can be incorporated into and compatible with the standards they are mandated to cover. This collaborative effort and shifting of services to the classroom can help lessen referrals made by teachers for the school clinician's services. It can also lessen the reluctance by teachers to allow a child to miss classroom time, especially if the child is also pulled out due to behavioral problems or other special services.

Flexibility in problem solving is critical for the school clinician, along with the ability to be creative and innovative in meeting the demands and difficulties of conducting play therapy.

SCHEDULING LIMITATIONS

School clinicians may encounter difficulty getting children released from their classroom setting for sessions. Careful coordination and collaboration with the classroom teacher is essential to work out a mutually agreeable time and day, with the least disruption to the class and the child's education. In addition, the play therapist has limited time available to offer services to so many children referred and mandated. Scheduling groups or play therapy sessions during lunch, before and after school, and during nonacademic times or recess can permit clinicians to more easily see the students throughout the day. This can also reduce or eliminate conflict with teachers over children missing academics.

Sessions may need to be limited to 30 minutes rather than the usual 45 or 50 minutes in clinics and private practice. Children who are being seen more for the developmental benefits of play therapy might be able to utilize 15-minute sessions twice weekly as readily as a full 30-minute session. These children do not need an intense relationship with the play therapist and may need instead to focus on a specific problem area or be seen for short-term or less severe issues. For instance, a child who has problems attending school because of a school phobia or recent family event (birth of a baby, death of a relative, parental hospitalization) could be seen for 5 to 10 minutes daily before school starts. Interaction with a supportive school clinician and time to work out concerns and relax using the toys and play materials would help ease the child's entry into the day's program. This initial contact and playful start to the day would help the child look forward to school and lessen the stress on the child. Short periods spent in the play therapy room a few times a week can also help children who have lots of energy, poor impulse control, or short attention span. Flexible scheduling or use of shorter sessions over a few days in the week also helps address the issue of absenteeism, particularly of children at risk or coming from disorganized homes. When a child is absent, the school clinician can reschedule shorter sessions more readily than if a large block of time was allotted only once a week. The use of short-term play therapy and play therapy groups can also help solve the dilemma of too many students and too little time.

SPACE LIMITATIONS

Ginott (1961) recommends 150 to 200 square feet for a play therapy room. Often, the school clinician does not have the luxury of this much space; often, there is no adequate space at all to have a play therapy room within a school. The school clinician may also need to travel to several different settings and may have no assigned room to use. Facilities may be inadequate, with no locking file cabinets, direct phone line, or comfortable chairs. Again, flexibility and creativity on the part of the play therapist can overcome these hurdles. The use of a vacant office or classroom, part of the cafeteria or library, a corner of a classroom, a hallway area, an unused workshop, a large storage closet or even an art room can be transformed, with a portable play therapy kit containing essential materials, into a play therapy space. Some therapists utilize the school stage in the auditorium or in the cafeteria. One school clinician converted a school bus into a play therapy office and used it to travel to various schools where services were given. Grants or special funding may provide money for a central location where children can be bused for therapy to help ease time constraints.

It is essential, however, that whatever space is utilized, it is sufficiently large and private for sessions to occur. Children's confidentiality and privacy must be guarded, and children should be told if others will be able to hear or see what they are doing.

LACK OF TRAINING AND/OR SUPERVISION

Adding to the school clinician's and teacher's burdens is the lack of availability of trained school clinicians who can meet the demand of treatment services and offer anger management skill training in the schools (Thomas & Holzer, 1999).

Consequently, school clinicians and teachers have become overwhelmed with the need to come up with practical solutions for dealing with the many referrals for school services. But many school counselors and teachers are ill equipped to use play therapy techniques in the counseling setting or classroom due to lack of training or knowledge of the field of play therapy. Many school clinicians, especially the paraprofessionals, may not have training specific to play therapy theory and play therapy techniques. Often, even in graduate psychology programs, there is little or no coursework devoted to play therapy. Some school districts hire paraprofessionals at a lower salary than a school clinician with a master's or doctorate, which allows the district to save money while trying to get more personnel to help the children. But sometimes the paraprofessional has no counseling education or training either. Monies for attending conferences and workshops in play therapy may be limited. With funding cuts, middle-management supervisors are being let go, which results in a lack of supervisors with psychological training and expertise. A school principal may be competent to offer administrative supervision, but such supervision is not adequate to address clinical and psychological issues. Many times the school clinician is the *only* person within the school building or district offering psychological services. A support network of school clinicians in the district, or among nearby districts, can help by forming a peer supervision group that could meet outside of the school day on a regular monthly basis.

The Association for Play Therapy was founded in 1982 in New York "to provide a forum for professionals interested in developing a *distinct group of interventions that use play as an integral component of the therapeutic process* for children in need" (2000a, p. 2). The mission statement of APT promotes

> (1) the understanding of play and play therapy, (2) the effective practice of play therapy through training, research and support, (3) the recognition, incorporation, and preservation of diversity in play and play therapy, and (4) the development and maintenance of a strong professional organization to accomplish these objectives. (2000b, p. 11)

State branches have formed to help further these ideals locally and to make training more readily available and accessible. APT has specific requirements for academic degree, training and supervision received, and direct clinical experience to obtain the status of Registered Play Therapist or RPT-Supervisor. School clinicians are urged to obtain training and supervision in play therapy and should not try to implement techniques (even from within this book) without it. It is unethical for school clinicians to practice play therapy or even utilize play therapy techniques when they are functioning beyond the realm of personal competence and training. Information about APT and local branches and workshop and conference training in play therapy can be obtained through Web sites and direct contact (see Association for Play Therapy, Inc., 2050 N. Winery Avenue, Suite 101, Fresno, CA 93703, www.iapt.org).

Areas of Special Consideration

Expense of Materials

Play therapy materials need not cost a fortune nor put a play therapist into debt. The specifics of what materials are most helpful and essential to have will be discussed in depth in Chapter 4. Even if the school clinician has only a small budget (or even none), there are many creative ways to obtain needed materials for your playroom and sessions. You can find many materials through garage sales, hand-me-downs from siblings or relatives, and thrift stores. The school Parent-Teacher Association can also be contacted for a grant for particularly expensive items, such as sand trays. Even notes sent home with students asking parents for particular toys and items can result in obtaining what you need. However, you must be selective. Do not accumulate junk or broken toys. Do not have valuable items in your room for children to use whose loss or damage will create an imbalance in the therapeutic relationship between you and the child. Think more of the therapeutic value of the item and whether it can be readily and easily replaced.

Noise

The problem of noise volume during sessions often arises. Children express their feelings loudly, both verbally and through the action of their play. Teachers and administrators may not tolerate the banging, shouts, or noise coming from the play therapy room, even though the amount of time spent on this mode of expression may be small in comparison to the time spent in quiet play or conversation. Limits on the child's behavior and volume of expression may be needed more often than in a clinic or private practice setting. Ideally, the space utilized for the play therapy process should be far from classrooms and administrative areas. This physical distance from the more controlled and less permissive classroom atmosphere helps to contrast and differentiate for the child, on a deeper psychological level, the more permissive, accepting atmosphere of the play therapy room (Schiffer, 1969). Also, physical distance from class-rooms and offices helps to minimize the disruption and sound to the classrooms. If this distance is not possible, the child needs to be reminded when the volume needs to be lowered. The play therapist will find it nec-essary to set more limits on the child's behavior than in another type of setting (clinic, private practice). More direction and explanation will be needed as to what is off-limits for the child. In addition, the play therapist will need to rethink the types of materials available in the room so as not to further add to conflicts over noise.

Teachers and administrators also must be educated about the process of play therapy. It is important to explain that it is the process of allowing children to express their feelings by using play therapy materials and tech-niques that allows for the resolution of issues and the gaining of self-control. Finally, giving permission and freedom to let out feelings, even in a noisy way, during the play process in the session lessens the likelihood of the child's acting out or becoming disruptive in the classroom setting.

Confidentiality

It is important for children to know at the outset of your work together that there is limited confidentiality of what they share with you. It is important to establish what the limits to confidentiality are, such as information that someone is hurting (physically or sexually abusing, threatening) the child, whether an adult or another child, or that the child is about to harm self or other. Children need to understand your role as a mandated reporter of possible abuse and neglect, and that you will have to file a report based on what they tell you. You should state that, if a report has to be made, you will explain it to them at that time and go over what the process entails. There may be times when it is difficult to know whether or not to make a report, and your decision to file one may be at odds with the principal, who may also be your supervisor. This alone can be a difficult task for the school clinician. It is important to have adequate supervision to help you process your decision and guide you in your legal requirements.

There may be times when you will need to share information with a parent, teacher, principal, or outside agency. The parent(s) and school personnel are ideally also part of your treatment team, working together in the best interests of the child. As the child is a minor, it is the parent who holds the legal privilege about communication. It is helpful to let the child know that there will be times, such as at school meetings and parent conferences, when you may have to share the child's progress during ses-sions or issues that are of concern, and that those adults at the meeting are all working together to help the child. However, you can help assure the child that his or her privacy can still be respected by not revealing exact details, words, and so on of sessions unless the child wants them shared. Instead, you could share themes and general information, getting the child's permission before the meeting about what to include.

SUMMARY

Since the turn of the twentieth century, when psychological services first entered schools, there has been a need for school clinicians to deal with the emotional and behavioral problems of children. Even 100 years later, school districts have a growing need to offer psychological services to address the dramatic rise in school violence, abuse and neglect, emotional disorders, family dysfunction, and societal stresses. There continues to be a shortage of professionals and paraprofessionals who have the expertise and training to deal with these issues. The benefits of offering play therapy in the school are many. The use of play therapy and play therapy techniques in the school and classroom, especially early on in the child's life and early in the problem stage, results in higher success rates and a lower financial burden for society in the future. The school system is the ideal setting to offer early intervention and preventive services, as well as a therapeutic milieu. Play, and consequently play therapy, is a natural way for children to express their feelings and emotions. The use of toys and various play materials allows for the development of expressive and affective skills as well as the playing out of life situations and traumas. Through the help of the skilled school clinician or teacher, the child can enhance self-esteem and problem-solving skills and reduce behavioral problems, which limit academic success.

There are many advantages and challenges in using play therapy/techniques in schools. It is hoped that the practical suggestions and examples supplied in this chapter will encourage school clinicians and teachers to try incorporating play therapy and play therapy techniques in their work with children in the schools. If such services were available in all school districts, in time the positive impact of an expanding therapeutic attitude throughout the school system would have a profound effect not only on teachers and administrators but, most of all, on all the children.

REFERENCES

Alexander, E.D. (1964). School-centered play therapy program. *Personnel and Guidance Journal, 43*, 256–261.

Anastopoulos, A.D., & Barkley, R.A. (1992). Attention deficit-hyperactivity disorder. In C.E. Walker & M.C. Roberts (Eds.), *Handbook of clinical child psychology* (2nd ed., pp. 413–430). New York: Wiley.

Association for Play Therapy, Inc. (2000a). *Membership directory: 2000–2001.* Fresno, CA: Author.

Association for Play Therapy, Inc. (2000b). *NewsLetter, 19*(2), 11.

Barkley, R.A. (1998). Attention deficit/hyperactivity disorder. In E.J. Mash & R.A. Barkley (Eds.), *Treatment of child disorders* (pp. 55–110). New York: Guilford Press.

Brandenburg, N.A., Friedman, R.M., & Silver, S.E. (1990). Epidemiology of child psychiatric disorders: Prevalence findings from recent studies. *Journal of the American Academy of Child and Adolescent Psychiatry, 29,* 76–83.

Centers for Disease Control and Prevention. (1998, August 14). Youth risk behavior surveillance–United States, 1997. *CDC surveillance summaries MMWR, 47*(No. SS-3). Atlanta, GA: Author.

Chess, S., & Thomas, A. (1986). *Temperament in clinical practice.* New York: Guilford Press.

DuPaul, G.J., & Stoner, G. (1994). *ADHD in the schools: Assessment and intervention strategies.* New York: Guilford Press.

Fagan, T.K. (1995). Trends in the history of school psychology in the United States. In A. Thomas & J. Grimes (Eds.), *Best practices in school psychology–III* (pp. 59–67). Washington, DC: National Association of School Psychologists.

Fagan, T.K. (2000). Practicing school psychology. *American Psychologist, 55,* 754–757.

Gage, N.L. (1990). Dealing with the drop-out problem. *Phi Delta Kappan, 72,* 280–285.

Ginott, H.G. (1961). *Group psychotherapy with children.* New York: McGraw-Hill.

Kantrowitz, B. (1997, Spring/Summer). Off to a good start: Your child. *Newsweek* [Special edition] 7–9.

Kottman, T. (1995). *Partners in play: An Adlerian approach to play therapy.* Alexandria, VA: American Counseling Association.

Kranz, P.L. (1972). Teachers as play therapists: An experiment in learning. *Childhood Education, 49,* 73–74.

Landreth, G., & Bratton, S. (1999). *Play therapy.* New York: Wiley.

Landreth, G.L. (1983). Play therapy in elementary school settings. In C.E. Schaefer & K.J. O'Connor (Eds.), *Handbook of play therapy* (pp. 200–212). New York: Wiley.

Maxfield, M.G., & Widom, C.S. (1996). The cycle of violence: Revisited six years later. *Archives of Pediatrics and Adolescent Medicine, 150*(4), 390–395.

National Center on Child Abuse and Neglect. (1994). *State statutes related to child abuse and neglect: 1993.* Washington, DC: U.S. Department of Health and Human Resources.

Osofsky, J. (1995). The effects of exposure to violence on young children. *American Psychologist, 50,* 782–788.

Perry, B.D. (1996). Incubated in terror: Neurodevelopmental factors in the cycle of violence. In J.D. Osofsky (Ed.), *Children, youth and violence: Searching for solutions* (pp. 124–149). New York: Guilford Press.

Perry, B.D. (1997). *Maltreated children: Experience, brain development and the next generation.* New York: Norton.

Ray, D., & Bratton, S. (1999). *Play therapy: What research says about play.* Association for Play Therapy, Inc. [Online]. Available: www.iapt.org/research.html

Safford, P.L., & Safford, E.J. (1996). *A history of childhood and disability.* New York: Teachers College Press.

Sanders, M.J., & Dyer-Friedman, J. (1997). Child abuse. In H. Steiner (Ed.), *Treating school-age children* (pp. 189–214). San Francisco: Jossey-Bass.

Schaefer, C.E. (1993). *The therapeutic powers of play.* Northvale, NJ: Aronson.

Schiffer, M. (1969). *The therapeutic play group.* New York: Grune & Stratton.

Shaw, R.J., & Feldman, S.S. (1997a). General principles and treatment. In H. Steiner (Ed.), *Treating preschool children* (pp. 1–26). San Francisco: Jossey-Bass.

Shaw, R.J., & Feldman, S.S. (1997b). General principles and treatment. In H. Steiner (Ed.), *Treating school-age children* (pp. 1–31). San Francisco: Jossey-Bass.

Slater, R. (1980). The organizational origins of public school psychology. *Educational Studies, 2,* 1–11.

Snyder, T.D., Hoffman, C.M., & Geddes, C.M. (1997). *Digest of educational statistics 1997.* Washington, DC: U.S. Department of Education, Office of Educational Research and Improvement.

Steiner, H. (Ed.). (1997). *Treating preschool children.* San Francisco: Jossey-Bass.

Surgeon General. (1999). *Mental health: A report of the surgeon general* [Online]. Available: www.surgeongeneral.gov/library/mentalhealth/chapter3/html

Thomas, C.R., & Holzer, C.E., III. (1999). National distribution of child and adolescent psychiatrists. *Journal of the American Academy of Child and Adolescent Psychiatry, 38,* 9–15.

VanFleet, R. (1998). Play therapy ideas No. 6: Family Enhancement and Play Therapy Center [Online]. Available: play-therapy.com/ideas6-html

Wright, J.D., & Devine, J.A. (1993). Housing dynamics of the homeless: Implications for a count. *American Journal of Orthopsychiatry, 65*(3), 320–329.

Zelman, A. (Ed.). (1996). *Early intervention with high-risk children.* New York: Aronson.

Zigler, E., & Lang, M. (1991). *Child care choices: Balancing the needs of children, families and society.* New York: Free Press.

CHAPTER 4

Play Objects and Play Spaces

ATHENA A. DREWES

THE SCHOOL clinician (school psychologist, social worker, school or area counselor, guidance counselor, teacher, or paraprofessional, such as child associate or youth and family worker) needs to carefully consider which toys and materials and space to utilize when working with children in play therapy or using play therapy techniques. This chapter focuses on the various guidelines for selecting the proper toys and materials, as well as how best to set up the play therapy room or office for working with children in a school setting.

RATIONALE

The central premise of play therapy, which mandates the use of toys when working with children, is that toys stand for the child's words, just as play is the child's language (Landreth, 1991). Play becomes a medium of exchange, comparable to the use of words as the adult's medium of exchange. But play is not therapy by itself, just as talking is not therapy by itself. All therapies require the formation of a therapeutic relationship, along with the use of a medium of exchange. The use of play helps establish a working relationship with children, especially those who lack verbal self-expression, and even with older children who show resistance or an inability to articulate their feelings and issues (Haworth, 1964). Play allows a child to "verbalize" conscious material and associated feelings. It can also be used to help the child act out unconscious material and thereby reduce or eliminate uncomfortable feelings and tension

(Haworth, 1964). Through the play activity, children can be helped to develop a way of handling themselves and managing behavior, which will continue to be valuable later as an adult. The school clinician is able to create a safe and encouraging therapeutic environment through providing material, opportunities, and encouragement to help children test themselves as individuals and thereby mobilize resiliency and self-healing abilities to deal with current and future issues.

The presence of toys and play materials in the room sends a message to the child that this space and time is different from all others. It indicates to the children that they are given permission to be children, and to feel free in being children, at their own pace and in their own way (Landreth, 1983). It is important that the school clinician obtain a diagnostic understanding of the dynamics of the child's personality, as this will guide which materials and type of play therapy strategy (directive or nondirective) are selected for a particular child (Haworth, 1964).

WHY CERTAIN TOYS ARE SELECTED

The literature abounds with various views as to which toys and materials should be selected and why, as well as how to utilize the toy to assist the child. The general consensus is that whatever material or toy is placed in the room (whether a play therapy room, an office, or a space on an auditorium stage), it is there for a specific purpose. The objects should be selected with the goal of allowing the child to be free to focus on internal processes, as well as allow for maximum expression (James, 1997). No object should be included just because it is a toy or a popular fad in the stores. The toys and materials are selected and placed in consistent locations within the room to create (1) a therapeutic atmosphere of trust (that the toy will be there each week); (2) predictability (it will be in the same location each week); and (3) a child's personal capability (the child does not need to ask for help and depend on the adult; James, 1997). Each time the child enters the therapeutic space, it is as though it were the first session, with everything back in its place, with no surprises, and with the opportunity to return to a previous play scenario or to start anew on something different. By removing the external distractions of misplaced toys, broken or missing toys, or complicated toys requiring dependency on others, the room becomes stress-free and the child can get down to the business of working through issues. "It is important to recognize that young children personify toys. They frequently assume the role of caretaker of these objects to which they have given special meaning. When they fear that the toys are not safe, they may also assume that they themselves will not be safe" (James, 1997, p. 78).

The toys need to be able to provide children with experiences in which they can feel successful, and so the toys must be durable and well made. The toys should pull for the child's interest and allow for a broad range of creative and emotional expression, as well as allow for verbal and nonverbal exploration and expression (Landreth, 1991). It is important that the school clinician avoid toys that children feel uncomfortable with or about. Children will pick up on the clinician's nonverbal communication and discomfort, and this will in turn impact on and even hinder the therapeutic relationship and interaction. No toy should be selected that cannot be replaced or is of high personal and emotional value to the clinician. The toys also need to be developmentally appropriate for the child, as children dealing with various emotional traumas may find themselves at a lower developmental than chronological age. The use of play as therapy can be directed to address developmental challenges and lags. Some children may need alternative methods to express their feelings; they may be more visual or kinesthetic processors. So, the use of tactile materials may be more appropriate in helping to develop expressive and affective skills.

Theoretical Reasons

The particular theoretical framework studied, followed, or used by your case supervisor or you in conducting play therapy will help to guide in the selection and arrangement of the toys and materials. Several noted individuals have offered different theories, writings, and techniques that have led to their being considered the pioneers in the field of play therapy. Those trained in their philosophy continue today to follow the guidelines they have established.

Anna Freud

Freud (1951) used toys primarily during the initial or introductory phase of treatment, to help woo children into the therapeutic process until they were able to verbalize their concerns directly. She believed that children were able to use fantasy to express thoughts before they could verbally do so (James, 1997). Freud indicated that the following toys and materials should be utilized: (1) sturdy wooden blocks of various shapes, with cars and trucks able to fit the blocks, which may in turn be made into buildings, houses, and roads; (2) fabric, needle, and thread to make blankets and pillows and clothes for dolls; (3) a collection of small animals, both wild and domestic; (4) finger puppets of firefighters, nurses, doctors, police, and other kinds of people who are in the child's life; (5) a small Lego set, a set of dominoes, and two decks of cards. In addition, safe scissors, rubber bands, toothpicks, scotch tape, a good stapler, pens, pencils, erasers, markers, crayons, and paper need to be available. The guiding principle is to offer the child tools for expression through play, but to have a minimal amount of toys. In this way, the toys and materials do not become so entertaining and gratifying that they get in the way of or create resistance to the therapeutic work (Siskind, 1992).

Melanie Klein

Klein (1955), on the other hand, had a separate box for each child to use each session, with initials (to protect confidentiality) on it. The box contained various miniature toys that were specific to the child's issues and that could be added to or deleted over the course of the year. She included the following items: small or miniature wooden men and women, small cars, trains, airplanes, animals, trees, bricks, houses, fences, paper, scissors, pencils, string, chalk or paints, glue, a knife that was not too sharp, marbles and balls, string, and clay. No mechanical toys were to be used. The goal was for the child to be able to utilize fantasy; thus, the materials should allow for use in a multitude of ways so that the children could express many different feelings and their personal story (James, 1997).

Clark Moustakas

Moustakas (1959), noted for his pioneering work in relationship therapy, suggested unstructured materials such as water, paints, clay, and sand to allow the child an opportunity to release feelings that have been pent up. The child would then be able to pound, hit, shape, and reshape the object, molding it into various images of the issues the child was dealing with. Moustakas believed that the unstructured nature of the items, especially in the early phases of therapy, were particularly valuable because they allowed the child an opportunity to express feelings indirectly at a time when the child was not ready to face those feelings openly. Aggressive feelings, he believed, could be displaced onto such items as darts, rubber or plastic knives, play guns, and swords. Rather than hurting others or themselves, the child could express extreme feelings through acts of stabbing, punching, shooting, cutting, killing, and attacking on objects or symbolically in play (James, 1997; Moustakas, 1959). Further, he suggested having family dolls and puppets available to allow for the working out of issues involving the family or siblings. In addition, Moustakas suggested having cars, trucks, tractors, checkers, paper, pencils, and boats to allow the child to play games and have "noncommittal activities until he is ready to express his feelings either indirectly and diffusely through the nonhuman items or directly through the family and other human figures" (p. 8). Moustakas felt the therapist should be nondirective in approach to allow children to freely express themselves and to choose materials.

Virginia Axline

Axline (1947), a nondirective play therapy theorist, believed that each child has within himself or herself the capacity for self-actualization. She believed there were three key components to the therapeutic work: the toys, limits, and the therapist's relationship and role. It was through the relationship between child and therapist that the child was able to be promoted and helped to grow emotionally. Axline wanted the child to have the ability to freely choose toys and materials, which were readily accessible in the room. The toys should be able to be used for family play and aggressive displays. The materials should be nonstructured, such as paints, clay, and water, and the toys should include animals, a telephone, and soldiers. She also suggested including a large sandbox that the child can sit in (James, 1997), as well as allowing the opportunity for dramatic play with a stage.

Violet Oaklander

Oaklander (1988) uses a Gestalt approach that emphasizes sensory experience. She includes materials that encourage access to feelings and allow for the connection between body and emotion to allow the child to develop congruence (James, 1997). She encourages the use of manipulative and imaginative toys and has created a variety of techniques that involve drawing with guided imagery and storytelling. Fantasy play is also encouraged through use of clay, wood, sand, and water.

Garry Landreth

Landreth (1991), like Axline, a nondirective play therapy theorist offers rules for the selection of the toys that enable the children to be themselves. Landreth states that

> toys and materials should be selected to facilitate the seven essentials in play therapy: (1) the establishment of a positive relationship with the child, (2) the expression of a wide range of feelings, (3) the exploration of real life experiences, (4) reality testing of limits, (5) the development of a positive self-image, (6) the development of self-understanding, and (7) an opportunity to develop self-control. (p. 117)

He further adds that "the rule is selection rather than accumulation" (p. 116). You do not want to wind up having a room cluttered with randomly selected toys, which will in turn slow down and even prevent the therapeutic benefits of the time you've spent with the child.

Charles Schaefer

Schaefer (1993) advocates using a prescriptive approach both to the therapy model chosen and to the materials used, as one standardized play therapy approach is not effective across a variety of symptoms and problem areas. Using the prescriptive approach, the school clinician creates an intervention strategy that is specific to the child's emotional issues and concerns.

Directive Play Therapy

Where a more directive approach may be needed, materials such as puppets, dolls, and various art supplies are useful in helping to guide a child to deal with a specific issue (e.g., sexual or physical abuse trauma, birth of a sibling, hospitalization, or death of family member or friend). Bibliotherapy and storytelling may also be employed. Social skills training and anger management, being more directive by nature, require use of therapeutic and common board games and a variety of creative expressive arts tasks, along with role playing and practicing of new skills.

SPECIAL POPULATIONS

Working with various populations will also pull for inclusion of various types of materials and toys. Ginott (1961) stated:

> Enuretic children should be given paint and running water, encopretic children should be given mud and brown clay. Children who play with fire should have cap guns, sparklers, and flashlights. All children should have miniature utensils for cooking and serving meals to sublimate oral needs; dolls that can be dressed and undressed to sublimate sexual needs; and punching bags, targets, and guns to sublimate aggressive needs. (p. 62)

Children who need to deal with aggression and angry feelings need aggressive-release toys (Landreth, 1991). This may include a "bop bag" or punching bag or clay for hitting and pounding. In addition, culturally appropriate toys, such as multiethnic, multicultural dolls and puppets and markers and paints with a variety of skin tones, are necessary to allow for exploration of ethnic and cultural issues and identity. Special population children, such as children who have physical or mental limitations or may be hospitalized, require modifications to the list of toys and an awareness by the school clinician of their differing needs and abilities.

The school clinician should also remember that the very nature or construction of the toy or material might determine and pull for a particular type of response and interaction from the child. Certain toys will automatically elicit a particular behavior. For example, the inclusion of a bop bag, a "bobo punching bag," or padded batakas will result in a child's expressing more aggressive feelings and actions through hitting, punching, and kicking than any other response. Dolls with baby bottles, on the other hand, usually elicit more nurturing and caretaking responses than aggression. It is important that the toys be carefully selected and thought through, especially during the initial stages of the therapeutic process, when the child is not sure how much to show of feelings or does not feel safe enough yet to express creativity (Landreth, 1991).

Toys to Avoid

Toys and materials to avoid for safety reasons include those that are sharp or pointed, contain glass, and are breakable. In addition, expensive, complicated, and mechanical toys and highly structured games should be avoided, as they tend to interfere with the child's free expression and creativity. Puzzles should be avoided, as it is easy to lose a piece, which then results in frustration, lack of success, and the prevention of closure for the child (Landreth, 1983). The school clinician should remove broken toys after the session and replace with others if possible, as broken toys and items wind up serving as a distraction and source of frustration for the child.

Recommended Toys and Materials

Landreth (1983, 1991) prepared a list of toys and materials he has found useful in working with children and based on over 25 years of experience in training students at the University of North Texas and as a therapist. Among the items on Landreth's (1983) list of the minimal requirements for a play therapy session, he includes:

> crayons, newsprint, blunt scissors, nursing bottle (plastic), rubber knife, doll, Play-Doh (or clay) . . . , dart gun, handcuffs, (20) toy soldiers, (two) plastic or tin play dishes and cups, spoons (avoid forks because of their sharp points), small airplane, small car, two play telephones, hand puppets (alligator, dragon or wolf) or bendable doll family, small cardboard box with rooms marked on the bottom and a door and window cut out, dollhouse furniture, small plain mask (Lone Ranger type), Nerf ball (rubber ball bounces too much), bendable Gumby, . . . popsicle sticks, pipe cleaners, pounding bench and hammer, old cap or hat, and egg cartons to stack, color or smash. (p. 206)

He also suggests having an inflatable vinyl punching bag toy and a dishpan-size plastic container with an inch of sand or rice on the bottom.

Landreth's (1991) more extensive list includes items such as doll bed, clothes, pacifier, chalkboard with chalk, wood refrigerator and stove, plastic food, broom and dust pan, building blocks, paints and easel, multiwheel riding toy, musical instruments (cymbal, drum, xylophone), hats (a variety, including firefighter's), zoo and farm animals, suction-tipped darts, toy machine gun, rope, medical kit, play money and cash register, hand puppets (various types of occupations, family members, and aggressive animals), Tinkertoys, and tissues.

The school clinician does not have to go broke to obtain all these items. Many can be obtained by checking out local garage and yard sales; contacting siblings, friends, and relatives whose children may have outgrown their toys; posting a list in the teacher's lounge; or sending a note home through the children in the school building or via the school's Parent Teacher Association requesting donations of the items you need. Sometimes, monies are also available through school budgets and special grants from the PTA or community businesses. As mentioned earlier, be selective and do not accumulate junk or broken toys.

SPECIAL CONSIDERATIONS

The Portable Play Therapy Kit

For those school clinicians who need to travel to several locations or do not have a permanent playroom to use, a portable play therapy kit is essential. However, you need to consider the space you have and how portable the items are. As noted above, Landreth (1991) has a minimal list of items for conducting play therapy, as the items allow for a wide range of use and expression by the child. James (1997), who has had extensive experience going to many school sites each week to work with children, developed her own system. She designates a group of children at each school building as helpers; they carry in the materials she has brought that day. She suggested bringing nonstructured media such as papier-mâché, egg cartons and paint, material for building projects (e.g., wood for birdcages, bits of rock or other objects); books for bibliotherapy; small toy family members, small toy animals, a folding dollhouse, puppets, clay, crayons, chalk, small cars and trucks, a small sand tray, a few board games (which were rotated weekly), and something unique or special to the group or child she was working with (so they knew she remembered the child's preferred color choice or subject).

I have found it helpful to include wooden blocks, clay with a small pounding hammer and laminated placemats, two to four puppets (one domestic animal, one aggressive animal, and two people), a portable folding magnetic dollhouse and magnetic city (see addendum), and a medical kit, in addition to the items suggested by James. I, too, recommend using a small portable sand tray. This can be a blue Tupperware bucket with lid that has about one to two inches filled with sand, or you can use a litter box or sweater box. The small people and animal figures can double as sand tray items. I have also found it very useful to own a folding luggage cart, the small kind that you can put a few pieces of luggage on and roll, which are sold at airports and luggage stores. I load up several items, tie them in place with elastic cords, and then pull it from the car into the building. If you do not have anyone to assist you in bringing in your material, you still can do so efficiently and without straining yourself.

CLAY VERSUS PLAY-DOH

Often, school clinicians and play therapists include Play-Doh in their list of materials, and so I want to share my personal experiences and recommendations. Although Play-Doh feels wonderful when new, and even smells good to some children, my experience has been that in a short while it will begin to dry out and then crumble. Inevitably, the children will mix the colors into a nondescript new color, which soon after loses appeal for them. Also, Play-Doh does not allow for hardening into a final and lasting product or being painted and having a design added. If you find Play-Doh essential in your list of objects to have in your playroom, by all means continue to use it. However, I suggest some alternatives and additions to consider; included in the addendum is a list of other materials and where they can be ordered.

I enjoy using clay with children; however, traditional clay must be kept damp in an airtight container or plastic bag. This type of setting breeds bacteria and salmonella, which may result in infection if a child or adult has an open cut or sore on the hand. Consequently, after much searching I have come across a clay created by Myrna Minnis called Oogly Clay. Her idea is for children (and adults) to make Oogly figures, consisting of a large head to which you could add spaghetti-like hair (by using a garlic press included with the clay), as well as all sorts of feathers, buttons, and so on to decorate it. This creation helps work on self-esteem and self-image, which the child can add to or change over time. The clay itself is remarkable, in that it does not require special conditions to keep it usable. You can keep it in a plastic box or bag, but it can also be kept out in the air; it does not require moisture or being kept damp. After a short time holding and kneading it with your fingers, it softens up quickly and becomes quite malleable. You can undo the creations easily or let them sit out without worrying about the clay hardening or crumbling and can use the clay for any other therapeutic ideas you have. However, the clay cannot be fired or baked.

Other marvelous materials include Crayola's Model Magic, which air dries. It is a nontoxic, soft, and malleable modeling clay that is lightweight and very pliable. It does not crack, cling to surfaces, or flake. It comes in white, which when left to air dry, can be decorated with tempera or watercolor paints and markers. Crayola's Dough is also nontoxic and air dries within two days if permanent creations are desired. It comes in bright primary colors and in large tub containers and smaller amounts, depending on your need. If you do not want the Model Magic or Dough to dry out, you must keep it in an airtight container.

Sculpey is a white polymer clay that is soft and easy for young children to mold. It will not dry out when exposed to air and stays flexible until baked in a regular oven. After baking, it can be sanded and painted with water-based acrylic paint. It also comes in bright, vivid colors that can be baked in the oven. After baking, it becomes hard with a smooth matte finish.

The addendum lists these materials and where you can obtain them. I do not receive any financial benefit from these companies, but I do find their materials very useful in working with children and am always on the lookout for time-saving, inexpensive, and therapeutically useful supplies.

Toys That Release Aggression

Aggressive children need the freedom and permission to express their anger, rage, frustration, and hostility in the safe and accepting setting of the playroom. They may play out shooting, killing, burying, biting, and stabbing in symbolic terms. However, there is often intense affect along with the angry and aggressive feelings that the school clinician may find unsettling. It is important that you know your own personal "comfort zone" around such intense feelings so as not to move in too quickly to stop or interfere with the child's expression.

There appears to be a philosophical and theoretical difference between play therapists in the East Coast and the West (notably Texas) regarding the use of certain toys and materials that elicit aggressive feelings. This is particularly notable regarding the inclusion of toy guns, rope, handcuffs, rubber or plastic knives, suction-tipped darts, dart guns, swords, and masks. East Coast play therapists tend to exclude them, thereby allowing the child's fantasy to utilize other materials symbolically, whereas the Texas and West Coast play therapists consider these materials indispensable. In part, this may relate to the fact that play therapists in Texas and the West follow Axline's (1947) child-centered approach, and the East Coast play therapists appear to follow Anna Freud's (1951) psychoanalytic approach more. However, with the recent increase in children bringing guns and knives into schools, as well as the terrible tragedies of school shootings and deaths by children, schools have begun instituting or reinforcing strict rules prohibiting guns and knives in the school. Students are often immediately suspended, with police contacted, if found with or even overheard stating that they plan on using or bringing in such items. Consequently, the school clinician needs to carefully think out whether or not to include such items as toy guns, swords, and handcuffs in the playroom or therapy room regardless of what philosophical or play therapy theory, orientation, or technique is followed. If you feel it necessary to include these items in your therapeutic work, school administration need to be informed, as they may need to support your decision to parents and staff. However, it may be hard for school personnel to understand, in light of school policy and historical social events, why you choose to include such items as a means of releasing angry and aggressive feelings. You will need to explain the benefits of the use of play therapy and play therapy techniques, especially in reducing acting-out behaviors of children in school and the classroom.

You also need to consider the children's feelings. They may feel conflicted if they perceive that there are two different standards, one imposed by the school and one followed by the school clinician. They may feel uncomfortable using such materials, knowing the real-life consequences outside of the therapy room. You need to weigh the value of each position and develop a clear and sound rationale for whichever decision you make.

Some children may need a release for angry and aggressive feelings and to be able to play out scenes of violence that they face each day (at home or in the community); in those cases, alternative toys to consider are padded batakas (overstuffed, padded, swordlike paddles) and a punching bag or bop bag that bounces back up after being hit. These still allow children the ability to communicate their angry and aggressive feelings and play out violent scenarios, but without jeopardizing school policy. I find it very helpful to have wooden blocks as part of my play therapy materials, along with clay. I encourage children to build up towers of blocks and kick them down, which offers the chance to be constructive and destructive, thereby releasing feelings of anger through action along with impact that the noise offers. I have children rip apart, smash, and pound on clay or shape it into figures. Placemats underneath help protect carpeting from ground-in clay and also lessen the noise from pounding on the floor. As a further step, these placemats are made with positive affirmations on them (e.g., "I am special" and "I am capable"), which the child can decorate. Then I laminate them and make them available to the children when they use the clay. The clay can also be used to throw down at the placemats or at a piece of paper with a target on it to help the child release anger.

DEALING WITH MESS

The school clinician needs to be aware of personal tolerance for mess and disorder, so that it does not interfere with or become imposed on the child's use of materials. The use of paints, sand, water, and clay, which can be messy, as well as the child's use of many objects at once, leaving the room in disarray, are inherent in play therapy but could become a deterrent to the school clinician. The clinician's tolerance and patience will be tested, especially if you have a strong need to always have the room neat, clean, and orderly. Mess and disorganization are necessary parts of the therapeutic process. However, the school clinician needs to allow ample time to straighten up and put the toys away. Axline (1964) recommended hiring a maid to clean up after each session as the best solution for keeping order and constancy between sessions. Another suggestion is to hire an intern or student helper (James, 1997) who could assist with this task, although it is rare that anyone has this luxury, and it usually falls on the person working with the child to maintain order. As noted earlier, everything in the therapy room is there for a purpose, and the toys are the equivalent of the child's words. Children should not have to search for objects each session or enter a constantly rearranged room that surprises and unsettles them. The room needs to be orderly and predictable in appearance. In addition, by the nature of the therapeutic process, the child is given permission to use the materials and roam freely without many restrictions. Consequently, school clinicians need to guard against revealing, through facial expression, body language, or direct verbalization, their discomfort when a child proceeds to dump toys on the floor or splash water.

SETTING LIMITS

Moustakas (1959) clearly states, "One of the most important aspects of relationship therapy is the setting of limits. Without limits there could be no therapy. Limits define the boundaries of the relationship and tie it to reality. . . . They offer security and at the same time permit the child to move freely and safely in his play" (p. 11). There are limits not only on the time frame of the session, but also on the use and care of the toys and materials. Children need to know when they have only a few minutes left to play (see below) and that all the toys and materials stay in the room at the end of the session; the toys are not taken home or borrowed. The child needs to be told "All the toys remain in the room. I know you would like to take them home with you, but they are to be used here." Limits also need to be set for children who become dangerous in their actions or appear to be manipulating and testing limits on how far they can bring chaos into the room. Children are not permitted to actively destroy objects or to physically abuse the therapist or his or her clothing (Moustakas, 1959).

Given the time and space limitations of play therapy sessions, the therapist could set up therapy "stations" in corners of the room (such as an art area, puppet area, dollhouse and doll area, and clay area) and establish at the outset the limit of using two stations per session. This works especially well if you have sessions that are only 30 minutes long as opposed to the traditional 45- to 50-minute time period. In addition, when materials are no longer being used because the child has moved on to new materials, the clinician can suggest putting the unused items back to allow for more space. This will help lessen the cleanup later.

CLEANUP TIME

There are different theoretical and practical points of view on whether the child should be enlisted to help in the cleanup process or whether the clinician should clean after the child has left the room. Some theorists (Freud, 1928; Jung, 1965) believe it is best to dismantle the materials after children have left the session, as their creation represents intrapsychic and unconscious communications. Others (Landreth, 1983; Moustakas, 1959) believe that cleanup should be the job of the school counselor or play therapist. "Requiring the child to clean up may result in a power struggle, or the child may feel punished for being messy" (Landreth, 1983, p. 204).

The process of cleanup can offer the clinician time to think about the session and the child on a conscious and unconscious level, which adds to the clinician's understanding of the therapeutic process. In a typical 60-minute therapy session, 45 to 50 minutes are usually devoted to the therapeutic process, with the remaining 10 to 15 minutes (after the child has left) spent cleaning up and putting items away in their prearranged places before seeing the next child. However, there may be times when sessions need to be much shorter and there is no time to clean up between seeing children. In these cases, the cleanup needs to occur with the child present during the last 5 or 10 minutes of the session. It is critical that the child be given a time warning before the session ends to know when cleanup will begin.

All sessions need to be structured to give the child a time reminder about 10 minutes before the end (making sure that will be enough time to actually clean up), for instance, "In five minutes the session is over" (if the therapist cleans up afterwards) or "We will need to begin to clean up in five minutes." In the second case, five minutes before the end, the clinician needs to state "It is now time for cleanup." The child can be enlisted to help, but it is the responsibility of the clinician to pick up the items and place them where they belong. By making the child solely responsible for the cleanup, power struggles can ensue, which can result in a negative impact on the therapeutic relationship and possibly in dragging out the session due to the therapist's having created a crisis situation.

PLAY SPACES

The playroom is specifically designed and standardized for setup and furniture to facilitate the therapeutic process. It is important that the play space create a warm and accepting atmosphere, as this is the first thing that impacts the child on entering. Creating an inviting, friendly environment takes planning, effort, and sensitivity to what the child's needs are, and, once accomplished, it should be safeguarded. The play space should not be used for babysitting or for siblings or other students to use it or even other staff members who are not working therapeutically with children (Landreth, 1991); otherwise, the space may be seen as just a play area that can be "borrowed" when needed. It is important for children and staff members to understand that the "play therapy relationship is a special emotional relationship that takes place in the special playroom" (Landreth, 1991, p. 128).

THE PHYSICAL SETTING

There is a diversity of professional and theoretical opinion regarding the physical setting and layout of the playroom. The general consensus is that whatever the dimensions, location, and so on of the play space, ideally it should be a particular space for regular meetings that the child comes to regard as his or her special place to play.

Melanie Klein

Klein (1955) suggested that the playroom have a washable floor and that it include a table with a few chairs, a small sofa, some comfortable pillows or cushions, a chest of drawers, and running water available. Each child should have a separate drawer containing miniature toys to use each session, which were added to or removed based on the needs of the child over the course of therapy.

Virginia Axline

Axline (1947) felt that therapeutic intervention could occur effectively in almost any type of setting, even the corner of a classroom or workroom. But she stressed that the ideal is a specifically designated and equipped room just for play therapy. The room should be sound proof, have easily cleaned walls and floors, and water available.

Garry Landreth

Ginott (1961) recommended 150 to 200 square feet as an ideal playroom, because the child is never too far from the therapist. Landreth (1991) agrees with the need for 150 to 200 square feet, as it is also sufficiently large for group play therapy with two or three children. Each child can move freely without physical contact, as well as having space to work alone. Landreth adds that long narrow rooms or larger spaces would not be effective, as the therapist would need to keep moving around the room to be close to the child; this would deprive children of the opportunity to come to the therapist when they wanted. Landreth lists other specifics for the playroom: (1) having no windows on the inside wall or in the door to ensure privacy; (2) vinyl tile squares on the floor for easy cleaning and easy and inexpensive replacement (carpeting should be avoided, as it is difficult to keep clean or get sand out of); (3) walls painted with washable enamel (preferably off-white, avoiding dark, somber, or even vibrant colors); (4) a sink with cold running water; (5) shelves on two walls to provide space for toys and materials to be displayed (with the top shelf no higher than 38 inches for small children to be able to reach without assistance or climbing); (6) a chalkboard with tray across the bottom, mounted to the wall approximately 21 inches from the floor; (7) sturdy child-size furniture made of wood or of a hard surface (a table and three chairs, with one adult size); (8) a storage cabinet with a countertop for painting, clay work, and so on. He also suggests, if possible, acoustical tile on the ceiling only to help lessen noise and make the room more soundproof, as well as a bathroom within the playroom. Landreth also feels that children need a place to escape to or hide from the therapist and suggests having the room arranged so children can find a way to be out of view when they feel the need to do so: "Such separation or rejection of the therapist is significant in the development of freedom in the relationship" (p. 128).

Diana Siskind

Siskind (1992), a psychoanalytic child therapist who follows Anna Freud's approach, suggests that the cabinets have doors and that those doors remain closed whenever the child arrives for sessions (except for the first session, so the child can see where the toys are). After the first session, it is then up to the child to seek out the toys. The open toy cabinet in the first session serves as a "transitional offering that affirms [the child's] sense of anticipation to this otherwise unfamiliar place" (p. 73). "The reason that the toy cabinet is never open in advance again is because while I have toys, playing with toys is not a requirement. It's voluntary, and having that toy cabinet open with all of the attractive baskets holding all sorts of toys is suggestive and even seductive" (p. 73). Siskind further states, "There is an implied expectation that the child should go over there rather than begin where he or she might have begun were those toy cabinet doors closed. The child should begin his session in the same way as the analysand begins a session—with absolutely no interference or suggestion. Any directives from the therapist, however silent and indirect, are a form of interference" (p. 73).

O'Dessie Oliver James

James (1997) states that the space should feel right to the individual, and suggests that 12 by 14 feet with built-in cabinets is suitable. She adds that a chair with rollers allows the therapist to move about the room as the child moves around. She suggests the cabinets be much like kitchen cabinets, at child height, with doors and a countertop with three separate metal sink-like "cavities" to allow for dry sand (3 by 4 feet), wet sand (3 by 4 feet), and cold running water (2 by 4 feet). The cabinets below should contain pull-out drawers with items to use at each sink area. On the opposite wall should be a mounted easel with cabinets above containing the paint supplies; the fourth wall should have cabinets for the dollhouse, blocks, and larger buckets of toys. James suggests painting the room light blue and covering the floor with washable linoleum. The playroom ideally should be located far from classrooms and administrative offices. This allows for less noise and fewer classroom disruptions from the child's activity.

ALTERNATIVE TYPES OF SPACES

Not all school clinicians will have a separate playroom available to conduct sessions. In this case, an office can be divided to contain a separate play therapy section. Other parts of the school building can also be utilized: a corner of the cafeteria or auditorium stage, a storage closet (such as an unused book storage room) or workroom, part of the nurse's office, a corner of a regular classroom, or an empty or temporarily unused classroom. Larger spaces will need to be defined and delineated through use of chairs, tables, a curtain, and so on to help limit the child from using the whole area. One school clinician used an old schoolbus converted into a traveling therapy room, as she had to go to various sites each week to see children. It is crucial that the child's confidentiality and privacy are maintained at these various types of locations. If others might overhear or see the child, the child needs to know so he or she will be aware of the lack of privacy. The school clinician may need to use a portable play therapy kit or have a special storage area where items in a box or covered bookcase could be left for each session.

PLAY THERAPY/TECHNIQUES IN THE CLASSROOM

Graduate-level teachers attending my School-Based Play Therapy course shared how useful it would be if all classroom teachers could use play therapy techniques in dealing with the emotional issues and behavioral problems of their students. In addition, they felt that play therapy techniques and interventions could be used to address specific problems of individual students or developmental issues of the whole class. Furthermore, these could help encourage problem solving and affective growth in the children.

It is important to realize that teachers are usually not trained in therapy. However, the literature (Kranz, 1972; Landreth, Homeyer, Bratton, & Kale, 1995) supports successful therapeutic work by teachers and teacher-therapists with children once they have obtained the necessary training and attended workshops or courses in theory and technique, along with receiving ongoing supervision to maintain the proper emotional distance as well as insight into the child's responses.

The graduate teachers were able to devise ways of utilizing work stations that already existed in their classroom as therapeutic stations to encourage play. Specific areas were designated as a family corner, block corner, art corner with table and chairs, feelings corner, and puppet and theater corner. The family corner would have dolls, kitchen utensils, furniture, and dress-up clothing. The block corner would have blocks but also small toys to set up towns, houses, and land. The puppet corner would have a variety of puppets, both people and animals (tigers, alligators, dragons, and also dogs, cats, rabbits). The art corner with table and chairs would have clay, a sand tray, a dollhouse with furniture and small doll family, drawing paper, and crayons. The feelings corner would have such items as bubble wrap (the type used for packing) for children to stomp on or pop with their fingers when upset, and a mirror for allowing the children to see how their faces look when angry, happy, and so on.

Overall, the room should be designed to be warm, inviting, and comfortable. A daily schedule for use of the stations would remain the same for most of the school year, allowing children to become more comfortable and independent in working in this setting and offering a sense of routine, constancy, and predictability to the day. A daily program would include special times when the teacher spends 10 to 15 minutes working with individual children on their issues, as well as several daily blocks of time that would include both free play and teacher-guided play. Classroom aides and special area teachers could also be utilized in helping the classroom teacher plan and implement the therapeutic play strategies. The school counselor could also collaborate with the teacher around supervision and strategies.

SUMMARY

Play therapy and use of play therapy techniques are an effective modality for helping children deal with emotional issues and behavioral problems. The school or classroom setting allows for more children to be helped than through outpatient services, and offers a setting that is known and comfortable. Utilizing play therapy in the schools maximizes the child's academic progress through the use of a consistent and predictable therapeutic setting and the play materials help in the natural expression of feelings and issues. This chapter has offered specifics as to the rationales and theories behind the selection of various therapeutic objects and materials, as well as the layout and furniture that should be included in the play therapy room. It is hoped that school clinicians and teachers will find these details helpful in setting up a play therapy room or environment in their school.

REFERENCES

Axline, V. (1947). *Play therapy: The inner dynamics of childhood.* Boston: Houghton Mifflin.

Axline, V. (1964). *Dibs: In search of self.* Boston: Houghton Mifflin.

Freud, A. (1928). *Introduction to the technique of child analysis* (L.P. Clark, Trans.). New York: Nervous and Mental Disease.

Freud, A. (1951). *The psychoanalytic treatment of children* (N. Proctor-Gregg, Trans., 3rd ed.) New York: Anglo-Books.

Ginott, H.G. (1961). *Group psychotherapy with children.* New York: McGraw-Hill.

Haworth, M.R. (1964). *Child psychotherapy: Practice and theory.* New York: Aronson.

James, O.O. (1997). *Play therapy: A comprehensive guide.* New York: Aronson.

Jung, C. (1965). *Memories, dreams, and reflections.* New York: Vintage.

Klein, M. (1955). The psychoanalytic play technique. *American Journal of Orthopsychiatry, 25,* 223–237.

Kranz, P.L. (1972). Teachers as play therapists: An experiment in learning. *Childhood Education, 49,* 73–74.

Landreth, G.L. (1983). Play therapy in elementary school settings. In C.E. Schaefer & K.J. O'Connor (Eds.), *Handbook of play therapy* (pp. 200–212). New York: Wiley.

Landreth, G.L. (1991). *Play therapy: The art of the relationship.* Muncie, IN: Accelerated Development.

Landreth, G.L., Homeyer, L., Bratton, S., & Kale, A. (1995). *The world of play therapy literature: A definitive guide to the subjects and authors in the field* (2nd ed.). Denton, TX: Center for Play Therapy.

Moustakas, C. (1959). *Psychotherapy with children: The living relationship.* New York: Ballantine Books.

Oaklander, V. (1988). *Windows to our children: A Gestalt therapy approach to children and adolescents.* Highland, NY: Gestalt Journal Press.

Schaefer, C.E. (1993). *The therapeutic powers of play.* Northvale, NJ: Aronson.

Siskind, D. (1992). *The child patient and the therapeutic process.* New York: Aronson.

ADDENDUM

RESOURCES FOR MATERIALS

Constructive Playthings   www.cptoys.com, 13201 Arrington Rd., Grandview, MO 64030-2886, 800-448-4115; FAX: 816-761-9295. Sculpey, Model Magic, and Crayola Dough.

Crayola   1-800-Crayola. Model Magic and Dough.

Crestwood Company   (414) 352-5678; Fax: 414-352-5679. Magnetic house, magnetic town, magnetic farm, magnetic zoo.

Myrna Minnis   Myrin Enterprises, P. O. Box 6211, Leawood, KS 66206; 913-649-1185. Oogly clay.

Self-Esteem Shop   4607 N. Woodword, Royal Oak, MI 48073; 800-251-8336. Puppets, bibliotherapy books, and all other books related to play therapy theory and techniques.

CHAPTER 5

Play Therapy in a Special Education Preschool

PATTI J. KNOBLAUCH

THE EMOTIONAL responses and adaptation of a child of preschool age are not always considered significant in our culture. However, people who work closely with young children know that therapeutic intervention assists children's coping skills and boosts developmental opportunities, whether at times of crisis, coping with ongoing matters, or meeting developmental challenges.

Children ages 3 to 5 years spend either two and a half or five hours, five days a week, in this special education preschool. This setting bridges home and the outside world, and for a time in the child's life becomes one of the child's natural environments. The play therapist collaborates with other significant adults in the child's life, including therapeutic and educational staff, parent/guardian, and any social agency that may be involved, to enhance benefits offered by this program to the child.

REFERRAL PROCESS

Children's play therapy eligibility in this setting is identified in one of three ways. Children may be referred following formal assessment and meeting at a local school district level. Then, play therapy is mandated in an individualized education plan (IEP). The IEP specifies that services be offered in either the special education preschool described throughout this chapter with play therapy and possibly other therapies (speech, occupational, physical, and vision) or that play therapy be offered within a regular private preschool that is located on site.

Alternatively, parents or members of the educational team may identify a child once the child is in our program. Then, either because of a crisis or because the child has only a short time left in the program, the child will be offered play therapy lacking the school district mandate but *with parental permission*.

THE PLAYROOM

The play therapy room is a separate space, usually smaller than the classrooms. Toys and materials that allow for self-expression, dramatic play, and relationship building should be available. Staples for this age group usually include a dollhouse, human and animal figures, babydolls and accessories, expressive art materials including paint, clay or Play-Doh, and markers, dress-up clothes (especially including a medical kit and material for capes), cars, trucks, play food, and some building materials. I like to include toys that offer opportunities for mastery, such as a ball and hoop and a few puzzles and simple games. The availability of sand, one container of dry and one of wet, is advised. Theme play kits, such as hospital, police station, and supermarket, for example, are also an asset and contain figures and miniature toys that can be used in the sand. A few books, pillows for either resting on or hitting, bubbles, and a container of water are also used frequently.

THE PLAY THERAPIST'S ENGAGEMENT OF CHILD, FAMILY, AND TEAM

Initially, a child is discussed at a team meeting led by the special education teacher. Next, I observe the child in the classroom setting. Then, I call the parent or guardian to introduce myself as a school psychologist and assigned play therapist for this child and explain that I like to keep in contact with parents of children with whom I work. I admit a working assumption that most people are unfamiliar with play therapy and offer to describe it. Very briefly, I draw a parallel between play therapy for children and talking therapy or counseling for adults. Then I say something like the following:

> Even typical preschool children have only been talking for a very short time, so they are not that good at using words to communicate. Even adults, who have used words for most of their lives, often have difficulty talking about their feelings and things in their lives that are uncomfortable

or confusing. Children whose development is not typical, then, need ways to communicate about their inner life other than solely with words. As it turns out, children do communicate through their play. Play therapists are trained to communicate with children through play and to facilitate development by playing with children.

I inquire of parents their view of their child, any concerns and goals they hold for their child, and the extent to which they want contact with me initially. Usually, I arrange to talk with them again a couple of weeks after I begin meeting with their child. A face-to-face meeting may be planned for or arranged.

THE PLAY THERAPIST'S PRESENCE IN THE CLASSROOM

It should come as no surprise that children vary greatly in their initial receptivity to the play therapist. I usually have been in the classroom, definitely in a different role than a teacher or assistant but also definitely not in an easily categorized role. I may or may not participate in an activity, and unless a question of safety is at hand, I do not engage in a disciplinary role. Children seem to notice that I take a few children with me to the "playroom," always the same few. I may talk or play with any of the other children, though.

ROUTINES, PARAMETERS, LIMITS, AND SAFETY

There are some formal aspects to arrange with both child and classroom teacher, such as when and for how much time we meet together (usually up to 30 minutes one or two times a week, as mandated by the child's IEP), how we leave and return to the classroom, and where we go when we leave the classroom (usually the playroom exclusively but occasionally to the playground or for a walk inside or outside).

There are also some playroom parameters that emerge. Children are invited to play with any of the toys they want, in contrast to the classroom, where toy choices are more structured or limited. Wet sand is not allowed to be mixed into the dry sandbox and vice versa (a typical temptation); instead, trays for mixing the sand are offered. Most important, the playroom must be a safe place. Common examples of how safety issues arise are when there are so many toys out that a child cannot walk without tripping and when so much water spills onto the linoleum floor that it causes slippery conditions. In these instances, I verbally reflect on the safety issue and offer to help rearrange things. Very often, children will watch me the first time and join me thereafter. The children seem to "get" that dumping toys all over the floor may be tolerated as part of a play process and the same with heavy splashing, yet the *play space* must be preserved, and that is my job as therapist. Intentional breaking of toys is discouraged; throwing of hard objects is redirected to throwing of soft objects, and therapist assault is redirected to doll or animal figures, Play-Doh, or pillows.

As in any therapeutic relationship, the importance of these structures (routines and limits) is to establish a reliable, expectable, and safe environment wherein free expression is intended, and to teach that some behaviors actually inhibit free expression because of the results of their actions. I have found that the mere setting of some limits is eminently useful both to reveal certain needs of some children and, as the relationship develops and the child demonstrates greater ego strength, for the feeling of mastery and positive identification.

COMPARING THE ROLE OF THE PLAY THERAPIST WITH THE ROLES OF OTHER STAFF MEMBERS

One of the main differences between what happens with the child and the play therapist and what happens with the child and other staff in school is the type of relationship that unfolds. In particular, the play therapist does not set goals having to do with activities, achievement, or concrete outcomes. For example, the object of playing a game may not be either to win or even to play by the rules; rather, it may be to offer the child opportunities to create rules, to break rules, to express aggression, or to develop a theme, depending on the situation. The play therapist is thinking about and sometimes commenting in play on feelings, relationships, involvement, separateness, identity, self-concept, likes, dislikes, dreams, fears, wishes, and safety and in these ways indicating the play therapist's contribution to the child's preschool experience and world. *I always try to assist the children in their play. I try to bring undivided attention to their physical, mental, and emotional expressions as they come in contact with and interact with their peer, adult, physical, and pretend environment.*

I may narrate what the child plays, mirror what the child does in either the same or a different modality, or offer materials or suggestions to draw out the play. I offer my actions always gently. I readily accept the children's rejections of my offers because I may be off-target, it may be the wrong time, or it may be that the child's style of receiving or processing information requires either time or some manner of conflict. In my experience, a child's rejection of an offer does not necessarily mean the intervention was unhelpful. A child may get back to it later on the child's own, be more receptive at another time as a result of hearing it more than once, or be practicing setting boundaries. I may even encourage children's rejections. I try to help children use the materials they choose in the playroom in ways that feel right to them.

In this setting, I do not initially explain play therapy or discuss the particular reason for the child's referral. Usually, children's difficulties outside the playroom become apparent either in their play choices or in their relationship with me, or both, and I address these through the play. Preschool children in a special education setting do not need to have a reason to visit the playroom. They see their peers and sometimes themselves go to offices for other therapies (or, from their viewpoint, other play situations). I find it unnecessary and burdensome to direct the preschool child's attention to what is essentially a natural process for the child, which is to express who they are and what is going on in their world through their play and behavior.

Once, when a child asked me why she comes to the playroom, I reminded her about feeling fearful when she first came to school, not wanting to play with the other children and asking for her mother a lot, which she remembered. Then, I contrasted that experience with how much she was currently enjoying being in school, playing with her new friends, the toys, and the activities. She seemed quite pleased with herself when I said that, so I added that I thought coming to the playroom helped her feel better. It was a very simple explanation that seemed to satisfy her. I left out many important things, including why she was concerned about her mother and how the content and level of her play had shifted from anxious nurturing to self-expressive and mastery-oriented. When I talk to children I try to remember that 3- to 5-year-olds usually have a limited attention span and listen best to what is relevant to their immediate experience.

SCHOOL INTERRUPTIONS TO THE THERAPEUTIC ENGAGEMENT

In a preschool setting, play therapy is part of an entire program in school, rather than an appointment parents arrange for and go out of their way to make happen. Unpredictable interruptions to the schedule are common, including meetings and emergencies, school events such as holiday parties and field trips, and school holidays, vacations, and snow days. As a result, the school play therapist's presence can in some ways be more remote from the child's life than a play therapist engaged by the child's parents. It also can be experienced as less accessible to the child. The following examples illustrate varying approaches to engagement, both initial and ongoing.

Engaging a Child Who Declines My Initial
Invitation to the Playroom

Jason is a 3-year-old who at first declines my invitation to the playroom. It is the beginning of the school year for this very young child. He attends the program for the full day, which in this case is five and one-half hours long. It can be expected that his separation from the familiar significant adults in his life presents a normal developmental challenge for him. Also, it is likely that he is still adjusting to the school routine in general and facing expectable feelings of insecurity. Because it is the beginning of the school year, he has not had an opportunity to observe a pattern of therapists taking children out of the class for 30-minute segments and returning with them. He has seen me only a few times before, observing quietly in his class. He probably has not noticed the office that we will use for play therapy. With these considerations in mind, I decide to offer Jason some practical information that may help him be more receptive to my invitation.

I explain to Jason that there are toys in the playroom, that we will be there just a short time, and that we will not be leaving the building. Jason responds by asking if he can bring his friend. I say not today. I do not want him to bring a friend that day primarily because I am attempting to establish the parameters of our new relationship. At a later date, I may be more open to his request for a friend, especially if I have a sense of its merit in our work. Jason then asks if he can bring the toy animals he has been playing with, and I say yes.

I am aware that Jason is seeking a "transitional object." A transitional object is widely understood as a physical object that a young child probably imbues with and perceives as having psychological qualities that support feelings of security. Common examples are the "blankey," the pacifier, and a special stuffed animal. Jason did not have a familiar, established transitional object from his home life or school available to bring to the playroom, but in the moment he attempted to create one to buoy his courage to do this new thing with this relatively new person. In work with preschool children, it is important to be sensitive to their practical needs for security.

Jason's negotiations with me about who or what he could bring and under what conditions he would accompany me are significant not just in relation to security needs and the setting of parameters. They also forewarned of his already learned pattern of attempting to manipulate and control relationships. However, in this initial encounter, my focus was on providing and working with the conditions that would allow the relationship to unfold and build.

In the playroom, Jason tells me the toy animals want to hide. I ask if they would like to hide in the dollhouse, which is on the opposite side of the room. In a young child's early visits to the playroom, I often avail myself of opportunities to point out the materials and possibilities for their use. I am aware that young children have a natural and vital interest in exploring their environment and finding out what is possible. Jason immediately brings the animals across the room to the dollhouse and begins to explore the house with them. In many subsequent sessions, Jason uses these toy animals in that house to communicate feelings about and to try to understand his home and family life.

Engaging a Child by Building Bridges between the Playroom and Classroom

I become Florence's play therapist in her second year of preschool, because her play therapist from the first year had taken a job elsewhere. Florence is 4½ years old at the time. She had been receiving services in the areas of speech, occupational therapy, and special education from the county since before preschool, due to severe delays discovered early in her life. Despite some developmental gains since her first year in preschool, she is still aggressive and isolated.

In Florence's first play session with me, she immediately chooses and engages play figures with purposefulness. She shows minimal response to my attention. Near the end of the play session, I let her know there are five minutes left before we return to the classroom. I routinely tell children this to give them a chance to create some kind of closure with their play if they choose and to give them a sense of control over the schedule. (Getting used to a schedule is, afterall, a primary focus of any early school experience.) Florence chooses to leave right away. As she reenters her classroom, she walks past the children sitting at a table and walks around the room facing the walls. When Florence is gently escorted to the table by an assistant teacher, she starts throwing things from the table. It takes a considerable amount of time and some rocking on her teacher's lap before Florence settles comfortably into the activity.

I am impressed by Florence's avoidance of interpersonal experience and her failure to successfully join the group on her return to class. I inquire of her teacher and learn that membership in the group and transitions between activities are, in fact, consistently challenging to Florence. I do not want her return to class after play or any other therapy to be repeatedly unsuccessful. Therapies are offered with the intent of supporting Florence's participation in her social life. To help Florence with her coming-and-going dilemma, therefore, I request that her teacher or an assistant come to the playroom after 30 minutes and join me in walking Florence back to the classroom. I share the plan with Florence.

As I walk Florence to the playroom for her second play session with me, I notice she faces and touches the walls all the way down the hall between her classroom and the playroom. I feel she is seeking a physical boundary, almost as a bridge between the two rooms and experiences.

At the close of the second play session, Florence's teacher helps me walk her back to class. Florence is initially resistant in words and body language, but partway down the hall she stops resisting. When Florence enters her classroom on this day, she walks right over to the snack table, chooses a seat, and joins the group for snack. At the close of the third play session, Florence is ready to leave after 30 minutes, and her teacher has not yet arrived. Florence initiates the transition and again successfully joins her class for snack.

Florence's teacher does not continue to escort her return; in fact, it is quite inconvenient for her teacher to leave class. Also, Florence's transitions in general change dramatically. She begins to take toys with her as transitional objects when she goes from room to room. At the door of her classroom, Florence ceremonially gives me back the playroom toy after showing it to all the classroom staff then saying good-bye to it and to me.

Engaging a Child Who Resists Social Initiatives

Celia is a bright and charming 4-year-old, presenting with significant motor planning difficulties, which interfere with her direct and positive engagement in almost all activities. Instead, tantruming, whining, verbal opposition, and a knack for argument are her regular responses to the initiation of activities and at transitions. She is still in diapers, does not drink from a cup, is fearful of using playground equipment, and often expresses that she "cannot" do what is being asked or offered. She often gets "stuck" and complains she cannot decide or does not know what she wants. As a result, adults tend to cater to Celia, which reinforces her resistant behaviors and fears.

I choose to pick Celia up for her first play therapy session from the park across the street from school one hot summer day because, having observed her already, I know she will welcome the relief from the playground and the heat. She readily walks back into school with me to the playroom. I notice that she seems more attentive to me and makes better eye contact when I am very active and dramatic in my gestures and verbal expressions. When toys we are playing with fall off the table, I make a game of seeing who can pick them up first. Although it is difficult for her to coordinate bending down, picking the toys up, and setting them upright again, she responds to my playful enthusiasm and seems pleased when I make sure she is more successful than I.

It appears to me that Celia feels a lack of mastery in the execution of many typical, age-appropriate activities and perhaps attempts to execute too much control interpersonally, resulting in quite a lot of frustration. As the early therapeutic relationship develops, I am seeking to offer Celia opportunities for freer self-expression and to provide feedback she might be able to use to see what control she does have.

In early play sessions, I invite Celia to make big gestures as a foil for the constrictiveness she usually exhibits. For example, I encourage her to dump boxes of toys onto the floor when she is looking through them. I reframe her typical "I can't" response as an "I choose" response. For example, she enters the playroom and says she is unable to choose what to do. I reflect, "You don't know what you want to do." When she chooses, she often immediately renegs, so I say "Oh, you've changed your mind." I use every opportunity to point out the control that is at her command. For example, she asks me how to play board games but does not understand the rules, so I tell her she can make up the rules, for she is in charge of how the play goes in the playroom. When she asks for, then rejects my offer, I say "You know you don't want to do that!"

Celia consequently does become clearer in her decisions. She decides, for example, that she wants to walk from the playroom back to her classroom by herself. Although unusual, I allow it, because Celia has missed many developmental opportunities to express independence. I suggest that she can walk back herself and I will stand at my door and watch her, which she accepts. I reflect to her that she is able to do some things by herself.

Around this time, I consult with the staff about Celia's whining and tantrums. I ask them to label her behavior, direct her to a part of the classroom separate from the group, and ignore her. I ask them to say "You're having a tantrum. You're whining and stamping your feet and shaking your hands. That's called a tantrum. Please go over there to have your tantrum, and when you're finished you can join us." I do this within earshot of Celia, so that she knows what to expect. I model it for the staff to show the matter-of-fact and nonpunitive tone that will be helpful. This turns out to be a very successful intervention.

Celia quickly reduces the amount of time she is being resistant and using for transitions. She begins to show a lot more interest in participating in activities. Over time, Celia chooses friends and participates in parallel play. She becomes directive in her play in the playroom and often elaborates themes into stories, when previously her stories consisted of categorization. She learns to use the bathroom and to drink from a cup, and she zealously enjoys the playground equipment. Her motor planning, still an observable difficulty, has improved greatly, because her receptivity to help in general, and to intervention from occupational therapy in particular, has grown.

Engaging a Child with a Communication Delay

Paul, an exuberant and adorable child, enters our school at age 3½. Both expressive and receptive communication skills are immature for his age, and his parents recognize that he becomes frustrated and aggressive when he is having difficulties communicating. Paul does say some words and make some word combinations, but his articulation and speed of delivery typically make his communications incomprehensible.

Paul comes easily to the playroom the first time and busily explores a wide variety of toys. Eye contact is rare, and he uses very little language. He does not want to leave at the end of the session. In the next few sessions, although Paul talks more and more, I do not understand him. He continues to throw himself into play excitedly and also begins to use expressive play, such as drawing and putting figures in the sand. In the fourth session, he says to me, "You play with me." He does not respond to my asking "What do you want me to do?" so I must find my way by mirroring his actions alongside him and tentatively trying to interact. Although he seems more satisfied by the mirroring, he does not seem really interested in what I do, just that I be active beside him.

Paul begins to express that he does not want to grow up, and this becomes the main theme in his play. He becomes possessive about the playroom, the toys, and my attention. When a peer accompanies him to play, either in the playroom or in the classroom, he has great difficulty sharing or waiting. I see that Paul has replaced the development of age-expected peer relationships with his vital interest in interacting with his play environment, quite possibly due to his communication frustrations. Other developmental tasks will be at risk also, as indicated by his opposition to the idea of growing up.

Paul has an active imagination and is clearly interested in expressing himself. In the play therapy experience he finds opportunities to satisfy this need. He spends many play sessions drawing, painting, setting toys in the sand, and telling stories. He encourages communication between me and his mother, frequently suggesting that I call her and ask her about something they did at home. I always comply and report back to him in the next session. Often, there is some underlying concern that Paul wants me to learn about.

For about a year, Paul holds tenaciously to not wanting to grow up. Then, in his play, there are indications of beginning identifications with being older. After that, he begins to use appropriate assertive skills with peers, making play with them more gratifying for him. In his sandplay, he allows a "kid" to join the previously insular family he had always worked with of "only mommy, daddy, and baby" (his words). In fact, he does have siblings, and rivalry had been significant. Finally, Paul begins to express pride in his impending transition to kindergarten and sometimes chooses to skip a play therapy session to remain with his class.

Engaging a Child Who Will Be Moving

Four-and-a-half-year-old Kendra attends our school for just about one and three-quarter months, midway through the school year, between two family moves. She presents as timid, soft-spoken, and quite anxious. Previous evaluations indicate a history of needs in social, language, cognitive, and fine motor areas, although her only area of service in our school is play therapy. She is on medication to help regulate erratic and inattentive behavior, which often interrupts routines at home. Kendra's parents reach out to me for parent counseling.

Kendra displays an immediate affinity for the playroom. She plays as if she has a plan, as if she has something on her mind. She pulls a chair up to the table with the dollhouse and plays there with family and pet figures for the entire length of the first session. As she plays, she narrates nearly inaudibly. I sit very close to her, am very attentive and mostly silent, except for just a few questions about associations between her play in the house and her home. She provides brief but reality-based answers. The content of her play is about setting up the house (e.g., furniture) and following routines, such as preparing and serving breakfast.

It is not difficult to engage Kendra in her work, but I feel I am missing out on something essential because I cannot hear most of what she says. I wonder about the possibility of her feeling let down by me, because maybe she is telling me something she wants me to know or respond to. She, however, appears satisfied for now to play out stories that occur in the home setting and have me as witness.

Her play takes two significant turns before her impending move is addressed. First, on occasion, she takes a few human figures and places them upside down in the sand, then knocks them over or buries them. She does this as if it is very funny. Again, although I have associations to the scene, I have no clue about the meaning of it to her in her current process. I respond by verbally reflecting her actions. My response feels passive and inadequate to me, but because she plays with decisiveness, I feel my role with her is to watch and wait and allow her to express herself. The other significant attribute I notice about Kendra's play in the playroom is that when a peer is present, she becomes more impulsive and childish and takes a follower role. This behavior underscores for me her need to feel confident and in charge during her individual play sessions.

It is not long, however, before Kendra will be moving again. When I find out the details, there are two sessions left. During the first of these, Kendra tells me that her father has gone early, for which, she says, she is glad. In her dollhouse play, the baby, the dog, and the sister "pee" and "poop" all over the house, repeatedly. No one can help, and the baby is left alone on the roof of the house. Kendra thinks this is all very, very funny. However, she listens and makes eye contact with me as I verbally reflect the helpless feelings of the players. She eagerly accepts my invitation to have a good-bye party for her in her next and last session, and she tells me what food and drink she would like to have.

We begin Kendra's last session by eating the cookies and juice for her party. She seems very happy! She tells me that the movers are packing and moving her things today. She also tells me with apparent pleasure that she has spoken to her father two times on the telephone. At the dollhouse, Kendra plays out a scene of chaos. Then she introduces a story about a little girl trying to make friends, but all the friends say no to her. So, she beats them down. I suggest some language to accompany the beatings, such as "I don't like you to say no to me." She seems to like this, then the friends say yes and no back and forth. Finally, the little girl makes a friend of a baby and they play in a "special crib."

I spoke to Kendra's mother after the final session. She verified that Kendra had been upset when her father left early and would not speak to him on the phone the first night he called. Then (after the play session), Kendra did speak to him two times, happily. She also related that the baby in Kendra's play referred to a neighbor who does have a "special crib" they play in together, whom Kendra is sad about leaving. I expressed my concern that Kendra feels alone and may be anxious about making new friends and moving.

As Kendra's play therapist in school for a short time, I was struck with the richness of the experiences she was attempting to explore and express in the playroom. Although her play seemed almost pregnant with meaning, in the short time we were together I did not find my way to formulating a significant intervention until the details for the move were clarified. At that time, the ritual good-bye party and the beginning trust that had evolved through my reliable attention to Kendra's self-expressions through play seemed to provide enough of a secure base for Kendra to tell me directly about her father's early departure, rather than allude to it with the doll figures. Then, combining dollhouse play and conversation together, I addressed Kendra's feelings about being left, about leaving old friends and making new ones. Finally, I told

Kendra's mother about Kendra's feelings, so that her mother would be in a position to understand the basis of Kendra's needs for emotional support, should Kendra's behavior begin to reflect an increase in anxiety at this time.

APPROACHES TO PLAY THERAPY IN PRESCHOOL

There may be many approaches to play therapy in preschool and many techniques that are utilized as cases proceed. In developing my style of intervention for this particular setting, I have found very useful the philosophy of floor-time, developed by Greenspan and Wieder (1998). In particular, floor-time philosophy begins with the establishment of rapport and proceeds through stages to facilitate interaction and discovery.

In my work, I rely on two basic tenets to guide me with each child and through each moment. The first is that *the child chooses the materials and the direction of the play*. The most limited child I have worked with chose only one activity, which was to play in the sand with his hands. Through this play, we were able to develop a productive and interactive relationship, expressing a range of affects, which we brought out of the playroom and into many different areas of the school. This was a child who had been referred for significant socialization problems, including hitting and biting. His limited choice of materials did not hinder the play therapy process, and may have contributed to his progress. Even a child's inability to choose guides the therapy, as in the case of Celia described above.

Allowing the child to choose the materials and direction of the play requires the play therapist to exercise keen observation skills, patience, and a willingness to serve in a capacity defined by the child. The play therapist may be asked to put on a cape and act out a superhero role or to pretend to submit to being yelled at and punished by the child enacting a parent role, for example. The therapist may spend a lot of time wiping up spills from a child's vigorous play on the water table, to watch and say nothing, to show how to use specific toys, to act as a scribe writing a note to a parent or teacher, to write a story, to read or tell a story, or to sing a song.

To allow the child to choose the materials and direction of the play supports the therapist's communication to the child that "this is about you and your process." Were a therapist to say that to a 3-, 4-, or 5-year-old, what would the child take it to mean? The child who repeatedly experiences it in action learns to understand and trust it. Many children will return to the same play materials session after session for periods of time. These toys and the play that they direct become their process.

The other tenet that guides me is that *the therapist creates opportunities for self-expression, assists in elaboration and exploration of themes, and supports resolutions and growth.* This is done by adhering to the parameters described earlier in the sections on routines and the role of the play therapist. By creating in the playroom and the therapeutic relationship a safe container for the child's potentially limitless use of materials and the relationship, the therapist fosters the child's self-expression. By bringing complete attention to the child's behavior, the therapist can judge whether to offer elaboration and exploration of themes. Sometimes, elaboration and exploration of themes are untimely, although whether that is so cannot always be known by the therapist. In the case of Kendra, described above, she seemed unmoved by the therapist's few comments in the first session about associations between her play in the playhouse and her real house. However, given that moving from, to, and away from a new house was a major theme in Kendra's life and became a significant focus in her therapy, neither therapist nor Kendra may have been able to judge the impact of the therapist's exploration of the theme in the first sessions.

I try to be acutely aware of overt signs of the child's resolutions and growth. When Celia asked to walk back to her classroom alone, I was eager to be agreeable. I never hesitate to offer positive feedback to children when the information pertains to a concrete activity that they can relate to. For example, in his play a child replaces animals with people for the first time, and states "I love people." I acknowledge that I notice this. In the following examples, I point out how the therapeutic process is guided by the child's choice of materials and direction of play on the one hand and by the therapist's creation of opportunities for self-expression, assistance in elaboration and exploration of themes, and support of resolutions and growth on the other, while offering play therapy in a special education preschool.

From Being Dinosaurs to Being Human: Development and Therapy Go Hand in Hand

Jason, a child who begins our program at age 3 years, is described earlier in this chapter as a child who declines my initial invitation to the playroom. Jason is in play therapy with me for two years, including through the summer. Over that time, he encounters typical developmental challenges, such as his separation from his parents when beginning preschool, described above. However, he is also challenged to cope with his father's mental decompensation, rejection of him, and eventual abandonment; with a brother who has emotional problems; and with his own speech and fine motor immaturities. Although Jason frequently rails against attending school, arguing with his mother and refusing to get dressed in the morning, the preschool experience, the staff, and especially his relationship with the play therapist provide Jason with a reliable, secure second-home-like environment to support his growth and development.

Jason's initial choice of materials, the animals that he brings into the playroom from his classroom, has already been mentioned. He continues to choose these animals and many others, which he finds in the playroom, especially a dinosaur family, as his main figures to play out stories for about a year and a half.

Jason uses the dinosaurs to depict and explore conflict among family members and to show his confusion and concerns. When I check in with Jason's mother, I find that although Jason's stories are often dramatized, the dynamics they reveal are true to life. Jason engages me in playing these stories with him. He assigns me a dinosaur to hold, move, and talk through. Together, as dinosaurs, we fight over space and ownership of the children, we try to make friends and play together, we take short trips. Jason begins to weave in comments about what is going on with his family. One day he tells me his mother has gone to court. "No, to China. I don't know where she is," he says, and puts his head in his hands. Around this same time he begins to appear very sad. This is in contrast to his usually zippy, engaging demeanor.

In the second year, Jason, now 4 years old, becomes more competitive, strongly tests limits, and often does not want to leave at the end of the play session. Partway through that year he begs to take home the dinosaur that he usually animates. When I say no he says, "But this is me." A couple of months later Jason asks for the dinosaurs and sets them aside. Then, he takes out the people figures and plays elaborately with them in many different scenes. In one, they are looking at animals in a zoo, and Jason says, "I love people."

In the spring of the second year, Jason changes the direction of the play. He develops a story in which I am a bad little girl who won't do her homework and whom he punishes. He yells loudly at me and sends me to bed. He tells me "I'm tired of this. I've had enough." Jason likes to play slight variations on this scene every session now. One day in the middle of this play, he threatens to leave me alone, with no aunts, grandparents, or uncles to go to. I play very quietly and sadly for a few minutes. Then I say, "I know you're not supposed to leave a little child alone. There's always supposed to be someone to take care of a little child, even if I have to go to the police for help." Jason calms down, then says, "Maybe I'll take you to the store and buy you a dinosaur," thereby mimicking a typical way in which his mother is comfortable showing affection and providing nurturance.

Because of my long-term involvement with Jason and his family and because of the confidence Jason appears to have in our relationship, I take risks, which I might not be inclined to take in another situation, when I attempt to elaborate and explore themes that Jason introduces. In the play, Jason as parent has threatened to abandon me as child. I know that Jason is struggling with fears of abandonment that are fueled by reality-based experiences. I feel it would help him to hear from me, role-playing the recipient of that threat, that I am confident of adult care, even if just on a survival level (e.g., the police).

In final sessions, Jason speaks to me realistically and directly, rather than through play, about missing his father despite his father's offensive behavior (which he details). He also expresses concern about not being understood by his mother. Intending to elaborate this theme and to support his growth, I introduce the term "daddy-types." I name several "daddy-type" people in his life already and suggest that he will meet and want to have relationships with others as he grows up and meets new people, including in the new school he is going to when he goes to kindergarten next year.

Chasing a Parent and Finding One's Place in the World

Vincent, nearly 4 years old, presents with moodiness and temper tantrums, including head banging, at home. He is very shy, is tactile-defensive, and has difficulty separating from his mother. He has lost two grandparents in the past year with whom he was close. Vincent has an older brother with special needs, and his father is often unavailable due to untreated emotional needs.

Vincent's first toy choices are of the human figures. He holds one male figure and gives me first two and then three (and, in later sessions, four) females to hold to follow his figure around. He sends his figure down a toy chute and mine follow. He talks about Halloween and suggests we hide our figures in the sand from ghosts. He goes to the dollhouse and makes our figures play hide and seek. Dad goes to work. Vincent asks me to find the baby figure. His play continues like this for several sessions.

Then Vincent introduces a dog figure, which he gives to me. He wants my dog to chase the father, and they keep getting separated. The chase occurs all around the playroom. One day, I elaborate the play by offering language for the dog. I say, "Where are you? Help me. I need you and want to be with you." Vincent wants me to repeat this as we play. In the next session, he explores many different toys in the playroom. Two sessions later Vincent provides further direction for the chase by adding a sister dog. He narrates that the brother dog goes to school on the bus and the sister misses him. He plays this, then adds a teacher and a grandfather in the classroom. Then he adds a friend, who is a tiger. He speaks about feeling scared in the classroom. In a subsequent session, Vincent identifies that the father is scared when he goes to sleep, and he gives the father figure a candle to take to bed.

The next week, Vincent plays that the big brother dog hides and runs away and the little sister dog has to find him, but is always unsuccessful because he runs away again when she comes upon him. I offer an elaboration by providing language again. I speak for the sister dog, whom I animate. I say I feel upset, mad, and sad. Vincent asks, "Why mad?" I explain, "Because my brother goes away and won't talk or play with me."

In a session soon after, Vincent directs the play further and more complexly. First, the sister dog chases a brother and an uncle. But Vincent hides the brother and uncle in the sand. Then the sister is looking for friends. Friends arrive and call her by very silly names, then laugh and run away. She is left without friends, brother, or uncle. A dinosaur comes who says he is going to help sister to find father. He brings her home. The dinosaur puts the brother in the doghouse and the father in the bed. The brother runs away. When the sister goes to the father, the father says to leave him alone. He says he is angry and needs to rest. I ask where mother is. Vincent says she is not there.

In tandem with Vincent's play sessions, I have phone contact with his mother. She requests help to schedule his bedtime and mealtime routines, which she successfully puts into effect. Then she discusses ways to offer him more time with peers who do not have special needs in order to encourage typical social behavior. This too, becomes a fruitful intervention. I report to her that Vincent appears to be seeking more of a relationship with his father and appears confused about his father's behavior. She verifies for me the relative availability of Vincent's father from time to time, and also that she had been away the weekend previous to Vincent's saying she was not there. She also explains that although Vincent is very patient with his brother, their play interactions are often frustrating due to his brother's interpersonal limitations.

In the beginning of work with Vincent, I sense his anxiety. Although he assigns me action in his play immediately, I nevertheless feel a sense of avoidance of relationship from him. I did not know about his relationship with his father at first. I follow Vincent's direction, often wondering where the chase might lead. In staying with him and talking with his mother, I learn that it is the chase itself that is the important relationship he needs to explore. I offer only a few words of elaboration on occasion, and Vincent is able to elaborate the theme on his own. The support I offer comes mostly through my talks with his mother, who, in seeing the emotional life of her child more clearly, is able to enact a stronger parental role. She adjusts routines, limits, and expectations to match his needs for regularity and typical social life outside of the home. Vincent easily meets each new challenge that she offers him.

SPECIAL ISSUES

TERMINATION

Children sometimes are discharged from play therapy midyear. More often, however, termination parallels the child's leave-taking from the program at the end of June or August. Termination is facilitated by the child's transition to kindergarten or another new school. The child is ending relationships with teaching staff, classmates, bus drivers, and often other therapists as well, in the context of anticipating new relationships because the child is growing up. These transitions are discussed as they arise in play therapy, usually beginning from three to six months before the child's last session. As in any therapy termination, our memories of our time together are reviewed.

The children may want to spend our last session together in a special way. Often, I suggest a party; they choose the refreshments and I supply them. Sometimes, they want to go to the playground or take a walk to a store (specifically, a bakery they have visited on walks with their class). Finally, I see the children at a "graduation" event, arranged by the school, which takes place at a park and is attended by parents as well. This is not an opportunity for therapeutic work, but represents a ceremonial occasion for the child when he or she can stand in relation to school, family, and the outside world at once. I make sure I connect with all of my clients with their families at this event to express my support for their "graduation" and to offer appropriate best wishes for their future.

GROUPS AND PEER CHOICES

Children may be seen individually or in a group. Almost always, if a child is assigned to a group for play therapy, I also see the child individually. It is in the individual play therapy relationship in the preschool that the parameters of the play therapy relationship are established as compared to the child's relationship with other staff in the school.

When seen in a group, either I join the child in the classroom or I take the child with one or two other peers into the playroom. The groups are small because of limited playroom space. It has become most comfortable for me, maybe due to habit, to see my preschool client with one other peer when working in the playroom. In that situation, I find I can focus easily both on the client's individual process and the interactions. Often, children want to choose the child who is to accompany them. Usually, I allow that; sometimes, I see two children together simply because they are both my clients and both are assigned to the same group.

I am often amazed by what occurs during preschool play therapy groups, therefore I do not labor too much over peer choices. I remember one group for which I paired two children because it was convenient for my schedule. I did not know if this pairing was going to offer anything to the children. Both children played alone in class, were soft-spoken, and appeared to lack socialization skills. In fact, the children did begin the first group playing completely independently, their backs to each other. By the end of the first session, I was surprised by their visual curiosity in each other's play. It was not long before they began exploring ways to develop relationships between their play in subsequent time together, both in and outside of their classroom.

PLAY THERAPY IN THE CLASSROOM

Play therapy in the classroom is different from play therapy in the playroom. In the classroom, the teacher is in charge, and the structure, routines, and kinds of relationships that the teacher establishes take precedent. In the classroom, when my clients ask me for direction, I direct them to their teachers.

When I work in the classroom, I try to come in during free play time rather than during circle, snack, art, or some other structured time. During free play, I am able to observe the child's choice of materials and direction of play. In the classroom, these choices include which play area the child chooses, how the child uses the large space available in the classroom, which peers the child interacts with, and the nature of those interactions. I may attempt to facilitate skills, to work as a coach, an advocate, or a role model.

The playground is sometimes an excellent choice of location for group play therapy. On the playground, children tend to have encounters with peers they might not otherwise choose to interact with. So many socialization skills are engaged: Children need to wait turns to go down the slide, to share toys in the sandbox, to indicate when they want to get off or on a bicycle or merry-go-round. There are always groups of children running to join anonymously, and simple imaginative play groups involving monsters or setting up a home. Many special needs children feel challenged by the play equipment and appreciate the company of an understanding adult to boost their confidence to take risks. Supporting new skills offers opportunities to contribute to the developing child's sense of self.

INVITING PARENTS INTO SCHOOL

Ideally, the play therapist would have the opportunity to meet with the parents of all the children who are seen. There are differences between children's behavior at home, in the classroom, and in the playroom. One child I see is shy and cooperative in class, but unruly and even dangerous at home; in the playroom, she shows both aspects. It can be useful to offer parents opportunities to observe their children in class and in the playroom. I always accompany parents while they observe and schedule time immediately afterwards to talk. Sometimes I offer a different spin on what we have observed, which can help parents understand their child differently. Sometimes, parents are moved to share additional information from home to further elucidate what we observe.

Whenever parents ask for guidance around specific issues, such as establishing a bedtime routine, giving up a pacifier, using the toilet, how to talk to their children about the other parent's involvement with the law, going back to work, or aggressive behavior, I encourage them to meet with me in person. I do this because I want to take a history and develop a plan with the parents that suits the individual child and family. Frequently, feelings or additional information pertinent to the question arise that are not obviously relevant when the request for guidance is initiated.

Occasionally, I suggest that parents accompany the child to play sessions for a specified period of time (e.g., for a few weeks). This can be helpful when their relationship needs support or when the parents are trying to understand how to play with their child in ways that support the child's development.

SCHEDULING EXTRA SESSIONS

In a school environment, there are many pulls to schedule extra sessions. As a full-time staff member, I am seen almost daily by the children, and they frequently ask to come to the playroom. They say, "I want to come to the playroom right now" or "I want to play in your sand right now." I always respond by telling them that they will be coming back to the playroom and that I look forward to that time. Typically, I remind them of their scheduled day or, if it is their day, that they have already been to the playroom or will be coming later.

SUMMARY: THE PLAY THERAPIST AS TEAM PLAYER

The play therapist in the special education preschool works as a member of a multidisciplinary team, which often feels like a community. Educational and therapeutic staff meet regularly, both formally and informally, to discuss children's progress. Joint observations are often conducted to share hypotheses. Interventions are sometimes carried out together.

In the context of this mutuality, the play therapist must determine what constitutes confidential information. Certainly, I honor when a parent, and more rarely a child, requests that I keep information in confidence. However, I may discuss the merits of the parent's sharing that information with the others on the child's team if it would be useful to support the child's progress.

Preschool children do sometimes specify that I keep what they say or do a secret from a parent or teacher. These secrets have always been about their developing sense of self and not about being placed in danger. Therefore, I have been able to honor their requests. On occasion, I have needed to tell a child that I have a concern about something he or she told me, and that I wish to speak to the parents about this. Children have always been receptive to this. I do share the contents of children's play with staff members if I feel doing so will enhance understanding of the child. Staff are usually very grateful to hear something that may not otherwise have been accessible to them and are always interested in the children's self-expressions.

Most striking and compelling to me about working as a member of the special education preschool community is how children's progress reveals gains made in all areas, and how gains from different areas are interwoven. Assertiveness skills help children who have articulation problems try to speak. Improved motor planning helps children feel more confident to climb play equipment with their peers. Developing trusting feelings enables a child to be more receptive to participating in therapies. Acquiring self-regulation habits enables a child to participate in a group during circle time. The multidisciplinary team in this setting works together to support the growing child who is faced with typical and with special challenges.

REFERENCES

Greenspan, S.I., & Wieder, S. (with Simons, R.). (1998). *The child with special needs: Encouraging intellectual and emotional growth*. Reading, MA: Addison-Wesley.

PART THREE

INDIVIDUAL PLAY THERAPY APPROACHES

CHAPTER 6

Child-Centered Play Therapy for At-Risk Elementary School Children

PHYLLIS POST

CHILDREN CHARACTERIZED by minority cultural status, low socioeconomic status, and living in crowded urban areas are at risk of academic failure and lifelong social problems. They face frequent changes in caretakers (Levy-Warren, 1994), impoverishment, neglect, and/or violence. They are often afraid of physical harm (Silverman, La Greca, & Wasserstein, 1995) and have a sense of ever-present crisis. They are exposed to drugs, incarceration of family members, and explicit sexual practices. The families of these children are often overwhelmed with the process of living and are unable to attend to their children's needs. These children enter our schools every day.

At-risk children begin school with fewer cognitive, social, and emotional school-readiness skills than non-at-risk children (Edlefsen & Baird, 1994). They attend "high-poverty" schools (National Center for Educational Statistics, 1997) and receive free or reduced-price lunch. They often exhibit lack of impulse control, short attention span, poor academic performance (Frick-Helms, 1997; Martinez & Richters, 1993),

---

This chapter is dedicated to the memory of Robert Wilson III, whose untimely death is a reminder that we need to cherish every moment with our children.

depression, and poor social skills (Post, 1999). Assisting these students during elementary school is critical to reduce the risk of their dropping out of high school (Bloom, 1981; Gage, 1990; Mann, 1986) and facing futures of unemployment, lower earning potential, health concerns, and emotional problems (Rumberger, 1987).

In this chapter, the following topics are addressed: play therapy with at-risk children, the referral process, goals of child-centered play therapy with at-risk children, and consultations with caregivers and teachers. All of the case illustrations are based on the author's experience conducting child-centered play therapy in schools composed predominantly of at-risk children.

PLAY THERAPY WITH AT-RISK CHILDREN

Child-centered play therapy provides one culturally sensitive counseling strategy appropriate for elementary school at-risk children. Through weekly play therapy sessions, children can express a wide range of feelings, test ideas, master tasks, and practice coping with problematic situations. Landreth and Sweeney (1997) best describe the universality of the child-centered play therapy approach when working with at-risk children:

> The child-centered approach is uniquely suited for working with children from different socioeconomic strata and ethnic backgrounds since these facts do not change the therapist's beliefs, philosophy, theory, or approach to the child. Empathy, acceptance, understanding, and genuineness on the part of the therapist are provided to children equally, irrespective of their color, condition, circumstance, concern or complaint. The child is free to communicate through play in a manner that is comfortable and typical for the child, including cultural adaptations of play and expression. (p. 25)

Studies that include play therapy as one component in an overall program of services dominate the research regarding the impact of play therapy on at-risk children. The results indicate that the children seem happier at home and at school, show improved concentration at school, handle fears more effectively (Albaum, 1990), exhibit greater self-control and self-acceptance (Trostle, 1988), and are absent from school less often (Baecher, Cicchelli, & Baratta, 1989). In a study examining the effects of child-centered play therapy on at-risk children, Post (1999) concludes that play therapy may be needed to prevent at-risk children from developing lower self-esteem and from reducing their sense of responsibility for their academic successes and failures.

REFERRALS

TEACHERS

Students are referred for play therapy because of inappropriate behavior in the classroom, depression, and low self-esteem (Post, 1999). Also, children labeled with Attention-Deficit/Hyperactivity Disorder or mental disabilities may feel unaccepted by their peers (Johnson, McLeod, & Fall, 1997). These students may feel frustrated and respond by acting "more labeled." When they disrupt their own and others' learning, they are frequently referred for play therapy. Thus, in the school setting, teachers make most of the referrals. Given their regular contact with the children, teachers know what happens in the lives of their students. They observe subtle changes in their behavior that can indicate upheaval at home.

For example, Morris, a large fifth-grader, had two brothers who were incarcerated. His teacher referred him to play therapy, indicating that Morris had been totally out of control since his third brother had recently gone to prison. He refused to do assigned classwork, did not stay on task in the classroom, and responded with extreme aggression when other students teased him about his size. Because of this teacher's awareness of the events in Morris's life, she referred him for play therapy.

PARENTS

Parents also refer children for play therapy. Children may have been troubled, but their behavior in school did not lead a teacher to refer them. For example, children who were quiet or withdrawn may have been experiencing emotional problems that could have affected their learning; however, they were not creating problems in the classroom. Chris was an excellent fourth-grade student. Her father died when she was 3 years old, and her mother remarried. Chris was extremely competitive and wanted to do everything well. Chris's mother was concerned about a sense of sadness and withdrawal she had noticed, and she requested play therapy for her.

OTHER SCHOOL PERSONNEL

In addition to teachers and parents, other school personnel, such as nurses and speech therapists, are key sources for identifying children who could benefit from play therapy. Through in-service experiences, school counselors can describe the rationale, goals, processes, and expectations for child-centered play therapy. In addition, noneducators in the school, such as secretaries and custodians, play important parts in the lives of children, so school counselors need to establish relationships with them.

One powerful example is shown in the case of Sammy. Sammy was employed as a helper. He drove children home when they were suspended or got sick. He had a regular monthly outing with children for a basketball game or pizza, and he hung out on the playground with them. The children in the school trusted Sammy and talked to him. Sammy had befriended Charles, a child who was being transferred to a management school because of his extreme and repeated aggressive behavior. In his final play therapy session, Charles related that there were two people in the school who cared about him: one was the special education teacher and the other was Sammy. In another instance, a fifth-grade elective mute went on his first outing with peers to a basketball game that Sammy hosted. Undoubtedly, Sammy's relationship with the children, and subsequently the counselor's relationship with Sammy, helped the counselor keep in touch with the needs of the children in that school.

GOALS FOR CHILD-CENTERED PLAY THERAPY WITH AT-RISK CHILDREN

Child-centered play therapy is not a set of skills; it is a way of being with children (Axline, 1947; Landreth, 1991). Children of every race and socioeconomic status have the same needs for understanding, safety, and attention. In child-centered play therapy, the goals for at-risk children are identical to the goals for non-at-risk children. However, the realization of these goals is more critical for at-risk children because of the intensity of their needs.

ACCEPTANCE

In child-centered play therapy, children are accepted and valued as they are. Through play, the counselor learns about children's experiences in a noninvasive, caring way. This approach can overcome barriers between the counselor and children that may result from cultural differences (Cochran, 1996). This goal of acceptance is particularly important for at-risk children. Because of their disruptive behaviors in the classroom, these children repeatedly receive critical feedback from teachers, school administrators, and family members. The acceptance, empathy, and genuineness of the play therapist give children the freedom to express their feelings and try out new behaviors. Through the relationship with the counselor, at-risk children begin to accept themselves. In turn, as they accept themselves, their classroom behavior frequently improves, and they become more accepting of others (L. Guerney, 1983).

Anthony, a third-grade child, demonstrated the strength of the accepting relationship in child-centered play therapy. He was referred to the school counselor because he did not respond to the teacher and refused to sit at his desk. The teacher suggested that the counselor use a behavioral contract with the child. The child was uninvolved in developing the contract and did not follow through on the behaviors that he contracted to do. After three sessions, the counselor decided to take Anthony to the playroom. He immediately became involved with the counselor and played with the toys. Anthony attended six play therapy sessions. According to the teacher, his classroom behavior improved dramatically (Post, 1999).

STABILITY AND CONSISTENCY

In contrast to a chaotic home environment, a goal of child-centered play therapy is to create a reliable and stable environment (Levy-Warren, 1994) for the children. The play therapy setting is consistent, the toys are consistent from session to session, and, most important, the counselor's way of being is consistent. This consistency for children at risk is a powerful therapeutic tool.

One first-grader, Jessica, demonstrated the importance of this stability. Jessica's father had just died, and her mother was a substance abuser. Her grandmother, who was her caretaker, needed intermittent hospital care. Jessica's home life was insecure. During session 1, Jessica smiled, played with several of the toys, and stood close to the counselor. When the session ended, Jessica's speech was barely audible, her teeth were chattering, and tears were in her eyes. The counselor responded to her feelings of sadness and fear of never coming back to the playroom. Session 2 resembled the first: Jessica played with some toys and interacted with the counselor; when the session ended, Jessica responded as she did after session 1. After session 3, Jessica did not express any fear or sadness about leaving the playroom. At the end of session 4, Jessica said to the counselor, "I don't get mad anymore when I leave the playroom because I know you will bring me back." The child left the playroom with a smile on her face. Jessica began to trust that she could count on some things in her life; in this case, it was play therapy.

SELF-CONTROL

Another goal of child-centered play therapy, which is also a goal for most parents, is to help children learn to exercise self-control. Greathouse, Gomez, and Wurster (1988) report that in their efforts to protect their children, Black and Hispanic parents tend to discipline them in authoritarian ways. Thus, although the goals of child-centered play therapy and the goals of parents are both to help children achieve self-control, the strategies are different. In the child-centered playroom, the children are in charge, within certain limits. Giving children the opportunity to assume responsibility for their own actions helps enhance their self-esteem. The messages they experience are "You can decide things for yourself," "You can be responsible," and "You are OK." These are powerful messages to children with behavior problems.

School counselors can help parents understand that in the child-centered play therapy environment, the child guides the experience. And it is this practice of decision making and control that helps children achieve greater self-control in other settings, such as the classroom and home. Working directly with parents of at-risk children through consultation and filial therapy is an ideal forum for achieving this goal.

The counseling goals for at-risk students established by the National Dropout Prevention Center (NDPC) include developing self-confidence, self-control, self-awareness, effective communication skills, problem-solving skills, and adaptability (Poidevant & Spruill, 1993). These goals are remarkably similar to those of child-centered play therapy (Axline, 1947; Landreth, 1991). Child-centered play therapy is certainly one way to help prevent at-risk children from dropping out of school.

INTERVENTIONS

The ideal way to help at-risk children is to provide support services to the children, their parents, and their teachers. Working in these avenues, the counselor acquires a more complete understanding of the child and can best coordinate efforts to help the child. The following types of interventions are addressed next: individual play therapy, group play therapy, consultation with caregivers, filial therapy, and consultation with teachers.

INDIVIDUAL PLAY THERAPY

The elementary school counselor can establish caring and genuine relationships with at-risk children in individual play therapy sessions. In this section, special considerations and typical play behavior of at-risk children are addressed.

Special Considerations for At-Risk Children

Because many schools in urban, disadvantaged neighborhoods consist of classrooms with a majority of needy, at-risk children, teachers face a tremendous challenge as they try to create positive learning environments.

After managing persistent disruptions in their classrooms, teachers typically welcome the assistance of the counselor. Because of the responses these children elicit from their teachers, they often enter the counseling relationship with apprehension and distrust. The child-centered play therapy environment provides the facilitative conditions of empathy, warmth, and genuineness (Rogers, 1951) necessary for helping these children work through many of the problems that affect their classroom behavior.

According to Landreth (1991), play is the child's language and toys are the child's words. Extending this metaphor, the child-centered playroom offers at-risk children more words than they usually have to explore their feelings and concerns. Landreth describes three categories of toys for play therapy: aggressive-release toys, real-life toys, and creative-emotional release toys. When working with at-risk children, counselors should include a variety of culturally appropriate toys, such as African American, Hispanic, and Native American dolls/families and multicultural markers providing a variety of colors similar to varied skin shades. These categories of toys work effectively with at-risk children, including upper elementary children in the 10- to 12-year-old range.

Landreth's (1991) advice about returning the toys to the same place before each session is critical when working with at-risk children. It is a concrete way that the counselor can provide consistency for the children. Because at-risk children may not have many toys in their homes, their disappointment is tremendous if they cannot easily find a toy (or a word) they need to use. For example, one fifth-grade child reported that she had never seen watercolors, and she eagerly sought them out during each of her 18 sessions. Similarly, many children entered the playroom and headed straight for the handcuffs. Reliable access to these materials provides children the optimal way to communicate.

In school settings with large populations of at-risk children, the rationale for including guns as one of the aggressive-release toys must be addressed with administrators, teachers, and parents. School counselors should help educate school personnel about the necessity of providing safe ways for children to deal with their life situations. This occurs through providing materials the children can use in play therapy to reenact actual, feared, or ideal experiences.

In the author's experience, at-risk children have expressed universal concerns for safety in their neighborhoods. Students mentioned fear of gangs; one child became anxious because she witnessed a rape; another child saw a drive-by shooting in a neighbor's front yard; one child was being held in the arms of his father when his father was killed by gunfire. Understandably, many schools prohibit any semblance of weapons, such as dart guns. Because aggressive-release toys are therapeutic for at-risk children, school counselors need to provide a variety of acceptable alternatives to toy guns, such as rubber knives, handcuffs, a bop bag, craft sticks, and modeling clay.

During the school day, the counselor sees the children in many settings outside of the play therapy room: in hallways, in the cafeteria, on the playground, and to and from the playroom. The counselor should maintain a therapeutic way of being when interacting with children in these different places, always being someone that children in the school can trust. For example, when one play therapist was walking a sixth-grader from the classroom to a play therapy session, the student told the counselor that he was sent to the assistant principal because of calling another student a name. The student shared that he had wanted to hit the girl, but he had used self-control and "just" called her a name. This would have been an inappropriate time for the counselor to discuss the painfulness of name-calling.

Themes in Play Therapy

Aggression.   Aggressive themes are dominant in the play therapy of at-risk children. What is most striking, however, is not that they play aggressive themes, but the intensity and persistence of their aggression. Children repeatedly play out scenes of fighting, killing, confrontations with police, and severe discipline, as the following cases illustrate.

Will, a 5-year-old, was referred because he was extremely aggressive toward other children in his classroom. He hit, yelled at, and bit other children. His speech was unclear. Importantly, his father was a police officer. During the first session, he told the counselor about a big knife at home that he could reach. Over the course of 12 sessions, Will's play was characterized by themes of good versus bad. He was always a good guy, and he spent most of his time shooting bad guys. In the playroom, Will played out his aggressive feelings; in turn, his aggressive behavior in the classroom subsided. At the end of his time in counseling, not only was his speech clearer, but his teacher reported that his behavior in the classroom had improved greatly.

Darius was a fifth-grader with an extremely strict father. His teacher described him as "quick to anger and slow to respond when called down." His play was characterized by extreme aggression of action figures: there were explosives, alligators attacking and eating action figures, and cowboy attacks. He attacked the bop bag so vigorously that it was destroyed 15 minutes into session 1.

Abraham was a fifth-grade African American who talked and moved incessantly in the classroom. In session 1, Abraham played a scene in which a father was mad that someone had killed his son. In sessions 2 through 6, he buried action figures in the sand, shouting that they were dead. In session 8, his play involved shooting, robbing, and killing both a father and a school principal.

Reenactment of What the Child Has Witnessed.   Similar to all children, the play of at-risk children is frequently a reenactment of what they have witnessed. The critical difference for these children, however, is that the play reflecting harsh struggles are not anomalies, as they might be with non-at-risk children. They are the norm, as the following cases illustrate.

Julius was a fifth-grader who had great difficulty focusing in class. Julius's brothers were incarcerated, and his play centered on violence and danger. In one session, his play involved a robber who was caught by the police, sent to jail, and escaped. There was a car wreck in which a policeman died. In play therapy, unlike in his real life, Julius was able to create "ideal" endings: the robber escaped; the policeman died.

Older children often talk about experiences in their lives while engaging in play. The counselor can use the same skills of responding and reflection to give children the freedom to express themselves through their words.

For example, Isiah played with handcuffs and small guns as he described his experiences with real guns. He talked of running from the police and not getting caught. He described when someone shot his toe. As he left the playroom one day, he told the counselor that he was afraid that someone could kill her in the mobile unit playroom. He noticed that there was no telephone there for her to call for help.

The experience of living in a violent neighborhood is seen through the play of at-risk children. John, a fearful second-grader, would literally run away if a teacher called him down. John played out a scene in which a child was hearing gunfire outside of his house. He described the "real" experience of a bottle crashing through his bedroom window. John made many items in the playroom into guns, and he kept these "guns" with him during his sessions.

Unstable Home Situations.   Children who live in extremely unstable home situations are at risk for academic failure and for problematic emotional well-being. The following examples demonstrate the difficulties these children bring with them to school.

Tina was in the fourth grade. She was born prematurely because her mother overdosed on drugs during the pregnancy. When Tina was 2 years old, her mother abandoned her and her two young siblings. A neighbor found the three children alone in the house four days later. Tina was adopted, but she still had contact with her biological mother. In her eight sessions of play therapy, Tina played with stuffed pets and focused on parent-child relationships.

Jacob lived with his great-grandmother; however, his mother, grand-mother, and great-grandmother were all significant in his life. In session 8, Jacob used the puppets to depict a family that he was robbing and shooting. He said that they were not dead. Jacob hung the father with the handcuffs and talked about how the children would have to be in a foster home because the mother was killed. Given Jacob's unstable home life, it is interesting to note the confusion of this story about who was alive and who was dead and his awareness of the possibility of going to a foster home if family members die.

Money.   Money was another dominant theme in the play of at-risk children. They played with the play money and the cash register; they put items on layaway. Many children put money in their pockets and wanted to take it out of the playroom with them. Jamal presented a typical pattern as he carefully counted the play money in session 4. In session 5, he immediately looked for the money when he entered the playroom and re-counted it. Before the winter break, Jamal said that he wanted clothes for Christmas and that if he had a lot of money, he would use it to pay his mom's light bill.

Knowledge of Sexual Behavior beyond Their Age.   At-risk children frequently live in small homes with many other people. Their play can reflect knowledge of sexual behavior that is beyond their level of development. Although counselors need to be alert to the possibility of sexual abuse, they must also balance that possibility with a worldliness because of exposure to sexual behavior of people in their homes and on television. For example, 7-year-old Jason repeatedly undressed one Barbie doll and put his tongue to the genital area. Another 8-year-old girl played out a scene in which dolls identified as Mom and Dad were on top of each other groaning.

Unfamiliar Abundance of Toys.   For many at-risk children, the play-rooms contain more toys than they have at home. When one child did not want to leave the playroom, the counselor said, "Your time here is special." The child responded, "What's special here is that you bought all of these toys." Another example occurred when Jerry was aghast at the number of toys in the playroom. He begged to take the toys home with him and shared that he had one action figure at his grandmother's house. He went on to say that his sister would love coming to this playroom. Jerry began session 2 stating that his sister became angry when he told her about the playroom.

Effects on Play

Aggressive Play.   As described above, children who are at risk have a strong need to express/release their emotions about their life experiences. The active release of tension, which at-risk children do in the playroom through aggressive play, frequently decreases their need to act out in the classroom. After participation in play therapy, many teachers comment that children are better able to focus in the classroom.

Reluctance to Play. At-risk children may be reluctant to play at the beginning of a therapy experience. Some may be overwhelmed with the variety and quantity of toys. It may take at-risk children several sessions to trust that the counselor's statement "In here, you may play with the toys in many of the ways you want" (Landreth, 1991, p. 162) is true and that they may choose to play or not to play. Accepting their decisions demonstrates to them respect and patience. In one case, Rebecca, a fifth-grader, chose to sit in the chair and play with a button on her shirt for eight sessions before she explored the toys in the playroom.

Repetitive Play. Many children who live in chaotic family conditions are content to repeat the same behaviors in the playroom (Levy-Warren, 1994). Repetitive play is a typical behavior of traumatized children (Schaefer, 1994). At times, their repetition appears to be joyless.

An example is the case of Keisha, a fourth-grader who had limited academic ability and was extremely shy in the classroom. Her grandfather frequently took her out of school early, and she helped him clean offices four afternoons each week. There was no evidence, but suspicion, that she was being sexually abused by her grandfather. Keisha had 17 play therapy sessions. During most of the sessions, she used the crayons to carefully construct the same picture: a building with doors and windows. She rarely spoke a word. The buildings varied in size. As the sessions progressed, the doors of the building gradually got bigger. During session 16, she drew a building with watercolors. She added a smiling red sun and red rays. The door of the house was extremely large. The building had purple walls and a green room, and a person stood beside the house. The teacher reported that Keisha had started speaking in class and seemed happier participating in class activities.

Limit Setting. Counselors should welcome the opportunity to set limits with at-risk children. It gives them a chance to control their behavior and behave responsibly, which are goals for play therapy. Limit setting with at-risk children occurs predominantly in three situations: when their behavior is excessively aggressive, when they want to take the toys, and when they do not want to leave the playroom.

With regard to aggressive behavior, Richard, a second-grader, was referred for play therapy because of hitting his teacher, hitting children, and an inability to focus in the classroom. In play therapy, he would pummel the room and shout at the counselor, "You need to be quiet!" Afterwards, he would become nurturing toward the counselor. On one occasion, he sat in her lap after completing this ritual. Limits were set to prevent him from hurting himself and destroying materials in the room.

After Richard released those feelings in the safety of the playroom, he seemed to feel great relief.

As for leaving the playroom, some children hate to leave the toys and the counselor, and others have difficulty making transitions to and from the playroom. Allowing children time to manage their own behavior requires time. For example, Michael attended 14 play therapy sessions. During the first eight sessions, it took about 15 minutes for Michael to leave the playroom. Directing him back to his classroom was challenging also. In a school setting, where the freedom allowed in the playroom is different from the requirements of a classroom, counselors should plan for the time required and consider this factor when scheduling children for play therapy sessions.

GROUP CHILD-CENTERED PLAY THERAPY

Group play therapy in the child-centered model is defined simply as having more than one child in the playroom. The goals are similar to those for individual play therapy, with the addition of enabling children to work on interpersonal relationships (Landreth, 1991). One challenge in a school setting is deciding when it is in the children's best interest to engage in group versus individual play therapy because most children are so excited to attend play therapy that they ask repeatedly to bring their friends and siblings with them to the playroom.

A powerful example of the impact of group play therapy came in the case of Joshua, a biracial fifth-grader who had been a self-imposed mute at school for three years. (Post, 2000). He did not talk with teachers or other students. For the first 14 sessions, Joshua was silent in the playroom. He never explored the toys. He sat in one chair and occasionally played with the modeling clay. Group play therapy was initiated with the goal of helping Joshua develop a much needed relationship with a peer. Joshua indicated that he would be interested in having Robert join him in the play therapy sessions.

During their first session together, Joshua laughed a lot, and Robert actively played with a gun and a puppet family and conducted a TV interview. Although Joshua did not speak during this session, he laughed and played with the toys for the first time. It appeared that Joshua was watching Robert to see how to play. He had selected a peer who talked continuously through the session. Joshua seemed to know what he needed to change.

Before the next session, Joshua and Robert were talking as they approached the playroom. When they entered the playroom, Joshua immediately explored the toys. He demonstrated interest in what Robert was doing. He communicated throughout the session with noises and gestures; again, no words were spoken in the playroom. During their fourth session together, the boys talked with each other and with the counselor. Joshua both responded directly to the counselor's interactions with him and initiated talking to her. Joshua and Robert both played actively. Joshua was speaking—just like other fifth-grade boys.

Consultation with Caregivers

Parents/caregivers are crucial members of a team to help troubled at-risk children. Because family is such an influential aspect in a child's life, if children's caregivers are not included in a partnership with the school, the potential for helping the children is limited (Edlefsen & Baird, 1994). Unfortunately, caregivers' involvement with at-risk children in school can be limited. Many parents are difficult to contact; most do not work at jobs where they have a telephone at their desk; they do not have email or fax machines. Much of the contact with parents is through notes in the children's backpacks—a clearly unreliable way to communicate. Many of the caregivers of at-risk children live in the same unstable situations as the children; thus, the logistics of transportation and child care can be challenging. Also, many caregivers feel uncomfortable relating to school personnel because of their own negative school experiences.

Given these obstacles, the challenge for the school counselor is to create a relationship with the parents. Strategies for school counselors are to call parents during the evening, use flextime to make home visits during the afternoon and evening, and create welcoming opportunities to get to know parents. A successful strategy in one elementary school with a predominance of children at risk was to offer a breakfast meeting before school and show a videotape demonstrating parenting skills. Because this event did not single out parents with troubled children, it gave the counselor the opportunity to interact with parents in a nonthreatening environment.

When counselors are able to meet with parents before children enter play therapy and discuss with them the goals for working with their children, parents are more likely to endorse the process. During this meeting the counselor should focus on establishing a positive relationship with the parent by inquiring about the parent's concerns for the child, stating what the counselor can do for the child, and asking what the parent hopes the child will be like when counseling is no longer needed. Providing parents with a written statement of the benefits of play therapy for their child often increases their involvement.

As play therapy progresses for children, counselors should try to contact parents at least once a month. If meeting in person is not possible, telephone contact is necessary. The goals of the consultation are to build an alliance with the parent and to work toward greater consistency between communication skills used in play therapy and those used by parents. During consultations, the counselor can listen to the parent's concerns, review information about the child's progress, and introduce some techniques that the parent might try.

The value of regular consultations is shown in the case of one parent who was having difficulty understanding how play therapy could help her 5′ 8″, 240-pound, 10-year-old son. This child's persistent behavior in the playroom was pouring sand to the top edge of containers and parading around the room to see if it would spill. In addition, the child had difficulty deciding what to do in the playroom. Although the counselor did not discuss these incidents with the parent to protect the confidential relationship with the child, she asked if her son "pushed her to the limit" and talked about the child's confidence in making decisions. The parent realized that in the play therapy, her son was actually working on issues that were central to his development.

FILIAL THERAPY

The parent-child relationship is critical to the health of children. Parents' sense of adequacy affects their interactions with their children as well as their children's development. Teaching parents skills they can use with their children empowers them to change and gives parents a sense of participation and accomplishment (Edlefsen & Baird, 1994). Filial therapy (Landreth, 1991; VanFleet, 1994) is one way to provide support to parents of at-risk children. Instead of counseling directly with the children, in filial therapy (B. Guerney, 1964) counselors train parents to conduct child-centered play sessions with their children. The training generally takes place in a support group format. Parents are taught, through modeling and feedback, the following skills: structuring play sessions, describing behavior, responding to feelings, responding to effort, returning responsibility to the child, and setting limits. One benefit of filial therapy is that the group discussions help create better child-parent relationships for all children in the family (Andronico & Guerney, 1967).

The following modifications of Landreth's (1991) filial therapy model were made in one school with a predominant population of at-risk children. First, because it was difficult to find parents to commit to attending 10 group sessions, the parents were chosen from those who were already in the schools for some reason, such as GED classes. Second, the only "homework" given to the parents was to conduct weekly play sessions with their children. Given the crowded, hectic lives of many of these parents, limiting the out-of-session experience to finding the time, space, and privacy for one play session each week was challenging in itself. Readings or exercises parents could conduct at home were provided for parents who wanted them, but all training activities occurred during the context of the filial sessions. Third, because these parents did not have access to videotaping equipment, time was structured during the weekly filial session for conducting actual play sessions in lieu of asking parents to videotape sessions in their homes. Thus, the parents were observed, live, by other parents in the group, and immediate feedback was provided. The outcome of this process was that parents felt tremendous support from other group members, and the process itself facilitated the development of group cohesion.

Parents were provided filial kits that included toys representing all of the toys necessary to conduct play sessions. These toys were a welcomed gift; two parents mentioned that these toys would be Christmas gifts for their children. In one case, Bertha was the custodian of her granddaughter, Ariel. Bertha also had a 6-year-old daughter of her own. During one group session, Bertha related that Ariel kept pulling out the toys from the filial kit, so she was having trouble following the recommendation to use the toys in the filial kit only during the play sessions. As she continued talking, she told us that the toys in the filial kit were the only toys that Ariel had. The play sessions gave the children both sacred time with a parent and toys that most of them had never had. The play sessions gave the parents both sacred time with their child and new skills. Parents reported that they felt closer to their children, accepted them more, and, most of all, appreciated tremendously the skill of limit setting as an alternative to harsher ways of disciplining their children.

CONSULTATION WITH TEACHERS

With the support of teachers, school counselors are able to access children for play therapy. Without their support, it is difficult to work with the children. Teachers understand the serious problems experienced by at-risk children, yet they still may find it troublesome to allow these "difficult" students to leave the classrooms to "play." Using terminology other than "play" might be helpful. More important, however, is consistent communication with teachers and administrators to help them understand the value of play therapy.

Working with at-risk children in a school setting has the obvious advantage of assisting numerous children who would not receive services outside of the school. An ideal play therapy schedule would be to see students once a week, but at-risk children often have high rates of absenteeism. This absenteeism, paired with other academic and attention problems, frequently results in the reluctance of teachers to allow these children to miss class time devoted to academic instruction. To address this problem, school counselors can schedule play therapy sessions during breakfast, recess, lunch, after school, and at other nonacademic times. In addition, counselors can vary the times for sessions so the children will not regularly miss the same academic subjects.

School counselors can present the basic concepts of play therapy during in-service sessions. It is helpful to (1) provide teachers with written material on the positive outcomes possible as a result of play therapy; (2) review the importance of confidentiality; (3) explain the process of retrieving and returning children to the classroom, including how to speak with the children after their sessions; and (4) arrange regular consultation meetings to discuss the child's progress.

Maintaining contact with teachers while children are in play therapy helps the school counselor recognize progress that is made in the classroom. This is essential because the ultimate goal of play therapy in schools is to help at-risk children become effective learners. Teachers need to know that they are a critical part of the helping process.

CONCLUSION

At-risk elementary school children typically come to school with attention and behavior problems. Because these problems can detract from their academic and social development, cause persistent school misconduct, and affect other children negatively (Hovland, Smaby, & Maddux, 1996), helping these children become involved and successful in school is essential. Child-centered play therapy is one way to help at-risk children.

Conducting play therapy with at-risk children in school has clear challenges. The crises in their lives are ongoing; they move frequently; they are absent often. Teachers question whether they should miss much needed instruction to "play." Parents may be difficult to reach and reluctant to become involved. In spite of these challenges, child-centered play therapy offers great promise for at-risk children.

That promise is grounded in the theoretical underpinnings of the approach (Axline, 1947; Landreth, 1991). Even in adverse situations, Axline (1964) demonstrates in the case of Dibs that children grow in a child-centered therapeutic environment. The goals of child-centered play therapy match the needs of at-risk children. Within the safety of the relationship established with the child-centered play therapist, at-risk children have a place where they can learn to express and cope with a range of feelings. They have a place where they assume responsibility for their own decisions. They have a place where they can succeed. Providing at-risk children, their parents, and their teachers a child-centered therapeutic environment gives these children—children who have the greatest risk of failing—an avenue for success.

REFERENCES

Albaum, J.S. (1990). *A cost-free counseling model for high-risk elementary students* (Report No. CG023092; ERIC Document Reproduction Service No. ED 327–788). Sacramento, CA.

Andronico, M.P., & Guerney, B.G. (1967). The potential application of filial therapy to the school situation. *Journal of School Psychology, 6,* 2–7.

Axline, V. (1947). *Play therapy.* Boston: Houghton Mifflin.

Axline, V. (1964). *Dibs: In search of self.* Boston: Houghton Mifflin.

Baecher, R.E., Cicchelli, T., & Baratta, A. (1989). *Preventive strategies and effective practices for at risk children in urban elementary schools.* Paper presented at the annual meeting of the American Education Research Association, San Francisco.

Bloom, B. (1981). *All our children learning.* New York: McGraw-Hill.

Cochran, J. (1996). Using play and art therapy to help culturally diverse students overcome barriers to school success. *School Counselor, 43,* 287–298.

Edlefsen, M., & Baird, M. (1994). Making it work: Preventive mental health care for disadvantaged preschoolers. *Social Work, 39,* 566–573.

Frick-Helms, S.B. (1997). Boys cry better than girls: Play therapy behaviors of children residing in a shelter for battered women. *International Journal of Play Therapy, 6,* 73–91.

Gage, N.L. (1990). Dealing with the drop out problem. *Phi Delta Kappan, 72*(4), 280–285.

Greathouse, B., Gomez, R., & Wurster, S. (1988). An investigation of Black and Hispanic parents' locus of control, childbearing attitudes and practices and degree of involvement in Head Start. *Negro Educational Review, 39,* 4–17.

Guerney, B. (1964). Filial therapy: Description and rationale. *Journal of Consulting Psychology, 28,* 303–310.

Guerney, L. (1983). Client-centered (nondirective) play therapy. In C. Schaefer & K. O'Connor (Eds.), *Handbook of play therapy* (pp. 21–64). New York: Wiley.

Hovland, J., Smaby, M.H., & Maddux, C.D. (1996). At-risk children: Problems and interventions. *Elementary School Guidance and Counseling, 31,* 43–51.

Johnson, L., McLeod, E.H., & Fall, M. (1997). Play therapy with labeled children in the schools. *Professional School Counseling, 1,* 31–34.

Landreth, G.L. (1991). *Play therapy: The art of the relationship.* Muncie, IN: Accelerated Development.

Landreth, G.L., & Sweeney, D.S. (1997). Child-centered play therapy. In K. O'Connor & L.M. Braverman (Eds.), *Play therapy: Theory and practice* (pp. 1–45). New York: Wiley.

Levy-Warren, M.H. (1994). Child's play amidst chaos. *American Imago, 51*, 359–368.

Mann, D. (1986). Drop out prevention: Thinking about the undoable. *Teachers College Record, 87*, 308–323.

Martinez, P., & Richters, J. (1993). The NIMH community violence project 11: Children's distress symptoms associated with violence exposure. *Psychiatry, 56*, 22–34.

National Center for Education Statistics. (1997). *Social context of education 1977* (Department of Education Publication No. NCES 97–388). Washington, DC: U.S. Government Printing Office.

Poidevant, J.M., & Spruill, D.A. (1993). Play activities of at-risk and non at-risk elementary students: Is there a difference? *Child Study Journal, 23*, 173–186.

Post, P. (1999). Impact of child-centered play therapy on the self-esteem, locus of control and anxiety of at-risk 4th, 5th, and 6th grade students. *International Journal of Play Therapy, 8*, 1–18.

Post, P. (2000). Play therapy with a selective mute child. In G. Landreth (Ed.), *Innovations in play therapy: Issues, process, and special populations*. Philadelphia: Brunner/Routledge.

Rogers, C. (1951). *Client-centered therapy.* Boston: Houghton Mifflin.

Rumberger, R. (1987). High school dropouts: A review of the issues and evidence. *Review of Educational Research, 57*, 101–121.

Schaefer, C.E. (1994). Play therapy for psychic trauma in children. In K. O'Connor & C.E. Schaefer (Eds.), *Handbook of play therapy: Advances and innovations* (Vol. 2, pp. 297–318). New York: Wiley.

Silverman, W.K., La Greca, A.M., & Wasserstein, S. (1995). What do children worry about? Worries and their relation to anxiety. *Child Development, 66*, 671–686.

Trostle, S.L. (1988). The effects of child-centered group play sessions on social-emotional growth of four- and five-year-old bilingual Puerto Rican children. *Journal of Research in Childhood Education, 3*, 93–106.

VanFleet, R. (1994). *Filial therapy: Strengthening parent-child relationships through play.* Sarasota, FL: Professional Resource Press.

CHAPTER 7

Sandplay Therapy in a Time-Limited School-Based Program

ANTHONY J. PABON

ULSTER INTENSIVE Day Treatment Program (IDT) is a 30-day strength-enhancing program. Its mission is to help students who are in emotional crisis. The focus is both educational and therapeutic: teachers address academic concerns by providing one-to-one tutoring and emotional support; a licensed clinical staff use a variety of modalities to help empower children, their families, and schools. Sandplay has been particularly useful in this time-limited setting. Students are referred to IDT by hospitals and schools. At least half of the children have been either physically or sexually abused; in one case, a child was being retraumatized when a perpetrator was about to be released from jail. Feelings of low self-esteem with accompanying feelings of anger, anxiety, and depressions are common in this population.

The school provides a setting for concerned parents to consult with teachers and clinicians regarding their child's academic, social, and emotional growth. Receiving therapy in a school setting reduces the stigma of emotional illness and also eases transportation difficulties. Failed appointments are substantially decreased.

The role of the therapist in IDT differs in many ways from the role of other therapists who provide clinical services to children in the school setting. The school social worker or psychologist usually works with students in either group or individual sessions, one or two times a week, but is not in classrooms on a daily basis. This milieu has added pressures and rewards. Student, teachers, and clinicians are in close contact six hours a day. The staff models behavior, eats breakfast and lunch with students, and provides group and individual therapy.

Each day begins with group therapy. Students are expected to maintain a daily journal with a minimal requirement that they record their day on a feeling scale of 1 through 10, 1 being suicidal and 10 feeling great. They are introduced to the technique of scaling during the intake interview.

INTRODUCING STUDENTS TO SANDPLAY THERAPY

The sand tray is introduced to each student along with his or her family during the intake process. While on tour of the two IDT classrooms, students are shown the play therapist's office. They view a large display of approximately 600 miniatures on open shelving and a sand table. Sometimes students can't resist and touch the sand and examine it; others look carefully at some of the miniatures. Although the majority of students are open to the idea of creating scenes in the sand, a few react with disdain.

The play therapist initially introduced the sand tray only to children from age 8 to 13, but when time allowed, older teens up to 17 were also given the opportunity to make a tray. Currently, each older teen does several sand trays as an adjunct to therapy appointments with the primary therapist. Play therapy, particularly sand tray therapy, is the primary modality used with the 8- to 13-year-old group.

A BRIEF HISTORY OF SANDPLAY THERAPY

Margaret Lowenfeld was the first to use sandplay as a therapeutic modality. She gives children the credit for the method she began to develop in 1929, which she called the World Technique (Bradway, Signell, Spare, Stewart, & Thompson, 1981). She worked in England during World War II, during the Nazi air raids, and tried to provide a safe place for children to express their personal and national trauma. Carl Jung was an influence on sandplay by encouraging his protégé, Dora Kalff, to study Lowenfeld's methods. For most of his life, Jung would sometimes play with mud and water when he was deep in thought and problem solving. Jung's other significant contribution to current sand tray therapy includes his theory of archetypes, images or fixed ideas that exist in the psyches of all peoples;

each archetype contains its opposite and thus has a positive and a negative pole (Carey, 1999).

Jungian therapists attempt to connect the conscious mind of the patient with archetypes that are the cause of personal suffering. Kalff was influenced by Eastern philosophy, which teaches that a direct question is never answered but is referred back to the student. This became her rationale not to interpret a sand picture to the maker, at least until such time that the maker was able to tolerate interpretations. She believed that interpretation became productive only when the ego and the self had established a positive connection. She referred to the sand tray as "the free and protected space"; she believed, as Jung had taught, that each individual had an internal drive toward wholeness and healing. Her methods were nonintrusive. Kalff was strongly influenced by the work of another Jungian analyst, Erich Neumann, who wrote about stages of psychological development that Kalff applied to her understanding of the trays her clients created. From its inception, sandplay work has been concerned with the development of the self and the balancing of positive and negative forces. The sand tray is an excellent method for understanding child development (Carey, 1999).

THE SAND TRAY THERAPY SESSIONS

Sexual Identity

Jake

During one intake, the toddler in the family touched the identified patient's crotch area. The 10-year-old appeared to react uncomfortably but with a facial expression that looked suspicious to me. I felt alerted. Was this just an innocent toddler's clumsiness, or was he communicating that the family had sexual abuse issues?

Jake's first tray was very artistic. He was drawn to the figure of Athena and other women; children age 10 would rather use *Star Wars* figures, cars, trucks, aliens, spacemen, cowboys, and farm animals, but here it seems we have Eros. This 10-year-old was dealing with enmeshment issues and his own sexual identity; the boy appeared to have conflicts about sexuality. The parents did not mention abuse, but it eventually came to light that some months earlier, a neighbor was molesting two female cousins of this boy. The cousins warned the boy not to tell his mother or they would get hurt by the perpetrator. Finally, the villain was caught violating the children by the girls' parent, and he was subsequently sentenced and jailed.

It seemed as if this boy's fantasy life emerged from a preconscious state to a conscious one earlier than his developmental age. Secrecy, fear, and forbidden and pleasurable libidinous feelings forced themselves into consciousness by this crime against his cousins.

LIVING IN A CRACK HOUSE

Sandra

Sandra, age 15, reported that she lived in a crack house for periods of her early childhood. When she created her first tray, she made several starts and stops as she explored the figures and then changed her mind when she found a figure she liked better. She liked the Disney characters and took quite a few of them out, telling me her favorite story was *Lady and the Tramp*. When asked what she liked about the story, she could not say. She watched it over and over when she was young and had to mind her younger sister and brother. She happened to see it again recently.

Then, she put the young lion son on top of a mound. She said that he belonged there. She then told the story of *The Lion King*. The cruel uncle baboon killed the Lion King and left the son without a father. She next said that she liked the aliens and told me about a ghost haunting the battered women's shelter as well as ghosts in other houses where she had lived. She relayed how her grandfather told one ghost to leave a new place they were moving into and it left.

As she worked in the tray mounding the sand and enjoying the feel of it, she told me that her mother used to drink a lot and that her mother's boyfriends were often abusive to her mother but not to her. She could not believe that all she had to do here was play. I listened and felt very present. I asked her if she was angry about all the caretaking she had done for her mother and siblings. She said that she did not mind her role because she knew no other and it was what was expected of her. I commented that I thought the sandbox might be just what she needed because she hadn't had much of a childhood and maybe it would be relaxing to use the sand.

She thought her next scene was beautiful. It was an undersea world where a mermaid was taking a bath, while some of the whales and sharks had food on their agenda. Would the mermaid be the prey, I wondered to myself, but, as if attuned to my feelings she said the fish were no danger to the mermaid. A walrus was on the mound where the young lion had previously sat. A small walrus was attempting to get up on the mound to be with the adult walrus. It seemed that the small walrus wanted to be noticed and cared for, and that could be the metaphor for Sandra's childhood. She then decided that the size of the figures could seem more real if they were seen at different depths in the sea, and so she saw her scene from another perspective.

During the session, Sandra also shared feelings about her recent hospitalization. She had a fright reaction and was retraumatized by the act of nurses restraining another patient soon after Sandra was admitted. The commotion and screaming caused her to have flashbacks to the domestic violence she had witnessed in her life in crack houses. She told me that she had torn the wallpaper off the hospital wall because she felt that she was a small child again in a crack house. As she described it, it seemed as if she had suffered from posttraumatic stress. After the session was over, she drew a large, colorful dragon, four or five feet high, on the classroom chalkboard. It was in motion, leaping and breathing fire. She thought it was beautiful. She shared a photograph of the tray she created with everyone.

Sandra had not lost her ability to play and she had mastered her scary feelings by placing some of her fears into ghost stories. *The Lady and the Tramp* had been her babysitter and was also part of her healing. This resilient child felt joyful after the session. The dragon remained on the board for weeks and was admired by all.

Trinket

Trinket, age 8, was in a crack house when she was 4. In her sand tray, she portrayed the characters from the *Wizard of Oz* as opposites (e.g., good and bad Dorothy and good and bad witch and good and bad scarecrow). Each of the bad characters had a little bit of good in them and each of the good ones had a little bit of bad in them. As she told the story, everyone turns bad, which she expresses by burying each figure. Finally, a wolf goes to get help, but he doesn't come back for two years. Everyone is so hungry that they could eat spiders. The figures were unburied for the photograph.

This is a story of deprivation and betrayal, likely an actual memory of not being able to trust anyone and feeling hungry for long periods of time while she was in the crack house. Trinket was at IDT because of her explosive temper. She was filled with rage and continued to be victimized and to victimize others in return. Ongoing sand tray therapy with such children has the potential of helping them master past traumatic experiences. Trinket returned to this theme of finding good and bad together in an attempt to integrate her feelings about her substance-abusing parents, her alcoholic relatives, and herself.

BRUTALITY

Amy

Amy, age 14, went to work quickly as she created her first sand tray. She liked the way the sand felt; she found it soothing to move it about, to make the surface choppy, to smooth it gently or to flatten it by pounding.

Amy reported that her house had burned down, yet, even though this was the most pressing concern she had at present, she would put the house and firefighters off to the side of the tray. I wondered out loud if she could move other feelings and events around in the same way she moved the burning house. She responded too quickly with "No!" In the center of the tray she placed a skeleton on top of its grave. A black metal fence surrounded the figure. An ominous figure in dark robes stood at the entrance to the cemetery she had created. Next to this, she placed a man on a motorcycle riding up the side of a ditch she had dug alongside the grave. Then she said, "It represents suicide, my right to take my life and do dangerous things."

In another area was a house surrounded by a white picket fence. In the enclosure was a happy couple (bride and groom), their children, a birdbath, and an eagle. These were the things she wanted in the future but had serious doubts that they could ever become a reality for her. The last figure placed in the box was a wrestler in camouflage clothing. "This is my father. He molested me." She placed this figure more or less in the center of the tray. She said she hated him but was confused because he was her father. The perpetrator had gotten away with his crime and now had a new family. At times, Amy wanted to see him, but her mother was adamant that this was not a good idea.

In her second session, she said that she had moved some things around in her life and was feeling better. She and her mom had discussed her desire to see her father. In this tray, she made everything positive. The bride and groom have figures behind them that represent their private love; birds, animals, and jewels are all around the couple. In response to this tray, I took the figure of the father she had used previously and said that he was missing. I wondered out loud if she could put the figure on the floor and step on it. "No," she responded, "I can't, he's my father." Through the family history I knew that this brutal father would slap his daughter if she refused to let him fondle her. Amy struggles to come to terms with her love for and hate of her father. She became more and more aware that all her thinking was colored by her relationship with her father and came to see this clearly in her trays. After doing a few trays, she also became more open to discussing her feeling with her mother and primary therapist.

SELF-MUTILATION

Mary

Thirteen-year-old Mary, who struggled not to cut herself and at times lost control, made a scene of skeletons and death to represent her dead feelings. By using the tray, she could give expression to her feelings three-dimensionally and share them more easily. Mary was not a young-ster who could express her feelings and thoughts verbally.

While Mary was at IDT it came to light that her stepfather was touch-ing her and making threats that he would kill her if she revealed what he was doing. This was the second time in her life she was sexually abused by a stepfather; the clinical assumption that her states of depersonaliza-tion were primarily related to her first victimization proved only par-tially correct.

After Mary's revelation of abuse to her mother, her stepfather was jailed. When he was quickly released on bail, he began stalking the family. He was jailed a second time, but he will get out again. Years of humiliation of having to keep this secret of nightly fondling while she pretended to be asleep have caused this child to withdraw deeply into herself. Using the sand tray helped her to begin to like herself again.

Lori

Lori was age 13 when she first entered IDT. She had been cutting herself, mutilating her arms; she had lost weight by refusing to eat. Her parents' separation for more than six months precipitated this teen's depression and anxiety. Her mother wanted to help her daughter, but she also needed to help herself, as they were both in crisis. The mother and daughter were enmeshed and boundary issues were present. When the parents recon-ciled, Lori's therapist became her mom's therapist. Her dad began drink-ing too much, and with a downturn in the economy, the family was forced to move in search of better pay. Lori was aware of the change that comes when you can't be Dad's little girl anymore. She said that it was uncom-fortable to smell alcohol on his breath at a family pool party.

Lori liked using the sand box; she called it her friend. She often pre-ferred not to use miniatures. For her first tray, she created six or seven mounds in the sand, describing these as obstacles a young person faces. A section of the tray did not contain these mounds; it represented the reso-lution of the problems. Pathways connected the obstacles. Eventually, the way became smooth.

Lori had trouble being critical of her parents. She presented as a very good child who loved her family and just wanted to do well in school. Mom continued to look for just the right therapist for Lori. At one point, Lori's mother even thought she might ultimately become a social worker. Lori thought her mom would make a good social worker. Lori would say, "She is so wonderful she can do anything." Lori liked the feel of the sand as she talked about issues. She was able to catch up on schoolwork and ap-peared less depressed at the end of her 30-day stay in the program. Un-fortunately, she had to return to IDT some time later.

At that time, Lori told me that one of the techniques she was taught while she was in the hospital was to take a shower or brush her teeth when upset instead of cutting herself. She added, with defiant undertones, that she could use water that was too hot or brush her teeth very hard and make her gums bleed. Lori was in the driver's seat and, in a sense, could outsmart any therapist. With this understanding, I said, "That's your coyote coming out." This metaphor was used to bring out the other side of the very good child she always tried to be. She would not acknowledge ever feeling angry and yet had good reasons to feel angry. Lori had had three therapists in the community and had been through the IDT program once previously. However, she elaborated a great deal more the second time about what she was going through. Lori had not revealed on her first admission that her boyfriend had been hitting her for the two years they were dating; she had finally broken up with him. Like her mother, she had tried to rescue men.

This time she made a sand scene with mounds similar to her first sand tray six months earlier. This story had a different ending: although the person got over many obstacles and the number of them lessened, there would still always be obstacles. The road to maturity is a difficult one.

In her next sand tray she drew large concentric circles in the sand. I was able to show her a picture in a journal that looked very much like what she had drawn in the sand. It was a picture that represented wholeness, and, indeed, she seemed to be on her way.

She was more rebellious on this second admission, not trying to be like her idealized mother, the Great Mother. The negative side of the Great Mother could keep her chained and deny her independence. Lori read about casting evil spells but told me you couldn't really cast a spell unless you picked the plants in certain seasons, in certain places, and of the right color. It was wonderful for this student to begin to express her anger in fantasy and verbally. She was developing a good sense of humor.

These brave female students who used depersonalization and cutting as a defense against feelings of deadness agreed that the sand soothed them; one called the sand tray her friend. The sand has a grounding effect for these victims. It helps these children feel more present and grounded.

THE ARCHETYPE OF THE SHADOW

I remember listening to the radio when I was 7 or 8. Television was just beginning to come into its own, but the radio still held sway as the primary source of family entertainment. For me, it seemed late (close to bedtime) and the voice would come on the air with the words, "The Shadow knows." Scary music enhanced the words. No doubt, these were moralistic tales by today's standards, as good always conquered evil. It was frightening to think that some form that can't be seen lurks everywhere and knows one's deepest thoughts and desires. For example, a child could think, "It's scary that I want to hurt my body, but of course I have bodily curiosity, I stole something, I want to get even, and so on." I can remember playing the Shadow with my brother and sisters, a composite of mummy (Mother) and a blind man's bluff; we would come upon each other and frighten each other.

As people are capable of so many cruelties to children as well as large groups of other people, it is ever important that we face our shadow individually and collectively. Children can use the sand tray to look at their shadow and the shadows of adults they know who are villains.

Billy

Billy at age 13 was using marijuana and alcohol and had gotten himself into legal trouble twice. As his court date approached, his behavior became more and more hostile. It initially started with his bullying younger children on the bus or wherever it was difficult to supervise him. He did not accept responsibility for his behavior. Billy's father, who managed to hold a job but to drink every night and weekend, had burned his son's forearm with a lit cigarette. Visits were stopped immediately, but Billy revealed that his father had been hitting him for some time. Billy acted out his anger but would deny it verbally.

Billy did a series of trays in which an out-of-control bus driver robs a bank and drives a bus full of children to Mexico. Fences, along with police and tanks block the Mexican-American border. The bus driver, a female with a flame thrower, attempts to blast the police away. This antisocial child's rage found expression in the sand tray, after which Billy successfully rode the bus for several more weeks.

The shadow can make itself known on the bus or playground or in the cafeteria, places where fragile children feel unsafe. The reasons are both obvious and subtle: these places are less structured and allow more social interaction. On the playground, you may yell, run, and meet up with peers who are not in your class; the teacher can't be in all places. The back door of the building and under the jungle gym are excellent places where a child can hide when there are several classes sharing the playground. The concept of the safe, protected space of the sand tray (Kalff, 1980) needs to be extended to all places where children are.

For the majority, the bus trip home may be fun, a chance to sit with a best friend and tell jokes, be excited about going home to play videogames or see a pet. In rural areas, some children have long rides home and take advantage of the time to nap. But sometimes, a child returning home may again be subjected to witnessing domestic violence. The playground bully role has now blossomed into its adult form. In another home, a perpetrator may be waiting for his victim to get off the schoolbus. A teen may feel isolated, lonesome, and depressed and suffer privately as he or she hears slurs about gays and lesbians that kids so often repeat, or jokes about weight, or any other difference children might ridicule.

Of course, it is foolish to believe that all aggression must be vanquished. It is part and parcel of the species and no doubt a necessary resource for survival. Education, social grace, and positive activity, however, ought to be offered as alternatives or adaptations for more primitive styles of behavior. The shadow, too, contains its opposite, and both poles need to be balanced. A child can depict negative feelings in the tray and attempt to master them instead of behaving like a bully or delinquent.

METAMORPHOSIS

Jeff

By the time this 17-year-old left the room, I was very sad and felt surprised by the level of pain his story could evoke in me. Prior to doing his first sand work, he announced to his classmates that he was going to play in the sand. This is a common announcement that teenagers make to classmates. To the teachers, it is sometimes interpreted as a statement about getting out of classwork.

In his scene, he had depicted a grandmother, a child, and a bearded wizard surrounded by a white picket fence. "The wizard is my grandfather. He is wise," Jeff said. The grandmother was obviously loving the child in her arms. Two boys and their dogs were playing baseball. Not far off were cows and chickens. Three figures of women were watching the scene: his grandmother, his mother, and his new sister-in-law. His mother was described as well-meaning; she was the good witch of the East. He remarked that his brother's wife is fat and he is not yet used to the idea that his brother is married.

He also had a row of three friends—an Indian, a spaceman, and a cowboy—and remarked that these friends were "straight" (non-drug-using) as opposed to "bent." They were all different from each other, and this seemed to spur a sense of wonderment as he stared at the figures. I believe these figures represent choices or his ways to be.

Jeff has been in rehabilitation for polysubstance abuse, including opioids and alcohol. At his grandfather's 80th birthday, though he planned to have only a few drinks, he got drunk. He was in denial about his ability to control his consumption of alcohol once he had his first beer.

Drinking was a violation of his parole; because of his drinking at the party, he was returned to the inpatient program a second time. He said that he felt totally humiliated. In an inpatient alcohol rehabilitation center, he learned that there was a hereditary connection between his alcoholism and his father's.

He next described a feeling of great fear. If he was with someone and they smoked marijuana, he could be violated by the probation department again, and this time he would be put in jail. Even if his auto broke down and he hitched a ride he could be in trouble, especially if there were drugs in the vehicle. Drug use and alcohol were common to nearly all the teenagers he knew. Using the tray, this teen could make visual his problem as he looked at the players in his life and how they affected his wants and needs.

His tray was one of loss: the grandparents were not functioning well, were getting senile; he wondered if his recently married brother would lose interest in him. He remarked, "I am not trusted. People say that all I do is related to the possibility of relapse. If I am tired, people want to know if I am doing drugs." It is likely he doesn't trust himself. He has missed out on school sports, a great love, as he had played on various teams all through high school.

He felt very depressed but added that he was not suicidal. He felt positive about the box, for though he spoke of all the losses, he wanted a bright future. He is happy about not being high and says that a couple of times a day he reminds himself that he feels good. The sand tray was shared with his therapist, who was surprised that this boy used the sand tray. The experience was enriching for both this older teen and his play therapist. As he left the office, he decided to add the figures of a caterpillar and a butterfly placed side by side, symbols of growth and metamorphosis.

CONTAINMENT IN THE SAND

Katie

Katie's hands were shaking. The new medication prescribed for her symptoms of manic-depressive illness proved toxic to this 10-year-old's body. She was coping as well as she could, but she was obviously scared and uncomfortable. Her mother was coming to pick her up from IDT to take her to the local hospital emergency room. I asked Katie to do a sand tray while she waited, hoping the feel of the sand would lower her anxiety and I could continue to observe her.

She asked me to bury her hands in the wet sand. I encouraged her to take control by requesting instructions on how wet she wanted the sand

and how high to pile it on her hands. She wanted it wet and up to her el-bows. At one point, she started to drool. I took a tissue and wiped her mouth. I had the image of a young bird reaching her neck up from its body while sitting in its nest, appreciating my gesture as if it were a morsel of comfort. The sand, now Mother Earth, held the shaking child and gave her comfort.

Billy

Ten-year-old Billy often wanted to be buried in the same manner as Katie. I sometimes wondered if this activity was therapeutic; certainly, it was a way of building rapport and reaching the child on a kinesthetic level. Be-sides which, the children had fun. I thought of it as cradling (Brody, 1993) the child, who was paradoxically held without being touched. With hind-sight, I see that the weight of the sand symbolically keeps impulses in check. I learned in my follow-up phone call 90 days after his discharge from IDT that Billy had stopped putting his hands on others.

Billy's aggression had been played down as a symptom during the in-take evaluation. The greater problem was said to be his school attendance. Billy would throw tantrums and his mother could not get him to school. The school guidance counselor was angry at the parents, thinking they were colluding. This year, Billy's educational level is also more realistic. He knew how to grow a garden and to fix some machinery, but reading and writing were harder for him. Billy shared one scary dream in which alligators and snakes came after him. After showing me his nightmare in a sand tray, he made no further mention of nightmares.

Paul

Paul suffered many ego weaknesses and demonstrated self-soothing activities that are often seen in autistic children. He was learning dis-abled and counted magically in the fashion of children with Obsessive-Compulsive Disorder. He could not let go of anger and, before coming to IDT, would attempt to strangle kids who knew how to goad him to come after them. Then he would get into trouble.

Paul, age 11, had me bury his hands; at one point, he wanted to get into the box. He play-acted as if he was going to climb into it so that he could be totally covered with sand. He then said that his hand was a snake and he promised an imaginary squirrel that he would not eat him if he came near. He laughed gleefully at the squirrel's folly. A wonderful meal for a snake.

Paul moved his arms and hands under the sand and had me put my fin-ger in the hollow that he created when he pulled his arms back toward his body. This was a game of deception. Eventually, the snake became a mother eating her squirrel children. I watched Paul after the session. He stood in a strong stance somewhat like a warrior pose. The teacher shot me a look as if to ask what was going on with him. The posture was odd, in that Paul appeared more grounded and strong. Children know just what to do with the sand and how to use it to heal themselves: "Trust the process" (Carey, 1999; Kalff, 1980).

USING THE TRAY WITH MORE THAN ONE CHILD

ENEMIES

George and David

While completing his sand tray, George, age 13, complained, "I don't like David [a child of the same age]. He doesn't want to be my friend. He is always messing with me." George was an intelligent seventh-grader diagnosed with Obsessive Compulsive Disorder. His behavior prior to enrollment at IDT involved threatening to harm himself by sticking a paper clip in an electrical outlet. He was argumentative and thought his sister was the family's "Little Miss Perfect." At times, George was effeminate and immature; he sang songs his classmates found annoying. He grimaced because of his Tourette's syndrome. I asked him if it would be OK if I invited David into the session and that they could each do a sand tray. I was surprised that he agreed.

David, who liked to use the sand tray, was more than happy to get out of doing his academic subjects. David does not like to do schoolwork and was about to fail for the year. I told David that George was willing to share his sand tray appointment with him. I would draw a line down the middle of the tray and they could each work on one side. George made a complex story involving a temple and intruders, and there was the usual ceramic toilet he liked to include in his trays. Typically, David made an army scene. After the Columbine shooting, he reenacted the tragedy in the sand. He seemed stuck in conflict with separating from his mother and rejection from his father. He, too, was a very bright child.

Just before the session was over, George placed a tiny bridge and a giraffe at the separation between his and David's scenes. George then dripped sand all over his scene. A motoric release of his tics had been done in each of his sand trays. The two boys got along better from this point and their bickering stopped. I took a photograph of their scene for each of them and suggested that they might look at it and think about it later in the week. David and George were able to transfer the ability to get

along in a sand tray session to the classroom, where they would sometimes play board games together.

FRIENDS

Anita and Carol

Anita, 16, and Carol, 17, wanted to make a sand tray together. I asked if
they would divide the tray in half or create one story. They elected to create a scene together. Very quickly, they had cowboys and Indians fighting. A man on a horse was on his way to rescue a drowning boy; the
naked figure was in the pond. Anita put mud on the figure's genital area
to cover it up.

I told them I was surprised that they used cowboys and Indians.
Stereotyping, I said that I thought boys would be more likely to choose
them. They agreed that they both had mostly played with dolls growing
up and both liked horses and had brothers. A cowgirl on a horse was not
involved in the rescue, only a cowboy. They spoke candidly about their
problems. Carol had used alcohol with her medication and she did not
feel very well that day. Anita told about her father just getting the word
from his doctor that he could drink alcohol, as his medical condition
had improved. He had won his bout with cancer. I suggested that they
look at their photographs of the tray during the week because one sometimes sees something in a different way. Anita responded that maybe
this was really a story about how each of them is feeling, so conflicted
and angry inside.

CONCLUSIONS

Sand tray therapy can be used with good results by persons of all ages. In
addition to dialogue with the therapist, individuals can readily use their
imagination and represent a problem in many aspects. In a single session,
a person can use figures to show conflict and pain and also depict elements of hope. A sense of humor and detachment are also possible. Trinket represented her pain symbolically by having a giant lizard eat Peter
Pan to represent what parentification has done to her childhood.

That children use toys to manage stress and try new roles is known by
all who come into close contact with children. Roles of mother or father or
teacher are often incorporated into children's play when a child dresses
up for the part. In the sand tray, a figure will be chosen and manipulated
to accomplish this same end. Sandra used the firefighters and police in
the tray to put out a fire and rescue the building's tenants. She expresses

hope about therapy and believes in the selfless hero. Youngsters who have been sexually abused report that the sand helps them feel grounded and present rather than depersonalized and dead. Students are immediately aware of the temperature and moisture content of the sand as well as their reaction to touching it. The mind and the body are present and respond simultaneously through visual and tactile sensations in addition to internal fantasy.

Students can quickly depict their problems in the sand tray for they and the therapist to see. Figures in the box may dialogue or be moved or additional elements added to suggest the next step forward in resolving conflict, as when George and David made their scenes. George placed a bridge and giraffe at the line dividing their scenes, representing his desire to be closer and to bridge their relationship rather than feel isolated.

Depressed students who can hardly verbalize, even with the help of medication, can use the tray to show conflict and open up their feelings to the therapist. All children who have used the sand tray reported that they felt good about their creations and what they did in the session. After a session, it is usual for them to feel better and to be surprised by what they have accomplished by creating a miniature world.

Children who are not confident academically can show others what they have created in the sand. It is a noncompetitive experience even in the classroom where children have seen each other's creations. The conscious and unconscious mind can be present and opposite aspects of the self can be depicted without the confines of ordinary logic. Metaphor, intuition, chaos, humor, and all the aspects of the self are regarded with respect. Use of the sand tray appears to depend only on the situation of the individual child or adult.

REFERENCES

Boik, B., & Goodwin, E. (2000). *Sandplay therapy.* New York: Norton.

Bradway, K., Signell, K., Spare, G., Stewart, C., & Thompson, C. (1981). *Sandplay studies.* Boston: Sigo Press.

Brody, V. (1993). *The dialogue of touch: Developmental play therapy.* Treasure Island, FL: Developmental Play Training Associates.

Carey, L. (1999). *Sandplay therapy with children and families.* Northvale, NJ: Aronson.

Erdoes, R., & Ortiz, A. (1984). *American Indian myths and legends.* New York: Pantheon Bools.

Fraiberg, S. (1959). *The magic years.* New York: Charles Scribner's and Sons.

Gil, E. (1992). *Outgrowing the pain.* New York: Dell.

Kabat-Zinn, J. (1990). *Full catastrophe living.* New York: Delacorte Press.

Kalff, D. (1980). *Sandplay.* Boston: Sigo Press.

Moustakas, C. (1953). *Children in play therapy.* New York: McGraw-Hill.

Satir, V. (1964). *Conjoint family therapy.* Palo Alto, CA: Science and Behavior Books.

Schaefer, C., & Carey, L. (Eds.). (1994). *Family play therapy.* Northvale, NJ: Aronson.

Webb, N. (Ed.). (1991). *Play therapy with children in crisis: A casebook for practitioners.* New York: Guilford Press.

Webb, N. (Ed.). (1993). *Helping bereaved children: A handbook for practitioners.* New York: Guilford Press.

Wilmer, H.A. (1987). *Practical Jung.* Wilmette, IL: Chiron.

CHAPTER 8

Play Therapy in a Residential Treatment Center

DAVID A. CRENSHAW and CHRISTINE FOREACRE

A PROFILE OF CHILDREN REFERRED FOR RESIDENTIAL TREATMENT

CHILDREN ADMITTED to a residential treatment center typically manifest a degree of behavioral and/or emotional disturbance considerably more severe than children who can be treated in community-based settings. Their clinical features are often multidetermined. Often, they come from families who have struggled with poverty and violence, substance abuse, and, sometimes, major psychiatric disorder in one or both parents. In addition to the environmental stressors, many of these children manifest neurobiological deficits that significantly affect their development and functioning. Language delays, speech and language impairment, sensorimotor integration weakness, attention deficits, hyperactivity and impulsivity are all common clinical features. These children often have extremely low frustration tolerance and inability to delay gratification. Their impulsivity is sometimes driven by neurological dysfunction and sometimes by emotional arousal, as they often cannot tolerate the powerful affect that gets triggered in them; this is particularly true for children with a history of trauma and/or abuse. There is a high frequency of sexual and physical abuse history in the residential treatment population, and often they exhibit the abuse reactivity syndrome (Johnson, 1988). They are prone to fusion of sexuality and aggression and a proclivity to reenact the abuse experiences. The sexual reactivity of these children poses an extreme challenge to the staff to maintain a safe, therapeutic environment. These children often manifest severe attachment problems that lead them to respond to closeness, affection, and nurturance with either anxiety, aggression, or overwhelming disorganization. This highly predictable pattern among children in residential treatment has been referred to as the "crisis of connection" (Crenshaw, 1995). It should be noted that although these children face many obstacles and have suffered many developmental imbalances, our experience has taught us to respect the resilience and courage of these children, who often eventually learn to trust and make attachments to adults as a result of the intensive treatment.

VALUE OF PLAY THERAPY WITH THIS CLINICAL POPULATION

Play is often a preferred modality of communication and working through the emotional distress of everyday life, and it is often the treatment of choice for children who have been exposed to abuse, violence, and/or trauma (Mann & McDermott, 1983; Terr, 1983). Play therapy for children who have experienced or witnessed violence or trauma can create a safe and gradual healing process that allows the child to experience a degree of control that is critical to youngsters who have experienced terror. Typically, children will use puppets, sandplay, dollhouse play, or dramatic skits that lead up to the trauma events or abuse experiences in their lives. Some youngsters may have experienced severe deprivation and will play out nurturing scenes in which they cook and feed the therapist or the puppets or stuffed animals. They may also play out scenes in which their nurturing needs are soundly rejected. An example of this is a scene in which the child goes to the store for groceries and the store is closed.

The following play scenario involved compensation for severe deprivation:

> Billy had just returned from a holiday home visit in which, due to unexpected circumstances, the family did not have sufficient food to celebrate the holiday. On Thanksgiving Day, this youngster ended up eating a stew served at a local shelter where his mother was temporarily staying. In the play session, Billy insisted on cooking a Thanksgiving feast for his therapist. It included turkey with all the trimmings and there was plenty of food. There was so much food that Billy insisted that we bring the Jolly Green Giant to the table to help us eat all the incredible abundance of food. Then suddenly, Billy stared in the corner with a shocked look on his face. He was staring at the high chair and he said, "Oh my God, we forgot to feed the baby!"

Obviously, Billy was identified with the baby that somebody forgot to feed and was compensating for his intense experiences of deprivation with this huge feast that could be consumed only with the help of the Jolly Green Giant. This child would not have been able to tell his story directly or through primarily verbal means. His symbolic play communicated his deep, unmet needs for nourishment both physically and emotionally and his longing for the idealized all-nurturing and giving parent who would provide him with all that he could ever want. Not only did this child lack the skills to communicate primarily by verbal communication, but much of the story that he played out was outside of his awareness at that point. Thus, the fantasy play allows the child to gradually come to understand better his or her emotional and social functioning. As O'Connor (1991) has pointed out, although play therapy can be the treatment of choice for many young children and especially those with histories of abuse and trauma, verbalization should not be omitted. O'Connor noted that verbalization aids in generalization and is essential for processing of trauma events.

Play therapy offers safety in the form of a symbolic haven to work through painful and difficult material, as well as pacing that reduces the risk of retraumatization. Because of this, play therapy is often the treatment of choice for young children in residential treatment, as these youngsters tend to be very impulsive and action-oriented. The playroom and materials allow these children an opportunity to express themselves in keeping with their natural proclivity toward action. Finally, many children in residential treatment function emotionally at a much earlier developmental stage than would be indicated by their chronological age. Often, the emotional issues that require mastery relate to early periods in their life and involve developing trust around the meeting of very basic early needs. Play therapy allows for the kind of regression that enables these children to participate in a potentially developmentally corrective and healing experience.

ADAPTATIONS OF PLAY THERAPY FOR A RESIDENTIAL TREATMENT CENTER POPULATION

ESTABLISHING A THERAPEUTIC ALLIANCE

Establishing a therapeutic alliance with severely emotionally and/or behaviorally disturbed children in residential treatment is often a difficult and lengthy process. Although there is frequently an initial eagerness to "go to therapy" to be like other children and to get the undivided individual attention inherent in therapy sessions, the actual formation of a working relationship can take many months. This is largely because these children have learned that closeness with others is hurtful, whether through physical, sexual, or emotional abuse or neglect (Gil, 1991). Thus, as they begin to feel a connection to the therapist, they also feel threatened and are likely to resist in a variety of ways, which might include acting-out behaviors, flight, or attack.

CREATING A SAFE THERAPEUTIC ENVIRONMENT

Of utmost importance in establishing a therapeutic alliance is the creation of a safe and secure therapeutic environment. This place should be predictable for the child, always the same. This sameness involves the infrastructure of therapy: location, time, physical setting, toys, rules and limits, and the therapist's presence. Ideally, each therapy session should take place in the same playroom on the same day and at the same time each week. The length of the session should be the same, usually approximately 45 minutes but sometimes shortened for a child who cannot tolerate the anxiety generated by the closeness. The same toys should always be there (unless the therapist chooses to add additional items for a particular child at certain stages in therapy), and the room should be tidy, always looking the same and never in disarray. There should be no sign of the previous child's presence in the room.

Scheduling

Given the scheduling difficulties and the high volume of shared usage of the playrooms by all the clinicians inherent in residential treatment centers, it is not always possible to achieve the above ideal. At times, sessions have to be changed to accommodate other scheduling needs of the child, which may also necessitate a change in location. Such an occurrence affords an opportunity to help the child deal with change. No matter how careful the therapist is to be consistent in the timing of sessions, there are inevitable violations of this (e.g., due to lateness) or interruptions due to illness or vacations. These occurrences afford the opportunity to work on prior losses or disappointments. For example, a therapist was recently late for a therapy session with a boy whose family has been very inconsistent in their visits with him. A simple statement by the therapist that her lateness must have made him think she wasn't coming led to a long discussion of his disappointments and anger when his grandmother did not come for her visits.

Toys

There are many differences in opinion about what toys should be included in the therapy room. These range from O'Connor (1991), who limits the number of play materials to five, to play therapists who have fully stocked shelves of toys and miniatures. In our treatment center, the playrooms are filled with materials that encourage projection and expressive fantasy play, including puppets, dolls and their accoutrements, art materials, cars and trucks, pretend food and kitchen items, sand trays, and miniatures. There are also therapeutic games and other board games for older children.

Limit Setting

Another ingredient in creating a safe and secure therapeutic environment is limit setting. Knowing what they may and may not do reduces the anxiety children feel. Similarly, knowing that the adult is in charge also helps children to feel safe. Rules for the playroom should be kept simple and to a minimum and generally should revolve around safety issues. Usually, a rule that includes the idea that no one and nothing can be hurt in the room will suffice. Clear boundaries in the relationship between child and therapist are also important. Another issue that often arises with the children in residential treatment is their wanting to take things from the playroom. We have a general rule that nothing may be taken from the room except what the child has drawn or made with clay.

An issue that is often debated in our residential treatment center is whether therapy should be confined to the playrooms or the therapist's office. The general guideline is that there should be careful consideration given to conducting sessions in other locations and that there should be a therapeutic reason to do so, such as circumventing resistance or diluting the intensity of the relationship of the child toward the therapist. With some of the more disturbed children, however, it has been found that sessions in the therapy rooms can be too anxiety-producing to be effective, and alternative settings or activities may be more effectively employed. These children typically have extreme difficulty forming attachments, have severe expressive and receptive language deficits, and have diffuse ego boundaries. It is often necessary with these children for physical distance to be present to gradually build trust and a therapeutic relationship. Going for a walk or playing in the hallway or on the playground may be more conducive to meaningful conversation and relationship-building than remaining in a therapy room.

COLLABORATION WITH THE MULTIDISCIPLINARY TEAM

Collaboration with the multidisciplinary team working with the child is an important function of the play therapist in a residential treatment center. Team members (including the direct care workers, teaching staff, and recreation staff) spend many hours a week with the child and can offer many observations and insights into the child you are treating. Likewise, you can share your knowledge of the developmental level, dynamics, defenses, and strengths of the child with the team and make suggestions for treatment. It is sometimes helpful to include a member of the multidisciplinary team in a therapy session. This can serve to help process a conflict or crisis that has arisen in daily living and can also help to build attachments.

ISSUES IN CONFIDENTIALITY

Confidentiality is always an important issue in play therapy in residential treatment. The child should be apprised of the limits of confidentiality early on in the course of therapy and care should be taken not to give false assurances of confidentiality. Children should understand that what happens in the therapy sessions is private, but that general statements about their progress will be shared with other members of their treatment team as part of the collaborative approach to their treatment. They should also be told that if they reveal previous abuse or things that could affect their safety or that of others, this will have to be shared with the relevant people. It is helpful to know that, often, when children ask questions about confidentiality, they are asking whether other children will be told about what they do or say in therapy. A firm promise of privacy about this can and should be made. When a play therapist has multiple clients within a family (e.g., siblings or the parent and the child), the therapist must clarify at the beginning the nature of the relationship with each person, explaining the differences between individual and family issues. No information about one family member can be disclosed to another without informed consent.

THE ROLE OF THE FAMILY

The role of the family in play therapy in a residential treatment center is important. The family is considered part of the multidisciplinary team, and their partnership and contributions can be of extreme value. Although they will not usually be physically present in their child's individual sessions, their emotional presence is strong. Their support and encouragement of the child to share thoughts and feelings can be vital to successful therapy; progress is limited in cases where the parents urge the child to keep secrets or subtly undermine treatment in other ways. Often, a child is involved in family therapy as well as individual play therapy; the interplay of the two modalities can hasten treatment progress, as issues discussed in family therapy can be further explored and processed in play therapy. In play therapy sessions, a child can think of issues to bring up in family sessions, can practice doing this, and can gain strength and courage by rehearsal. In some cases, family play therapy has been a useful modality; much information can be gleaned about the functioning of a family while watching them play. This includes, but is not limited to, the affect of the parents and the child, intrusiveness of parents and child, compliance with the therapist's directions, and communication among family members (Gil, 1994). Play in a family provides for a shared enjoyable experience that also lowers defenses. There are a wide variety of play therapy techniques that are applicable to family sessions, including Family Puppet Interviews (Gil, 1994), projective drawing exercises, and Mutual Story Telling (originated by Richard Gardner, 1968).

A TREATMENT PROTOCOL FOR PLAY THERAPY IN A RESIDENTIAL TREATMENT CENTER

JOINING AND EGO STRENGTHENING

It is crucial that a strong therapeutic alliance be established with the child before work on the more painful and trauma-related issues can begin. It is important in the beginning to establish safety, which includes appropriate limits, as described above and, teaching self-soothing and self-calming skills and relaxation techniques (O'Connor, 1991). Also, it is important to work on building defenses (Crenshaw, 1990; Mordock, 1991). Vulnerable children who are easily triggered and flooded by affect that they cannot regulate need direct teaching and modeling in coping skills and reinforcement of adaptive defenses. This principle is a key tenet of our philosophy of residential treatment (Crenshaw, 1990). Often, this can be done within the metaphor of the play (Mordock, 1991). For example, a child may be in the process of playing with the dollhouse and suddenly a fire breaks out and the child becomes anxious because of the breakthrough of aggressive impulses and wants to stop playing. At that point, the therapist could suggest that they get the firetrucks to the scene to put out the fire and call an ambulance in case anyone is hurt. Such an intervention on the therapist's part models for the child, within the metaphor of the play, the defense of undoing when faced with overwhelming aggressive impulses. This same attitude and approach is taught to all staff working in the residential treatment center, whether teachers or child care workers, so that children who get easily overwhelmed with their impulses and emotions are taught adaptive coping skills and emerging defenses are reinforced. Direct care staff and teaching staff in a residential treatment center work under enormous pressures and stress, so they have the opportunity frequently to demonstrate and model adaptive coping strategies from which the children can learn. In addition, in therapy with children who have faced abuse and trauma, it is important to teach adaptive use of trauma-related defenses such as compartmentalization and dissociation (Gil, 1991; James, 1989). Compartmentalization allows children who otherwise might easily be overwhelmed by their emotions to set aside painful material until they are more comfortable in dealing with it; this reinforces their sense of control and mastery. Dissociation, which is a commonly used trauma defense, needs to be brought under the conscious control of the child, as described by Gil. Gil emphasizes the need to teach the child a name for the experience of dissociation, such as "spacing" or "zoning out." This enables the child to identify and talk about the experience more easily. It should also be normalized, because everyone experiences some degree of dissociation in the course of every-day life; it is the degree of dissociation that is problematic for children who have experienced trauma. Children need to be engaged in dialogue about when it is helpful for them to dissociate and when it is not. Teach-ing them alternative ways of coping with the anxiety and powerful emo-tions triggered by memories or reminders of the trauma is crucial. Strategies can be taught to help them reorient and focus when they are able to observe themselves dissociating.

EXPLORATION OF THE TRAUMA

It is important to use what James (1994) describes as invitational therapy when exploring trauma in children. As James explains, children find it very hard to initiate discussion or play that reveals their abuse and/or trauma experiences. Therefore, the therapist has to be active and directive in creating opportunities for unburdening and to gradually elicit the af-fect. Thus, during the relationship-building and ego-strengthening stage, the therapist may follow the child's lead and use a child-centered ap-proach. In trauma work, however, it is important for the therapist to be more directive. Children, like adults, are ambivalent about disclosing or confronting the abuse and/or trauma in their past. They may be fearful of the intense emotions surrounding the original experiences, yet they may have an equally strong desire to unburden and to have their pain wit-nessed by others. Often, children will give clues to their readiness to con-front the painful experience more directly by the nature of their play scenarios, which become more and more transparent and thinly disguised in relation to the original abuse and/or trauma experiences. Clinicians need to assess the ego strength of the child prior to making interpretations that require the child to confront the trauma directly. One important clue to the child's capacity to handle the powerful affect associated with the trauma events is the amount of disruption and emotional spillover follow-ing the session. If a child is unable to cope or function in the classroom or living group following the therapeutic play session in which the trauma events were approached through symbolic play, this would strongly suggest the risk of retraumatization due to flooding and reinforcement of the child's sense of helplessness and powerlessness. The child's breaking off play in the middle of a trauma-related scenario is also an important indication of lack of readiness to directly face the trauma. It is important for all play therapists to be aware of the guidelines for identifying posttraumatic play (Terr, 1981) and for intervening with posttraumatic play (Gil, 1991). A child stuck in repetitive posttraumatic play is expressing vulnerability and lack of sufficient emotional resources to process the trauma in a more direct manner.

It is important to pursue the details of spontaneously expressed memories and dreams to facilitate access to the child's affect. It cannot be emphasized enough that pacing is crucial due to the risk of flooding. Acute traumatic reactions are often seen in the endless repetition of violent play scenes. The therapist needs to intervene when the repetitions are only reinforcing the sense of powerlessness and to offer alternative solutions for mastery and resolution.

REPAIRING THE SENSE OF SELF

Trauma survivors experience painful feelings of shame, guilt, and self-blame that have to be countered with affective intensity to have any impact (B. James, personal communication, 1993). In other words, the negative messages that the child has received during the course of early development are imprinted with such emotional intensity that simply talking in a calm way does not begin to counterbalance the negative message. James (1989, 1994) has suggested some creative therapeutic interventions to accomplish this purpose. During this stage, the therapeutic focus shifts to rebuilding self-esteem and developing a realistic view of self in relationship to others and a separate identity that is not crystallized around victimization and trauma. It is important to help children view themselves in the context of a larger life than is defined simply by the trauma events.

RESTORING CONNECTIONS AND BUILDING ATTACHMENTS TO OTHERS

Following the intensive individual work, or in conjunction with it, it is important to widen the circle of trusted people in the child's life. In residential treatment, it is sometimes overlooked how important are the child's relationships to teachers and child care workers, even if the child does not acknowledge this. Likewise, it is critical to be sensitive to the potency of loss and separation for these children, because in many cases they have experienced multiple losses in their early life. Frequently, a child will be triggered into a crisis by some kind of shift in the residential context, such as a favorite child care worker or teacher being on vacation or another child leaving the placement for home.

In family work, the focus is on restoring connections between the child and the family and healing the hurt that relates to disconnection, separation, and sometimes violence in the family. It is extremely important that a firm expectation be established that we will talk about the trauma within the family (A. Fussner, personal communication, 1998). It is also critical that the parents be able to convince the child that they want to and are able to hear the pain of the child as he or she expresses the details of personal feelings and experiences (A. Fussner, personal communication, 1996).

DEVELOPING A FUTURE ORIENTATION

In the concluding phase of therapy, it is important to help these children develop a sense of a positive future, to highlight their strengths and resiliency, and to create hope. It is also crucial to recognize and honor the spiritual dimension in the healing process (James, 1989). James has indicated that this is especially critical with children who have experienced abuse and/or trauma. James states, "They need to feel that there is a core to their being that cannot be lost or taken away, and that they have an inner wisdom upon which they can rely" (p. 211).

TRANSFERENCE AND COUNTERTRANSFERENCE

Children in play therapy in residential treatment settings tend to relate to the therapist by extreme projections. Often in the beginning, the therapist is idealized and seen as an all-providing figure available to meet the child's every need. The child longs for the good mother who will make up for all of the experienced deprivations in early life. When the inevitable frustration comes, and the child becomes aware that the therapist cannot meet all of his or her intense needs and longings, the therapist tends to be devalued and viewed as rejecting, hostile, and abandoning. This all good or all bad manner of viewing the therapist mirrors the way the children tend to view themselves. The intensity of these needs can evoke powerful feelings in the therapist, resulting in countertransference reactions that can be unhealthy if unexamined. Often, the therapist becomes the recipient of the child's intense rage at unmet needs. In addition, children may identify with a cruel or destructive figure in their past, which may lead them to respond to any warmth or caring on the part of the therapist in a violent or mocking manner. If these projections are interpreted too early, they will be experienced as a massive rejection (Boston, 1983). These children often discourage therapists and have a way of making therapists feel inadequate, helpless, rejected, and hopeless—the very feelings these children themselves have found intolerable. In understanding these children, it is important to recognize the typical pattern of identification with the aggressor. Anna Freud (1937) defined identification with the aggressor "as representing a way of mastering fear of a dreaded external object by assimilating or identifying with it" (p. 118). Some children are so caught in their identification with the aggressor that they derive enormous gratification from the sense of power they experience as the active aggressive one instead of the terrified, helpless one. Rage and anger also serve as primitive distancing techniques. At times, the degree of rage expressed by the child reaches sadistic proportions and may stir powerful counter-transference feelings in the therapist, who may find it very hard to witness or to be the recipient of such intense hostility. Even more distressing is the often intense abandonment depression that underlies the rage. When this happens, the therapist may be frightened by the intensity of the child's despair and hopelessness. It is crucial that the therapist receive adequate support and supervision to be able to see the child through these intense phases of therapy and the powerful affects that emerge. Hardy (1998) has described the intense rage associated with invisible wounds that children feel who have experienced oppression and domination along with learned voicelessness. Hardy conceptualizes the job of the therapist as helping children to break their silence and find their voice. The therapist needs to facilitate children in expressing the underlying rage and depression, even though these powerful affects can be very frightening to the therapist when the children begin to find their voice. One of the important advantages of residential treatment is the availability of a team approach and the network of support available to both children and staff. Without the support of colleagues and supervisors, the intensive work with such severely disturbed children could be overwhelming to even the most experienced therapist.

CRITICAL ISSUES IN PLAY THERAPY WITH CHILDREN IN RESIDENTIAL TREATMENT

INABILITY TO ENGAGE IN SYMBOLIC PLAY

Some children, because of the extreme deprivation and/or trauma they have experienced, may not be able to easily symbolize or to enter into symbolic play. Deprived children may have lacked the stimulation and encouragement to engage in imaginary pursuits and may also have been delayed in their cognitive development. As a result, they may approach the toys in the playroom in a concrete and literal manner without giving the objects a symbolic function. Such a child may just simply engage in repetitive motor play such as building a tower with blocks and knocking it down or ramming trucks repeatedly into the wall. In such cases, the play therapist will need to model for the child the use of imaginary and symbolic play to help the child develop the action of the play into a story. The play therapist may need to demonstrate puppet play or fantasy play scenarios to help stimulate this capacity in the child. Children who have been exposed to trauma may be reluctant to engage in fantasy and to use their imagination due to the frequent reminders that relate to their painful experience. For these children, it is almost as if they cannot afford an inner life (Boston, 1983). Gradual desensitization will be necessary for these children to overcome their fears about drawing on their inner life and engaging the capacity for fantasy and imaginary play.

IDENTIFICATION WITH THE AGGRESSOR

Children who have been exposed to violence often respond by adopting the defense of identification with the aggressor. Turning from the help-less, powerless position to that of the aggressor, children feel empower-ment and a sense of control that was lacking in their real-life experience. Children with this history, however, sometimes become caught in their identification with the aggressor and become overgratified in this role to the point that it is difficult for them to give it up. In some cases, the ag-gression acted out is carried to sadistic proportions, which may cause considerable discomfort for the therapist and is not helpful for the child. This process is parallel to what Terr (1983) described as posttraumatic play. The child literally becomes "stuck" in this form of play; the play loses any therapeutic value and requires the therapist to intervene. The guidelines offered by Gil (1991) for intervening with posttraumatic play are useful also in intervening with children who have become rigidly identified with the aggressor and repetitively play out such identifica-tions with little or no variation. It is important that the therapist not per-mit this play to continue past the point where the empowering value is overshadowed by the reinforcement of a faulty and unhealthy identifi-cation with a cruel or persecuting aggressor. The gratifications from adopting such a powerful role are undeniable, particularly for children who have been terrorized, and giving up these gratifications may be dif-ficult. The goal of the therapist should be to introduce variation in the play and redirect the child to a different role. It is possible to do this at times within the metaphor of the play. For example, if the child is using the alligator puppet to terrorize all the other puppets, the therapist may ask the child to switch and play the role of the superhero who comes in and saves the other animals and sends the alligator away. In this instance, it is important to stop the scene as soon as the child has played out the superhero intervention so that he or she does not then switch back to identification with the aggressor. The other puppets can offer considerable reinforcement to the superhero to counteract the enormous gratifications obtained from the identification with the aggressor role. Such an intervention might need to be repeated numerous times before the child is ready to give up exclusive preoccupations with the identification with the aggressor.

This rigid identification with the aggressor is reminiscent of Boston's (1983) concept of double deprivation, in that the children suffer not only the deprivation related to external circumstances but often deprive themselves further by their crippling defenses, which cut them off from sources of satisfaction. Boston describes the essence of this double deprivation as the identification with an unfeeling, cruel, abandoning parental figure; in the child's inner world, this figure tends to be perceived in other people. Consequently, these children tend to push away and provoke rejection in those who would befriend them or attempt to help them. They live in a context of cumulative deprivation and attendant rage. Because the compounded effect of the negative polarities of the identification with the aggressor defense can be devastating, it is important for the therapist to intervene once it is clear the child is stuck in this pattern of rigid defense.

PREVALENCE OF SEXUALIZED BEHAVIOR

A relatively high proportion of children in residential treatment have experienced sexual abuse in their history. As a consequence, in the play therapy sessions, children may engage in sexualized behavior or even seductive behavior toward the therapist. They may have difficulty distinguishing between affection and sexuality, and sometimes aggression and sexuality are fused in these children. At times, the children may be simply overstimulated by their premature sexual exposure and victimization and engage in a pattern of sexually reactive behavior. This can be very stressful for the play therapist who may not know how to respond. It is important in the case of sexually reactive behavior that the therapist establish that the playroom is a safe environment for both the child and the therapist and that it is not appropriate for the child to engage in such behavior. In the past, these children may have been told that they had to engage in such behavior for adults to like them or to bestow special favors on them. The therapist can empathize with the child's difficulty in controlling these behaviors and agree to work with the child on ways to develop better control. The therapist can suggest that at the point the child starts to engage in sexualized behavior, the therapist will stop him or her and the therapist and child will take a brief break from the session to practice together relaxation techniques such as deep breathing. Also, they will reflect on alternative ways for the child to express feelings of affection or excitement. These can be practiced with the therapist, who can provide prompts when he or she anticipates the breakthrough of sexualized behavior. This places the therapist and the child in a collaborative alliance, with the goal of helping the child gain more effective control over the sexualized behavior.

Children also reenact their traumatic sexual experience in the course of play therapy. These abuse reenactments are attempts by the child to gain mastery over the original experience, which was overpowering at the time. Gradually, the children are able to master the powerful affects often related to the victimization experience(s). If the child is engaged in compulsive repetitions of the trauma event without variation or indications of movement, it is important to follow the guidelines by Gil (1991) to interrupt the posttraumatic play. When the child has moved on and no longer experiences a compelling need to play out the sexual traumatization, it is often helpful to work with the child on empowerment and prevention of future victimization. It is important to emphasize what the children have learned in terms of protecting themselves and to highlight resources available to them, both internal and external, to prevent further occurrences. It is also helpful to identify the period of traumatization as a brief portion of the child's total life course that need not be a defining event in terms of the child's identity.

Children also work through their sexual trauma in a symbolized way that provides a safe distance from the actual experience. The ability to symbolize and to maintain distance suggests the development of more adequate defenses in the children that allows them to approach this material without being flooded or overwhelmed. An example of a symbolized play scenario in which sexual trauma was the core issue follows:

> In Roberto's scenario, people brought their animals to a pet store, but instead of these animals being sold to others, they were killed. The therapist introduced the idea of the "animal rights" people coming to the rescue, and so a truck pulled up in front of the pet store. Roberto permitted only the babies to be saved. The truck started down the road and the babies

were scared because they were afraid the animal rights people would kill them. The truck flipped over and the animals fell out. Then they were placed on a conveyor belt and led down a chute, where they were all chopped up and killed.

Here, it is obvious that the child is dealing in a very dramatic and extreme way with issues of trust and betrayal and violence. This child had been prostituted by his mother for money and drugs. He had been forced to perform sexual acts with men and women when he was between the ages of 4 and 6. The degree of violation, violence, and trauma is well symbolized in the baby animals' being placed on the conveyor belt to be chopped up by the supposed animal rights people. It took many repetitions of similar play scenarios and interventions on the part of the therapist to introduce the idea that not all caregivers and helpers are violent, abusive, and unworthy of trust. Change was slow, as one would expect in a child with this degree of sexual trauma.

PRACTICAL TECHNIQUES IN PLAY THERAPY WITH CHILDREN IN RESIDENTIAL TREATMENT

Children in residential treatment need to be taught the language of feelings (A. Fussner, personal communication, 1995); Fussner has stated that these children experience feelings like "a wind blowing through their systems." In other words, they are unable to differentiate feeling states that often flood or overwhelm them. Some children of trauma experience alexiathymia, a disturbance in which one is aware only of the physiological aspects of affect, such as increased heart rate, but unable to name or give symbolic representation to an emotional experience (James, 1994; Krystal, 1998). In these children, the capacity to understand and identify emotions is impaired; they are able to describe how another child might feel in similar circumstances but cannot describe their own emotional experience except for its physiological components. As James (1994) points out, alexiathymia inhibits learning from one's emotional experiences. James also notes that intense affect related to trauma inhibits and blocks the ability to verbally communicate one's experience. She further explains that "traumatizing experiences appear to be encoded in the primitive, non-verbal part of the brain, thus explaining the inability to verbalize the experience" (pp. 14–15). As a consequence of these inhibitions and lack of capacity to verbalize in young children, particularly those who have been traumatized, it is crucial to help children identify and find a language for their feeling states and to find safe ways for them to express these feelings through play, drawings, puppets, or sandplay. Other creative methods such as working with clay may be very helpful for some children. These techniques reduce the pressure on the child to verbalize, but it is important that verbalization not be omitted (O'Connor, 1995). Verbal processing of trauma to the extent possible facilitates generalization outside the therapy session and reduces the amount of work that the child may be required to do at later developmental stages (O'Connor, 1995). Children exposed to extreme abuse and trauma as well as significant losses will do best with what James has described as a developmentally sequenced model of therapy. For example, a child who has experienced the death of a parent in early life may be able to process that enormous loss only to a certain point at age 5. At age 10, the child will understand more and have the cognitive capacity and emotional resources to go further in terms of grieving the loss. In adolescence, the teen can understand death in a more adultlike manner: to appreciate death as inevitable, universal, and lasting past one's own lifetime. At this point, the grief may take a new form, as death is appreciated in a new way. In residential treatment, this developmentally sequenced approach requires the therapist to adopt realistic expectations and to understand that children may be limited by their cognitive and emotional limitations in how far they can go in addressing past traumas. The techniques described in this section, however, are useful to the play therapist in assisting the children to go as far as they can at their stage of development.

TEACHING THE LANGUAGE OF FEELINGS

Basket of Feelings

The basket of feelings technique (James, 1989) is useful in helping children in residential treatment increase their ability to verbalize feelings and to understand that they can feel several ways and in different intensities about the same event. In this exercise, therapist and child write down feeling words on separate pieces of paper. The child should think of as many as possible, with the therapist contributing two or three to make the effort a collaborative one. When this is completed, there might be seven or eight different pieces of paper with such words as angry, sad, scared, happy, excited. The next step is to place different numbers of crayons or markers on each piece of paper to signify and quantify the amounts of different feelings the child has based on a benign, nonthreatening scenario. Then, the therapist tells the child about a time that evoked various feelings and places the amount of markers on the papers to indicate each of the feelings. For example, the therapist might tell about a time when her dog ran off and was missing for a few hours. She might then put a large handful of markers on *angry*, an even larger amount on *worried*, a few on *sad*. The therapist would then explain why and how the feelings pertained to the situation; for example, she might be worried the dog would get hurt. After this, it is the child's turn. The child can pick his or her own scenario or use ones suggested by the therapist.

Time Line

This technique uses color and affect pairing to help children express the various feelings they had at different times in their life. It is useful to encourage the sharing and verbalization of memories, to put the events in order and perspective, and to attach feelings to these events. This technique has been especially helpful with children in residential treatment who have had many different out-of-home placements in their short lives.

Have children draw a horizontal line across a piece of paper with small vertical lines to indicate different ages or times in their life. They should then fill in the different times and the memories about what happened at each point. The children should then choose different colors to represent various feelings. For example, a child might choose blue to represent sad, red to indicate angry, and yellow to mean scared. After these pairings have been made, the next step is for the children to color in the time line so that the colors reflect the feelings they had about each memory or time in their life.

Pick-Up Sticks

This technique (McDowell, 1994) uses the well-known game of pick-up sticks to help a child verbalize feelings and events. The game is played in the usual way, with the addition of the following: the colors of the sticks are paired with different feelings by the child, and whenever a stick is successfully picked up, the player tells of a time when he or she felt that feeling. Therapist and child take turns doing this until all sticks are picked up. Children in residential treatment find this game attractive and fun to play, so it is a popular activity. In addition to encouraging the language of feelings and the verbalization of events from life or problematic situations, this game is helpful in teaching the impulsive, action-oriented child to slow down. It teaches problem solving, planning strategy, and control.

Feeling Maps

A technique that has been most useful with children in play therapy in residential treatment has been the Gingerbread Person/Feelings Map (Drewes, in press). This exercise, sometimes referred to as the Gingerbread Person, involves pairing colors with different feelings, then coloring in a gingerbread figure in terms of the proportion of each of those feelings the child has experienced in relation to some event in his or her life. These exercises are extremely helpful in enabling children to express mixed feelings, which is a difficult concept for young children to grasp. Harter (1983) describes the developmental progression in children that leads eventually to appreciating that one can have opposite feelings directed toward the same target.

Color Your Life

A strategy developed by O'Connor (1983) is called the Color-Your-Life Technique. Children are given a blank piece of paper and asked to depict emotions that go with each color using either crayons or markers. Then they color their life according to how much they have felt each of these emotions. This is another art strategy that enables children to reveal in a creative way what they would find extremely difficult to share verbally. It is important, however, in processing the art productions to elicit the feelings of the child verbally to the extent that the child is capable and willing.

Puppet Play

In many ways, puppet play is the backbone of play therapy. It is a method that seems to be inherently attractive to children, many of whom will use the puppets spontaneously or with only minimal encouragement from the therapist. It provides the "stage" for children to tell their story, to express feelings, and to work out conflicts and behavioral issues. It is easy for children to identify with various puppet characters and to project their own thoughts and feelings onto them. Puppet play can be used in several ways with play therapy. Children can be given free rein to tell whatever stories they want with the puppets; this is useful initially to help the children feel comfortable and to explore how to express themselves freely. Another way to use puppets is for the children to tell a story, followed by the therapist retelling the same story with a slightly different ending so as to gradually change the children's perception of events, improve their coping strategies, or build defenses. Or the therapist may suggest a theme for the play. For example, the therapist might ask children to "tell a story about a time when you felt sad" or "tell a story about what happened last weekend." Another approach is for the therapist and the child to each have one or two characters to converse about a subject. It is much less threatening for a child to have bear and elephant, for example, talk about a traumatic event than to do so directly. It is helpful to have a variety of puppets available, including aggressive animals (e.g., alligator, lion, snakes), shy and quiet animals (e.g., turtles, birds, kittens), magical characters (e.g., dragons, wizards, princesses), and people representing various family members and various professions (e.g., police, firefighters).

DRAMATIC PLAY

Everyone has seen little children engaging in dramatic play, taking on a role and pretending to be something or someone other than themselves. A boy might be a fireman and heroically put out a raging fire. A girl might pretend to be a mother, feeding and caring for various children. This sort of play helps children express their inner thoughts and feelings as they play out experiences. For all children, but especially for those in residential treatment, it helps to weaken the impact of affective pressure and helps children assimilate the traumatic experiences from their past. It provides an opportunity for them to turn a passive experience into one in which they can be an active participant who can control, direct, and master the situation.

The therapist can learn much about the child by watching this play which, just in itself, can be curative. The therapist also can help the child by commenting on the play, by taking a role within the play, or by introducing alternative solutions or endings. As stated earlier, the therapist should intervene when the child's symbolic play becomes repetitious and does not move forward toward resolution. It is helpful to have a wide variety of props for symbolic play in the playroom, including dress-up clothes, dolls, a dollhouse, doctor equipment, cars and trucks, and food and kitchen equipment. Experience has shown that the neglected and abused children in residential treatment are drawn to the food, dishes, and kitchen appliances and spend a lot of time playing out themes of nurturance. One 8-year-old girl whose mother had died and who had been emotionally and physically neglected as well as abused by her father, often played out the following scene in which she was the mother and the therapist was the daughter: It was the daughter's birthday but she did not remember this, and the mother, in secret, concocted an elaborate birthday cake and then presented it with much pleasure to the child, who was surprised and delighted.

In addition to free and spontaneous symbolic play, the therapist might direct the child in dramatic play. For example, the therapist might say "Pretend you are a (animal, princess, sports hero) and tell a story," or might ask the child to show what he or she would do with a magic wand.

SANDPLAY

The therapeutic use of a sand tray and miniatures was first developed by Margaret Lowenfield in the 1920s and was later expanded and popularized by Dora Kalff (1980), a Jungian analyst. In this technique, the child is asked to create a scene in the sand tray, choosing from a wide selection of miniatures. The therapist observes the process, after which child and therapist might discuss the scene and might also take a picture of it. What the child does in the sand tray is considered symbolic of his or her psyche. The therapist interprets the child's selection and placement of miniatures and tracks the changes in this as the child moves through developmental stages.

Sandplay is appealing to children, and the tactile experience can be therapeutic in and of itself. It is a helpful technique for children in residential treatment, as it provides a way to express emotional issues and communicate nonverbally and can help to overcome reluctance and resistance. It also provides distance for the child and a safe place in which to symbolize, project, and displace strong and perhaps negative emotions. The sand tray, miniatures, and sand provide natural limits and boundaries for the children, which enhance the feeling of safety within which they can experience control and gain mastery (Homeyer & Sweeney, 1998).

PROJECTIVE DRAWING TECHNIQUES

A technique contributed to the play therapy literature by Ellie Breslin is a projective drawing based on a story about a boat in the ocean facing a storm. The story allows children to depict, through their identification with the boat, their feelings regarding their existential position in the world. The drawing often is helpful in revealing the degree of threat and vulnerability the children are feeling with respect to the personal storms in their life. The degree to which the boat is strong or weak is indicative of children's perception of their own resources to cope with adversity.

Another extremely useful projective drawing is described by Oaklander (1988) in her excellent book *Windows to Our Children*. The drawing is in response to a story about a child going into a cave in which there are doors on each side, and each door has a name on it, including a door that has the child's name on it. The child is asked to picture what is on the other side of the door with his or her name on it. The drawing, which is referred to as the Your Place drawing, allows the child to project wishes, fantasies, and longings in depicting what would be in his or her place on the other side of the door. This story and projective drawing often reveal what is missing or longed for by the child. In some cases, it may depict the actual circumstances of the child's life, such as a barren or isolated place with little human contact; in other cases, it may express a compensating fantasy in which a child, for example, depicts a room full of toys when his or her life is filled only with deprivation. These projective drawing techniques enable children to depict feelings that they would have extreme difficulty verbalizing directly. In many cases, these feelings are outside of awareness.

Teaching Binding and Compartmentalizing Defenses

Children in residential treatment need help with developing the defense of binding/compartmentalizing. This defense is helpful in coping with overwhelming trauma. One strategy to facilitate this defense enables the child to put boundaries around material too painful to deal with at any given time. The garbage bag exercise described by James (1989) is an intervention where children place in a garbage bag descriptions of events in their life that are very hard to discuss. The therapist is left "holding the bag" from session to session and the children are invited to pick out a piece of paper or index card each session depicting a topic or event that they are able and willing to talk about at that time. This helps children avoid being flooded or overwhelmed with affect and at the same time provides an invitation to explore the painful issues when they are able to do so. It also reinforces a sense of control in the child. James (1994) has referred to this approach as invitational therapy, in that the child is encouraged to talk about painful areas but only after the child has given explicit permission as the material is approached.

Variations of this technique have been developed in our residential treatment center. In one, children have been encouraged to make boxes that they then decorate and put a lid on and place within the topics or events they need to discuss but are afraid to do so at the time. The box is typically kept in the possession of the therapist and brought to the session each time; the children are encouraged to lift the lid and take out one of the topics that they are prepared to address. Another variation is to make a large envelope that children are invited to decorate that contains index cards on which are written the painful topics; once again, the envelope is opened at each session and the children are encouraged to choose one of the topics to talk about if they are able to do so.

Drawing Strategies to Enable Children to Face Fears Associated with Posttraumatic Stress Disorder

A drawing technique called Party Hats on Monsters (Crenshaw, in press) has been developed to help children desensitize to their fears. This technique involves gradual and titrated exposure to the fearful objects, including frightening dreams and intrusive imagery, associated with Posttraumatic Stress Disorder. It has been very useful with a wide range of children because it involves an active mastery approach in the context of doing an activity (drawing) that most children enjoy. The technique involves having children gradually approach, through successive drawings, the scary part of their dream or daytime imagery, allowing for gradual exposure and desensitization. As an added step, they alter or modify the drawing by bringing in helpers, including superheroes, that enable them to feel safe. This latter step involves an active mastery approach and highlights symbolically both the inner and external resources of the child.

STORIES AND METAPHORS

Mills and Crowley (1986) offer guidelines for constructing therapeutic stories and metaphors that can be enormously useful with children in residential treatment because they allow for addressing an affectively loaded issue in a safe and often enjoyable context for the child. The senior author has used Mills and Crowley's story of the "Three-Legged Dog" on many occasions with children and families who have suffered loss. It is a story that inspires a great deal of hope and encouragement to those who have experienced a death or major loss in their family. A story entitled "Johnny Rabbit's Father Dies" (Crenshaw, 1995) articulates and normalizes the range of feelings that children experience when faced with the death of a family member. A story developed specifically for children in residential treatment to help them cope with the feelings related to termination in therapy is called "Jose and Pete on the Mountain" (Crenshaw, Holden, Kittridge, & McGuirk, 1991). This story is intended not only to help children express and identify with the range of feelings experienced at the end of an intensive period of therapy, but also to highlight what they have gained and can take with them as they move on to the next step. A novel feature of this story allows for the children to participate and to add their own version to some of the adventures of Jose and Pete. Climbing a mountain together is a useful metaphor for capturing the process of doing therapy with children in residential treatment.

SUMMARY

This chapter has described some of the unique and special characteristics of children in residential treatment and some of the attendant challenges of doing play therapy with this population. Clearly, play therapy with such severely challenged children should never be done in isolation. Close collaboration with teachers, child care workers, and the entire multidisciplinary staff of social workers, nurses, psychiatrists, psychologists, speech and language therapists, art therapists, and recreational therapists is absolutely essential for success. Often, play therapy is done in combination with other modalities of therapy, especially family therapy, group therapy, and sometimes art, music, and drama therapy. We have identified the adaptations of traditional techniques of play therapy necessary to be effective with this clinical population. A treatment protocol for play therapy in a residential treatment center has also been described, along with the typical transference and countertransference issues that arise. Clinical issues that are stressful for all play therapists, even experienced ones working with children in residential treatment, are described along with practical techniques that have been useful with this population. The challenges of this population are many, but the rewards of seeing children learn to trust again and to make attachments make this work extremely meaningful and presents lessons for the therapist in therapeutic courage and perseverance.

REFERENCES

Boston, M. (1983). Technical problems in therapy. In M. Boston & R. Szur (Eds.), *Psychotherapy with severely deprived children* (pp. 1–10). London: Routledge.

Crenshaw, D. (1990). An ego supportive approach to children in residential treatment. *Perceptions*, 5–7.

Crenshaw, D. (1995). The crisis of connection: Children of multiple loss and trauma. *Grief Work, 1,* 16–21.

Crenshaw, D. (in press). Party hats on monsters: Drawing strategies to enable children to master their fears. In H. Kaduson & C. Schaefer (Eds.), *101 favorite play therapy techniques.* New York: Aronson.

Crenshaw, D., Holden, A., Kittridge, J., & McGuirk, J. (1991). Jose and Pete on the mountain. In J. Mordock (Ed.), *Counseling children: Basic principles for helping the troubled and defiant child* (pp. 215–219). New York: Continuum.

Drewes, A. (in press). The gingerbread person/feelings map. In H. Kaduson & C. Schaefer (Eds.), *101 favorite play therapy techniques.* New York: Aronson.

Freud, A. (1937). Identification with the aggressor. In A. Freud (Ed.), *The ego and mechanisms of defense* (pp. 117–131). London: Hogarth Press.

Gardner, R. (1968). The mutual storytelling technique: Use in alleviating childhood Oedipal problems. *Contemporary Psychoanalysis, 4,* 161–177.

Gil, E. (1991). *The healing power of play.* New York: Guilford Press.

Gil, E. (1994). *Play in family therapy.* New York: Guilford Press.

Hardy, K. (1998). *Overcoming "Learned Voicelessness."* Workshop presentation at the Family Therapy Networker Conference, Washington, DC.

Harter, S. (1983). Cognitive-developmental considerations in the conduct of play therapy. In C. Schaefer & K. O'Connor (Eds.), *Handbook of play therapy* (pp. 95–127). New York: Wiley.

Homeyer, L., & Sweeney, D.S. (1998). *Sandtray: A practical manual.* Canyon Lake, TX: Lindan Press.

James, B. (1989). *Treating traumatized children: New insights and creative interventions.* Boston: Lexington Books.

James, B. (1994). *Handbook for treatment of attachment-trauma problems in children.* Boston: Lexington Books.

Johnson, T. (1988). Child perpetrators: Children who molest other children. *Child Abuse and Neglect, 12,* 219–229.

Kalff, D. (1980). *Sandplay: Mirror of a child's psyche.* San Francisco: C.G. Jung Institute.

Krystal, H. (1998). *Integration and self-healing: Affect, trauma, alexiathymia.* Hillsdale, NJ: Analytic Press.

Mann, E., & McDermott, J. (1983). Play therapy for victims of child abuse and neglect. In C. Schaefer & K. O'Connor (Eds.), *Handbook of play therapy* (pp. 283–307). New York: Wiley.

McDowell, B. (1994, September). The pick-up sticks game: Adapted to facilitate affective expression. *APT Newsletter, 13,* 1–2.

Mills, J., & Crowley, R. (1986). *Therapeutic metaphors for children and the child within.* New York: Brunner/Mazel.

Mordock, J. (1991). *Counseling children: Basic principles for helping the troubled and defiant child.* New York: Continuum.

Oaklander, V. (1988). *Windows to our children.* Highland, NY: Gestalt Journal Press.

O'Connor, K. (1983). The color-your-life technique. In C. Schaefer & K. O'Connor (Eds.), *Handbook of play therapy* (pp. 251–258). New York: Wiley.

O'Connor, K. (1991). *The play therapy primer.* New York: Wiley.

O'Connor, K. (1995). *Ecosystemic play therapy for victims of child abuse,* Workshop presented at summer Play Therapy Institute. Teaneck, NJ: Fairleigh Dickinson University.

Terr, L. (1981) Forbidden games: Post-traumatic child's play. *Journal of the American Academy of Child Psychiatry, 20,* 741–760.

Terr, L. (1983). Play therapy and psychic trauma: A preliminary report. In C. Schaefer & K. O'Connor (Eds.), *Handbook of play therapy* (pp. 308–319). New York: Wiley.

CHAPTER 9

Theraplay® for Classrooms

DORIS M. MARTIN

THE PURPOSE of this paper is to introduce Theraplay® for use in classrooms by teachers or counselors. Theraplay® is an effective play therapy system developed by Ann Jernberg of the Chicago Theraplay® Institute and later adapted for group use. Theraplay® promotes healthy self-esteem and meaningful relationships in the classroom through playful, planned activities that require the adult to depart from the traditional adult roles. Theraplay® addresses children's needs for challenge, stimulation, structure, and nurturance and acknowledges the necessity of meeting those needs at the developmental, not chronological, age. Theraplay® provides classroom teachers a way of rethinking negative interaction patterns and provides children with positive models and new ways of being with others.

> Eric turns and kicks Juan, who had accidentally tripped Eric as he came running into the room.
>
> Latisha and Margaret complain to their teacher, "We don't want Shana to work with us. She's so mean!"
>
> Crouched under a table, Joel shakes his fist in warning and yells at curious peers who venture too close, "Leave me alone!"
>
> The music teacher announces, "These three boys disrupted the whole class!"
>
> Curled up on a beanbag chair during silent reading, Norma twists a strand of hair, sucks her thumb, and stares into space.

Scenes similar to these occur in nearly all preschool and primary grade classrooms. Increasingly, teachers are faced with children whose behaviors disrupt their own and their peers' ability to learn and reduces their own ability to function as successful members of a group (Garbarino, 1995). Throughout the school-age years, the classroom teacher and increasingly the child's peers play an important role in supporting the child's emerging sense of self (Greenberg, 1989).

Earliest social interaction patterns are learned from infancy as parents and other caregivers attend to their children. Personal realities of divorce, unemployment, homelessness, or physical difficulties such as fatigue, disabilities, or stress may make appropriate caregiving very difficult for some families. Parents whose own basic needs are unmet or who are experiencing traumas in their lives frequently have difficulty rallying the resources needed by their young children. Children who routinely fail to receive the support they need frequently grow to see themselves as unworthy and ineffective (Ainsworth, 1989). These beliefs underlie many of the destructive social patterns that children carry out in interactions with teachers and peers.

THEORETICAL BASIS
FOR THERAPLAY®

By acknowledging the necessity of meeting children's primary emotional needs, Theraplay® provides classroom teachers with a way of interrupting negative interaction patterns and provides children with the experience of positive models. Children who focus much of their attention on unsuccessful social negotiations have little energy left for academic challenges (Best, 1980). Compounding young children's difficulties in dealing with peers is their egocentrism or their limited developmental ability to assume the role or perspective of others. Children whose early experiences include models of prosocial behavior and whose basic wants and needs have been met are able to function successfully in social interactions. For those children whose families have been unable to support their social-emotional development, the school experience becomes a critical second chance.

According to an NEA report (Merina, 1991, p. 4), only one fourth of the states require elementary school counselors, and of those, a counselor may serve as many as 1,700 students. Says Nancy, a kindergarten teacher, "We are very fortunate to have a full-time counselor for 350 students. The counselor sees six of my children for 30 minutes a week." Meanwhile, these children contributed to the near chaos in Nancy's classroom as they demanded immediate and unconditional attention from their teacher. Though counseling was helpful, for these children it simply was not enough. These children had learned all too well the kind of behaviors that demand attention. Still others had learned that passivity and refusing to participate seemed to be the safest path. Faced with what seemed like insurmountable needs of children and despite 30 years of successful teaching experience, Nancy questioned, "Could I be empowered to deal with these children within my own classroom?"

Phyllis Rubin, a special education teacher, asked this same question while studying at the Theraplay® Institute in Chicago in 1978. By experimenting with Theraplay® techniques in their own classrooms, Rubin and her colleague Jeanine Tregay collaborated in developing a group Theraplay® model for teachers to use in their own classrooms (Rubin & Tregay, 1989). Theraplay®, developed by Ann Jernberg (1979), is based on the theory and practice of Austin des Lauriers's play techniques of intrusiveness, body and eye contact, and a focus on an intimacy between the child and therapist. Theraplay® was further influenced by the work of Viola Brody (1993), whose therapeutic work with children emphasized active physical contact, physical control, singing, and meeting the child at his or her developmental, not chronological, level.

The interaction strategies of Theraplay® are modeled on a healthy caregiver-infant relationship. Jernberg maintains that the basic needs of nurturing, structure, intrusion, and challenge must be met before a child can progress further in development (Rubin & Tregay, 1989). Jernberg classified caregiver behaviors essential for healthy infant development into four categories:

1. Structuring: limits, defines, forbids, outlines, reassures, speaks firmly, labels, names, clarifies, confines, holds, and restrains.
2. Challenging: teases, dares, encourages, varies, chases, plays peek-a-boo, offers a cheek for grabbing, makes noises for imitating, and wiggles a finger for catching.
3. Intruding: tickles, bounces, swings, surprises, giggles, hops at and pounces at baby.
4. Nurturing: rocks, nurses, holds, nuzzles, feeds, cuddles, envelops, caresses, lies next to, and hugs the baby. (Jernberg, 1979, p. 62)

Ideally, all children would experience the above interactions in relationship with their parent(s) or other primary caregivers. Most children, however, grow up in circumstances that are less than ideal. The absence of nurturing, intrusion, challenge, and structure in parent-child interactions leads to behavior that is maladaptive (Jernberg, 1993). Without these experiences, children are likely to have difficulty forming secure attachments to others and frequently display aggressive, whiny, overly demanding, or withdrawn behavior (Sroufe & Fleeson, 1986).

Classroom teachers seldom have the luxury of focusing their attention solely on the withdrawn or the disruptive child and are often trapped into reacting to negative behaviors rather than proactively leading the child into positive experiences. The planned activities of the brief classroom play sessions (Theraplay®) reduce the negative effects of earlier unmet needs by offering direct and concrete opportunities for nurturance, intrusion, challenge, and structure in real time.

THE PLAY SESSION

Sessions are planned so that all children are included, reinforcing the sense that everyone in the class is a valued and important member of the group. Noncompliant, boisterous, or aggressive children are often viewed by themselves and their peers as "different" or "bad" because of the negative reactions they elicit from teachers and children. In the play session, however, the adult explicitly and sincerely welcomes each child just as he or she is.

Sessions are balanced between the novel and the routine, making them inviting for children and usable for experienced teachers with a minimum amount of preparation. Four simple rules are followed to create a positive atmosphere and safe environment for the group (Rubin & Tregay, 1989):

1. "No hurts": This rule serves to remind children that no one is to inflict injury on another, whether physical or emotional, intentional or unintentional. If an accident or injury should occur, it is immediately attended to by the adult and the participating child(ren). This rule provides for a safe zone where everyone works together to prevent injuries of any kind.
2. "Stick together": Stick together is a way of illustrating the interdependence of group members. We need each other and we help each other out.
3. "Have fun": This rule sanctions the importance of adults and children having fun together. Play, including physical contact, is a necessary activity for all children. In Theraplay®, the adult is encouraged to play with the children, not simply to watch over or guide them.
4. "The adult is in charge": Children feel safe when someone older and wiser is in charge or is responsible. This is most significant in combating the inverse relationships many children experience when the adult family members relinquish authority inappropriately or fail to provide for the child's basic needs, forcing premature independence.

The first three rules are shared with the children and are reviewed at the beginning of the session and as necessary throughout. The last rule is for the teacher and is made explicit to the children only through the teacher's actions.

The group session consists of three parts: the opening, planned activities, and the closing. The beginning and closing rituals of the session provide children with the consistency of an undeviating beginning and clear ending—a predictability that is reassuring to children (Rubin & Tregay, 1989). Teachers also welcome the ritual because it provides a ready structure that simplifies planning. The simple and playful structure of the session provides needed relief for teachers and children from the typical school routine.

Ideally, Theraplay® sessions are conducted two to three times a week for about 20 to 30 minutes, depending on the group's ability to sustain its collective focus. A helpful rule of thumb is to keep initial sessions brief and build the length gradually as children become accustomed to the format. Establishing a regular time and providing Theraplay® on a regular basis throughout the school year optimizes its benefits by heightening children's anticipation of and expectations for the sessions. However, outside demands on classroom time and schedules are often unavoidable. Conducting Theraplay® sessions irregularly and infrequently is preferable to none at all and can have significant benefits for individuals as well as the group.

OPENING RITUAL

The opening ritual includes the singing of a song and "checkups." The song, used consistently at each session, serves to mark the beginning of this time together when all of the children and teacher(s) come together in a circle on the floor. The session may take its name from words in the song (e.g., the Sunshine Group from "You are my sunshine"). The song selected should represent the idea of group togetherness or appreciation for others. Following the song, the rules are explained or reviewed as necessary. One teacher of young children adds a playful and literal context for demonstrating the "sticking together" rule by pretending to put glue between the children's knees. Children quickly grasp the meaning of "no hurts" to include hurt feelings; likewise, the rule "have fun" needs little explanation.

The opening proceeds with "checkups." This part of the opening ritual is perhaps the most crucial of all. Seldom are we invited to share with others any pain that we feel; society has trained even the youngest among us to quip "Fine" when another inquires "How are you?" For that reason, each child is asked the question "Do you have any hurts?" Children who respond yes are asked to identify their hurts. Often, children will indicate a scrape or bruise on their skin, which the teacher then soothes by gently rubbing a small amount of baby lotion around the area of the hurt. Some children will describe hurt feelings, and still others will say that they have no hurts. The group applauds each child for not having hurts or for having had the hurts soothed. This is the time when each child has the supportive attention of the whole group. The group leader includes the other children by inviting their attention to the one whose turn it is. Eventually, children can take on this role by asking the child next to them if he or she has any hurts and so on around the circle. The nurturing that takes place in checkups builds trust and cohesiveness for the rest of the session.

PLANNED GAMES/STRUCTURED ACTIVITIES

This part of the session consists of planned activities that, as Jernberg states, "enhance self-esteem and increase trust in others through concrete, personal, positive experiences" (1979, p. 126). This portion of the session contains elements of surprise and is purposely structured with constantly changing and varied activities to pique the children's interest (Martin & Lahman, 1999). Because the activities are intended to be playful and active, the children may tend to get boisterous. Creating new variations and providing new games rather than repeating the same thing helps the teacher to stay in control, thus following the rule "The adult is in charge."

Activities are selected to meet the underlying needs of the children. Although a specific activity may be chosen with a particular child in mind, the activity will be fun and beneficial for all of the children. In most cases, each child should be directly involved and encouraged to actively participate; however, depending on the activity, the amount of time required, and the level of adult supervision and participation demanded, adjustments may need to be made. For example, the group may be involved in coaching and guiding a blindfolded child through a maze of obstacles. Different roles might be assigned according to what each child needs to experience, so that all are participants, but not necessarily all children, will repeat the same roles. Anticipating children's desire to be included and their demand for equity, leaders may announce at the start that additional opportunities will be available in another session. Activities requiring this much time and attention and the need for postponement are best avoided.

Most activities meet more than one need and thus can be tailored to individual needs during the session. It is important to remember that the focus is on meeting children's real needs, which may represent unmet needs from a much earlier time. Thus, children of a wide range of ages can benefit from activities that on the surface may seem more suitable for younger children. To keep sessions manageable for young children, most will involve only one activity per session; however, depending on the simplicity of the activity and time needed, two or three different activities may be presented in one session.

Examples of activities that can be used to meet children's specific needs are described below.

Nurturing

Theraplay® session begins with the nurturing in the opening song and continues through checkups. Nurturing benefits all children, but it is critical for children who appear to be "angry at the world," such as the child who is aggressive or noncompliant. Aggressive and bullying children generally believe that no one likes them, and thus their negative interactions become a self-fulfilling prophecy. These children are especially in need of nurturing. Nurturing may take the form of simply noting, "How beautiful your two big brown eyes are!" A simple nurturing activity involves gently rocking a child suspended in a blanket by the rest of the group. The children might even sing a simple lullaby or love song to the child being rocked. In this lullaby, however, neither the cradle nor the "baby" will fall down; as always, the group is reminded to look out for each others' safety. The nurturing that takes place facilitates the group feeling of being at home, that is, in the best sense, a place where one is appreciated unconditionally (Sinclaire, 1994).

Structuring

Structured activities are especially significant for children who operate with little or no internal sense of structure. Such children may run wildly in the room or regularly test their teacher's limits. Structured activities are very specific, with explicit rules and the expectation that the directions will be followed. To avoid getting into verbal explanations or using the confrontational no, teachers anticipate attempts of manipulation and ward them off with paradoxical statements or challenges and confidently proceed with the activity as planned. For example, a child who is making a face might be challenged to make an even more scary face; in so doing the teacher incorporates the behavior rather than banishes it.

An example of a structured activity is one using colors that the children are wearing. The leader announces the color and either one by one around the circle or all at one time children are told "Touch the color blue." Additional challenges can be imposed by naming a particular body part required to make the contact, for example, "Touch red with your head." Because of the physical nature of the activity, this is a good time to remind children to be gentle and to ask each other, "Are you okay?" Third-graders noted another kind of hurt when several children refused to touch a peer even though she was the one closest to them wearing the stated color. This prompted a later discussion about exclusion and what it means to be rejected, a hurt with which most children can identify. This incident also suggested to the adult that the rejected child could benefit from additional opportunities for being nurtured.

Intrusion

Children who are rigid or withdrawn may benefit from intrusion activities such as face painting. To keep the focus on the children, supplies are kept to a minimum. In this case, a cotton ball becomes the "paintbrush" and the imaginary paint is any color that the leader or children can imagine. Applying the "paint," the leader may model for the others, "I'm going to take some of this sparkling aqua and very softly make a flower on each of your cheeks. Does that tickle? Oh, and I think that this lovely lemon yellow will be just right for your perfectly round chin." Each child then gets to paint another child or the children can be paired and paint each other. At the end, a mirror is passed around so that the children can see their own beautiful smiles and their beautifully "painted" faces.

Challenge

Children who are timid and fail to initiate interactions with others may be supported in a blindfold lead, a trust-building activity. A handkerchief or scarf is placed over the child's eyes. The group then leads the child around the room. Children are encouraged to give directions, to ask how the child feels, and to reassure him or her that they will prevent any hurts. Another challenge activity is the partner stand. A pair of children sit back to back with their arms interlocked. The challenge is to cooperatively stand up without unlocking the arms. Depending on the group, all children might be doing this simultaneously. Doing one pair at a time allows the group leader to focus attention on each pair, but it has the disadvantage of taking longer. Once a pair has completed the activity, they can assist and coach their peers to success.

A simple group activity that nurtures, challenges, and intrudes is the tower of hands. In small groups, a tower is made by taking turns adding a hand to the stack. When the last child's hand is added to the top, the bottom hand is pulled out and placed on top. The lotioning of everyone's hands before the game adds to its appeal and is, for most children, a soothing and pleasant experience. The lotion can be applied individually or can be done in pairs, each child taking a turn at lotioning another. Care must be taken to avoid lotions that may cause allergic reactions, such as highly perfumed or colored lotions.

CLOSING RITUALS

After the structured activities, it is time to bring the session to a close. A calming, quieting activity is planned, such as sticking knees together again or passing gentle cotton-ball tickles around the circle. The closing rituals restore the group calm and provide a transition to the rest of the daily routine. The final activity of the closing ritual is the food share. A small cracker or other bite-size snack is placed into each child's mouth, symbolizing the care and intimacy of being nurtured with food. For children who resist this intimacy, the teacher may take the child's hand in his or her own to place the cracker in the child's mouth. In later sessions, the teacher may place a cracker in each child's hand, and one by one, going around the circle, each child will feed his or her neighbor. To address the issue of hygiene, a moisturized wipe may be included as part of this ritual to allow children to clean their hands prior to the food sharing. The food exchange is not intended to replace snacks.

The final activity is the singing of the closing song, which may be the same or different from the opening song. Songs that involve words of appreciation for each other are especially appropriate. Children often respond to the closing song by spontaneously putting their arms around each other or holding hands as they sway to the music. The session is now officially over, but, as Nancy noted, "The effects of the session flow over into the entire day." During a class discussion about the responsibilities of a family, a kindergarten child noted, "Just like we're a family!" confirming that the children were becoming aware of the cohesiveness that was supported by the Theraplay® sessions in their classroom.

SPECIAL CONSIDERATIONS

The decision to begin Theraplay® sessions in the classroom must be carefully and thoughtfully considered. The teacher should determine how confident and comfortable he or she is entering into play activities that deviate from the traditional role of teacher. During the Theraplay® session, the teacher, although still very much in charge, is also a participant in the play activities.

The sessions are intended to provide teacher and children with ample opportunities to maximize physical contact; however, children who have been known to have been or are suspected of having been sexually or physically abused need to be treated with sensitivity and in consultation with the school counselor. The physicality of the games is a way to help children experience positive touch. Children who have experienced positive touch are better able to recognize touching that is inappropriate. Games involving lots of physical contact may be questioned by parents and other professionals as inappropriate for the classroom. To reduce confusion and potential conflict, parents should be informed of the benefits of Theraplay® and invited to participate. The support and assistance of the school counselors can be invaluable during the session as well as by providing follow-up with individual students. Whenever possible, two adults should participate in the Theraplay® session (Martin, 2000). Jernberg claims that one person would find it very difficult "to observe, manage, interact, initiate, and still remain cheerful throughout the entire session" (1979, p. 130). The skills of the teacher, the needs of the children, and the availability of support will determine whether and how often a teacher will attempt Theraplay® in his or her classroom.

How often the session should be scheduled and which activities are included in each session are a matter of the teacher's professional judgment. Generally, Theraplay® is more effective if sessions are scheduled several times a week. However, there is no magic formula nor is there a prescription for matching particular activities with children's particular behaviors. Tobin reminds teachers, "Your ability to accurately perceive a child's inner needs is the source for the most effective interventions available to you" (1991, p. 42). Teachers must rely on their own and their colleagues' expertise to discern the underlying needs expressed through children's maladaptive behavior and through careful observation determine which activities can best help meet those needs (Martin & Lahman, 1999). Apart from the specific need a particular activity may fill, general criteria include playfulness, active involvement, noncompetitive interactions, simplicity, and novelty (Rubin & Tregay, 1989). Games or activities are chosen because they tap into affective and social aspects of behavior, not isolated academic skills (Fluegelman, 1981; Kami, 1980; Rubin & Tregay, 1989).

CONCLUSION

Good teachers have always known that they need to provide children with more than academic instruction (Sinclaire, 1994). However, despite the recognized importance of children's emotional and social development, teachers are seldom expected to plan for and include activities in the curriculum that intervene in affective growth. One teacher just beginning to use Theraplay® strategies concluded, "I have finally realized that no matter how hard I try to reach these children academically, little of what I intend can be learned until the needs for nurture, structure, intrusion, and challenge have been satisfied." The strategies of group Theraplay® sessions require a departure from the traditional role of the teacher and from the usual activities of the classroom, a departure that is necessary so that teachers can teach and all children can learn.

Although many children do come to school with social and emotional development that is more than adequate to function effectively with their teachers and peers, many do not. The children whose relationship skills and accompanying sense of self have not developed to where they are "at home" in the classroom stand to gain immensely from participating in Theraplay® sessions, but they are not the only ones. All children benefit from having an attentive and available adult with them during the many hours spent in school. Our society is in great need of individuals who can help mediate and resolve conflicts and who care for and nurture others. The process of offering nurturing in a group context such as a classroom where children and adults spend significant time together can mean the difference between having children who develop a group identity and a sense of belonging and having children who grow up seeing themselves as isolated and disconnected. Theraplay® is a way of acknowledging the importance of affect in the lives of children, something that good teachers know intuitively. "Teaching with love" is the unconditional regard deserved by every child as we conduct a Theraplay® session. Lisa Goldstein writes, "It [teaching with love] has the potential to transform the field of early childhood education, giving authority to the emotional, interpersonal work that is at the heart of teaching young children" (1997, p. 168). The demands of the school curriculum are significant, but perhaps none so critical as helping children to become healthy, caring, and cared for members of a community.

REFERENCES

Ainsworth, M.D.S. (1989). Attachments beyond infancy. *American Psychologist, 44,* 709–716.

Best, R. (1980). *We've all got scars: What boys and girls learn in elementary school.* Bloomington: Indiana University Press.

Brody, V. (1993). *The dialogue of touch: Developmental play therapy.* Treasure Island, FL: Developmental Play Training Associates.

Fluegelman, A. (1981). *More new games.* Garden City, NJ: Doubleday.

Garbarino, J. (1995). *Raising children in a socially toxic environment.* San Francisco: Jossey-Bass.

Goldstein, L.S. (1997). *Teaching with love: A feminist approach to early childhood education.* New York: Peter Lang.

Greenberg, P. (1989). Learning self-esteem and discipline through play. *Young Children, 44*(4), 28–31.

Jernberg, A.M. (1979). *Theraplay: A new treatment for using structured play for problem children and their families.* Washington, DC: Jossey-Bass.

Jernberg, A.M. (1993). Attachment formation. In C.E. Schaefer (Ed.), *The therapeutic powers of play* (pp. 241–266). Northvale, NJ: Aronson.

Kami, C. (1980). *Group games in early education.* Washington, DC: National Association for the Education of Young Children.

Martin, D.M. (2000). Teacher-led Theraplay in early childhood classrooms. In E. Munns (Ed.), *Theraplay: Innovations in attachment enhancing theraplay.* Northvale, NJ: Aronson.

Martin, D.M., & Lachman, M. (1999). *Games that heal: Activities for use in Theraplay.* Unpublished manuscript, James Madison University, Harrisonburg, VA.

Merina, A. (1991). The counselor's in. *NEA Today, 10*(5), 4.

Rubin, P., & Tregay, J. (1989). *Play with them: Theraplay in groups.* Springfield, IL: Thomas.

Sinclaire, C. (1994). *Looking for home: A phenomenological study of home in the classroom.* Columbia, NY: Teachers College Press.

Sroufe, A., & Fleeson, J. (1986). Attachment and construction of relationships. In W.W. Hartup & Z. Rubin (Eds.), *Relationships and development* (pp. 51–71). Hillsdale, NJ: Erlbaum.

Tobin, L. (1991). *What do you do with a child like this? Inside the lives of troubled children.* Duluth, MN: Whole Person Associates.

PART FOUR

GROUP PLAY THERAPY AND SPECIAL POPULATIONS

CHAPTER 10

Crisis Intervention Activity Groups in the Schools

MAXINE LYNN and DANIELLE NISIVOCCIA

THIS CHAPTER addresses the use of goal-focused activity groups with children who are experiencing crisis. The school is an ideal arena for crisis intervention because it is a natural cross-section where the child and family must interface with formal institutions (Congress & Lynn, 1994; Meyer, 1976). Schools should provide crisis intervention services to students because children need to be freed from the debilitating effects of major crises in order to learn. Children need to find a safe place and protection from their own anxiety and the anxiety of adults in their lives. An activity group offers comfort, support, and the opportunity to work out their feelings.

The authors present a conceptual framework for crisis intervention activity groups. We provide the basics of getting a group started and illustrate activities and the dynamics occurring in groups through examples from practice. Included are the role of the leader as well as the limitations associated in doing this work.

Children face the developmental crisis of separation from the parent as they begin school. Solving this normatively supplies tools for future problem solving and establishes a connection and trust in school personnel. Children look toward school to help them cope with and learn from the various crises that life brings, such as the loss of a parent or sibling,

environmental disasters like hurricanes, floods, or fires, familial violence, and acts of violence in the community and/or the school itself.
Children do not innately have the coping skills to handle major crises. Instead, Mary daydreams in class, Christopher hides in the closet or
punches Tyrone, Annie starts a tantrum over a missing pencil. These children have put learning on a back burner.

One may wonder whether the school should deal with crisis intervention utilizing a group modality. Children in school are in a group environment. For the school-age child, the peer group is a place for trying out
new skills. Schools host large numbers of children and are a place where
children create informal groups. The group is the natural milieu of the
child. In this setting groups are an effective way to reach more children
in a shorter time frame. Beyond teaching academics, schools are venues
for teaching social skills as well as interpersonal communication and the
values of democratic citizenship. Schools today have become even more
important in the development of the emotional health of children because
of changing family structure and the numbers of parents working to
make ends meet.

ACTIVITY GROUPS DEFINED

Activity groups have a long history in both social group work and group
therapy tradition (Middleman, 1968; Shulman, 1999; Slavson & Schiffer,
1975). Slavson and Schiffer noted that children who have experienced
emotional difficulties benefited and also changed when exposed to a
nondirective approach in which a room is set up with play objects and the
children enter into a play situation with a therapist who follows the members' lead. In social group work, the activity is a tool used to achieve an
outcome. It also has benefits in itself, with no hidden agenda. Activity is
also the means to help a child effectively cope with a crisis.

The process of relating and communicating through the relationships
among members and between members and the leader is also through
activity. The activity can be used to help the group achieve its goals.

The activity group modality uses play/art materials and games to reach
and connect with the child. In addition, group activities promote healing
through such therapeutic factors as being "all in the same boat," univer-
salization, cohesiveness, mutual aid, and problem solving (Shulman, 1999;
Yalom, 1985).

To fulfill the purposes of a crisis intervention group, a short-term,
goal-focused, structured model related to a specific crisis should be developed. In this way, the group dynamics and some of the issues are limited. The crisis theme becomes the bond that holds the group together. A

directive leadership style works best, using preplanned activities that take into account the stages of group development, the particular crisis, the gender and age range of the children, and their individual needs Nisivoccia & Lynn, 1999).

REVIEW OF CRISIS INTERVENTION LITERATURE

CHILDREN AND CRISIS

Perhaps more than any other time in history children are now experiencing crisis situations that are private events—such as the death of a loved one, moving into a shelter, or witnessing domestic violence—or public events that impact a group, such as violence in the schoolyard, a natural disaster such as a flood or hurricane, or the death of a classmate or teacher (Roberts, 2000). With greater publicizing of events and access to mass media, the rise of violent acts in the United States, and the many personal tragedies that modern families are encountering, few children escape the emotion and pain of stressful life events. Thus, there needs to be a greater focus on working with children who have experienced a major crisis.

Stress itself is not detrimental; in fact, it creates opportunities for learning and growth. However, stressful events can precipitate a crisis reaction whereby children experience temporary feelings of severe acute distress, helplessness, confusion, shock, denial, disbelief, or depression. These feelings may be expressed as disorganized or agitated behavior. Roberts (2000) defines a crisis as "a period of psychological disequilibrium, experienced as a result of a hazardous event or situation that constitutes a significant problem that cannot be remedied by using familiar coping strategies" (p. 7). Because children have fewer coping strategies than adults, they may be unable to reduce the discomfort.

In making an assessment of a child who has experienced a crisis, the following factors are pertinent (Webb, 1999): (1) the proximity to the crisis; (2) the presence of loss factors; (3) the physical injury/pain; and (4) the presence of life threat. School-age children are particularly vulnerable in their ability to cope with the anxiety due to their age, developmental phase, cognitive and verbal skill level, immature defenses, and lack of life experience (Wainrib & Bloch, 1998). Often, the anxiety accompanying the crisis exceeds the child's ability to adapt. Webb notes how anxiety precipitated by a crisis situation can paralyze or seriously interfere with a child's usual functioning. Children often require interventions to relieve their anxiety and learn new methods of coping to deal with stressful life situations (Nisivoccia & Lynn, 1999; Webb, 1999).

THE BASICS OF CRISIS INTERVENTION

Crisis intervention theories assume that the child's symptoms are a sign of experiencing disequilibrium that will be time-limited. Therefore, intervention is focused and short term, usually 1 to 12 sessions. The literature notes the differences between interventions directed to the initial phase of restoring equilibrium, which reduce the subjective discomfort, and crisis resolution, which results in cognitive understanding and mastery, new coping and adaptive skills, and resources to utilize in the future (Roberts, 2000). Parad and Parad (1990) define crisis intervention as aimed at

> actively influencing the psychosocial functioning during a period of disequilibrium in order to alleviate the immediate impact of the disruptive stressful events and to help mobilize the manifest and latent psychological capabilities and social resources of persons directly affected by the crisis for coping adaptively with the effects of stress. (p. 4)

With children, some of these coping capabilities are not yet in place and need to be learned.

The primary aims of the interventions are to cushion the stressful event by immediate emotional and environmental first aid and to strengthen the child in his or her coping and integrative struggles through immediate therapeutic clarification and guidance during the coping period (Wainrib & Bloch, 1998). Interventions are directed at four tasks: (1) physical survival and safety; (2) expression of feelings; (3) cognitive mastery; and (4) behavioral/interpersonal adjustment (Nelson & Slaikeu, 1990). To facilitate the child's work toward resolution, interventions should be empowering and action-oriented. The acronym ACT is helpful in remembering the urgency and the components of intervention in the crisis situation: the worker and client attend to action, cognition, and relevant tasks. In essence, they ACT (J. Lee, personal communication, July 23, 2000).

Crisis intervention assumes immediate intervention, a supportive environment, and the worker's self-awareness of how the crisis has affected him or her directly or vicariously (Gilliland & James, 1997; Parad & Parad, 1990; Roberts, 2000; Wainrib & Bloch, 1998). The developmental steps of crisis counseling call for defining the crisis early on, examining its multidimensional impact, and addressing the child's immediate needs for safety and protection. Actions are aimed at helping the child explore his or her perceptions, feelings, and emotions regarding the crisis. One needs to validate the feelings and experience through verbal and nonverbal means. Focused exploration is used to determine the child's perception of the precipitating events and whether the crisis event is defined as the child's own or someone else's problem. Problem solving provides alternatives and options that are considered in dealing with the crisis. Action steps (tasks) are explored and generated. Interventions are directed to build on strengths and enhance coping skills and self-image. Last, resources and referrals are put in place. This completes the utilization of the ACT principle in crisis intervention.

CRISIS INTERVENTIONS IN THE SCHOOLS

The past five years have seen an alarming increase in violence in the schools. To address the explosion of crisis situations, schools have taken both reactive and proactive approaches. In reaction to violence in the schools, crisis protocols have been developed and crisis curriculum with trained special district and school-based crisis teams have formed to handle and debrief students in such situations. Examples include aggressive and hostile students in the classroom and violence and murders (Callahan, 1998). A proactive, preventive response has been to develop didactic materials to teach children about such social ills as tobacco, drugs, alcohol, and AIDS, as well as techniques for handling conflict. These efforts have included nonclassroom material utilized by teachers, nurses, school psychologists, social workers, counselors, and administrators. There is a need for more literature on engaging children in the social environment and the medium in which they are most comfortable: play peer groups.

LIMITATIONS TO CRISIS INTERVENTION ACTIVITY GROUPS

There are limitations in doing crisis intervention activity groups in the schools. Informed permission is required in all work with children and youth. Sometimes during the immediacy of a crisis this becomes overlooked. Therefore, one needs to find a quick, efficient way of getting permission.

The confidentiality issue is a big concern. The group worker needs to clearly define the limits of confidentiality in relation to school personnel and parents, which can differ (Congress & Lynn, 1994). Workers need to share certain information with teachers, administrators, guidance counselors, and parents about possible harm to the child (such as child abuse). The group members need to know this. At the same time, the children need to be able to keep certain things confidential in the group, and school personnel and parents need to understand this so they do not become suspicious.

School personnel and parents are often affected by the crisis situation, and their concerns and anxieties add to the child's feeling unsafe.

The crisis period is often characterized by overall chaos and instability, so there is a need to create a holding environment that is calm and protected. School personnel, parents, and group leaders need to work through their own issues regarding the crisis.

Self-determination is a fundamental principle of social work practice (Freedberg, 1989). During a crisis period, this may be limited with children participating in a group experience in which they prefer not to be involved. One needs to both maximize the right to self-determination and provide a supportive structure for dealing with the crisis.

The crisis may affect many more children than can be accommodated in groups. Priorities need to be set to determine who needs the services most.

These groups can generate a great deal of feelings and intensity, which may spill into the classroom or the home. The groups may raise other issues that may need to be dealt with, such as cultural diversity, familial dilemmas, socialization concerns, and environmental problems. The group may create needs for individual intervention or referral or advocacy. All involved need to be ready and able to deal with these issues.

GROUP DYNAMICS

STAGES OF GROUP DEVELOPMENT

All groups experience the dynamics of the stages of development (Garland, Jones, & Kolodny, 1973; Henry, 1992). In an activity group, the tasks of each stage happen while the activities are occurring; thus, the activity takes on the dual purpose of facilitating the developmental dynamics of the group process and dealing with content. Therefore, it is important to have an understanding of the specific stage the group is in to effectively choose and utilize the activity and understand a member's behavior.

A four-stage model represents the development of the group (Nisivoccia & Lynn, 1999). The beginning phase deals with getting acquainted and establishing what we are here for (purpose); what we are going to do here (contract); what the rules are (contract and norms); defining commonalties (all in the same boat); and issues of confidentiality. In crisis groups, the commonality is that each child has experienced a similar crisis, such as witnessing a murder or suddenly being homeless. It is important to develop preliminary empathy through the worker tuning in to the meaning of the event and to the children's feelings and behavior (Schulman, 1999).

In all group beginnings, approach-avoidance is common behavior. Most children are concerned about being liked and accepted by their peers. It is not uncommon for a child to complain and ask "Why do I have to be here.

I'm missing music," or "Are these cookies for us?" or "Can I hug you?" They may also feel at sea as they struggle with how to cope with the crisis, and anxious as they anticipate having to disclose about the event they wish to deny. An example of this is, "It's OK that my sister's dead, I still have another one." They may also be ambivalent about sharing their feelings and concerns regarding the crisis event and act as though nothing different has happened. These children will need to feel that the group and the leader are providing a safe and nurturing environment.

The beginning is critical, as it sets the context for the group. A primary concern is trust. Through the use of activities, the tasks of beginnings include making a clear contract, developing ground rules, encouraging sharing of experiences and feelings, building cohesion, and creating a safe environment. All need to occur. Activities must also be focused on building relationships and motivation to participate. Such activities as decorating and exchanging name tags or drawing a picture of one's family (if that is not the arena of crisis) can facilitate belonging, sharing, and trust.

The second stage involves more sharing of content related to the crisis and self-disclosure of feelings. Power and control issues and testing the worker and members are heightened as each child attempts to establish his or her place in the group (Fatout, 1996). It should be noted that there is usually less intensity and depth of the stages of group development and member behavior when groups meet for one or two sessions and/or are open to new members. Younger children's interactions may be less intense and more benign than older children's. The combined tasks of moving into content and relationships often result in behaviors such as subgrouping, fighting, fleeing, and scapegoating. Roles, rank, and relationships become primary issues for the group and often result in conflict. Although the members should be supported as they experiment with testing issues, the worker must also set clear, firm limits. Activities should address and deal with conflict, develop empathy, and allow for participation in decision making. Such activities include "rumor clinic," giving the group a name, what a "good hand/bad hand" can do, and role play. The worker needs to reduce obstacles so that the middle or work phase can develop.

The next phase is where the work of the group and its members takes place. There is more give and take, acceptance, and a sense of the power of the group. Intimacy and cohesion increase. Members disclose more about their experiences and feelings regarding the crisis and how it has affected them. As the members feel that they are heard and supported by one another and the worker, risking, sharing intimate feelings, and mutual aid increase. Problem swapping and solving occurs with more acceptance of individual differences; this includes generating and exploring alternatives about the crisis and developing an action plan when appropriate. Members' strengths are utilized as a resource to enhance coping and adaptation and facilitate crisis resolution. Such activities as enactment of a story, using a theme such as "scared" to make a group poster, creating a group song or poem, and playing tic-tac-toe using wishes facilitate the tasks of the work phase.

The ending of the group involves separation and reflection. The group reviews the meaning of endings . For most people, and especially for children who have experienced a loss such as of a loved one or physical location, the end of the group may bring up feelings of abandonment, denial, anger, fear, sadness, or regression. It is a time when the gains are integrated in each member's thinking and behavior and the group experience is evaluated. Such activities as composing a group letter, writing and exchanging cards or photos, and writing one thing each member got and did not get from the group help bring closure. The process of conflict resolution and growth is well on its way. Resources and opportunities for discussing ongoing issues and feelings regarding the crisis are given.

ROLE OF THE LEADER

The leader needs to be clear on the purpose of the group and feel comfortable enough with the crisis issue. This means dealing with or saying the taboo, such as "All of you have just recently lost a loved one," and dealing with highly charged material such as talking about a teacher's being murdered by a student. Throughout the life of the group, the leader should model concern and empathy and act as a conduit for the members in making emotional connections with each other.

The leader must also create a safe environment for children who have experienced crisis. Leaders must be active throughout the life of the group. They must take on multiple roles such as protector, supporter, educator, therapist, director, and mediator. Initially, the leader will have to take on a more protective role; this includes setting limits and providing structure. Members may exhibit dependent and regressive behaviors and the leader should be nurturing and accepting. The leader must allow and channel the members' testing behaviors; these include issues of power and control and patterns of dealing with authority. This requires taking on pivotal and mediating roles to support the group's maturational process, allowing expressions of differences, and mediating members' conflicts. Each member should be encouraged to join in but allowed to proceed at his or her own pace. Serving food during the group may enhance the feeling of being given to.

GETTING THE GROUP STARTED

A school's primary purpose is education; although the emotional health of a child is important, fostering it is not the primary goal. Therefore, it is most important to develop a working relationship with the school personnel. The worker not only needs to be there for the children but needs to be connected with the teachers, administrators, and other staff members who are affected by the crisis. They too are concerned that the child is not performing at an optimum level.

A joint partnership is formed when the worker explores with the involved personnel the activity group's purpose and projected outcome and includes the staff in the planning of scheduling and content. It is important that teachers are informed that after the group, members might behave in unexpected ways. A meeting with school staff should be set up. The personnel need to know about confidentiality contracts and what may or may not be shared. The staff should be invited to give their perspectives and be made to feel that they are included. They are the referral source.

Group formation around a crisis situation needs to be done quickly. A simple permission slip that can be attached to a child's notebook could be sent home. The teacher or guidance counselor should be asked to follow up. One needs to remember that all children need parental permission.

The following nuts and bolts of getting started are ideal, and some school settings may not be able to accommodate them. In situations that are less than ideal, the leader must be prepared for extra issues to be dealt with before and in the group.

Below the age of 14, boys and girls should have separate groups to prevent distracting additional dynamics from operating. There are more developmental differences in children from year to year. Therefore, whenever possible, one should keep a close age range together (within a two-year frame). Unless one is doing a group with siblings, one should generally not include one sibling pair. Groups do best with 8 to 12 members; in groups with fewer members, the dynamics can intensify and become more familial, and one member's absence is felt more. In larger groups, it is hard for individual needs to be met and macrodynamics can occur.

Referrals can come from several sources, such as teachers, guidance counselors, school nurses, administrators, and parents. With older children, one could use a self-referral method where a worker explains the purpose of the group and children place their names in a box.

Depending on the nature of the crisis, one may have to assess the need either to limit membership or to provide other services. In situations where a child has lost all coping ability, one needs to provide immediate individual attention and referral to a mental health clinic. In a crisis that requires a great deal of individual interventions to provide safety, the group may not be the best modality. If there are too many children requiring the service, one must assess who is most in need based on symptoms, outside supports, and the intensity of that crisis on the individual.

ILLUSTRATION OF THE USE OF ACTIVITIES

Getting Acquainted, Purpose, and Contract: A First Group Meeting

Looking somewhat upset, seven girls ages 10 and 11 came into the social worker's office. The room was arranged with chairs around a table. The social worker, Ms. Ramsey, invited them to have a seat. There were markers and crayons on the table along with some five-by-eight cards. Five of the girls were not in the same class and did not know one another; two were in the same class. This was their first group meeting.

Ms. Ramsey began the group by welcoming them. Kenika, an African American girl, stated loudly, "I didn't do nothing." Lisa, an Italian girl, responded, "Me neither." Judy said toughly, "Yeah, Ms. Ramsey, why did we get sent down here?" The social worker responded, "I know that you all must be nervous about coming here. You did not do anything wrong. You've expressed a lot of concerns to your teachers about Cameron (a 10-year-old female student), who was attacked the other day on the way home from school by several boys. Your teachers asked your parents if it would be OK to invite you to a group to talk about your concerns. We will be meeting at this time [a class period] once a week for the next six weeks. Would you like to do this?"

Structure, Norms, and Confidentiality

Paula, originally from Costa Rica, said sternly, "What if we don't want to talk, do we have to stay?" Another girl quietly said, "Yeah." Ms. Ramsey responded, "No," the group is strictly voluntary. Each week we will do an activity together, have a snack, and talk about the activity. If you don't feel like doing the activity you don't have to. What we talk about in the group is private, between us, and will not be shared outside of this room. If I do have to share something that we talked about, I will talk to you about it first."

Several of the group members demanded the snack immediately, others sat quietly, and one complained about missing gym. The social worker allowed the girls to have the snack, asking for volunteers to assist her. She sensed that they were anxious and the snack would help lessen anxiety and encourage nurturing feelings.

Ms. Ramsey then introduced a getting acquainted activity, as everyone in the group did not know each other. She asked them to take a five-by-eight card, fold it the long way and, with the markers and crayons, write the name they liked to be called and color or decorate it any way they wished. She explained that after they did that, each would tell the other members about their name tag. While picking up the card, Kenika stated, "Crayons are for babies." The other girls and Ms. Ramsey began decorating their name tags and having the snack.

When everyone was finished, the worker asked if each of the girls would introduce herself and tell the group about her name tag. The worker also participated in the sharing of her name tag and the design on it. Some of the designs included on the name tags were flowers and stick figures. The girls seemed to be enjoying getting to know each other through the activity. When they got to Kenika, she explained that she had drawn "a knife with blood coming off it, cause that's what I'd do to any boys who tried to touch me!"

DEALING WITH THE CRISIS AND TABOO ISSUES

Talking about the crisis situation is critical. It may include taboo subjects or highly emotionally charged material. The crisis situation must be included in terms of purpose and why the group was convened. The activity facilitates the process and tasks of the beginning stage of group, as illustrated next.

Ms. Ramsey responded, "It sounds like you feel you need to protect yourself." Kenika explained that she had "sneaked a knife out of the kitchen just in case some boys try to mess with me." The worker empathized and asked the other members how they were feeling about what had happened to Cameron. Several responded that they were "really scared." Ms. Ramsey validated their feelings. She suggested that they list on the blackboard one thought or feeling that they had about what happened to Cameron. The girls began to respond when Kenika yelled, "Can I write it on the board?"

ENCOURAGING RELATEDNESS AND COHESION: WEATHERING THE STORM

The social worker brought a group of eight fourth- and fifth-grade boys into an empty classroom. Two days earlier, the nearby trailer court where the boys lived had been partially destroyed by a tornado. With their families they were living in the school gym and a nearby church. There were no fatalities. The worker explained their commonality, that all of them had been invited to the group because they had experienced losing all or part of their home to the tornado and were currently in temporary housing. She also explained the purpose of the group (to express their feelings about the effects of the tornado, etc.). Several boys gallantly expressed feelings of not caring and toughness about the event. The worker suggested that they begin by creating a mural of how it looked before the tornado and how it looked now.

DEALING WITH POWER AND CONTROL: IS THERE A PLACE FOR ME?

All groups go through a power and control stage, including short-term groups. Sometimes, the issues generated in this stage parallel real-life power and control issues.

A Tier II shelter opened in the vicinity of the local school. Formerly homeless women and children were to be housed for up to one year or until permanent housing was found. The administration had to find space in classrooms for 70 additional children, which created an organizational dilemma for an already overcrowded school. The children chosen for the group were powerless over the life events that created homelessness and the overcrowded classrooms. This is a third session of nine 8- to 10-year-old girls, all of whom had to adjust to the crowded school and a new living arrangement. The initial sessions dealt with their concerns about being in a group and the stigma of living in the shelter.

When the leader entered the room, she noted that three girls were absent. There was a lively discussion about some of the group members being involved in a lunchroom fight and how one member called the lunchroom monitor "a name."

A teacher brought in Candice, the girl who had started the fight. One of the other absent members also showed up with a big stain on her outfit. Carol, looking at Candice, started angrily and yelled, "You're here. Well, I'm not staying." Candice yelled, "Don't!" Holly asked, "What happened?" Rosa quickly jumped in to tell the story of how Candice got angry when the lunchroom monitor refused to let her eat lunch because she had lost her pass. Then Candice pushed into the line and knocked several trays over, messing up Carol's and Karla's clothes and causing the three girls to begin fighting. Several of the members jumped in and further embellished the story.

Carol yelled, "Shut the hell up. Just shut up. I don't want to hear this." She covered her ears. The worker asked curiously, "I wonder how this is helpful to anyone?" There was a brief silence, which Candice broke when she angrily yelled, "I do not want to be in this damn group anyway." The worker reflected Candice's anger. Candice responded that she was angry, saying heatedly, "That bitch let other kids eat lunch who lost their lunch pass but she wouldn't let me. Everyone was laughing!"

The worker noticed that Holly had taken an apple out of her pocket and had given it to Candice, who grabbed it. The members were anxious. The worker decided to serve the snack. She then suggested the girls role-play what happened but to think of different endings. The girls staged the scene with Candice as the monitor; Rosa and Alicia played the girls whose trays were knocked over; Carol played Candice (after protesting). They proceeded to plan the scenario. The discussion was lively with heated debate. What emerged from the scenario was that the girls felt they didn't fit into the school yet and were viewed as "different." Several shared being very dependent on the school lunch as a major meal. Several shared that they couldn't always wash their clothes in "the new place," so that getting messed up was a "big deal." Candice said sadly that she could not remember where she left her pass and feared never having lunch. The worker offered to intervene so that Candice would get lunch. She also empathized with the members "feeling different" and generalized about how stressful moving and going to a new school are for anyone.

As the girls played, they relaxed. Carol and Candice made peace. The worker ended the meeting with the following activity. Paper was distributed and members drew both their hands. One hand was a good hand and one was a bad hand. They were instructed to fill one hand with what a good hand does and one with what a bad hand does. These activities calmed down some of the anxiety and gave opportunities for the girls to problem-solve and express positive and negative feelings. The initial activity plan was put on hold. The worker will also have to follow up with the school personnel who were struggling with these additional children with special needs.

Dealing with Work Phase Issues: A Drive-by Shooting

The work phase is a problem-solving period. It is often characterized by intense intimacy and sharing of emotional issues.

The following is an excerpt from a 10- to 11-year-old boys' group. The group was formed after a classmate was killed in a drive-by shooting. At the previous meeting, the boys were upset that the school was making the students go through metal detectors. Two of the group members were stopped because they had knives on them "for protection."

The boys entered the group room and sullenly greeted the worker, Mark, who asked, "Well, what's happening?" Carlos responded that "school sucks." Monte chimed in, "Yeah! They treat us like we're in prison." Willi added "Like we can't even protect ourselves. Who do they think they are?" Mark stated, "Hold it, who's 'they'?" With bravado Al replied, "All of you who don't have to live here day after day." Mark asked, "I'm part of the they?" Al strongly stated, "You sure the hell are." Willi, somewhat protective of Mark, said to Al, "I don't think you meant that." Al affirmed that he did mean that and confronted Willi on telling him what he meant.

The group was able to raise issues in relation to the worker and also disagree with each other. This demonstrates a middle phase trust level. The lack of control and powerlessness they felt in an unsafe neighborhood was profound. Yet, the group was a place where they could earn and utilize power. To confront peers as well as the worker's power without violence was a positive experience.

Florio admitted that he was "pissed." Using what was happening in the group, Mark praised Florio and the other members, saying, "Well, guys, I think that you have picked the group's theme and work for today." Carlos looked at Mark and said, "You get to leave this place while we get to stay and get killed. It's actually a government plot to do away with poverty. One by one we will be shot or knifed and then there will be no more of us to make any more of us." One of the members was rapping his hands on the table and the other one was whistling. The worker took this opportunity to suggest that they create a rap song. Carlos laughed and reminded them that he's no Dr. Dre (a rap singer) and Al teasingly responded, "You're no poet either!"

The worker, attempting to validate their experiences and feelings, said, "Hey, don't the rap singers tell it like it is?" There is a moment of silence. Al sadly replied, "No one's going to listen to us." Enthusiastically, Mark let them know that he will listen and they will listen to each other. Monte proudly claimed that his brother's band "gets gigs" and that "maybe we can sell it!"

The boys settled down and created a rap song and, while they did this, worked on feelings of fear and rage. The worker needed to tolerate a great deal of anger, including the frequent use of curse words. Mark interrupted at one point to help the members also focus on the loss of their classmate and loss in general. This introduced the topic for further discussion. The theme was worked into the song. They created two versions, one for themselves and one that was presented to their class.

WORKING ON TERMINATION: CONSOLIDATING THE GAINS

Termination issues in crisis groups take on a powerful dimension. If the worker has provided a successful group experience, the children are going to feel the impact of separation very seriously, especially if the crisis involved a loss (Webb, 1985). The group may have also provided one of the few nourishing experiences the children have had and they may wish for more crises to occur so that the group can continue. This speaks to the importance of ongoing groups for this population.

The worker needs to help the children transfer their learning to other situations, feel the success of what they have accomplished, and recognize that they can turn to peers and other adults.

One can view termination as an ending or a beginning. It is a graduation with an opportunity to celebrate accomplishments as well as a time to explore feelings of sadness and loss.

Termination can be dealt with through activity and rituals. We suggest that in short-term groups, the issue should be introduced and worked on in the last third of the meetings. Therefore, in a three-session group, it will be the third meeting; in a twelve-session group, the tenth session.

Activities can include the following: Members may draw a pictorial map of where each member felt he or she started and where each member is now. They can create a group poem to which everyone contributes. Members may draw each other's names out of a box and then make a card for that person; a variation is making cards for all of the members.

The boys' group was asked to write on separate pieces of paper something they got from the group and one thing they wished they had gotten. They then read these aloud and decided whether they agreed or disagreed with the statement. Some of the statements were provocative; for example, they wished they had gotten "better ways to conceal a knife and sex lessons." Yet, they agreed they had gotten from the group a better understanding of "being pissed," had made friends, made something, and learned that a White man can be OK (i.e., the worker).

As a way of reflecting and bringing closure, members have created posters with the skills they learned or an artistic depiction of their experiences in the group. A graduation or good-bye party can also help members recognize the ending and celebrate their gains. It is important that members feel they have dealt successfully with the crisis situation and know that is why the group is terminating.

SUMMARY AND RECOMMENDATIONS

In a world of increased adversity, children have a greater potential to experience crisis situations. These experiences can have short- and long-term effects that are manifested in the child's behavior and social and cognitive development. Schools have the potential to ameliorate those effects and enhance the child's ability to bounce back by providing goal-focused activity groups. The following recommendations are made to develop and improve social work services for children who experience crisis:

- Recognize and respond quickly to the crisis.
- Provide groups for parents as well as children.
- Debrief staff about the crisis.
- Educate school personnel about the content and process of the children's activity groups.
- Teach those who work with these groups about the use of activity programming.
- Recognize culturally diverse ways that children cope.
- Utilize staff who are sensitive, structured, but flexible and "play-friendly."

Children demonstrate that they are remarkably resilient (Bernard, 1997). The use of goal-focused activity groups can provide opportunities to enhance a child's resilience. Activity groups recognize and build on strengths, create a natural environment for discussing positive and negative feelings, promote problem solving and decision making, and increase support and mutual aid. Coping and adaptation are thereby increased.

School acts as a second family to many children; it is their home away from home. Although the primary responsibility of the school is educational, it touches and provides a safety net for every aspect of a child's life. By developing opportunities for group peer experiences for children who have experienced a crisis, the school provides an educative, supportive, protective environment that can increase a child's learning potential and growth.

REFERENCES

Bernard, B. (1997). Fostering resiliency in child and youth: Promoting protective factors in the school. In D. Saleebey (Ed.), *The strengths perspective in social work practice* (2nd ed.). New York: Longman.

Callahan, C. (1998). Crisis intervention models for teachers. *Journal of Instructional Psychology, 25*(4), 226–234.

Congress, E., & Lynn, M. (1994). Group work programs in public schools: Ethical dilemmas and cultural diversity. *Social Work in Education, 16*(2), 107–114.

Fatout, M. (1996) *Children in groups: A social work perspective.* Westport, CT: Auburn House.

Freedberg, S. (1989). Self determination: Historical perspectives and effects on current practice. *Social Work, 34,* 33–38.

Garland, J., Jones, H., & Kolodny, R. (1973). A model for stages of development in social work groups. In S. Bernstein (Ed.), *Explorations in group work* (pp. 17–71). Boston: Milford House.

Gilliland, B., & James, R. (1997). *Crisis intervention strategies* (3rd ed.). New York: Brooks/Cole.

Henry, S. (1992). *Groups skills in social work: A four-dimensional approach* (2nd ed.). Pacific Grove, CA: Brooks/Cole.

Meyer, C. (1976). *Social work practice.* New York: Free Press.

Middleman, R. (1968). *The non-verbal method in working with groups.* New York: Association Press.

Nelson, E., & Slaikeu, K. (1990). Crisis intervention in the schools. In K. Slaikeu (Ed.), *Crisis intervention: A handbook for practice and research* (2nd ed., pp. 329–347). Boston: Allyn & Bacon.

Nisivoccia, D., & Lynn, M. (1999). Helping forgotten victims: Using activity groups with children who witness violence. In N. Webb (Ed.), *Play therapy with children in crisis* (2nd ed., pp. 74–103). New York: Guilford Press.

Parad, H.J., & Parad, L.G. (1990). *Crisis intervention* (Book 2). Milwaukee, WI: New York Family Service Association of America.

Roberts, A.R. (2000). *Crisis intervention handbook: Assessment, treatment and research* (2nd ed.). New York: Oxford University Press.

Schulman, L. (1999). *The skills of helping individuals, families, groups, and communities* (4th ed.). Itasca, IL: Peacock.

Slavson, S.R., & Schiffer, M. (1975). *Group psychotherapies for children: A textbook.* New York: International Universities Press.

Wainrib, B.R., & Bloch, E.L. (1998). *Crisis intervention and trauma response: Theory and practice.* New York: Springer.

Webb, N.B. (1985). A crisis intervention perspective on the termination process. *Clinical Social Work Journal, 13,* 329–340.

Webb, N.B. (1999). *Play therapy with children in crisis* (2nd ed.). New York: Guilford Press.

Yalom, I. (1985). *The theory and practice of group psychotherapy* (3rd ed.). New York: Basic Books.

CHAPTER 11

Play Therapy for Children of Alcoholics

JAMES G. EMSHOFF and LAURA L. JACOBUS

It has been estimated that 26.8 million children of alcoholics (COAs) currently live in the United States. Of these, over 11 million are younger than 18 (National Association for Children of Alcoholics, 1998). Our understanding of the effects of parental alcoholism on children continues to grow. Originally, many within the substance abuse field assumed that young children were unaware of parental alcohol abuse and were relatively unaffected by its presence (Anderson, 1987). However, more recent work within the field has acknowledged that alcoholism is a disease that affects the entire family system. Although recent work has highlighted the fact that there are many individual differences in the degree to which parental alcoholism affects children, it is also clear that there are many common vulnerabilities shared by these children.

Although there is considerable variation in both the form and severity of symptoms (Steinglass, 1979, 1981), alcoholic families can generally be characterized as dysfunctional (Kumpfer, 1987; Sher, 1987; West & Prinz, 1987). There is often a great deal of denial of the alcoholism and its attendant problems, as well as an air of secrecy when it is acknowledged (Ackerman, 1978, 1983; Woodside, 1982). Latham (1988) has documented lower overall family health, including a general negative mood and tone to the family environment. Despite a tendency for alcoholic parents to deal with their children in a rigid manner, there is a general lack of social order and organization (e.g., fewer rules and schedules) than in other families (Kumpfer, 1985, 1986). Indeed, the atmosphere in an alcoholic home is often more upsetting to children than the actual drinking behaviors per se (Wilson & Orford, 1978).

The above family characteristics and the concept of family systems have implications for the characteristics and behaviors exhibited by COAs. Children are often considered the most vulnerable of the family members to the adverse effects of familial alcoholism (National Institute for Alcohol Abuse and Alcoholism [NIAAA], 1981). COAs have also been shown to be at an increased risk for a wide range of behavioral and emotional problems, including addiction to alcohol and other drugs, depression, anxiety, school failure, delinquency, and difficulty getting along with their peers (Adger, 1997; Emshoff & Anyan, 1989; Sher, 1991). This lack of friendship and poor family relationships combine to give COAs an overall lower sense of support and higher levels of loneliness than other children.

Although this brief review of the literature has indicated that COAs are at an increased risk for a wide variety of social, emotional, and behavioral difficulties, it is important to note that these findings cannot be generalized to individual children. Not all or even a majority of COAs will manifest these dysfunctional characteristics (Sher, 1987). Instead, the vast majority of COAs are remarkably well-adjusted. Thus, counselors working with COAs must remain cognizant of the fact that knowing that a child can be labeled a COA offers relatively little information about that particular child's adjustment or development. Instead, counselors must investigate and consider specific experiences and risk factors that may contribute to a COA's likelihood of experiencing a significant disturbance. Knowing that a child has experienced alcoholism in his or her family should not be used to label a child as deviant or even potentially deviant. Instead, counselors should utilize this information in a responsible manner and use this classification as a challenge to gather more specific information regarding a particular child's experiences.

THE IMPORTANCE OF PLAY FOR COAS

Therapists have long understood the importance of play for the developmental growth of all children. Because of the many responsibilities and stresses that are associated with parental alcoholism, COAs are likely to be involved in a wide variety of experiences that may limit the amount and quality of play they engage in. Play therapy can provide counselors with a set of tools that allows them to work with children in a manner that directly addresses many of the issues that these children face.

Lack of Positive Role Models

Alcoholic parents are often emotionally neglectful and provide less support to their children than do their nonalcoholic counterparts (Allen, 1990). In addition, alcoholic parents are likely to demonstrate less competent parenting skills than other parents. The generally disruptive environment that often accompanies an alcoholic household may result in these children's receiving considerably less attention, positive regard, and discipline than other children (Edwards & Zander, 1985). As a result of these neglectful behaviors, COAs are likely to have experienced fewer adult role models for fun and play than have other children. Therapists using play therapy can serve as excellent adult role models for COAs searching for healthy modes of play.

Parentification

Although there are a wide variety of possible outcomes for children who grow up or live with an alcoholic parent, there are several symptom patterns that are frequently encountered among these children. One common symptom that is often witnessed among COAs is parentification. Parentification, or role reversal, refers to the process by which children assume adult responsibilities in the family structure.

Although COAs often appear to be successful and well-adjusted to the outside world, these children often suffer as a result of the extraordinary responsibilities they assume in the family structure. Alcoholic parents may frequently be unable to care for themselves, much less perform daily activities such as cleaning the house, cooking nutritious meals, and caring for younger children. COAs often assume these responsibilities themselves. Because of the many responsibilities that are often shouldered by these children, COAs often seem older than they really are. These children have often been praised and rewarded for acting "grown up" and "taking care" of the family. As a result of the burden of these added responsibilities and their perceived inability to alter their parent's behavior, parentified children are likely to demonstrate feelings of low self-esteem and strong feelings of inadequacy.

Play therapy can prove to be an extremely beneficial form of treatment for these tremendously burdened children to experience an environment in which they can act in an age-appropriate manner. Unlike other traditional forms of therapy, play therapy can provide children with a therapeutic outlet that can allow COAs to work through their problems in a safe, healthy environment while providing them with an opportunity to engage in the play and fun that they have been missing.

LEARNING HOW TO PLAY

Because of these numerous responsibilities, COAs may experience fewer opportunities to interact with other children on a meaningful basis. Parentified children who have assumed partial or full responsibility for a household are likely to have less time and energy to play with peers than will other children. Cork (1969) interviewed 115 children who were living in an alcoholic home and noted that many of these children reported being extremely reluctant to invite peers to their home because of their unstable, chaotic, and often embarrassing home environment. In addition, COAs reported being reluctant to socialize at a peer's home because of their reluctance to reciprocate the invitation. Because of this reduced opportunity for socialization, COAs may demonstrate reduced levels of developmentally appropriate social skills compared to their peers. This lack of socialization and reduced social skills have been shown to be related to higher levels of social isolation and withdrawal, both of which have been shown to contribute to a person's later risk of substance abuse (Sher, 1991). These risk factors may prove especially disturbing in COAs, as they also have elevated levels of other risk factors.

Play therapy can offer children an ideal environment in which they can learn and practice play. By providing children with a setting in which play is not only allowed but encouraged, therapists can help COAs learn to play in a manner that fosters both creativity and imagination. In addition, interventions that utilize play therapy techniques in a group format can offer COAs access to peers and socialization skills that they may have been missing.

PERFECTIONISM AS A SYMPTOM

Another symptom that is frequently encountered among COAs is perfectionism. Perfectionistic children learn very early that the easiest way to win approval within and outside the family structure is to demonstrate excellence in all areas of life. Through this perfection, these children demonstrate to the world that their family is "OK."

This perfectionism comes with a heavy price. Perfectionistic children often demonstrate compulsive behaviors and elevated levels of anxiety and are wary of risk taking. Developmental research has consistently demonstrated that children need to be able to take risks and make mistakes if they are to learn normal, healthy coping strategies (Burns, 1989; Smith, 1990). Children who are too afraid or unwilling to take these risks are at risk of becoming rigid, unyielding adults.

Play therapy can help these children by offering them a safe environment in which risks can be explored with minimally adverse consequences. Because there are no right or wrong ways to play, counselors can help perfectionistic COAs to explore their environment in a setting that does not threaten their need for perfectionism. Hammond-Newman (1994) suggests that these children often enter play therapy uneasy and uptight, choosing games that allow them to retain a sense of control over their environment. Through play therapy, these children can come to give up some of this control and expose the pain and hurt that underlie their mask.

EXTERNALIZING SYMPTOMS

Research has also demonstrated that COAs are at high risk for externalizing symptoms, including aggressive and antisocial behaviors (Sher, 1991; Windle, 1990). Although there is significant disagreement within the literature concerning the origins of these behaviors (e.g., see Kendler et al., 1995), there is considerable evidence documenting the negative effects of these behaviors. Sher and Trull (1994) demonstrated that aggression may serve as a mediator in the relationship in the transmission of alcoholism between parent and child. Thus, therapy strategies that serve to reduce levels of aggression and antisocial behaviors among COAs may be able to influence the transmission of this disease between generations. Aggressive and delinquent adolescents have also been shown to develop friendships with other aggressive and delinquent peers. As a result, aggressive, antisocial COAs may have significantly less exposure to competent, age-appropriate social skills.

Wegscheider (1981) notes that although the majority of these children appear angry and defiant, these children are actually using these behaviors to mask the more difficult emotions of rejection and inadequacy. Play therapy can prove to be an extremely beneficial tool for children who have demonstrated aggressive and delinquent behaviors. Play therapists can help these children to improve their self-image by offering them the positive attention and approval that they so desperately seek. Play therapy can also introduce these children to positive, healthy ways of coping with the stresses of living in an addicted household that can serve to replace the child's negative behaviors. Finally, because these children are likely to demonstrate significant social skill deficits as a result of their association with other delinquent peers, antisocial COAs can often benefit from inclusion in a group play therapy program. By offering these children an opportunity to develop and practice healthy social interactions with non-delinquent peers, group play therapy can greatly assist these children.

Hammond-Newman (1994) suggests that these children may enter play therapy unwillingly and may demonstrate aggressive and destructive play strategies. However, through play therapy, these children can come to share the hurt and pain that is masked by these acting-out behaviors.

INTERNALIZING SYMPTOMS

Another class of symptoms commonly witnessed among COAs is internalizing disorders. COAs have been shown to be significantly more depressed than other children, as well as demonstrating lower levels of self-esteem (Sher, 1991; West & Prinz, 1987). These children often withdraw from both family and peer interactions. This withdrawal is somewhat functional for these children, in that they can remove themselves from many of the negative effects associated with parental alcoholism.

This withdrawal can have severe consequences. Because these children can be ignored by their family, they tend to demonstrate low self-esteem and isolation. In addition, because these children spend so much time alone, hiding their feelings from their family, lost children often demonstrate significant deficits in social and communication skills (Wegscheider, 1981).

Play therapy can prove to be an excellent choice of therapy for these children. Because they are isolated from their family, children who internalize can also benefit from the attention and approval that play therapists can offer them; they also benefit from peer play therapy groups. These children are isolated not only from their family, but also from their peers, and as a result they can often benefit from the social interaction and social skills that these groups may foster. Hammond-Newman (1994) suggests that although these children may enter play therapy shy and timid, play therapists can help them by engaging in parallel play techniques. Slowly, these children can learn to trust their therapist and reveal their inner pain.

Although these profiles suggest that there are numerous coping strategies utilized by children to deal with the effects of parental alcoholism, there are also numerous similarities among these children. Many COAs learn to deny and minimize the effects of parental alcoholism on their lives. Because of this, some COAs have difficulty verbally expressing their feelings (Ficaro, 1999). COAs also tend to display low self-esteem in response to their inability to control their family situation and a perceived inability to gain positive attention from their family without resorting to manipulative tactics. These tactics tend to limit the degree to which many COAs interact with peers on a meaningful basis. This reduced interaction tends to limit the degree to which these children develop and practice healthy, competent social skills. Play therapy can assist counselors in addressing these difficulties in a manner that is approachable and understandable by children.

PLAY THERAPY: HOW IT CAN HELP

Play therapy provides counselors with an opportunity to assist COAs in a developmentally appropriate manner. The specific content of the play therapy session will vary considerably according to the needs of the individual child. Therapy should be guided by a desire to help COAs reduce their denial, abandon unhealthy coping roles, and release emotions and feelings related to their predicament (Hammond-Newman, 1994). An examination of how play therapy can accomplish these goals follows.

Whatever form of play therapy is utilized, counselors should remain sensitive to feelings of powerlessness experienced by COAs and utilize play therapy techniques that emphasize choice and foster a sense of empowerment among this population (Oliver-Diaz, 1988). Ficaro (1999) suggests that one way to allow children to retain a sense of control over the process is for the practitioner to assure the children that they are in control of the play therapy process and that they can terminate the sessions after a few meetings if they desire.

ESTABLISHING TRUST

An important goal of play therapy techniques is to establish a sense of trust between the counselor and client and to assist COAs in increasing feelings of trust in other settings. Because they have often experienced unreliable, inconsistent parenting techniques, COAs are likely to be distrustful of many individuals, especially adults. Play therapy offers practitioners an opportunity to connect to COAs in a manner that can serve as a foundation for trust building. In addition, therapists can utilize a number of exercises that foster trusting relationships (Landreth, 1991; O'Rourke, 1990).

WORKING WITH CHILDREN'S AMBIVALENCE ABOUT DISCUSSING THEIR PARENTS' BEHAVIOR

Another important goal of play therapy is to break through the denial and shame that many COAs experience as a result of their parents' substance abuse problems. Group play therapy can often prove beneficial in this process, as it can help these children understand that they are not alone in their dilemma and that they are not responsible for their parents' inconsistent, and perhaps abusive, behaviors (Cable, Noel, & Swanson, 1986). Play therapists can also facilitate this process by displaying an understanding of the child's circumstances and reassurance that what the child is experiencing is a normal reaction to parents' behaviors.

ALLOWING CHILDREN TO WORK THROUGH THEIR FEELINGS IN A CREATIVE FASHION

Because many COAs learn to minimize and deny their feelings, they may have difficulty expressing themselves in traditional, talk-based therapy techniques (Ficaro, 1999). Play therapy offers these children an opportunity to express their feelings and emotions in a creative, emotional fashion that may prove more comfortable for them. Play therapy additionally may benefit children who appear to be rigid and perfectionistic. By allowing these children to explore their worlds in a setting in which the pressure to "succeed" has been removed, counselors may be able to help them learn to increase their flexibility and spontaneity.

OFFERING CHILDREN EDUCATION AND INFORMATION REGARDING ALCOHOL ABUSE

Another goal of play therapy for COAs is to help these children learn about alcohol-related issues in a developmentally appropriate manner. Although the amount and type of information that a child is able to handle will vary depending on a child's developmental level and maturity, counselors can use play therapy techniques to address some of these important issues with their clients. Therapists can construct and utilize games and techniques that teach and allow children to practice skills for living with an alcoholic parent. One situation that many COAs experience is driving in the car with an intoxicated parent; practitioners can utilize play therapy techniques to address the dangers associated with driving under the influence and help children understand and practice skills that can help them avoid this situation.

In addition, therapists can utilize play therapy techniques to help children understand the idea of COA risk status in a developmentally appropriate manner. It is important for COAs to understand that having an alcoholic parent does not ensure that they will become alcoholic themselves; however, it is also important to convey the information that these children are at higher risk for alcoholism and substance abuse. It is estimated that anywhere from 13% to 25% of COAs will eventually become alcoholic themselves (Cotton, 1979). However, children who are aware of their risk status drink significantly less (in both quantity and frequency) than do COAs who are unaware of this information (Kumpfer, 1989).

MODES OF PLAY THERAPY

Play therapy occurs in a variety of therapeutic settings and uses a variety of therapeutic techniques. Group therapy and family therapy represent two common settings in which play therapy techniques can be applied to COA populations. Although group play therapy techniques are easily applied to a school setting, family play therapy is infrequently used in school settings. Many schools believe that families are outside their scope of interest and prefer to restrict their focus to the child. However, schools may occasionally wish to conduct interventions that utilize family play therapy techniques. If this is not appropriate or feasible, schools may wish to refer families to an external therapeutic setting where family play therapy techniques are utilized.

GROUP PLAY THERAPY

Whereas many play therapists choose to work with children on an individual basis, there are several advantages to working with children in a group setting. Although many practitioners believe that children should be seen for several individual sessions initially, group-based play therapy can offer practitioners an ideal environment for children to learn and practice a wide variety of skills that can assist them with the difficulties of being a COA. Because these skills are learned and practiced in environments that are similar to those in which they may later be practiced, children may be able to transfer these skills more easily to other settings.

Group play therapy is often the preferred treatment strategy for working with COAs. Group therapy can aid COAs by allowing them to break through many denial issues that are associated with having an alcoholic parent. By sharing their experiences and stories with other children, COAs can come to understand that they are not alone in their plight and so reduce feelings of shame, isolation, and guilt (Dies & Burghardt, 1991).

In addition, group play therapy can benefit children by offering them a number of other sources of social support. Social support is a natural result of group participation. As children share common reactions and discover that they share similar coping mechanisms, group cohesion is built. This cohesion and support may be especially important for COAs, who often face more than their share of problems with less than their share of support. Although individual play therapy techniques can offer children a considerable amount of support from their counselor, these are children who will generally benefit from as much support as possible. By offering these children a number of additional sources of support, group play therapy may assist these children in dealing with the difficult issues that they face on a daily basis. Furthermore, there is evidence that children may benefit not only from receiving support, but also from offering support. Some research demonstrates that programs that allow participants to both provide and receive support have the most positive outcomes (Maton, 1987). Sweeny (1997) suggests several additional benefits that may be achieved through the use of group play therapy:

- *Group play therapy can encourage children to develop a therapeutic relationship with the counselor.* Withdrawn or unsure children can watch other children participating in activities and building a trusting relationship with the counselor. By observing these activities, withdrawn children may be more likely to engage in the play therapy process and develop a trusting relationship with the counselor.
- *Children have the opportunity to develop and practice interpersonal skills in a group setting.* Many COAs may not have had the chance to develop and practice developmentally appropriate social skills, and group play therapy can prove to be an excellent opportunity for counselors to assist these children in this process. Counselors can utilize games and activities that allow children to learn and practice these skills in a group environment. Group play therapy allows children ample opportunity to practice these skills, and the skills may be more likely to be transferred to other settings.
- *Group play therapy offers children the opportunity to learn vicariously through others.* By allowing children to witness the play, growth, and insight of other children, group play therapy offers children increased opportunities to understand their own behaviors. In addition, by receiving feedback from other children, group play participants have increased opportunities to reflect and understand their own behaviors.

SCHOOL-BASED PLAY THERAPY

Because of the large number of COAs in school, school-based play therapy programs typically occur in a group format. Parent involvement is typically not required or logistically feasible for this type of school-based intervention and may not be desirable for some youth. Although these programs acknowledge the importance of parental rehabilitation, school-based programs usually recognize that this goal lies outside the scope of their authority (Ackerman, 1983). Therefore, these programs typically work only with COAs, helping them build a set of skills and competencies that can assist them in dealing with issues surrounding parental alcoholism. If appropriate, school-based play programs can refer families to outside counseling services and treatment.

Virtually all young children are involved in the school system on some level. Thus, the school provides therapists and counselors an important environment in which to identify and intervene with children of alcoholics. In addition, schools are a logical point of intervention with this population because it is the environment in which problems relating to parental alcoholism may be the most consistently discernible (Dies & Burghardt, 1991).

Benefits

School-based programs may benefit children by offering them consistent, nonstigmatizing access to programs that they might not otherwise attend. Many children, particularly COAs, have limited access to out-of-school programs, especially when transportation is difficult. Additionally, children may resist attending programs that are based in traditional mental health settings because of the potential for stigma and embarrassment.

Detection Issues

However, counselors working in this setting also face numerous challenges in detecting affected children. Because many of the symptoms exhibited by COAs are not unique to this population, identifying COAs without overidentifying often proves to be a difficult challenge without some type of referral (Ficaro, 1999).

Crowley (2000) suggests that counselors should use a wide net in identifying children at risk for these problems. By focusing their attention on children who are exhibiting school-related problems, counselors and school personnel will ultimately identify COAs. Because school counselors are not typically aware of family substance abuse problems in the home, counselors should focus their efforts on all children who are demonstrating disruptive behavior. By assessing these affected children, counselors can ultimately detect and treat children who are suffering from family addiction problems. However, it should be noted that a large number of the difficulties associated with being a COA (e.g., depression, anxiety, perfectionism) might not be visible to many school personnel. Consequently, specific types of COAs may be systematically ignored if only external problematic behaviors are used as a screen. Teachers and other school officials should be given information and training on how to identify COAs as well as other at-risk children.

One way to ensure that interventions identify as many affected COAs as possible is to err on the side of overidentification. Emshoff (1989) describes a video technique that maximizes student awareness and participation while minimizing stigmatization and threat. The technique involves exposing all children in a school to a video that dramatically portrays an alcoholic family. After the film, students participate in a brief discussion about the film, and interested students are invited to attend a longer discussion group later in the day. This longer discussion group should initially focus specifically on the film and then gradually move to more personal issues surrounding the children's experiences with parental alcoholism. Toward the end of the discussion, children can be informed of and invited to attend an ongoing group to deal with issues surrounding alcoholism.

This recruitment technique allows school personnel to identify COAs with as little stigma as possible. Children participating in these groups are not clearly identified as COAs but rather as children who are interested in the subject. If asked, children can claim that they are participating in the discussion group out of curiosity, or simply to skip class.

The CAGE

In addition to this recruitment technique, there are several well-developed screening measures that can be used to identify COAs. One such established measure that can be used with younger students is the CAGE questionnaire (Ewing, 1984). The CAGE questionnaire is a brief, four-question instrument originally designed to measure an individual's own alcohol problems. The CAGE instrument asks whether the respondent has ever "felt the need to cut down on your drinking," gotten "annoyed at criticism about your drinking," "felt guilty about your drinking, or something you have done during drinking," or "had an eye-opener first thing in the morning." The CAGE has also been used to allow children to provide a report of another individual's drinking habits. By simply altering the wording of each question so that it refers to the behavior of family members, school officials can quickly gain insight into potential alcohol problems in the child's home. Because this measure is so brief, school officials should not use it as the sole diagnostic measure when determining COA status. Instead, school officials should use positive responses on this measure as an indication to perform a more detailed assessment.

The CAST

Another common screening device appropriate for school settings is the Children of Alcoholics Screening Test (CAST; Jones, 1982). The CAST is a written, 30-item self-report questionnaire that asks children and adolescents to report their feelings and experiences related to parental alcohol abuse. Youth respond to each question using a yes or no format. The CAST is useful mainly with older children and adolescents but has also been used to screen adult children of alcoholics. The CAST is an extremely valuable tool in that it asks respondents to reflect not only on their parents' drinking behaviors, but also on their own reaction to and feelings about these behaviors. For a more detailed analysis of screening measures for COAs and issues surrounding detection, see Werner, Joffe, and Graham (1999).

Labeling

Another important issue for counselors working in a school setting is the potential for labeling. Although it is well-established that COAs are at increased risk for a number of difficulties, it is also clear that the majority of COAs are well-adjusted and demonstrate no significant difficulties (J. Crowley, personal communication, April 2000). In addition, research has demonstrated that mental health professionals are more likely to view a child as demonstrating pathological behaviors if they are aware of a family history of alcoholism, regardless of the child's actual behavior (Burk & Sher, 1990). Considering the dangers that exist for labeling to negatively affect COAs, mental health professionals should exercise caution in accepting referrals from school personnel. Mental health professionals should work closely with school personnel to explore the dangers of labeling to ensure that the proper children are being referred for treatment.

Ethical Issues

Confidentiality is another ethical issue that counselors working in a school environment must consider. School-based programs offer many advantages, but they also limit the degree to which confidentiality may be maintained. Although teachers and other school personnel will likely be aware of the purpose of school-based programs, counselors should make efforts to protect the confidentiality of children participating in these programs. Teachers and parents should be instructed that the content of such programs will remain strictly confidential and that the details of a child's participation will not be divulged, except in cases where the child poses a risk to self or others.

Another way to help ensure confidentiality is to refer to the program in vague terms rather than as a "group for children of alcoholics." For example, counselors may wish to refer to the program as "a stress and coping group." By referring to the group in these terms, counselors are likely to include children in the group who do not have an alcoholic parent. Although this may appear problematical, involving non-COAs in the group can be quite useful. Given the prevalence of alcoholism, it is likely that all children could benefit from discussions surrounding alcohol-related issues. Most children are likely to know an alcoholic individual, or will in the future. By allowing all interested children to participate, schools can reduce the stigma attached to the intervention as well as offer important substance abuse information to a wider base of children than a program that restricts its focus to COAs.

Parental Consent

Crowley (personal communication, April, 2000) suggests that counselors working in a school environment should carefully consider issues surrounding parental consent to participate in these programs. Although some researchers have argued that school-based interventions working with COAs do not require parental consent or notification, the vast majority of counselors working in a school setting are cautious of such claims and choose to obtain consent.

Obtaining such consent can present school mental health professionals with several difficulties. Because of the many disturbances that occur in an alcoholic family, it may be more difficult to secure consent for COAs to participate in school-related programs than for other children. In addition, although some parents may recognize the necessity of these programs and may actually refer their child for treatment, some parents, especially actively addicted ones, may resent the school's involvement in what they consider "family business."

J. Crowley (personal communication, April, 2000) suggests that school counselors should emphasize to parents the fact that these programs can address specific symptoms presented by the child, and de-emphasize the fact that these programs also deal with the underlying cause of these problems: parental alcoholism. By helping parents understand how play therapy can help their child reduce anxiety, depression, anger, or shyness rather than "deal with family substance abuse issues," school counselors are more likely to appeal to these parents and receive permission for the child's continued participation.

Another possibility offered by J. Crowley (personal communication, April, 2000) is to secure passive consent from parents for children to participate in such a program. School personnel using passive consent procedures often send out a "laundry list" of activities that children may be exposed to during the school year. Parents are instructed to inform the school of any program that they object to and do not want their child involved in. Parents who do not typically respond to information sent by the school are not likely to respond to this notification and will passively consent for their child to participate in any listed school activity. The use of such procedures remains somewhat controversial in the academic community, and each school must weigh the relative merits of instituting such a policy in their own school district.

Scheduling

Counselors working in a school setting must also carefully consider the scheduling of interventions. Although many schools desire that such interventions be scheduled after school hours so that children do not miss class, this is not always feasible. Children, particularly COAs, may have limited access to after-school interventions, especially when transportation is difficult. Parentified COAs may also be unwilling or unable to take time away from their responsibilities at home to attend after-school activities. To ensure adequate participation in interventions targeted at COA populations, schools should consider conducting these activities during the school day. Interventions conducted during school hours can address concerns that children will suffer academically by rotating the day and time of the intervention. By ensuring that children do not systematically miss one class or subject more often than another, school officials can work to ensure that schools adequately address children's academic and socioemotional needs.

Staffing

School-based interventions working with COAs must also carefully consider staffing issues. Interventions are often conducted by a variety of school personnel who may vary in terms of training and expertise on COA issues. Schools that wish to employ an intervention utilizing play therapy techniques must carefully consider the characteristics of the specific program when selecting appropriate personnel to staff the program. Interventions that are highly structured and rely heavily on predesigned programs may be less concerned with the specific training and supervision of their staff than are interventions that deal mostly with interpersonal issues. Interventions that are highly structured should instead be more concerned with the relationship and rapport that the program staff has with the students.

Utilizing teachers in school-based interventions may also pose special problems. Schools may wish to ensure that students are not involved in interventions that are staffed by their regular teachers; teachers may have a very difficult time separating their roles of teacher and "therapist." If this approach is chosen, schools must work carefully to emphasize confidentiality issues and techniques to minimize labeling.

Termination

Counselors should also remain cognizant of the difficulties that the termination process may present to a COA. Because their own parents have often cared for them on an inconsistent basis, these children are especially vulnerable to feelings of abandonment at the termination of counseling. Therapists should explore the child's feelings about the process and allow the client to express fear and uncertainty at the prospect of termination. Benedict and Mongoven (1997) suggest that the termination process is often made easier by allowing the child to take home something tangible from the play therapy room. Often, counselors and children create a toy or game for the child to retain ownership over. This memento serves not only to remind children of the progress they have made in the course of their play therapy experience but also offers them a mechanism for continuing the process of play after the sessions terminate.

School-based play therapy interventions must also be aware that the school calendar can strongly impact the termination of the play therapy process. School calendars understandably are rigid and do not take into account a child's progress in therapy when dictating the scheduling of the school year. Children may be forced to terminate play therapy at the end of the school year even if they are only beginning to make progress. Likewise, school-based interventions may be targeted toward children in specific grade levels and children may be ineligible for participation in these interventions at the end of a school year, even if they are continuing to make progress. Counselors working in a school setting should carefully explore these issues with students and give the children considerable notice that the sessions may be terminated. If needed, counselors should consider referring children to outside agencies for assistance during the time when school assistance is unavailable.

EXAMPLES OF HOW PLAY THERAPY WORKS

The vast majority of play therapy techniques that are used in group play therapy can be used in school-based play therapy groups. In addition, school-based play therapists can incorporate play therapy techniques into academic and extracurricular subjects such as music and art that children participate in on a regular basis. Although the variety of play therapy techniques that can be adapted for use in schools is limitless, presented below are several techniques that lend themselves well to a school environment and specifically address some of the issues that are often faced by COAs.

One technique that can be used with a range of ages is the feelings game. This technique is extremely popular in the play therapy literature, and numerous versions of the game exist. The purpose of the game typically is to help children gain a better understanding of their feelings, specifically regarding alcohol-related issues. A simple version of the game involves children creating a series of masks or pictures that depict various emotions that children might experience. Children are encouraged to pictorially represent as many different emotions as they can name. Once the drawings are complete, children are encouraged to represent their own emotions according to the pictures they have created. Children also are often asked to practice imitating facial expressions that mirror the emotions they have chosen. This game is designed to aid children in understanding the sometimes complex emotions they experience, as well as helping children to gain a more complex vocabulary for expressing such emotions.

Another technique that can help COAs deal with real-life problems is a simple card game that allows children to dramatize situations that may occur in alcoholic families. The counselor and children typically work together to create a series of situations that COAs may experience. The situations may run the gamut from the common (e.g., parents fighting) to the more serious (e.g., child sexual abuse). These situations are then transferred to cards, which are distributed to various members of the group. Children are asked to work with other members of the group to dramatize the situation depicted on their card. At the end of each dramatization, counselors ask the group to respond to each situation. Special emphasis can be placed on responding to the complex emotions that are triggered by each scene, as well as increasing situational problem solving by having children offer a number of potential solutions to each of the depicted difficulties.

Play therapy techniques vary widely in structure. The previous two techniques were relatively structured and most suitable for use with older children and adolescents, but there are a wide variety of less-structured techniques that are appropriate for use with younger children. Many of these techniques, which often include items such as puppets, sandboxes, and art supplies, emphasize allowing children to use play therapy as a creative outlet for their shame and anxieties. By offering young COAs the rare opportunity to express themselves through play, therapists can provide these children with some relief from the stresses associated with being a COA, as well as gain a better insight into the difficulties plaguing these children.

FAMILY PLAY THERAPY

Although most school-based interventions for COAs employ a group modality, occasionally it may be possible to engage the entire family in an intervention or refer the family for treatment elsewhere. Counselors widely accept the fact that alcoholism is a disease that affects the entire family and that the full effects of family alcoholism cannot be appreciated without examining the entire family system (Robinson, 1989). Family play therapy may be an attractive therapy option for working with COAs because a major focus of the family therapy process is strengthening the parent-child relationship (Van Fleet, 1994). COAs often develop distant, serious relationships with their parents; by offering families a supervised, healthy environment in which to engage in enjoyable and therapeutic games, family play therapy may strengthen the often difficult relationships that are created by substance abuse.

Family play therapy also offers the advantage of allowing parents to witness and understand the consequences that their addictive behaviors have on their family. Counselors can instruct parents on the importance of play for child development and ways in which play can be encouraged in the home environment. By involving the parents in the play therapy process, counselors may be able to increase the probability that these skills will be transferred to the home environment, where they are greatly needed.

However, family play therapy is clearly not appropriate for all families. Hammond-Newman (1994) suggests that family play therapy may be inappropriate for use with parents who are actively addicted. Parents frequently deny the effects of their addiction until they are at least six months into recovery (Hammond-Newman, 1994). Thus, parental involvement in the play therapy process may hinder its progress more than aid it. To this extent, counselors considering using family play therapy techniques should consider the specific dynamics of the family involved and whether they lend themselves well to this technique. Parents that are still in denial regarding their addiction and its effects on the family may not prove ideal candidates for this type of therapy. However, their children may still benefit from the play therapy process. Black (1982) argues that children who are living with actively addicted parents may be the most in need of play therapy and the haven that it provides. One potential solution to this difficulty is to restrict family play therapy participation to the nonaddicted parent if possible.

CONCLUDING COMMENTS

This chapter emphasized the potential benefits of using play therapy with COAs. Because of the numerous responsibilities that are often associated with living in a substance-abusing household, COAs typically receive fewer opportunities to engage in this fun than do other children. Play therapy allows these children to participate in activities that not only provide them with a relief from the pressures of being a COA, but can also be designed to address many of the risk factors these children experience. As a result of the denial and shame that is often associated with living in an addicted household, COAs may initially feel uncomfortable expressing themselves verbally and may view play therapy as a more approachable, comfortable, and developmentally appropriate forum in which to discuss, and eventually heal, the many different pains that these children experience.

Schools provide counselors with an excellent environment in which to conduct interventions that utilize play therapy techniques. Schools are a logical point of intervention with COAs because many of the difficulties that are associated with parental alcoholism may be readily observed in a school setting. In addition, schools can provide counselors with consistent, nonstigmatizing access to children whom they otherwise might not be able to reach. By taking advantage of the many opportunities that schools provide, counselors can work to design and implement interventions that benefit this complex population.

REFERENCES

Ackerman, R. (1978). *Children of alcoholics: A guidebook for educators, therapists and parents.* Homes Beach, FL: Learning Publications.

Ackerman, R. (1983). *Children of alcoholics.* Homes Beach, FL: Learning Publications.

Adger, H. (1997). *The role of primary care physicians* [On-line]. Available: http://www.health.org/nacoa

Allen, B. (1990). *Children of alcoholics.* Springfield: Illinois Prevention Research Center.

Anderson, G. (1987). *When chemicals come to school.* Troy, MI: Performance Resource Press.

Benedict, H.E., & Mongoven, L.B. (1997). Thematic play therapy: An approach to treatment of attachment disorders in young children. In H. Kaduson, D. Cangelosi, & C.E. Schaefer (Eds.), *The playing cure: Individualized play therapy for specific childhood problems* (pp. 277–315). Northvale, NJ: Aronson.

Black, C. (1982). *It will never happen to me.* Denver, CO: MAC.

Burk, J.P., & Sher, K.J. (1990). Labeling the child of an alcoholic: Negative stereotyping by mental health professionals and peers. *Journal of Studies on Alcohol, 51,* 156–163.

Burns, D.D. (1989). *The feeling good handbook.* New York: Plume.

Cable, L.C., Noel, N.E., & Swanson, S.C. (1986). Clinical intervention with children of alcohol abusers. In D.C. Lewis & C.N. Williams (Eds.), *Providing care for children of alcoholics: Clinical and research perspectives* (pp. 64–79). Pompano Beach, FL: Health Communications.

Cork, M. (1969). *The forgotten children.* Toronto, Canada: Alcoholism and Drug Addiction Research Foundation.

Cotton, N.S. (1979). The familiar incidence of alcoholism: A review. *Journal of Studies on Alcohol, 40*, 89–116.

Dies, R.R., & Burghardt, K. (1991). Group intervention for children of alcoholics: Prevention and treatment in the schools. *Journal of Adolescent Group Therapy, 1*, 219–234.

Edwards, D.M., & Zander, T.A. (1985). Children of alcoholics: Background and strategies for the counselor. *Elementary School Guidance and Counseling, 20*(2), 121–128.

Emshoff, J.G. (1989). A preventative intervention with children of alcoholics. *Prevention in Human Services, 7*(1), 225–253.

Emshoff, J., & Anyan, L.L. (1989). From prevention to treatment: Issues for school-aged children of alcoholics. In M. Galanter (Ed.), *Recent developments in alcoholism: Children of alcoholics* (Vol. 9, pp. 327–346). New York: Plenum Press.

Ewing, J.E. (1984). Detecting alcoholism: The CAGE questionnaire. *Journal of American Medical Association, 252*, 1905–1907.

Ficaro, R.C. (1999). The many losses of children in substance-abused families: Individual and group interventions. In N. Webb (Ed.), *Play therapy with children in crisis: Individual, group and family treatment* (pp. 294–317). New York: Guilford Press.

Hammond-Newman, M. (1994). Play therapy with children of alcoholics and addicts. In K. O'Connor & C. Schaeffer (Eds.), *Handbook of play therapy: Advances and innovations* (Vol. 2, pp. 387–407). New York: Wiley.

Jones, J. (1982). *Preliminary test manual: The Children of Alcoholics Screening Test.* Chicago: Family Recovery Press.

Kendler, K.S., Walters, E.E., Neale, M.C., Kessler, R.C., Heath, A.C., & Eaves, L.J. (1995). The structure of the genetic and environmental risk factors for six major psychiatric disorders in women: Phobia, generalized anxiety disorder, panic disorder, bulimia, major depression, and alcoholism. *Archives of General Psychiatry, 52*, 374–383.

Kumpfer, K.L. (1985, October). *Prevention approaches to adolescent substance use/abuse.* Paper presented at the American Academy of Child Psychiatry Institute on Substance Abuse and Adolescence, San Antonio, TX.

Kumpfer, K.L. (1986, April). *Family-focussed prevention interventions for children of alcoholics.* Paper presented at the National Council on Alcoholism Annual Forum: Alcohol and the Family, San Francisco.

Kumpfer, K.L. (1987). Special populations: Etiology and prevention of vulnerability to chemical dependency in children of substance abusers. In B. Brown & A. Mills (Eds.), *Youth at high risk for substance abuse.* Washington, DC: U.S. Department of Health and Human Services.

Kumpfer, K.L. (1989). Promising prevention strategies for high-risk children of substance abusers. *Office for Substance Abuse Prevention High Risk Youth Update, 2*, 1–3.

Landreth, G. (1991). *Play therapy: The art of the relationship.* Muncie, IN: Accelerated Development.

Latham, M. (1988). *Relationship patterns of female offspring of alcoholics: An examination of intimacy and individualization in marriage.* Unpublished doctoral dissertation, Georgia State University, Atlanta.

Maton, K.I. (1987). Patterns and psychological correlates of material support within a religious setting: The bidirectional support hypothesis. *American Journal of Community Psychology, 15,* 185–207.

National Association for Children of Alcoholics. (1998). *Children of alcoholics: Important facts.* Rockville, MD: National Clearinghouse for Alcohol Information.

National Institute for Alcohol Abuse and Alcoholism. (1981). *Fourth special report to the U.S. Congress on Alcohol and Health from Secretary of Health and Human Services* (DHHS Publication No. ADM 81–1080). Washington, DC: U.S. Government Printing Office.

Oliver-Diaz, P. (1988). How to help recovering families struggle to get well. *Focus, 11*(2), 20–21, 49–50.

O'Rourke, K. (1990). Recapturing hope: Elementary school support group for children of alcoholics. *Elementary School Guidance and Counseling, 25,* 107–115.

Robinson, B.E. (1989). *Working with children of alcoholics: The practitioner's handbook.* Lexington, MA: Lexington Books.

Sher, K.J. (1987, December). *What we know and do not know about COAs: A research update.* Paper presented at the MacArthur Foundation Meeting on Children of Alcoholics, Princeton, NJ.

Sher, K.J. (1991). Psychological characteristics of children of alcoholics. *Alcohol Health and Research World, 21*(3), 247–254.

Sher, K.J., & Trull, T.J. (1994). Personality and disinhibitory psychopathology: Alcoholism and antisocial personality disorder. *Journal of Abnormal Psychology, 103*(1), 92–102.

Smith, A.W. (1990). *Overcoming perfectionism: The key to a balanced recovery.* Deerfield Beach, FL: Health Communications.

Steinglass, P. (1979). The alcoholic family in the interaction laboratory. *Journal of Nervous and Mental Disease, 167,* 428–436.

Steinglass, P. (1981). The alcoholic at home: Patterns of interaction in dry, wet, and transitional stages of alcoholism. *Archives of General Psychiatry, 8*(4), 441–470.

Sweeny, D. (1997). *Counseling children through the world of play.* Wheaton, IL: Tyndale House.

Van Fleet, R. (1994). Filial therapy for adoptive children and parents. In K. O'Conner & C. Schaefer (Eds.), *Handbook of play therapy: Advances and innovations* (Vol. 4, pp. 371–385). New York: Wiley.

Wegscheider, S. (1981). *Another chance: Hope and health for the alcoholic family.* Palo Alto, CA: Science and Behavior Books.

Werner, M.J., Joffe, A., & Graham, A.V. (1999). Screening, early identification, and office-based intervention with children and youth living in substance-abusing families. *Pediatrics, 103*(5), 1099–1112.

West, M.O., & Prinz, R.J. (1987). Parental alcoholism and childhood psychopathology. *Psychological Bulletin, 102*(2), 204–218.

Wilson, C., & Orford, J. (1978). Children of alcoholics: Report of a preliminary study and comments on the literature. *Journal of Studies on Alcohol, 39*(1), 121–142.

Windle, M. (1990). Temperament and personality attributes among children of alcoholics. In M. Windle & J.S. Searles (Eds.), *Children of alcoholics: Critical perspectives* (pp. 217–238). New York: Guilford Press.

Woodside, M. (1982). *Children of alcoholics.* Albany: New York State Division of Alcoholism and Alcohol Abuse.

CHAPTER 12

Playing the Unspeakable: Bereavement Programs in the School Setting

RUTHELLEN GRIFFIN

LITTLE IS written on the development of bereavement groups in schools. Writings focus on crisis-oriented, short-term support and recognition of behavioral and emotional responses by grieving children. Staff tolerance for behavioral and academic changes occurs early in the grieving process, but decreases as staff begin to believe it is time for the child "to get on with life" (Nelson-Feaver, 1996). Despite the reluctance and resistance to discuss death with children, staff and parents need education about this concept, the grief reactions of children, and the importance and helpfulness of ongoing support for grieving children.

The value of groups such as these is great. By allowing children to grieve and express feelings related to the deaths in their lives, a dialogue for healthy sharing and support among peers is encouraged. The sessions at times are educational, honestly answering questions and concerns children may have about rituals and processes related to death and illness. Providing children with correct information, not misinformation that might be supplied by their friends, decreases fears that may manifest physically and emotionally. Through participation in these groups, positive changes can occur. For example, body symptoms connected to feelings about the loss can quickly disappear; parents often see behavioral and relationship shifts happen as well.

216

These programs are preventative in nature. Helping children express feelings and experience support from others can only aid them in the future when these skills will be needed again. Together, children learn that their responses and feelings are valued and heard. Each may learn to respect the responses of others, to develop listening skills, and to help others in need when appropriate. Group members begin to possess the ability to empathize with, understand, and nurture one another.

Finally, in this child-appropriate forum, adults recognize and support children's vulnerability. Together, all explore the universality of death, the result being a decreased feeling of isolation related to our experience.

This chapter presents a group approach that uses play therapy and the creative arts therapies as vehicles for facilitating child bereavement programs in school settings. It explores important influences on group development, offers content to facilitators, and makes recommendations for involvement and communication with parents and school staff. Some successful techniques from this author's group experiences are cited.

GROUP PHILOSOPHY

An indirect approach to the subject of death and related feelings is developmentally appropriate for children. Symbol and metaphor used in play and the arts can at times create a safe distance and a nonthreatening language for exploration. This allows children to begin piece by piece to make sense of the personal and universal experience of death. With exciting materials and playful interactions, children's fear decreases while they experiment with the possibilities, impossibilities, wishes, and realities of their lives. Children are encouraged to participate in a supportive experience that provides the correct information and answers questions they have about death.

Warm-up techniques or "ice breakers" begin to pave the way for serious work. For example, when asked to line up according to height, size of feet or hands, or length of hair, the group constantly changes, and children discover that they have more in common with others than they realized. The categories are endless: everyone who is wearing white could stand in one area of the room, everyone wearing black in another part; anyone who had a pet die could stand in yet another spot. Questions can be posed about the pets: What were their names? When did they die and how? Stories and names begin to emerge as children list dogs, cats, horses, birds, lizards, fish, and turtles. One boy recounts how upset he was when his mother flushed his fish down the toilet; several children nod their head in understanding and sympathy. In response to "Anyone who has had a death in their family, come stand here," the entire group moves to that spot. This is a very powerful moment, as the children see they are not alone in their grief. As one child said, "I don't want anyone to have to go through what I did, but it sure feels good to know that other kids know how I feel."

Directly involved children begin to process their world by manipulating concrete materials and developing symbols and metaphors. They move their body to create an understanding of experiences and feelings that have been in the body, sometimes nameless and overwhelming. They become increasingly aware of their unconscious and share their story. Verbal processing is sometimes interwoven, but is not necessary; it may be extensive or minimal, depending on the developmental ability or willingness of the child.

This model supports individual as well as group expression. The therapist nonintrusively facilitates the group in its unfolding process as well as on the individual's terms. Each moment is spontaneously acknowledged and is led by the group in its unique process. One needs to trust the process and adopt the attitude that what is happening has meaning and is important to the group. At times, however, it may not be clear what is occurring! We help the children remain in unclear, uncomfortable, blank spaces, not knowing, and allow time for issues, feelings, and the creative to emerge. We don't jump in making our own metaphors or using words to fill space for the group. We help contain the group and stay with our uncomfortableness and theirs. For example, a group of seven children were moving creatively in the room; they moved in different directions, at various tempos, stretching high and low. I waited, watched, and listened. A boy slapped his hands together, saying "I killed it"; someone stomped on the floor, saying "There, I killed an ant." I stopped the group, saying, "The ant is dead. What will we do?" Someone said, "We'll have a funeral for the ant!" How do we have a funeral? They dug an imaginary hole, put the ant in a box, lowered it, and filled in the hole with shovels full of imaginary dirt. All were involved. Some picked flowers to strew on the grave; some cried. "There," said a boy, "the ant is buried. Now we need a stone." They made a stone that they engraved with fingers swirling in the air, then created a ceremony and memorial for the ant. We stopped moving and sat in a circle on the floor. I asked the children about their experiences in the cemetery or at the funeral. Stories tumbled out as they eagerly contributed personal details and questions about the process. By gently guiding the group and individual ideas, I helped them develop a story that had personal and group meaning.

Finally, honesty and openness are important aspects of this model (Carroll & Griffin, 1997, 2000). Children need to be given information on their level of understanding. Information should not be vague or misleading;

concrete words need to be used when explaining death; euphemisms such as "gone away" or "passed away" only confuse children. A story was told to me by the aunt of a 5-year-old whose grandmother had died. The little girl waited for her aunt to be present at the wake. She refused to move or talk to anyone else until she arrived. Upon arriving, her aunt sat next to her, asking the child, who was quite distressed, what was wrong. The child said, "They said she has gone away, but she hasn't gone anywhere— she's right here!" An adult's choice of words did not help this child become more clear about her experience. During these sessions, children are given permission to question and to express emotions. Supporting adults must be role models, demonstrating honesty and openness about their feelings of grief. Remember, this is an opportunity for children to share and to remember the deceased. By creating, participating, talking, and listening to others, they can begin to transform feelings, and gain control over an uncontrollable experience. Finally, permit bereaved children to heal in their own time. Their growth is a personal process that requires unique support.

ORGANIZING GROUPS: HOW TO BEGIN

Laying the groundwork for the formation of school bereavement groups is very important. Community and school counselors can work together to support each other and to ensure successful development of this project. Administrative support and approval are needed. It is vital to find staff who will follow through, assuring implementation of the group.

An initial meeting, with a written proposal outlining theory, philosophy, goals, referral process, projected population, methods, as well as a tentative outline for each group session, will help clarify information for discussion, encourage questions and planning. Recommendations made at this time for initial staff in-service and plans for in-services (and CEUs) can be presented. Education is paramount. During in-services, participants must be informed of the necessity to address grief and related issues in school. Making school personnel aware of the ways death can affect a child's ability to function academically and behaviorally in the classroom can help children and teachers. Staff need to know about the existence of groups. An explanation of the session's purpose, goals, and possible activities clarifies their appropriateness. All can be encouraged to make referrals to the school counselor (or social worker), who can screen the children. Staff need to know that group leaders are classroom resources who can answer questions and provide information and ideas when requested; these individuals can also provide further support when necessary. People should be discouraged from handling these situations on their own. All are encouraged to contact the school counselor, who will create a list of possible group members. The social worker or counselor may already have a list. Children should not be ruled out if there are no apparent "problems" despite the death or if the death is not recent.

A letter about the group is then sent to parents, with permission forms for involvement. Letters are followed up by phone calls one to two weeks after the mailing. Meetings for parents are scheduled before the beginning of the group. At these meetings, questions and concerns about the sessions can be addressed.

The school counselor is responsible for screening children and gathering basic history of children who attend the group. Intake forms can be developed or found in the literature (Fitzgerald, 1995). This may include a brief family history, information about the death/deaths in the family (who died, when, how, who told the child, whether the child attended the wake or funeral, and the nature of the relationship with the deceased). A short history with time frames related to other changes in the children's lives is helpful in determining the complexity of their grief. This could include other losses by death, separation/divorce of parents, moving, fires or thefts, job changes of parents, or deaths of pets. This can be followed by a behavioral checklist (Fitzgerald, 1995) that pinpoints areas of concern or change since the death(s) occurred. The initial collecting of data is more accurate and informative for parents and counselors if gathered with the child, parent, and counselor before the initial group meeting. It can serve also as a record of progress made at the end of eight sessions.

SCREENING

Together, counselors need to scrutinize referrals made to the group. At this time, counselors must consider whether each child is capable at this time of being in a group or whether in fact he or she needs individual counseling. Hyperactivity and behavioral problems need to be considered. All concerned need to determine if any child would disrupt the group making it unsafe for others; the result might be members' inability to focus in the sessions. Are behaviors related to the deaths that occurred or are they long-standing problems that need to be addressed elsewhere? Is bereavement a priority for this child? The maturity level of children also needs to be considered. Sometimes, 5-year-olds can participate in groups; sometimes, they need to wait until they are 6 or 7. These factors should be considered in conjunction with the number of referrals and possible configuration of group members. If a child requires more one-to-one help, you may consider finding another staff member or volunteer to participate in the group. Perhaps the group could be split into smaller groups and separate sessions. Leaders need to experiment with possibilities, while being flexible and adventuresome. Of course, all need to be realistic, tailoring groups according to the children's needs.

LOGISTICS

In-school bereavement groups ideally occur toward the end of the school day or after school. This ensures that children are not required to return directly to class to focus on schoolwork. However, groups at other times of the day are feasible, because group process includes winding down to make transitions easier. Sessions are 45 to 60 minutes for eight consecutive sessions. The children may repeat them as many times as deemed necessary by staff (sometimes, children do not want to leave). Ages of participants vary; schools, now separated into grammar and intermediate, creating reasonably spaced chronology. Children who have experienced a recent or not so recent loss by death and are able to be contained in the group are eligible. Group size can vary from five to eight children with two adult facilitators. This ensures the possibility that one-to-one intervention for behaviors, special work, or handling of unanticipated situations can occur. Ongoing observations of group and individual processes can also occur from two perspectives. The consistent space used for the group needs to be private.

A large "Do Not Disturb" sign should be placed on the door and all intruders need to be confronted or escorted from the room, if necessary. Ideally, the room should be somewhat contained, with as few distractions as possible (i.e., toys, equipment). This decreases the necessity of having to constantly control disruptive or off-task behavior. Facilitators can restructure the space, if necessary. Large spaces with high, echoing ceilings are not conducive to this format. Large spaces can be reorganized by marking clear boundaries. The school counselor is responsible for finding the space and for communicating with staff and administration about the privacy of this group area.

Basic materials for groups include balls of different sizes, textures, and weights; scarves, stretch bands, carpet squares, boom box, tapes, and CDs can be used for movement and games; construction paper, glue, scissors, crayons, markers, paints, yarn, and decorative materials are needed for art. Other miscellaneous supplies include carpet squares, puppets, small toys, stuffed animals, pillows, books and story tapes about death, shoe boxes, large envelopes, clay and equipment for pounding and squeezing, balloons, and plastic packing bubbles. More materials may be required if special projects are planned.

WHAT YOU NEED TO KNOW

To facilitate these groups in the most effective manner, there is much therapists need to be able to know or access. Facilitators must understand child development and child/adolescent bereavement/grief theory and identify the child's developmental process with regard to the understanding death. The therapist must have an ability to develop groups that are nonverbal, using therapies such as movement/dance, art, poetry, drama, music, and play. Working with symbols and metaphors that arise in these sessions and understanding and spotting nonverbal content that expresses issues and feelings help counselors understand the child's path toward healing. Counselors must know how these connect to theory and help to determine the therapeutic response. Besides this, the facilitators must be familiar with group process theory and its implementation. The result is an open-minded, accepting attitude that enables the adult to facilitate and support what arises. An ability to control behavior in groups is mandatory and usually learned through practice and experience. Personal experience with death, hospice programs, and the dying process allows one to be familiar and to empathize with a variety of death experiences; these experiences also increase one's ability to feel comfortable with the subject. One's attitudes about death, as well as personal red flags that are raised when various issues arise, need to be processed before the group begins, and should be revisited on an ongoing basis and analyzed with the objective eye of a supervisor, therapist, or peer group. Such preparation allows one to speak comfortably and directly about many death-related topics with children.

One needs to be familiar with and be able to answer questions about the dying process, types of death, medical terms, and procedures (e.g., murder, suicide, cancer, stroke, AIDS, bypass surgery, I.V., radiation). If you don't know, find a resource who can provide you with the answers you need. Therapists need to discuss traditions and rituals related to death, such as wakes, funerals, cremations, and burials. Children often want to know some information about processes performed by funeral directors. Familiarizing yourself with death-related terms such as casket, vault, cremation, morgue, burial, gravestone, cemetery, and corpse allows you to present and explain some of the vocabulary to children when the need arises. Facilitators should be familiar with a variety of materials, books, resources, toys, and possible activities for bereavement groups. Being able to create appropriate activities with the materials at hand allows the therapist to be spontaneous, creative, and appropriate in each moment.

Finally, for those providing support to bereaved children, we need to remember that we can't take the children's pain away. We can only help them with their process. Remember that you must also take care of yourself in this process. Give yourself time to debrief, incorporate activities and lifestyles that nurture and sustain you in your important and difficult work.

DIFFICULTIES TO OVERCOME

Often, in the process of creating bereavement groups in school, there are a number of issues that need to be dealt with and that may prevent the actual formation of groups. These include an overworked/stressed staff who feel they cannot take on another project or responsibility. Often, one sees much initial interest with no follow-through: staff appear enthusiastic, then ambivalent, sometimes evasive, not returning phone calls or responding to agreed time frames.

Some school systems prefer to "handle it themselves," denying the relief and need of outside help. This resistance might also be a reaction to grief, an unwillingness to broach this difficult topic, or an underlying belief that children should be protected from death ("Why open a Pandora's box?"). Some think if children say nothing, they are doing well. Staff may also believe that a bereavement program is not important, that this is not the role of school personnel, or that there should be a time limit as to when grieving children "should get on with their lives." Resistance may be related to lack of experience, education about death, or unresolved personal issues or fears that shape attitudes and approach to death.

Other glitches may occur, such as lack of administrative support or lack of understanding of the system by the outside agency or counselor. Space and funding continue to be problems to be resolved with a certain amount of persistence, grant writing or community support, and flexibility. At times, parents refuse to become involved, dropping off their child to be taken care of, not acknowledging their own grief or not allowing their child to become a part of these groups. Much of their resistance and many of their attitudes are similar to those previously stated.

CONTENT OF GROUPS

Group content varies according to the needs of individuals in the group (see Table 12.1 for an example). With each lasting 45 to 60 minutes, the first two sessions are devoted to bonding and trust building, introducing the topic of death and the person who died; sessions two through six focus on issues and feelings and stories connected to the death and the

Table 12.1

Sample 8-Week Bereavement Group

---

grammar school, 7 children

3:00 P.M.–4:00 P.M. (after school)

2 adults: school counselor and community bereavement specialist

SESSION 1

3:00–3:15	Snack (brought in by parents each week). Talking about why children are present, how long the group will last, rules of group (developed with children).
3:15–3:30	Ice breaker: learning names, favorite food, color, etc.; throwing ball—name of person who died, how they feel about being in the group.
3:30–3:50	Art project: draw something about themselves and share with the group.
3:50–4:00	Group circle: movement; How do you say good-bye with your body to group members? Group mirrors activity.

Give parents flyer *Children and Grief* (Carroll & Griffin, 2000).

SESSION 2

3:00–3:15	Snack; discussion: How was the week? What did people do? Reiterate rules.
3:15–3:30	Movement warmup: trying on peoples' movements or favorite exercises; refreshing reminder of people's names (look for any themes related to death that may arise).
3:30–3:40	Art: What is your favorite activity or food? What was the deceased's? Draw two pictures depicting these preferences. Share with the group.
3:40–4:00	Game "Shuffle Your Buns" and goodbye.

Homework: Ask people to bring next week pictures or mementos of those who have died. Remind parents when they pick the children up.

SESSION 3

3:00–3:15	Snack and sharing of pictures and mementos.
3:15–3:30	What kind of weather do you feel like today? Show with hand, then body, group guesses how each person feels.
3:30–3:50	Discussion or writing: Write the different feelings that a child could feel if someone in his or her family died. Read the pieces of paper, show faces that describe what the word means. Draw a picture that shows the kind of weather you felt like when the person in your family died. Share with the group.
3:50–4:00	Group movement: moving and freezing into goodbye statues.

Parent Homework: Wear an item that belonged to the deceased or bring a memento if you don't have an object to wear.

SESSION 4

3:00–3:15	Snack and sharing pieces of clothing and mementos.
3:15–3:30	Story: *A Terrible Thing Happened* by Margaret M. Holmes.

Table 12.1 *(Continued)*

3:30–3:50	Discussion of body symptoms children may experience after the death. Draw your body and on the inside put the symptoms that you felt. Share with the group. Do people have symptoms now? Discuss. What do you do to feel better?
3:50–4:00	Moving with scarves to music.

Parent Homework: Bring in favorite stuffed animal, blanket, or pillow.

SESSION 5

3:00–3:15	Snack and sharing stuffed animals.
3:15–3:30	Story: "The King Has Goat's Ears" (about secrets).
3:30–3:50	Do you have a secret about the death that occurred? Is there something you are afraid to say? Write it down or draw it on a piece of paper. Mix the papers up. Therapists hide all the papers, on the count of 3, children open their eyes, look for the secrets, bring them back to the circle, put them in a pile. Therapist reads them anonymously. Anyone ever feel like this? Raise your hand. Discussion.
3:50–4:00	Moving single body parts as fast as you can, then changing to slow motion.

Article for parents: On Children and Grief (Internet).

SESSION 6

3:00–3:15	Snack. Have people thought this week about the person who died? Does anyone have a favorite story about that person?
3:15–3:30	Movement improvisation: looking for themes that arise.
3:30–3:50	Using clay, make a scene about the death of the person in your life; share.
3:50–4:00	Bat the balloons, movement with balloons in group.

Parent-Child Homework: Make an Emotional First-Aid Kit; explain to parents and children; show example.

SESSION 7

3:00–3:15	Snack. Sharing of First-Aid Kits.
3:15–3:30	Creating safe places in the room.
3:30–3:50	In safe space, draw a picture of the place you go to feel good, what you do, what you might eat, the objects you use. Share.
3:50–4:00	Remind group next week is last session—"Memorial Search." What do they want to do? Hand sandwich.

Parent-Child Homework: Bring in pictures of person who died that could be used in a small personalized scrapbook.

SESSION 8

3:00–3:15	Snack. Remind that this is last session.
3:15–3:30	Goodbye dance: circle dance, connecting, taking turns leading, coming together, paring, jelly roll.
3:30–3:50	Make small decorated books, using pictures and artwork in memory of people who died. Share.
3:50–4:00	Circle saying goodbye, hand squeezing. What do you remember about the group? What did you like the most? What did you like the least?

deceased and education about death; finally, sessions seven and eight consider coping skills in the present and future. Memorials are created to those who have died, and participants say good-bye to each other. For example, making worry dolls out of clothespins or toothpicks, yarn, feathers, and other decorative materials for the children's use at home can create objects on which to displace their worries. The dolls can be named, their special powers of protection identified. We can enumerate the kinds of worries people might have since the deaths occurred. Worries such as the surviving parent dying, being afraid of the dark or of someone breaking into the house are not unusual for bereaved children. The dolls created are often ancient- and archetypical-looking; some are modeled after superheroes seen on TV. All are unique with amazing abilities.

According to Corr (1995) and Schonfield (1993), the number of death topics is vast: Their ideas include: the concept of death as universal, inevitable, unpredictable, irreversible, and nonfunctional; beginning to make sense of what happened; identifying, validating, expressing in constructive ways strong reactions to death; commemorating the life that was lived; to go on living and loving; coping skills; and considering some continued form of life.

CONCEPT OF DEATH

When observing the group, its individuals, and their developmental levels, one must identify which parts of the concept of death to explore. Group art projects and puppet shows can be powerful after reading stories or folk or fairy tales that include death. For example, some children created a story about a person who died suddenly in a car accident, how the family was told, how the family responded, and how the person was waked and buried. Puppets were named, one aspect of each person's story was included in this fictional puppet version. Many stories can be found that attempt to explain why death exists, or the nature of death itself. These stories can begin the group creative process that conjures images of death and may bring up many feelings for the children.

While moving creatively, children may explore the meaning of being dead or alive. They often play at being dead versus being alive. What does it mean to be dead? Some hold their breath for periods of time, only to realize that they are alive; some lie very still. Then we discuss the difference between being dead and alive.

Children have created a drama about the struggle between life and death using scarves of various colors to represent their concepts. White represents life or God, red or black the devil and death. They choose a metaphor and begin to create interactions between characters playing at life and death. Yet many adults believe children don't think about death! During this session counselors could introduce different thoughts about death for discussion with children. For example, is sleeping like being dead? Why is it different? The counselor needs to create and discuss both play and talk, which lead to more understanding.

Helping children to make sense of death is a long process. It is therapeutically important to repeatedly tell the story, play out the event and begin to put the experiences together to make a whole picture. The group hears stories, and each member remembers his or her own. Part of our job is to help the children break down these difficult experiences into digestible chunks. Ask them to remember a point in time during or after the death that sticks in their minds; then fold a piece of paper into six blocks to create in cartoon format what they remember clearly or not so clearly. Showing the story and pictures to the group, saying one thing about the process or picture may help children experience a very important beginning that accesses the pain, memories, or strong feelings. All are encouraged to be verbal or nonverbal; some may choose not to tell their story, but all are listening. The group leaders support all responses.

ADDRESSING FEELINGS

Validation of strong feelings can be done with simple body drawings: have children draw their body and how it felt the day of their person's death. The body knows what our consciousness does not; body symptoms may indicate something is not being expressed. Discuss the normalcy of the children's reaction and point out the similarities; these are important aspects of this process. What do these symptoms look like? If you became one symptom and danced like it, how would it dance? What would it sound like? If you could take it out, what size would it be? How would you take if out of your body? How would you show the group? How would it smell or taste? What would you do with it if you could? What color would it be? How would it feel in your hands? Encourage interaction with the symptom; explore it using different senses, not just the mind. What does that symptom have to say to you? Does it have advice? During this activity, symptoms are pulled out of the body with much effort and affect. Symptoms are found in stomachs, hearts, heads, and throats. The grief is sometimes gooey, dark and gray. It sticks to you when you touch it and then adheres to other parts of your body. Before you know it, you are covered with it and can't wipe it off. It is cold and sends chills through your body. It takes the group to unstick you. Some children want to flush it down the toilet, burn it, lock it in the closet, put it under the rug, or give it to people they don't like; others want to save it to look at when they feel like it. These metaphors are rich in feeling and meaning.

Follow the process, it always leads to the surprising, as demonstrated by this example of "the man with a thousand hearts." Children began drawing their symptoms in a large body, adding headaches, stomachaches, jittery feelings, and broken hearts—many broken hearts. Several boys (whose fathers had suddenly died from heart attacks) began drawing more and more hearts, saying "This man has a thousand hearts. That way, if one stops working every year he will be able to stay alive for a thousand years"—wishes for their fathers.

Commemorating the life that was lived can be difficult if a person died after a long illness. Sometimes it is hard to remember positive, healthy days. How was life with that person? Lives can be commemorated in group sessions by making bricks out of cardboard then painted in memory of the person who died. Create a brick wall with all those names and dates of birth and death. A wall of styled fluorescent bricks can be built and later can serve as a backdrop for a larger ceremony at the end of the group.

How do children cope? Many children will have developed their unique forms of coping. Providing children with an opportunity to share their techniques is helpful in the group. Trying out new ideas in the group supports the children's emerging healthy practices. Discuss, imagine, and draw safe places that children have at home or elsewhere. They can draw pictures of themselves in their beds at home, under beds, in closets, or in forts they make in the woods. Encourage children to use these quiet places to center themselves during difficult times. What objects or activities make you feel better? Have them bring these to the group to share. You can also make dream catchers or worry dolls. Identify who helps the children through difficult times. Help them develop a list of do's and don'ts for adults (their advice to us is "Not so much kissing!").

If the group decides to explore some aspect of continued life, one needs to remember that all religious beliefs need to be supported. This is often the first time children become aware that others have beliefs different from theirs. Some children are shocked and scandalized. Movement and dance are good media for exploring the concept of heaven, for example. Questions may be posed to encourage creative, thoughtful, and spontaneous responses: Where is heaven? What does it look like? What's there? How do you get there? What do you do when you are there? How does it feel? Do you have questions about it? What are the answers? What advice does heaven have for you? Follow the flow; the group interest will take you through the varied terrains and experiences, perhaps to a heaven with water bubblers or cloud escalators. The final question, of course, is How do we get back to Earth? We can't remain in heaven.

TRUST AND SAFETY

A creative climate for expression is developed while building a foundation of trust and safety. The environment, with clear, group-made rules, sets the stage for free expression. New group members can be included up to the second session. Children create bonds, begin to respect each other's responses, and are encouraged to listen and question. They are not allowed to become physically or verbally abusive; this often occurs with siblings and limits need to be enforced consistently.

The issue of trust is ongoing and tantamount to the development of the group process. Time must be taken with each group, but especially in the beginning of the session, for children to create group bonds and become acquainted with each other as well as with adults in the group. The purpose of the group, topics that may be covered, and general format must be made clear, along with the rules. Questions are encouraged and answered honestly.

By simply throwing a variety of balls of different sizes and weights or surprising objects (e.g., scarf, rubber chicken, stuffed animal) to people in the group, calling their names and making eye contact, begins to acknowledge the developing bonds. Use sound, eye contact, and movement. During one group, we asked students to show us unique movements they could make with their faces. Children crossed their eyes, touched their tongue to their nose, giggled, and laughed. We all tried these funny faces, laughed, and became closer. Asking personal and impersonal questions of each child while throwing the ball encourages spontaneous participation. What's your favorite food? Color? Hobby? What do you hate to eat? All aim at breaking the ice and newness in the group.

Initially, children are told that their contributions are voluntary. If they would like to "pass," it's OK. This rule is usually tested very quickly in groups. For several meetings, two brothers chose to respond to most questions posed about their father's sudden death by saying "That's classified/top secret information." It was quite some time before they were able to express their pain outwardly.

Group "trust temperament" can be measured during trust-building activities in which children's reactions and interactions on a nonverbal level can be observed and assessed. If one or two children shove or disrupt group functioning, I recommend proceeding cautiously, until trust is established. For example, in a trust circle, all were standing with shoulders close; one at a time, each person, with his or her eyes closed, was passed around the group. An 8-year-old girl consistently shoved people into the middle of the circle and was unable to let the group pass her gently back and forth; another boy had no interest in supporting others in the group and would have let the child fall on the floor when passed to him. This lack of trust and ability to support need to be acknowledged, talked about in the group, and modeled for the children. Adults are encouraged to be actively involved in the group process and activity. The metaphors experienced in this activity are core elements of group support: helping to hold each individual through group support and cooperation by listening, being attentive, respectful, and caring, while each individual allows the group to support his or her weight. The child doesn't have to stand up by himself or herself during this process.

Why proceed cautiously? Why trust? What happens when trust is not established and assured? Children withdraw, and may begin off-task discussions and behaviors; sometimes conflicts break out in the group. When these behaviors occur, the group is not able to explore the topics effectively. In contrast, when too much is revealed too soon, anxiety in the group can increase, resulting in a shutting down of group members and a decrease in the development of group process. A girl of 7 burst into the group during the first session, revealing everything about the very recent death of her grandfather. She repeated this the second session, shutting down in the third, after which she dropped out of the group. When she left, we had to begin again for the remaining fearful group members.

"Do Not Disturb" signs should be posted on the door and interruptions should be discouraged. A consistent space, that is, the same room, makes the group feel safer; the children begin to feel safe and take comfort in the predictable after having been in an out-of-control, unexpected situation with the deaths that occurred.

The group and the individuals are encouraged to go to the edge of their difficulty. This can then be relieved by retreat into a place of safety and less revealing or threatening activity. A 7-year-old was asked to draw a picture about the time she was told that her mother had died from cancer. She was able to talk about it for a short period, but was unable or unwilling to draw what was said and her reactions. She could, however, draw a picture about things she did with her dad later that day, after she had been told about her mother's death: they played cards, checkers, and basketball. Too much anxiety in the group will decrease the likelihood of involvement and disclosure. Children need to return home or to class in one piece, feeling in control of their emotions. At the end of especially anxious sessions, release activities can help shift the focus and relieve tension. Jumping on plastic packing pillows or breaking small plastic packing bubbles with hands and fists is fun and requires focus and use of one's whole body. The children love this activity, and it helps transition to leaving.

Ongoing awareness of the group's ability to feel safe needs to be gauged by the facilitators. Appropriately nurturing, less-threatening activities may at times need to be introduced. This may reflect the group's reluctance to continue with difficult topics. For example, a tug of war between the children and adults naming each side Yes or No may be an appropriate metaphor. It decreases fear in the group by being less direct and requiring the use of the entire body to release tension. These types of groups can become dances of advance and retreat do not forge ahead with a predetermined plan.

RESISTANCE

If necessary, acknowledgment and support of resistance to involvement in the group needs to be immediately addressed and explored. One can directly ask children how they feel about coming to the group, or simply ask them to anonymously write on a piece of paper how they feel about being present. Pieces might be wadded up, folded, then placed or thrown in the middle of the circle; a volunteer then reads the papers, asking people to raise their hands if they feel that way. Often, children say that they do not want to be present. This was obvious in the case of two brothers, who literally sidestepped into the room, their backs on the wall in the hall. In the room they proceeded to stand in a corner, refusing to participate; they reported having headaches and stomachaches. Other children may not want to discuss painful experiences and refuse to respond in any way to requests of the group. In the case of two sisters, until we found a metaphor that reflected their unwillingness to share, little sharing was done. These girls responded to my request and metaphor that they make a fort to protect themselves. They proceeded to build a fort from furniture and blankets in the room. It was barricaded and only they could see out through peepholes. No one could see in; they protected themselves. When people came too close to the barricade, the girls threw wads of paper at the "attackers."

Reluctance to be involved can be demonstrated in many ways: disruptive behavior, off-topic discussion, changing the topic, continued "passing," refusal to share or be involved, withdrawal or seeming boredom, appearing not to hear, pairing with others to create conflict in the group, or seeing adults in the group as enemies.

MAINTAINING CONTROL
IN THE GROUP

Euphoria is not an unusual reaction by children when they discover they are allowed to express their feelings. However, euphoria can often escalate, making it hard for them to return to more difficult, focused responses. It can also create an unsafe climate, where individuals can get hurt and others may withdraw; this is not a climate that encourages vulnerability. Therefore, certain environmental structures and activities can be easily applied within a larger space to help control the group. Letting children choose their "spot" with carpet squares or masking tape boundaries assures the counselor that the children will return to their spots as the group's energy begins to escalate. Directing the children to freeze into feeling statues, statues on the ground, or statues on their spot helps. Asking them to move like lead, molasses, or a heavy weight, using their entire body or just certain body parts, or pretend being stuck on the ground by glue or Velcro shifts the energy. These experiences can be translated into feelings related to the death in their family. Did anyone feel very heavy and tired after the person in their family died? What would this statue look like? How would it move? What feeling do you feel when you are heavy and slow? Does anyone feel this way today? Make a group statue; try to move as a heavy, tired group, then freeze into a statue when the facilitator says freeze. Part of the group can observe, learning that feelings can be expressed in different manners.

Containing the group in part of the room may be necessary in large spaces with high, echoing ceilings. At different times, the group can be broken into pairs or smaller groups that later return to the larger group. Doing an activity on the floor or eliciting early developmental movement such as crawling or rolling can literally ground children. Moving from large to small shapes on the floor can be explored as a movement metaphor expressing how small they may have felt at the time of the death. The use of pillows, stuffed animals, and blankets in which to wrap up creates a safe, contained, nurturing space. Kids love playing baby, sucking their thumb, talking baby talk, throwing baby temper tantrums, curling into a fetal position; these are all acceptable ways to regress, to express feelings by returning to their centers and safe places in difficult times. Punishment is not a way to control these groups. However, specific rules need to be consistently reinforced. Individuals may be requested to sit in a specific place in the room until they are able to return to the group.

EXPRESSION OF STRONG FEELINGS

When children follow directions and listen, a climate of safety is developed in the group. Only then can we begin to work with strong feelings. Clear guidelines (with the help of the group) need to be stated when implementing activities that access anger, for example. We must create an opportunity for children to express strong feelings in constructive and safe ways. The expressions need to be specific, focused, and contained. For example, ask children to write on pieces of paper what made them mad about the death in their families, then ask them to put the paper in a balloon into which the feeling is blown; then the balloon is blown up and tied. The metaphor in this activity is obvious. Ask children to bat the balloons around, then one by one to jump on the balloons, while each person is instructed to think about what made him or her mad. All individuals are requested to read what was written. A discussion on the topic or general consensus as to who also felt this way can be determined by raising hands for those who prefer not to talk or discuss. Examples of statements written on these papers have included "I'm mad he didn't take care of himself"; "I'm mad he's dead"; "I'm mad the doctors didn't save his life like they are supposed to"; "It should have been someone else."

RETURNING TO THE CLASSROOM

Counselors need to make time to help shift the group and to transition smoothly to the classroom or home. This way, children can experience some control of their emotions. Cool-downs or predictable rituals developed by the group can be nurturing, welcoming, and calming at the end of a session. For example, by making a "hand sandwich" and stacking hands on top of each other; the hands may float up and away to wave good-bye. By slowing down breathing in the group; or by pairs sitting with their backs against each other, the counselor can instruct the children to breathe together or to focus on their breath, which then brings the children to a calmer center. Acknowledging good-bye verbally or nonverbally with sound and creative waves, which are mirrored playfully, will help set the scene for leaving. Use a check-in at the end of the group by asking for one word that describes today's group; children then reflect their experiences of feelings, activities, and group process. We sum up the experience quickly and spontaneously. Making a sound that expresses how children feel at that moment can be revealing. Creating a special group wave or handshake reflects all parts of the whole. The focus changes from internal to external. Ask kids to look at people while holding hands in a circle, then pass the squeeze; this can signal the end of the session. All members might be asked to talk about what they will be doing that night or even in the next hour.

COMMUNICATING WITH PARENTS
AND STAFF AT SCHOOL

The issue of confidentiality in children's groups arises repeatedly. How can one maintain contact with adults and provide helpful ideas and information that can be used with the children in other settings? Initial contact with parents must be informative and clear. Often, parents need to be assured that this will be a safe situation and that it will not traumatize their child. Parents can be provided with handouts containing a description of the group, the tentative plan for upcoming sessions, and an explanation of the group philosophy. Questions need to be encouraged and answered honestly. Brochures may be developed that provide helpful information. Parents should be informed that these groups are confidential and that, unless there are reasons for all to be concerned, they will not be told verbatim what the child has said, but that the child will be informed and/or consulted about facilitators speaking with parents. Behavioral intake forms that are pre- and postassessments can be completed with the child and parent.

"Homework" is given to group members, and parents are encouraged to become involved in this process. This could include making an Emotional First-Aid Kit (developed by M.L. Carroll, 1995, Camp Jonathan). What things do you need to be comforted after the death of a person in your family? Children have included Harry Potter books, special quilts made by family members, their blankets, computer games, pictures of family members, and special objects given to them by someone they love. Children may be asked to wear an item of clothing or to bring in pictures or items that belonged to the deceased. One boy brought in his father's large T-shirt; he said he sleeps in it every night and if he smells it closely, it smells like his father. The presence of hands-on, concrete items again brings up feelings and stories for all involved.

Parents can be given short explanations of activities done in groups. Discussion at home should be encouraged. The importance of parental involvement needs to be emphasized. This can be very difficult for the parents, who are grieving themselves.

Weekly handouts to parents (and school staff) should be short and informative. They could include articles on bereaved children (Carroll & Griffin, 1997), the child's developmental understanding of death (Seager & Spencer, 1996), a brochure on children and grief (Carroll & Griffin, 2000), what to do on holidays, or topics of interest from parents and staff. Many appropriate articles can be found on the Internet.

Open, ongoing discussion of home and school behavior as well as affect needs to be encouraged. Adults can be encouraged to voice their observations, hunches, and feelings. Counselors can help to explain what parents report by explaining child development and children's grief literature, and making suggestions for home. Wrap-up meetings with parents, upon completion of the group, can answer questions and concerns. Facilitators can at that time make further recommendations or referrals. The postscreening test can also be completed and discussed at this time. Parents and staff need to be informed that these groups are often just the beginning for children and that their grief work will continue with different time frames and on different levels as they mature.

OTHER WAYS TO BE INVOLVED IN SCHOOLS

Death and grief are not popular topics in schools or in our culture in general. However, discussion needs to be more open. Educating staff about the child's grief can help children and adults move forward in life. Kids who have not been directly affected by death can learn; some day, death will be an experience for them, too. Large gaps in awareness and information can be filled in with facts that can decrease fears and dissolve myths about death. For example, a 7-year-old boy was convinced that his father had been buried alive because he had been found by him with his eyes open after he had died. His 7-year-old friend confirmed this information. He had difficulty believing our information that contradicted that of his friend. Staff in-services that provide information in the schools about grief and children's reactions are necessary. Ways to interact with students who have experienced a death and how to use their classmates' involvement could be invaluable. Teachers can share what has been done by peers and at other schools. In-services can include staff's personal reactions to death and attempt to help staff reflect on their ability or willingness to provide support for grieving children.

Health classes in high schools can include a section on life and death. Students need to be encouraged to openly share reactions, concerns, questions, and philosophies. Poignant collages have been created by high school students that reflect the distress they feel related to personal losses as well as to loss as a result of war, famine, and disaster. Education can be provided about funeral parlors, cremation, cemeteries, burials, and the dying process. Trips can be taken to funeral homes and cemeteries to educate and to stimulate discussion.

Initially, individual counseling services should be provided to children who cannot function well in a bereavement support group. Counselors can provide ongoing support for the children while explaining the process to counseling staff. Talks to PTAs aimed at parent education and support of programs such as these can begin to open this often avoided topic to more individuals.

SUMMARY AND CONCLUSIONS

Honesty, openness, and lack of secrecy on the topic of death needs to be encouraged in schools. The universality of death needs to be acknowledged and discussed. It is our duty to be child advocates, educating children about this important aspect of life. Discussion with schools about the reluctance to broach these topics needs to be approached gently.

The presence of supportive adult role models is essential. Adults must help children process grief and its experiences while providing information. Children should not rely on peers for support and information. These role models do not have to be the parents, who may also be grieving and may not be emotionally available at the time.

Many difficult situations can be seen as opportunities for learning, the beginning of self-reflection, and creative expression. Protecting children is not helpful; it often confuses them and distorts their perceptions of reality. Can we really prevent children from learning about death? Is there really an opportune time to discuss death?

A young boy, whose father had committed suicide, was not told by his mother. Several years passed and he began making up facts of his father's death. His stories were quite distressing. All adults were upset, yet no one would tell him what happened. The child was criticized for what was not explained to him by adults. How will this continue to affect this child? Wouldn't the difficult truth have been better for everyone in the long run? Children are already familiar with aspects of death—from nature, TV, the news, and computer games. This is not an unfamiliar topic to young minds.

Finally, education, expression, and support lead to prevention. Children begin to learn to express difficult feelings (that they don't have to fear) in safe ways. Children learn about the facts related to death and as a result become less fearful. As adults, they will cope with and process difficult situations in communicative and successful ways. In short, educate parents, staff, and children, and all can continue to grow.

To do this, we need to be open to a number of difficult questions: Why aren't services being provided? What do we fear? What is our culture's influence on this dilemma? What is important in our lives? How does evading this topic actually affect one's ability to function and relate? And, most important, how can these services be provided?

REFERENCES

Carroll, J. (1995). Non-directive play therapy with bereaved children. In S. Smith & M. Pennells (Eds.). *Interventions with bereaved children.* Great Britain: Athenaeum Press.

Carroll, M.L., & Griffin, R. (1997). Reframing life's puzzle: Support for bereaved children. *American Journal of Hospice and Palliative Care, 14,* 231–238.

Carroll, M.L., & Griffin, R. (2000). *Children and grief.* Litchfield, CT: Friends of Hospice.

Corr, C.A. (1995). Children's understanding of death: Striving to understand death. In K.J. Doka (Ed.), *Children mourning, mourning children* (pp. 3–16). Washington, DC: Hospice Foundation of America.

Doka, K.J. (1999). *Living with grief at school: A practical guide for schools.* Washington DC: Hospice Foundation of America.

Doka, K.J. (2000). *Living with grief: Children adolescents and loss.* Washington DC: Hospice Foundation of America.

Fitzgerald, H. (1995). Developing and maintaining children's bereavement groups: Part Two. *Thantos, 20*(4), 20–23.

Grollman, E. (1995). Grieving children: Can we answer their questions? In K.J. Doka (Ed.), *Children mourning, mourning children.* Washington, DC: Hospice Foundation of America.

Holmes, M.M. (2000). *A terrible thing happened.* Washington, DC: Magination Press.

Nelson-Feaver, P. (1996). Be tolerant to grief in the classroom. *Thantos, 21*(2), 16–17.

Schonfield, D.J. (1993). Talking with children about death. *Journal of Pediatric Health Care.*

Seager, K., & Spencer, S. (1996). *Meeting the bereavement needs of kids in patient families: Not just playing around.* Waterlook, IA: Ceder Valley Hospice.

Silverman, P., & Worden, W. (1992). Children's reactions in the early months after the death of a parent. *American Journal of Orthopsychiatry, 2*(1).

Stevenson, R. (1995). The role of the school: Bereaved students and students facing life-threatening illness. In K. Doka (Ed.), *Children mourning, mourning children* (pp. 97–111). Washington DC: Hospice Foundation of America.

Tait, D., & Depta, J. (1993). Play therapy group for bereaved children. In N. Webb (Ed.), *Helping bereaved children: A handbook for practitioners* (pp. 169–185). New York: Guilford Press.

Ward-Zimmer, D. (1999). Grief as a metaphor for healing. Paper presented at the Dying and Grieving Horizons of Hope conference, Springfield, MA.

CHAPTER 13

Use of Play Therapy
for Anger Management
in the School Setting

BARBARA A. FISCHETTI

CONTROL OF anger has become increasingly prominent in the news media. Shootings by children and adolescents in Arkansas, Colorado, Kentucky, Michigan, Mississippi, Oregon, and Pennsylvania demonstrated the effects of uncontrolled anger in school settings. The loss of life precipitated by angry youth has led to a nationwide search for its causes and effective interventions to offer children and adolescents to stem the tide of future violence.

The literature suggests that there are approximately 6 to 9 million youngsters in the United States with serious mental health problems (Friedman, Katz-Leavy, Manderscheid, & Sondheimer, 1996; Lavigne et al., 1996). Brandenburg, Friedman, and Silver (1990) noted that the prevalence rate of emotional disorders in our youth ranges from approximately 14% to 22%.

The 1999 Surgeon General's report to the nation emphasized that childhood is an important time to offer preventive services to children. Prevention would include reduction of risk, prevention of onset, and early intervention (Surgeon General, 1999). In spite of these recommendations, Roberts (1994) noted that most children in need of psychological services did not receive treatment. Burns et al. (1995) noted that only one in five children with serious mental health issues were involved in treatment.

The 1997 Youth Risk Behavior Surveillance System (YRBSS) conducted by the Centers for Disease Control and Prevention (1998) highlighted the prevalence of suicide, attempted suicide, and weapons or threats at school. This survey, completed by 16,262 students across the nation, indicated that 20.5% of students had seriously considered suicide, 15.7% had made a plan, and 7.7% had attempted suicide. The Surgeon General (1999) noted that suicide is the third leading cause of adolescent deaths. With respect to school violence, the survey found 4% of students missed school because they felt unsafe, 8.5% of students had carried a weapon to school, 7.4% had been threatened or injured at school, 14.8% had been in a physical fight at school, and 32.9% had property stolen or damaged at school. The Mott Foundation (1996) noted that homicide was the second leading cause of death for 15- to 24-year-olds. All of these statistics illustrate the reason for the nation's concern with children's and adolescents' inability or difficulty with anger management.

Additionally, 3% to 5% of children are diagnosed with Attention-Deficit/Hyperactivity Disorder (ADHD; Wolraich, Hannah, Pinnock, Baumgaertel, & Brown, 1996). This behavioral disorder can be highlighted by impulsivity and hyperactivity that can make anger management difficult for children and adolescents. Finally, children who experience disruptive disorders such as Oppositional Defiant Disorder (ODD) and Conduct Disorder (CD) demonstrate aggressive behaviors such as disobedience, defiance, physical fighting, and loss of temper. Prevalence rates for ODD have been noted to fall between 1% and 6% and for CD between 1% and 4% (Shaffer et al., 1996).

In spite of the need for early and effective treatment of children and adolescents for ameliorating anger, Thomas and Holzer (1999) emphasized that there is a shortage of trained clinicians to meet this demand. Burns et al. (1995) found that 70% of children received treatment for emotional difficulties from the schools. Catron and Weiss (1994) found improved treatment access by offering services in the schools. Hoagwood and Erwin (1997) supported that schools were the primary site for the delivery of mental health services.

In light of the research advocating mental health services in the schools and the prevalence of mental health issues involving anger management, play therapy offers the school clinician and children a viable service delivery system to ameliorate anger. Landreth (1991) emphasized the importance of school personnel (school psychologists, school counselors, and school social workers) utilizing play therapy for elementary school children. He described play therapy in terms of its assistance in helping children be available for learning.

Individual and group counseling of students in schools by school psychologists, school counselors, and school social workers utilizing play therapy techniques for anger management provides children the opportunity to work through issues, learn new skills, and meet with greater academic success. School clinicians also provide family treatment that can help the child and the family in the home environment. Very often, treatment is of short duration due to staffing in the schools and is directly related to the difficulty impeding academic learning. Play therapy techniques helpful to the therapeutic process with children and adolescents include but are not limited to child-centered play therapy, release play therapy, game play therapy, cognitive-behavioral play therapy, role playing, relaxation training, and play utilizing the media of paint, clay, balls, social skill training, and specific anger management activities.

REFERRAL FOR COUNSELING IN THE SCHOOLS

Children with anger management problems are usually easily recognizable in the schools. Referrals are generated by parents, discipline records, teacher referrals, self-referrals, and child study or special education teams. Behaviors commonly associated with anger management issues include physical aggression, impulsivity, peer difficulties, poor social skills, and, at times, poor academic performance. Children manifesting these difficulties are often found in the principal's office or absent from recess or a fun activity. Teachers often utilize behavior management techniques, consultation with school personnel, instructional changes in the classroom, and parent conferencing to intervene with angry behaviors. If these interventions do not bring about behavioral and academic change, a referral is often made to counseling personnel in the schools.

The school clinician often observes the students in the classroom or the general school environment prior to meeting them. The clinician may log inappropriate behaviors to establish a baseline prior to school and counseling interventions. The clinician then obtains all available information relative to the anger difficulties manifested in school. Parents are interviewed to assess behavior at home and obtain developmental information. The school clinician may also work with the parents in developing a home program. The child is then interviewed to obtain his or her perception of the school difficulties. After all relevant information is gathered, the school clinician with the help of the school team generates an intervention plan for the student. This plan is always shared with parents and the referred student. If the plan includes counseling, written parental permission is obtained as well as verbal student permission.

Whenever play therapy techniques are to be utilized with elementary school children, the book *A Child's First Book about Play Therapy* (Nemiroff & Annunziata, 1990) or *The Special Playroom: A Young Child's Guide to Play*

Therapy (Gilfix & Heller Kahn, 1999) is read to or with the student. This provides for a smooth transition to the therapy process and encourages the student to ask questions relative to the therapy experience. For students at the secondary level, a discussion is held regarding the treatment process to encourage their participation and ease their transition to counseling.

COUNSELING IN THE SCHOOLS

Many schools have a playroom that allows the school clinician to work with a child utilizing play techniques. Very often, this room is the clinician's office that has been adapted to foster play as a therapeutic agent for children. One standardized play therapy approach for children is not effective in the schools. Time elements, client issues, and school structures significantly impact a clinician's ability to provide play therapy for students in the schools. A prescriptive approach enables the school clinician to specifically prescribe intervention(s) that address a child's emotional issues. This prescriptive approach to play therapy has been advocated by Dr. Charles Schaefer (Oliver James, 1997). The following approaches to play therapy are useful for planning treatment for children demonstrating anger management issues.

CLIENT-CENTERED PLAY THERAPY

For the clinician who has the opportunity to provide children with time to pursue their issues and personal growth, client-centered play therapy offers a viable choice of treatment. Axline (1969) highlighted the importance of the basic tenets of nondirective play therapy for use in the schools. Children are seen weekly for approximately 45 minutes. This approach can also be utilized in conjunction with group counseling and parent counseling techniques.

Client-centered play therapy has at its core the belief that children have the inner capacity for self-actualization. The therapist develops a relationship with the child that promotes and assists the child in his or her search for emotional growth. This therapeutic approach was originally introduced by Carl Rogers (1951) and further developed for children by Axline (1947) and Dorfman (1951). The play therapist needs to create a strong relationship with the child that is safe and secure. This fosters a therapeutic relationship in which the child can experience negative emotions and pursue growth. Three key features to this approach are limits, toys, and the therapist's role. Perry (1993) provided a complete description of this approach.

CASE EXAMPLE

A boy who had been sexually molested was demonstrating aggressive behaviors in school. Classroom management techniques were not successful in ameliorating or reducing the aggression demonstrated in the classroom and in the general school environment. Coordinating with the outside therapist, the school clinician provided weekly play therapy sessions designed to allow the child to work through his anger at school. This student frequently utilized the Bobo doll, drawing, and other toys to displace his anger toward the perpetrator. After the initial sessions, he began to produce drawings depicting bombing the assailant. A reduction of aggressive behaviors was noted in the classroom and school environment. This child continued to participate in play sessions for the remainder of the school year. As the school year progressed, he expressed more positive themes and seemed to be experiencing all parts of the self. The aggressive behaviors previously noted were not evident the succeeding school year.

RELEASE PLAY THERAPY

This type of play therapy was originally developed by Levy (1938) and extended by Hambidge (1955) as structural play therapy. The goal of this therapy is to assist the client in reenacting a stressful event. This fosters the child's ability to work through the event and release the anger or pain associated with it. Landreth (1991) noted three forms of activities for release play therapy: "(1) release of aggressive behavior in throwing objects or bursting balloons or release of infantile pleasures in sucking a nursing bottle; (2) release of feelings in standardized situations such as stimulating feelings of sibling rivalry by presenting a baby doll at a mother's breast; (3) release of feelings by recreating in play a particular stressful experience in a child's life" (p. 30).

This type of play therapy can be selected for children who have experienced a stressful event that resulted in the demonstration of anger at school and home. The number of sessions is dependent on the youngster's ability to benefit from the therapeutic process. These sessions are offered weekly for approximately 45 minutes; sessions can be offered more frequently as needed.

CASE EXAMPLE

An elementary school bus was involved in an accident on the way to school. The driver was killed and most students were taken to the hospital by ambulance. The youngsters were initially seen as a group and the medium of drawing was utilized to begin the process of integrating the experience. Individual play sessions were planned for each student as necessary. One student began to demonstrate aggressive behavior toward his peers and siblings after the accident and to experience nightmares. For this student, the opportunity to reenact the bus accident and the discussion of the feelings associated with the accident significantly helped to reduce the anger demonstrated in school and the nightmares at home.

COGNITIVE-BEHAVIORAL PLAY THERAPY

This type of play therapy is based on both cognitive and behavioral theories of emotional development (Knell, 1993). Behavioral therapy utilizes the concepts of antecedents, reinforcers, contingencies, and social learning theory; cognitive therapy helps children learn to change their own behavior, change cognitions, and become part of their own treatment. The therapist and the child develop goals for treatment. The therapist selects play materials and activities that will facilitate the meeting of the therapy goals. Braswell and Kendall (1988) described the methods utilized by this approach to include modeling, role playing, and behavioral techniques.

For individual counseling of students with disruptive behaviors, Bodiford-McNeil, Hembree-Kigin, and Eyberg (1996) developed a 12-session model of short-term cognitive-behavioral play therapy. This approach utilizes behavioral and cognitive techniques that includes systematic desensitization, positive reinforcement, shaping, differential reinforcement of other behavior, modeling, self-monitoring, recording dysfunctional thoughts, confronting irrational beliefs, and bibliotherapy. Play therapy process skills as well as strategies for managing disruptive behavior are also part of this therapeutic approach. The 12-session format contains a child's work and play activity as part of the therapy structure. Additionally, homework is assigned after each therapy session. Finally, parents are taught play skills and conduct special play sessions with their child on a daily basis.

CASE EXAMPLE

A child was referred for counseling due to impulsive behaviors demonstrated in the classroom and on the playground. The child's impulsivity resulted in disagreements with peers, temper tantrums when the child did not get his way on the playground, aggressive behavior, whining, and tattling on peers. The child's parents noted negative behaviors at home that included physical aggression with siblings and neighborhood children, frequent breaking of household rules, and sleep difficulties.

The child was seen for 12 treatment sessions; each session lasted approximately 45 minutes. In keeping with the previously described

Table 13.1

Sample Play Therapy Sessions Treatment

Session 1	Discussion of treatment goals with the child; read the book, *A Child's First Book about Play Therapy.*
Session 2	Week in review: began to identify feelings; played the Talking, Feeling, and Doing game.
Session 3	Week in review: practiced "I feel . . ." statements; began to identify when angry times occurred and what happened at these times.
Session 4	Week in review: read the book *Sometimes I Like to Fight, But I Don't Do It Much Anymore;* played the Feelings game.
Session 5	Week in review: made feelings thermometer; identified events or triggers of anger.
Session 6	Week in review: learned the "count to 10" and other anger management techniques; played the Anger Control game.
Session 7	Week in review: completed the Who's Responsible for Feelings? activity; read the book *The Very Angry Day Amy Didn't Have.*
Session 8	Week in review: learned the steps to decision making; played the game Breaking the Chains of Anger.
Session 9	Week in review: role-played triggers or events that lead to anger management difficulties and utilized appropriate anger management techniques; played game of student's choice.
Session 10	Week in review: student selected a play medium to demonstrate an understanding of feelings and an appropriate response to these; played game of student's choice; began to discuss termination.
Session 11	Week in review: taught the student progressive relaxation techniques; utilized playhouse to share anger management difficulties at home and a resolution to them.
Session 12	Week in review: review of previous sessions with emphasis on steps to decision making, identification of feelings, anger triggers, and techniques to utilize in anger management situations; read the termination part of the book *A Child's First Book about Play Therapy.*

Table 13.2

Sample Additional Play Therapy Treatment Sessions

Session 13	Reviewed with parent the concepts of developmental tasks and reflective listening. Observed a 10-minute play session between the parent and child and provided feedback. Homework for the session: Play for 10 minutes each day with the child and complete practice sessions 2 and 3 from manual.
Session 14	Reviewed with parent the concepts of reinforcement, parent messages, and structuring. Observed 10-minute play session and gave feedback. Homework: Continue play session daily and complete practice sessions 4, 5, and 6. Began the discussion of termination with parent.
Session 15	Reviewed play therapy techniques of limit setting, consequences, and setting rules with parent. Observed 10-minute play session between parent and child and provided feedback. Homework for the session: Play with child daily for 10 minutes and complete practice session 8 Selecting the Proper Response. Continued the discussion of termination.
Session 16	Reviewed previously taught play techniques. Observed 10-minute play session between parent and child and gave feedback to parent. Celebrated termination. Homework: Continue daily play sessions.

short-term treatment approach, each session contained a child's work and a child's play segment. An additional four sessions were held with the child and parent to begin the process of teaching the parent play skills and providing coaching to assist in their development. Table 13.1 offers a description of each session.

The four additional play sessions were designed to teach the parent skills to work with the child at home in daily play sessions (see Table 13.2). Skill development emphasized reflective listening, parent messages, structuring, limits, rule setting, and consequences and was based on the work of Louise Guerney (1978). Exercises for homework were selected from the book, *Parenting: A Skills Training Manual* (Guerney, 1978).

SUMMARY OF INDIVIDUAL PLAY THERAPY TECHNIQUES

Each referral for anger management difficulties requires the development of a treatment approach specifically designed to address the referral questions. When planning treatment interventions, there are a plethora of play therapy techniques that can be helpful to the therapeutic process. Play therapy techniques useful for anger management difficulties can be found in *101 Favorite Play Therapy Techniques* (Kaduson & Schaefer, 1997). Examples of play therapy techniques described in this book include: The Rosebush, Beat the Clock, Tearing Paper, The Anger Shield and Knocking Down the Walls of Anger. Each technique offers the client an opportunity to address and work through anger management issues specific to his or her development. The therapist selects play activities which will facilitate the therapeutic process.

Many of the aforementioned play therapy techniques as well as others can be useful for individual as well as group counseling. The school clinician selects appropriate techniques relative to the treatment goals of the child or children. Teachers are often helpful in assisting the student with generalizing new behaviors. Stop-and-think steps or steps to decision making are often posted in the classroom and children are prompted to utilize these steps in situations that provoke anger difficulties in the classroom, the cafeteria, and on the playground.

Games, toys, and books that are useful for practice of anger management issues are available from the Creative Therapy Store at (800) 648-8857 and ChildsworkChildsplay at (800) 962-1142.

GROUP COUNSELING IN THE SCHOOLS

Many school systems offer group counseling to students demonstrating anger management difficulties. These groups are predominately skill-based, and play therapy is utilized as an adjunct to and part of the therapeutic process. Children are referred for groups by teachers, parents, and themselves. Group size ranges from six to eight students. Groups meet weekly for approximately 12 to 20 weeks for 45 to 50 minutes. Gumaer (1984) noted that groups need to meet at least 10 times to be effective for children. Parental permission is obtained for group counseling sessions. Students may participate in both individual and group counseling. Parent training and classroom social skills training may also be offered with group counseling.

COGNITIVE-BEHAVIORAL GROUP PLAY THERAPY

A number of curriculum-based counseling programs are available for use with children demonstrating anger management issues. Many of these programs contain play therapy techniques; if not, play therapy techniques are utilized as an adjunct to these groups. For children demonstrating impulse control issues, *Cognitive-Behavioral Therapy for Impulsive Children* (Kendall, 1992a) has proven effective for ameliorating impulsive behavior. This treatment modality, originally designed for individual therapeutic intervention, was adapted for group format. The treatment approach contains 20 sessions. Play therapy techniques incorporated into the sessions include role playing, bibliotherapy, games, puzzles, drawing, modeling, storytelling, pretending, and making a commercial. Each student receives a *Stop and Think Workbook* (Kendall, 1992b). The group leader determines the appropriate sessions to teach the concepts. Some groups may require more sessions, and others may require fewer than the 20-session format.

This program teaches students specific steps to problem solving. These include the following:

1. What am I supposed to do?
2. Look at all the possibilities.
3. Pick an answer.
4. Check out your answer.
5. Tell yourself, "I did a good job!" (Kendall, 1992a, p. 3)

These steps are utilized throughout the counseling sessions. To improve generalization outside the counseling environment, these steps are posted in each classroom and students are encouraged to employ them on a daily basis. The program has additional lessons (Kendall & Bartel, 1990) that can be used with an entire classroom to reinforce the concepts. The school clinician and the teacher may elect to coteach these additional lessons to assist in the teaching of problem solving in the classroom. This approach helps students generalize the problem-solving techniques to other environments. Play techniques are also utilized with the classroom lessons and include role playing, puzzles, and games.

For children exhibiting specific anger control difficulties, group counseling offers an opportunity to learn specific skills and the opportunity to utilize these skills with peers prior to doing so in other environments. For children ages 10 to 17, *Cognitive-Behavioral Therapy for Aggressive Children: Therapist Manual* (Nelson & Finch, 1996a) offers a 17 to 27 sessions group counseling series designed to teach anger management skills to students. Each student is given *"Keeping Your Cool": The Anger Management Workbook* (Nelson & Finch, 1996b) for use in the counseling sessions. For students who demonstrate the need for additional instruction and intervention, the program has available *"Keeping Your Cool" Part 2: Additional Sessions for the Anger Management Workbook* (Nelson & Finch, 1996c).

This program integrates cognitive-behavioral therapy and utilizes play techniques for reinforcement of concepts. Nelson and Finch (1996a) noted that the program contains six basic components for anger training: cognitive change, arousal reduction, behavioral skill development, appropriate anger expression, moral reasoning development, and use of humor. Techniques utilized in the program include self-talk, relaxation training, role playing, problem solving, assertion training, and humor. It is important to emphasize that the program is flexible and additional play techniques can be integrated into the program as necessary for an individual and for a group of students. Anger management games such as Overheating or Breaking the Chains of Anger are often useful to play with students in the group during the course of treatment

A problem-solving sequence is taught to the group of students:

1. Stop: What's the problem?
2. What can I do? Brainstorm solutions.
3. Evaluate: What's the best solution?
4. Act: Try it out.
5. React: Did it work? (Nelson & Finch, 1996a, pp. 42–43)

The problem-solving steps are posted in the classroom to assist with generalizing the new behaviors to other environments. This program is particularly useful as it can be utilized with elementary, middle, and high school students. The Anger Coping Program (Lochman, Dunn, & Klimes-Dougan, 1993) is an additional cognitive-behavioral program useful for group counseling in the schools that includes play therapy techniques such as role playing, discussion, videotaping, and play activities.

CASE EXAMPLE

Five students were grouped for counseling due to anger management issues, impulsivity, and short attention span. The school psychologist chose to utilize the Stop and Think program for the group and the teacher's version in the classroom. Additionally, bibliotherapy, role playing, and the therapeutic use of games were part of the counseling process. Games included Overheating, the Anger Solution Game, and the Talking, Feeling, and Doing Game.

Students were seen weekly for 45-minute sessions for approximately 20 weeks. Classroom lessons were co-led by the school psychologist and the teacher for 15 weeks. Students reported that the problem-solving techniques assisted them in delaying their need for immediate gratification. They frequently employed the techniques not only in school but also at home. At the beginning of the following school year, three students self-referred for an additional group, noting that they needed to review the problem-solving process to help

them be successful in school. These students were allowed to participate in a review program of the skills, and therapeutic games were employed to practice anger management interventions.

CHILD-CENTERED GROUP PLAY THERAPY

As noted earlier, child-centered play therapy focuses on the child and the
therapeutic relationship rather than the referring problem. Landreth
(1991) identified the objectives for child-centered play therapy:

1. Develop a more positive self-concept.
2. Assume greater self-responsibility.
3. Become more self-directing.
4. Become more self-accepting.
5. Become more self-reliant.
6. Engage in self-determined decision making.
7. Experience a feeling of control.
8. Become sensitive to the process of coping.
9. Develop an internal source of evaluation.
10. Become more trusting of self. (Landreth, 1991, p. 80)

Children, therefore, are free to choose what they will work on during the
play therapy sessions. The child drives to self-actualize and the play therapist trusts that the child can chart the path. Limit setting, toys, and the
role of the therapist continue to be critical to the therapeutic process.

Landreth and Sweeney (1999) discussed this approach to play therapy
relative to group size, group selection, group playroom, and play materials. Additionally, they emphasized that the length, duration, and frequency of sessions are dependent on the age and needs of the children. In
general, sessions can meet once or twice weekly and run approximately
45 minutes per session. This approach can be utilized in the schools but
may be met with questions by teachers and administrators because the
therapist is perceived as not directly teaching the students to control their
anger in a planned, programmatic way. It is important that the therapy
sessions not be used as a reinforcer for appropriate behavior nor in a response-cost way for inappropriate behavior in school or in the classroom.
Students are involved in counseling regardless of their behavior.

CASE EXAMPLE

A school psychologist assigned as a consultant to a preschool program
was asked to work with three children referred for counseling due to

conduct issues, withdrawn behavior, and school phobic reactions. These children were grouped and seen twice weekly for 30-minute sessions for 15 weeks. A child-centered play therapy approach was employed by the school psychologist. Additionally, the school social worker met with the parents to discuss childrearing and discipline issues at home.

After the 30 sessions, the school psychologist noted a significant reduction in inappropriate demonstrations of anger; less anxiety was demonstrated; and positive social skills were noted in the classroom. The parents reported fewer discipline problems with their children at home; parents also noted more positive sibling relationships.

SOCIAL PLAY IN THE SCHOOLS

Classrooms provide an arena for encouraging the appropriate use of anger management techniques and socialization of students. Social play allows students to practice social behaviors in a controlled, supervised manner. Social play has been defined as "the technique of leading a group of people in a series of games, so that individuals experience, learn, and develop positive social attitudes and skills" (Aycox, 1985, p. 5). Social play helps students be the center of attention, to get to know one another, to learn to cooperate with one another, and to resolve anger or aggression.

Aycox (1985) outlines more than 50 games that can be utilized in classrooms with students to encourage social skills, reduce anger and hostility, focus attention on students, encourage cooperation, and allow students to employ dramatic skills. Aycox notes that social play will help students to:

1. Learn positive social behaviors.
2. Learn to increase self-control.
3. Be more socially organized.
4. Learn to develop gratification and control impulses.
5. Learn to enjoy the here-and-now and feel worthy of feeling pleasure.
6. Advance communication both verbally and nonverbally.
7. Foster a positive attitude toward writing and speaking as good ways to express feelings instead of acting out.
8. Learn the value of cooperating and supporting peers in the classroom community.
9. Learn to rely on intrinsic values and not prizes.
10. Increase use of mental imagery building.
11. Learn body coordination free of stressful performance anxiety.
12. Gain experience in social problem solving.

13. Be able to modulate shifting between active and calm state.
14. Adopt a happier and more respectful view of school and eliminate name-calling, fighting, and vandalism. (p. 92)

The school clinician selects appropriate social games to introduce to the class. The goal of early games is to get to know each other; later games proceed to establish group cohesiveness. Games can also focus attention on individual students. Finally, games that focus on anger resolution can be introduced to the class. These games assist students in resolving anger and help them manage future anger issues. As stated by Aycox (1985), "The optimum resolution of anger takes place in the social realm, not in the individual, one-to-one mode, and . . . cultural, social activities (play, dance, and drama) are the most effective forms of controlling anger in humans" (p. 77).

There are a number of social games that are helpful for anger management: Alphabet Volleyball, Broom Hockey, Bull in the Ring, Caboose Dodgeball, El Tigre, Guard the Chair, How Do You Like Your Neighbor, Line Tug O'War, Pris, Steeple Chase, Strideball, Swat, and Wave the Ocean. The school clinician visits the classroom twice weekly and leads the class in social games, which can occur during recess time so that students will not miss instructional time. In many cases, social games can be used as an adjunct to individual and group counseling. As noted earlier, counseling interventions are selected based on individual and group treatment goals. Social games encourage the emotional growth of an entire class.

CASE EXAMPLE

A school psychologist was asked to consult with a teacher who was encountering many discipline issues in the classroom. At the point of referral, three of the students in this class were involved in group counseling for attentional issues, and one student was involved in individual counseling due to anger management issues. The school psychologist helped the teacher develop a management plan for the class and suggested that the class would benefit from social games to increase group cohesiveness and cooperation. These games would also assist the previously referred students to improve their social skills and help them with anger resolution skills.

The teacher agreed to the new management plan and the introduction of biweekly social game sessions. The school psychologist led the social games; the teacher and class participated in the games. Games designed to help the class get acquainted were introduced initially; these were followed by games that encouraged group cohesiveness, intimacy, being the center of attention, and anger resolution. Games were played with the class for the entire school year, and the teacher began to lead games as the school year progressed.

The teacher reported that the students had fewer discipline referrals, more group connectedness, and greater empathy toward each other after the introduction of social games. The students noted less difficulty getting along with others and fewer anger resolution difficulties. The principal and playground monitors highlighted that the students demonstrated fewer verbal and physical disagreements on the playground, greater empathy toward students in other classrooms, and greater tolerance for frustration.

SUMMARY OF GROUP PLAY THERAPY TECHNIQUES

Group counseling integrating play therapy techniques provides students the opportunity to learn new skills, self-actualize, grow emotionally, and work through anger management difficulties. Group counseling in the schools often provides specific skill development and utilizes play therapy techniques to reinforce skills in the therapy session. As in individual counseling, the school clinician chooses counseling interventions specific to treatment goals. The student(s) may also participate in individual or family counseling if appropriate.

ADDITIONAL PLAY THERAPY INTERVENTIONS

Many programs and games are available that incorporate play in working with anger management issues. The reader is encouraged to review programs and games as to their usefulness in the schools and as a therapeutic agent for children. *The Anger Control Tool Kit* (Shapiro, Shore, Bloemaker, Kahler, & Schroeder, 1994) and the *I Can Control My Anger Kit* (Pinkus & Rolland, 1995) are two programs that incorporate a multi-modality approach to working with children with anger management issues. The former program includes 38 techniques for the school clinician to choose from when working with the angry child. It is recommended that the therapist choose techniques covering six different modalities: affective, behavioral, cognitive, developmental, educational, and social. Techniques that incorporate play include storytelling, the turtle technique, the self-calming technique, feelings charade, the hot seat, substituting behaviors when angry, role playing, and catharsis. The program also contains a videotape that reviews eight anger control techniques. The latter program also recommends that the clinician choose interventions from six treatment modalities: affective, behavioral, cognitive, developmental, educational, and social. Play activities include the Coping with Anger Target Game, Face It Card Game, Problem-Solving Cards, two story books, and Listen Up Card Game. The school clinician designs the treatment program for the individual child by selecting at least one treatment goal from the six modalities. Activities are chosen to work on these goals.

CASE EXAMPLE

A 9-year-old boy was referred to the school psychologist for anger management issues. Activities were chosen from *The Anger Control Kit* that addressed the six treatment modalities. These included the feelings charade, the turtle technique, storytelling, self-calming technique, role playing, bibliotherapy, a feelings thermometer, drawing, playing with clay, and others. The child was seen for 15 sessions. The teacher reported that the child demonstrated less impulsive behavior. The child was observed to be less ostracized by his peers and more involved in play activities on the playground.

SUMMARY

The present chapter reviewed play therapy techniques useful for anger management issues. Individual counseling techniques suggested for therapeutic intervention included client-centered play therapy, release play therapy, cognitive-behavioral play therapy, and developing an individual treatment approach incorporating play therapy techniques based on individual student treatment goals. Group counseling techniques included client-centered play therapy, cognitive-behavioral play therapy, social play, therapeutic games, and the use of specific programs designed to ameliorate anger management difficulties that incorporate play techniques.

A prescriptive approach to play therapy was recommended for addressing a student's needs specific to anger management difficulties. Interventions may include individual play therapy, group play therapy, and family counseling. Additionally, special play sessions between parent and child were discussed to assist with anger management difficulties at home. Specific case examples were shared to illustrate the play techniques. Finally, specific play therapy techniques were identified for potential inclusion in a treatment program.

REFERENCES

Axline, V.M. (1947). *Play therapy: The inner dynamics of childhood.* Boston: Houghton Mifflin.

Axline, V.M. (1969). *Play therapy.* New York: Ballantine Books.

Aycox, F. (1985). *Games we should play in school.* Byron, CA: Front Row Experience.

Bodiford-McNeil, C., Hembree-Kigin, T.L., & Eyberg, S.M. (1996). *Short-term play therapy for disruptive children.* King of Prussia, PA: Center for Applied Psychology.

Brandenburg, N.A., Friedman, R.M., & Silver, S.E. (1990). Epidemiology of childhood psychiatric disorders: Prevalence findings from recent studies. *Journal of the American Academy of Child and Adolescent Psychiatry, 29,* 76–83.

Braswell, L., & Kendall, P.C. (1988). Cognitive-behavioral methods with children. In K.S. Dobson (Ed.), *Handbook of cognitive behavior therapy* (pp. 167–213). New York: Guilford Press.

Burns, B.J., Costello, E.J., Angold, A., Tweed, D., Stangl, D., Farmer, E.M., & Erkanli, A. (1995). Children's mental health service use across service sectors. *Health Affairs, 14,* 147–159.

Catron, T., & Weiss, B. (1994). The Vanderbilt school-based counseling program. *Journal of Emotional and Behavioral Disorders, 2,* 247–253.

Centers for Disease Control and Prevention. (1998, August 14). Youth risk behavior surveillance: United States, 1997. *CDC Surveillance Summaries* MMWR, 47 (No. SS-3). Atlanta, GA: Author.

Dorfman, E. (1951). Play therapy. In C.R. Rogers (Ed.), *Client-centered therapy: Its current practice* (pp. 235–277). Boston: Houghton Mifflin.

Friedman, R., Katz-Leavy, J., Manderscheid, R., & Sondheimer, D. (1996). Prevalence of serious emotional disturbance in children and adolescents. In R.W. Manderscheid & M.A. Sonnenschein (Eds.), *Mental health United States, 1996* (pp. 77–91). Washington, DC: U.S. Government Printing Office.

Gilfix, J., & Heller Kahn, N. (1999). *The special playroom: A young child's guide to play therapy.* Unpublished manuscript.

Guerney, L.F. (1978). *Parenting: A skills training manual.* State College, PA: Institute for the Development of Emotional and Life Skills.

Gumaer, J. (1984). *Counseling and therapy for children.* New York: Free Press.

Hambidge, G. (1955). Structured play therapy. *American Journal of Orthopsychiatry, 25,* 601–657.

Hoagwood, K., & Erwin, H.D. (1997). Effectiveness of school-based mental health services for children: A 10-year research review. *Journal of Child and Family Studies, 6,* 435–454.

Kaduson, H.G., & Schaefer, C.E. (Eds.). (1997). *101 favorite play therapy techniques.* Northvale, NJ: Aronson.

Kendall, P.C. (1992a). *Cognitive-behavioral therapy for impulsive children: The manual.* Ardmore, PA: Workbook Publishing.

Kendall, P.C. (1992b). *Stop and think workbook.* Ardmore, PA: Workbook Publishing.

Kendall, P.C., & Bartel, N.R. (1990). *Teaching problem solving to students with learning and behavioral problems: A manual for teachers.* Ardmore, PA: Workbook Publishing.

Knell, S. (1993). *Cognitive-behavioral play therapy.* Northvale, NJ: Aronson.

Landreth, G.L. (1991). *Play therapy: The art of the relationship.* Muncie, IN: Accelerated Development.

Landreth, G.L., & Sweeney, D.S. (1999). The freedom to be: Child-centered group play therapy. In D.S. Sweeney & L.E. Homeyer (Eds.), *The handbook of group play therapy* (pp. 39–64). San Francisco: Jossey-Bass.

Lavigne, J.V., Gibbons, R.D., Christoffel, K.K., Arend, R., Rosenbaum, D., Binns, H., Dawson, N., Sobel, H., & Isaacs, C. (1996). Prevalence rates and correlates of psychiatric disorders among preschool children. *Journal of the American Academy of Child and Adolescent Psychiatry, 35,* 204–214.

Levy, D. (1938). Release therapy in young children. *Psychiatry, 1,* 387–389.

Lochman, J.E., Dunn, S.E., & Klimes-Dougan, B. (1993). An intervention and consultation model from a social cognitive perspective: A description of the Anger Coping Program. *School Psychology Review, 22,* 458–471.

Mott Foundation. (1996). *A fine line: Losing American youth to violence.* Flint, MI: Author.

Nelson, W.M., & Finch, A.J., Jr. (1996a). *Cognitive-behavioral therapy for aggressive children: Therapist manual.* Ardmore, PA: Workbook Publishing.

Nelson, W.M., & Finch, A.J., Jr. (1996b). *Keeping your cool: The anger management workbook.* Ardmore, PA: Workbook Publishing.

Nelson, W.M., & Finch, A.J., Jr. (1996c). *Keeping your cool, Part 2: Additional sessions for the anger management workbook.* Ardmore, PA: Workbook Publishing.

Nemiroff, M.A., & Annunziata, J. (1990). *A child's first book about play therapy.* Washington, DC: American Psychological Association.

Oliver James, O. (1997). *Play therapy: A comprehensive guide.* Northvale, NJ: Aronson.

Perry, L. (1993). Audrey, the Bois d'Arc and me: A time of becoming. In T. Kottman & C. Schaefer (Eds.), *Play therapy in action: A casebook for practitioners* (pp. 5–43). Northvale, NJ: Aronson.

Pinkus, D., & Rolland, A. (1995). *I can control my anger.* Plainview, NY: ChildsworkChildsplay.

Roberts, M.C. (1994). Models for service delivery in children's mental health: Common characteristics. *Journal of Clinical Child Psychiatry, 23,* 212–219.

Rogers, C. (1951). *Client-centered therapy.* Boston: Houghton Mifflin.

Shaffer, D., Fisher, P., Dulcan, M.K., Davies, M., Piacentini, J., Schwab-Stone, M.E., Lahey, B.B., Bourdon, K., Jensen, P.S., Bird, H.R., Canino, G., & Regier, D.A. (1996). The NIMH Diagnostic Interview Schedule for Children Version 2.3 (DISC-2.3): Description, acceptability, prevalence rates, and performance in the MECA Study. Methods for the Epidemiology of Child and Adolescent Mental Disorders Study. *Journal of the American Academy of Child and Adolescent Psychiatry, 35,* 865–877.

Shapiro, L.E., Shore, H.M., Bloemaker, M.A., Kahler, D.S., & Schroeder, J.M. (1994). *The anger control tool kit.* Plainview, NY: ChildsworkChildsplay.

Surgeon General. (1999). *Mental health: A report of the surgeon general* [On-line]. Available: http://www.surgeongeneral.gov/library/mentalhealth/chapter3/html

Thomas, C.R., & Holzer, C.E., III. (1999). National distribution of child and adolescent psychiatrists. *Journal of the American Academy of Child and Adolescent Psychiatry, 38,* 9–15.

Wolraich, M.L., Hannah, J.N., Pinnock, T.Y., Baumgaertel, A., & Brown, J. (1996). Comparison of diagnostic criteria for attention-deficit hyperactivity disorder in a county-wide sample. *Journal of the American Academy of Child and Adolescent Psychiatry, 35,* 319–324.

CHAPTER 14

Use of Developmentally Appropriate Games in a Child Group Training Program for Young Children with Attention-Deficit/ Hyperactivity Disorder

LINDA A. REDDY, PRISCILLA SPENCER,
TARA M. HALL, and ELIZABETH RUBEL

CHILDREN WITH Attention-Deficit/Hyperactivity Disorder (ADHD) are frequently disruptive and difficult to manage in the classroom and on the playground. The list of common inappropriate classroom behaviors is long; these children will often call out, leave their seat without permission, provoke other students, hand in messy or incomplete assignments, and fail to stay on task. Children with ADHD often have difficulties initiating and maintaining relationships with peers, siblings, and adults.

Current estimates suggest that 3% to 5% of all school-age children have the disorder, translating to at least one child with the disorder in an average classroom (DuPaul & Stoner, 1994). Nearly all children with ADHD

Preparation for this manuscript was support by grants 2-022627 and 2-022682 from the Society for the Study of School Psychology and a University Faculty Research Grant awarded to the first author.

exhibit significant academic underachievement (Anastopoulos, Guevremont, Shelton, & DuPaul, 1992) and an estimated 20% to 30% have a learning disability (Anastopoulos & Barkley, 1992). If untreated, the long-term outlook is poor. Up to 30% of children with ADHD who do not receive treatment do not complete high school and are at a higher risk for substance abuse, juvenile convictions, automobile accidents, and interpersonal problems (Barkley, 1998). These children present unique academic and behavioral challenges to school personnel and often require specially tailored social interventions.

SCHOOL-BASED SOCIAL INTERVENTIONS FOR CHILDREN WITH ADHD

The majority of school-based treatments for children with ADHD are individually based, focusing on techniques that allow school personnel to adapt their curricula to the needs of a specific child. Few programs include group-oriented interventions (e.g., developmentally appropriate games) that allow practitioners to target social and academic deficits in natural settings (DuPaul & Eckert, 1997).

School-based treatments for children with ADHD can be grouped into two general categories: contingency management and cognitive-behavioral treatments. A contingency management program establishes positive and negative consequences for targeted behaviors. Rewards and punishments can be provided by teachers and/or parents for school behaviors, creating links between actions and consequences. One contingency management program, the Attention Training System (ATS), developed by DuPaul, Guevremont, and Barkley (1992) is an individually based response-cost intervention that allows a child to earn or lose points based on his or her behavior. The ATS device is placed on the child's desk and displays his or her cumulative points earned. Points are added at a fixed interval, and the classroom teacher can deduct points with a remote control device. The ATS has been found to improve on-task behavior and academic productivity for elementary school boys.

Another common and effective technique is the daily report card, which allows parents to implement positive/negative consequences for school behaviors at home. The daily report card also fosters collaborative parent-teacher alliances by systematically communicating a child's daily progress toward academic and behavioral goals. This approach has led to improvements in social behavior, hyperactivity, attentiveness, and self-control (e.g., McCain & Kelley, 1993; Pfiffner & O'Leary, 1993). Several contingency management guides designed for classroom teachers are available (e.g., Barkley, 1990; DuPaul & Stoner, 1994; Pfiffner, 1996). Overall, contingency management programs are effective in improving individual classroom behavior, but gains tend to dissipate once treatment is withdrawn (e.g., Anastopoulos & Barkley, 1992; DuPaul & Eckert, 1997; DuPaul, Guevremont, & Barkley, 1992).

Cognitive-behavioral interventions help ADHD children develop self-control and problem-solving skills by examining and correcting the thoughts that lead to actions (Kendall, 2000). They can be used in both individual and group formats for treating a broad range of behaviors, including impulsivity, social skills, intrusiveness, and anger management. Cognitive-behavioral interventions in general are adult- rather than child-directed, in that adults initiate and guide the therapeutic process.

Common cognitive-behavioral interventions used with ADHD children include self-monitoring, self-instruction, and self-reinforcement (Anastopoulos & Barkley, 1992). Self-monitoring programs teach children to keep track of on-task and off-task behaviors and reward themselves for classroom compliance. Accurate self-evaluation is determined by matching teacher ratings. Self-monitoring approaches improve on-task behavior and academic productivity and are typically individually based, providing children with skills to remain at their desk for independent study. Self-instruction, or self-statement modification, involves teaching a child appropriate problem-solving skills by modeling the performance of a task while stating planning strategies aloud. The child then performs the task and engages in similar overt verbalizations. Self-reinforcement techniques teach children to reinforce themselves with tangible and/or intangible rewards after completing a goal or a step toward reaching a goal (Anastopoulos & Barkley, 1992).

Research on the efficacy of cognitive-behavioral interventions has been mixed. Although early studies reported its effectiveness with this population (e.g. Douglas, 1980; Kendall & Braswell, 1985), the majority of the outcome literature reports modest gains that fail to generalize to the classroom setting (Barkley, 1998; Pfiffner & O'Leary, 1993). Pfiffner and O'Leary speculate that this failure to generalize may be due to differences between treatment goals and classroom expectations, as well as the brevity of the training provided. Treatment goals more relevant to the children, such as peer acceptance or social skills, may generate more motivation and treatment success. Others assert that young ADHD children lack the motivation to adhere to the strict treatment regimens (Anastopolous & Barkley, 1992; Barkley, 1998). Perhaps cognitive-behavioral interventions are not intrinsically appealing and motivating for young ADHD children, which can interfere with treatment success.

Therapeutic techniques like developmentally appropriate games (DAGs) that are potent, relevant, and enjoyable to young children may increase motivation and skill development. Barkley (1998) recommends that treatment focus on "the performance of particular behaviors at the *points of performance* in the natural environment where and when such behaviors should be performed" (p. 65). That is, treatment is most likely to be effective when skills are taught in contexts in which children work and play. Group-based DAGs are an effective way to capture ADHD children's interest and motivation while teaching them important skills in natural settings such as school, home, and playground. DAGs provide children the opportunity to interact naturally with peers and learn appropriate behaviors in the context in which they will be used. DAGs offer school personnel valuable information on *when* and *how* social problems occur among children. Treating children in a natural play setting also increases the likelihood of maintaining and generalizing treatment gains over time (Hoag & Burlingame, 1997).

USE OF DEVELOPMENTALLY APPROPRIATE GAMES WITH ADHD CHILDREN

School-based DAGs enhance children's socialization through group contact, increase self-confidence through group acceptance, and provide recreational and leisure time activities (Reed, Black, & Eastman, 1978). For young ADHD children, DAGs offer an important means to acquire new skills, practice previously learned information, and experience a stimulating environment in which to share and practice skills with peers and adults.

DAGs are gross motor activities that are based on three principles: (1) each child has the opportunity to participate at his or her own ability level; (2) as each child plays the game, opportunities to participate increase; and (3) children who vary in ability can interact positively with each other (Torbert, 1994). DAGs can build children's sense of accomplishment, creativity, and positive regard for themselves and others, while teaching them important life skills for work and play (Torbert & Schneider, 1993). Children who participate in group games share an affiliation through which they can encourage others' growth in positive social interactions (Torbert, 1994). DAGs also present challenges to children that encourage them to persist and try alternative solutions (Bunker, 1991).

SCHOOL-BASED RESEARCH ON DAGS

Research has shown that DAGs significantly improve participation, cooperation, social skills, self-esteem, and visual-motor skills of regular education, emotionally disturbed, and perceptually impaired children more than do traditional school-based games (Ferland, 1997). For example, Bay-Hinitz, Peterson, and Quilitch (1994) studied the impact of DAGs and competitive games on the participation and cooperative group behavior of 70 preschoolers. Games were implemented 30 minutes per day, five days a week, for 50 days. Children who participated in DAGs exhibited greater participation and prosocial behavior than children who participated in traditional competitive games. Similarly, Orlick (1988) investigated the effects of DAGs and traditional group games on the cooperative behavior of 87 kindergartners during classroom instruction and free time. The children participated in games for 30 minutes per week for 18 weeks. Cooperative behavior during classroom free time increased significantly for those children provided DAGs, but not for those children provided traditional group games.

Garaigordobil and Echbarria (1995) examined the effects of a cooperative game program on the social behavior and self-concept of 178 children (ages 6 and 7). Treatment consisted of 22 play sessions during the course of an academic school year. Games were designed to enhance children's cooperation, sharing, symbolic play, and feelings of self-worth. Significant improvements were found in classroom behavior such as leadership skills, cheerfulness, and sensitivity/respect to others. Reductions in aggression, apathy, and anxiety were also reported.

Schneider (1989) assessed the impact of DAG play on the self-esteem of 36 kindergarten students. Self-report was measured through teacher ratings and child self-report. Likewise, classroom teachers rated each child on the same measure. Half of the sample participated in 15 to 20 minutes of free play for 17 sessions; the other half participated in DAGs for the same length of time and number of sessions. Teacher and child self-reported ratings of self-esteem improved among those students who participated in DAGs rather than in free play.

The influence of game play on the social behavior of children diagnosed as emotionally disturbed has also been investigated (Hand, 1986). Two groups of children, ages 10 to 12, were systematically observed during recess. One group participated in traditional games, where success was defined as the defeat or elimination of others, and the other group participated in DAGs. Games were implemented three times per week for 16 weeks. The children that participated in the DAGs were less verbally and physically aggressive and less often asked to leave the group activities than the children who participated in the traditional games.

Research has suggested that children with perceptual impairments may also profit from DAGs. For example, Reed et al. (1978) investigated the effectiveness of a parent-child group training program for perceptually disabled children ages 6 to 12. Children in the group had few friends, seldom participated in peer group activities, and were verbally and physically aggressive. Games were designed to enhance social skills and perceptual-motor abilities (e.g. visual-motor skills, visual acuity, and body awareness). The program consisted of one-hour sessions held twice a week for 16 weeks. Parent ratings revealed improved peer interactions at home and school such as greater participation during games, willingness to follow rules, and fewer verbally and physically inappropriate behaviors.

Despite the potential benefits of DAGs on children's social and emotional development, few studies have investigated their effectiveness with ADHD children. Investigators have recently begun studying the benefits of DAGs as part of a multimodal treatment program for young ADHD children (e.g., Files, Reddy, Rubel, Judd, & Spencer, 1999; Reddy, 2000; Reddy et al., 1999). DAGs afford young ADHD children opportunities to learn new skills through participating in structured peer group activities that are mentally and physically challenging. These games are flexible, require minimum equipment, and can be easily modified to meet specific individual and classroom needs. DAGs can be designed to enhance young children's social skills, self-control, and stress and anger management.

DESIGNING SCHOOL-BASED DAGS FOR ADHD CHILDREN

DAGs can be easily designed for the school, home, and playground. We offer a nine-step approach for designing games:

1. Identify the social, cognitive, and emotional needs of each child and the group as a whole.
2. Assess the skills required of each child to successfully participate in each game.
3. Design/select games that allow each child to participate at his or her own ability level.
4. Design/select games that enable children who vary in skill level and experience to interact positively with each other.
5. Design/select games that provide children increased opportunities to play.
6. Evaluate the space and equipment needed for each game and identify available resources in the classroom/school.
7. Determine the number of adults and children required for effective and safe participation in each game.
8. Assess the skills and knowledge required for adults to successfully implement the game.
9. Provide adult therapists with training as needed.

Children's needs and capabilities must be carefully considered when designing games for ADHD children in a group and/or classroom context. In general, children's needs can be conceptualized in three areas: social, cognitive, and emotional. Examples of social needs include children's ability to share themselves and belongings with others, take turns, play cooperatively, ask for help, and help others. Cognitive needs consist of the child's capability to understand and follow directions, identify personal and shared space, and attend to detail. Emotional needs include children's ability to identify feelings in themselves and others, use words to express feelings, and manage stress and anger.

A number of assessment strategies can be used to identify individual child and group needs. For example, standardized assessment instruments (e.g., Child Behavior Checklist, Social Skills Rating System, Kaufman Screening of Early Academic Learning), direct observation during structured and unstructured play activities, and consultation with school personnel familiar with each child are particularly useful.

MUSICAL CHAIRS

Schools use a number of traditional games that can be easily redesigned as DAGs. For example, the game Musical Chairs is a traditional game familiar to preschool and elementary school children. In looking at the objectives of Musical Chairs, the following is apparent: (1) the winner is the child who is fast enough to get to an empty chair and/or dislodge another child from a chair; (2) limited positive interactions take place between children who vary in ability level; (3) participants are not encouraged to help others, share personal space, and play cooperatively; and (4) as the game unfolds there are decreased numbers of opportunities to participate, and once a child fails to secure a place on a chair, the chair and child are eliminated.

Following the three principles of DAGs and the nine-step approach previously outlined, the game Musical Chairs can be redesigned as a cooperative training activity for young children. For example, the same basic setup and game design can be used. Instead of chairs, towels or carpet squares can be randomly spaced on the floor. The game starts with one towel per child. The children are instructed, as in Musical Chairs, that the music signals the need to move off the towels into the general space, and when the music stops each child must be on a towel. Controlled movements are required and encouraged. The use of imagery can also be added as needed. For example, the towels are described as "islands" and the general space is described as "water." The children can also be told that as they play the game, "the tide" slowly comes in, making the area on the islands smaller. When the music starts, all children must "swim slowly" in the water (i.e., general area), and when the music stops, they must climb onto an island. Every time the music stops, one towel is folded or removed, reducing the size of the islands. An island can hold as many children as is safe practice. These instructions encourage children to share personal space appropriately, help others, and practice self-control.

The first principle of DAGs indicates that each child has the opportunity to choose to participate at his or her ability level. Children who feel more confident in their ability to secure a place on an island may be observed moving further away from the islands. Conversely, children who feel less secure may stay close to the islands. Both options are acceptable. In addition, each child chooses how to move when the music plays. For example, one child might skip, another might crawl slowly, and another may pretend to float. All movements displaying self-control are allowed.

The second principle of DAGs requires that opportunities to play and practice skills increase as the game proceeds. The games offer children endless opportunities to participate because elimination of a player is not an option. When the possibility of elimination is removed, children become active members of the group and exhibit greater cooperation, cohesion, and problem solving.

The final principle of DAGs indicates that children who vary in ability can interact positively with each other. In the islands example, the game has been designed so that more than one child can safely be on an island. By knowing the individual child's and group's needs, school personnel can determine how many children can comfortably share one island. The children quickly learn that the islands must include more than one person for everyone to be out of the water. Children will invite others onto an island, create different ways to include children, and become enthused over trying to accomplish this goal as fewer islands become available. The game ends when all children are on a predetermined number of islands.

DAGs are usually as novel to children as they are to the adults who are presenting them. DAGs such as islands become rewarding and successful learning experiences when children's needs are carefully considered. When first playing this game, children with ADHD may exhibit poor self-control and prosocial skills. This can be observed when some children are unable to safely share the islands with others. If this occurs, one may choose to increase the number of islands used at the beginning of the game. A ratio of two children per island helps orient the children to the game. As children become familiar with the rules and process of the game, their ability to participate in the game will flourish. For many children with ADHD, this is unlike any other experience they have had with peers and it takes time for them to familiarize themselves with these new feelings and behaviors.

ADHD CHILD TRAINING GROUP CURRICULUM

A child specialty training group that uses DAGs, in part, to train young ADHD children (i.e., ages 4.5 to 8) is briefly presented. The ADHD child training group (Reddy, 2000), a multimodal psychoeducational intervention, was partially based on the seminal work of Bandura's (1973) social learning theory and behavior-deficit model, Torbert's (1994) cooperative games, and Goldstein's (1988) skill streaming approach.

CURRICULUM FOCUS

The group curriculum addresses three specific needs: social skills, self-control, and anger and stress management. Skill development is fostered through participation in DAGs and the teaching of skill sequences, a set of behavioral procedures designed to enhance social competence in children (McGinnis & Goldstein, 1997; Reddy & Goldstein, in press). Each skill is broken down into its behavioral steps, which are modeled by adults and role-played by children during group sessions. Collectively, the behavioral steps illustrate the implementation of the skill (e.g., using nice talk: a. approach the person in a friendly way; b. use a friendly look; c. use a friendly voice). Skills taught include using nice talk, following directions, sharing with others, helping others, asking for help, identifying and coping with scared, sad, and angry feelings in yourself and others, controlling impulses, ignoring provocation, managing stress and anger, dealing with boredom, using brave talk, accepting consequences, dealing with being left out, and being a good sport.

TEACHING STRATEGIES

Teaching strategies include (1) modeling: adult therapists demonstrate behaviors and skills; (2) role playing: guided opportunities to practice and rehearse appropriate interpersonal behaviors; and (3) performance feedback: children are frequently praised and provided feedback on how well they model the therapists' skills and behavior. Skill transfer and maintenance-enhancing procedures that are particularly helpful include (1) overlearning: correctly rehearsing and practicing skills learned over time; (2) identical elements: children are trained in real-world locations (e.g., schools, playground, peer groups) with children and adults they interact with on a daily basis; and (3) mediated generalization: teaching children a series of self-regulation skills such as self-evaluation, self-reinforcement, and self-instruction. For a detailed description of the child group training curriculum, see Reddy (2000).

TRAINING SESSIONS

Children's training takes place once a week for 10 consecutive training sessions, 90 minutes per session. Approximately six to eight ADHD children are trained in each group. We find it helpful to have one adult therapist for every two children. A token economy system is used to encourage the children to master new skills, follow directions, and promote their self-confidence. The group has three goals: follow directions, use my words to express my thoughts and feelings, and keep my hands and feet to myself. Children are given one sticker/point for each of the three goals they accomplish by the completion of each group session. Time-out ("break time") is modeled by therapists and used as a positive self-control technique.

The implementation of DAGs plays a critically important role in enhancing children's motivation and skill development. The following DAGs were designed for young ADHD children who exhibit significant deficits in social skills, impulse control, and anger/stress management.

TECHNIQUES FOR SOCIAL SKILLS—MEETING AND
MAKING NEW FRIENDS

Clap Your Hands

The game begins in a circle with each child clapping the syllables of his or her name. For clarity, each child/adult should freeze momentarily at the end of his or her name and then begin again. Together, the group also claps out each child's name. Adults must model the activity and provide encouragement. Next, children whose names have the same number of syllables form groups. Children who have difficulties discerning what group they belong to can receive help by having the whole group clap the child's name to assist him or her in determining which group he or she belongs to. Each group then has a "group clap" in which they present their special clap (determined by the number of syllables) as they say their names aloud, in unison, to the other groups. This game allows children of varying levels of ability to participate and interact without being eliminated. Having all group members clap each participant's name affords children many opportunities to introduce themselves and remember others' names. (This game also teaches turn taking, attention, eye-hand coordination, and memory and language skills.)

Swedish Meetball

The group sits in a circle on the floor. Each child slowly rolls a ball to another player. Each receiver says his or her name. This continues until each child has been both the roller and receiver. Once names are remembered, each receiver has a choice: to say his or her name when receiving the ball or have a group "shout." A group shout occurs when the receiver gains possession of the ball but chooses to remain silent. The rest of the group must call out the receiver's name before the ball is again passed. Each child has the opportunity to choose to participate at his or her own level of ability by choosing which child to roll the ball to. There are numerous opportunities to participate in the rolling of the ball, saying others' names, and the group shout. If a child is having a difficult time remembering names, the group shout reinforces this skill without singling out a specific child. (This game also teaches turn taking, attention, eye-hand coordination, and memory and language skills.)

Monkey in the Blanket

The game begins with the group forming two teams. Each child, in his or her own team, is given a number in secret. If the children have difficulty remembering their numbers, they can be written in the palm of one hand. The numbers should not be revealed to the other team. The first team stands with their back to the second team. Each child in the second team holds up a blanket as a wall. Behind this blanket is the member of their team assigned the number 1. On command, the other team turns to face the first team and decides who is the "monkey in the blanket." The decision is based on team consensus with the help of an adult. Impulse control and following directions are practiced when each child learns not to shout out his or her first guess. An adult can help the children with this by instructing them to count aloud to the number 3 before making their decision. If they are incorrect, they are allowed to guess again after a team consensus, until they are correct. After each correct decision, the other team receives the blanket and follows the same procedure. The game ends when each child has been the monkey in the blanket. (This game also teaches turn taking, memory, number recognition, counting, group problem solving, and language skills.)

TECHNIQUES FOR SELF-CONTROL

The Freeze Game

The game begins with the group standing in a circle a few feet apart from each other. When the music starts, each child moves slowly around the room. When the music stops, each child must freeze like a statue. Music can be varied to emphasize staying in control at different speeds. Children who are able to move in the general space without bumping others are praised. As children become more experienced at these skills, a group challenge can be introduced. For example, the group can be challenged to move to the music and freeze after two minutes without touching each other. If there are three touches during this time, the group receives three points. The challenge is to move again for two minutes and try to decrease the number of touches or points.

The freeze game allows children with varying abilities many opportunities to interact with each other. In our experience, children will start to encourage each other to avoid receiving points. Groups who become competent in moving under control can have the size of the general place decreased as an additional group challenge. (This game also teaches auditory and visual acuity and group problem solving skills.)

The Cotton Ball Game

The game begins with the group standing around a table a few feet apart from each other. An adult therapist demonstrates how one's breathing can impact one's environment. The adult shows slow and fast breathing through a straw. Each child receives a straw and cotton ball and practices moving the cotton ball by breathing through the straw. Next, the group is divided into two teams, standing on opposite sides of the table. A line is drawn or placed down the middle of the table. On command, each child tries to get his or her cotton ball into the other team's area (on the other side of the line). Because cotton balls are continuously moving back and forth, the children constantly are trying to rid their side of the cotton balls. On occasion, children run out of breath and require small breaks. Group challenges can also be presented. For example, the teams could try to get all the cotton balls on one side, have an even amount of cotton balls on both sides, or keep all the cotton balls on the table during a specified period of time. Children participate at their own level of ability, blowing as many or as few cotton balls as they are comfortable with. The team and group challenge allows children of different abilities to have many opportunities to positively interact. (This game also teaches turn taking, impulse control, fine motors skills, and group problem solving.)

Islands

As previously described, islands is a captivating group game that fosters a number of important life skills such as helping others, asking for help, sharing/respecting the personal space of others, taking turns, and controlling one's hands and feet. (This game also teaches impulse control, attention, group cohesion, problem solving, and gross motor skills.)

Techniques for Self-Control and Stress Management

I Am a Balloon

The adult therapists introduce the idea of feeling relaxed and demonstrate "hard and soft arms and legs." Children are asked to identify ways they relax at school and home. Children are asked to stand apart in the play area. They are told that they are balloons with no air in them and they are to shake loose and collapse. An adult models the skills to the children. The adult announces that he or she has an air pump that can blow up each balloon. The adults make the "ssshhhh" sound, indicating that air is being pumped into the balloons. Ample time for each balloon (child) to fill up with air is provided. Point out how each child chooses a different shape and way to blow up. Questions posed to the group may include Are you completely filled up with air? and Show me how filled up your balloon is, but do not allow it to drift away. Suddenly, the adult announces that each balloon has a small leak, using the "sssssss" sound to indicate air being released from the balloon. An adult models letting the air out as the balloons (children) slowly deflate and collapse on the ground. Imagery can also be included such as putting patches on each balloon and blowing them up again, balloons mirroring each other, and having children pretend to be air pumps. (This game also teaches visual and auditory acuity, attention, and fine/gross motor skills.)

The ZZZZZ Game

A pretend story about children going to sleep is read to the group. The sound "zzzzzz" is made by an adult, indicating that it is time for the group to go to sleep. Each child chooses a safe place on the ground. Questions to pose include How do your bodies feel when you're asleep? How do your arms and legs feel? After the children are able to simulate sleeping for a short time, an adult mimics an alarm clock going off (rrrriinngg!!). Children are encouraged to move safely when the alarm goes off. The children jump up and move to another part of the room, where they choose another safe spot to fall slowly back asleep again to the sound of "zzzzzz." Discussion revolves around how different their bodies feel when they are pretending to sleep and when they hear the alarm. All children participate throughout the game. (This game also teaches impulse control, fine and gross motors skills, and attention.)

The Pop Up Game

The game begins with the group dividing into two teams, the Rabbits and the Bears. Each team is asked to practice the movements their animal makes. The groups then sit on the floor and an adult stands in front of them with a stuffed rabbit and bear behind his or her back. When a team's animal is held up, that team must "pop up" and make the appropriate animal movement. For example, when the rabbit is held up, the Rabbit team hop in place, pretending to be rabbits. When the bear is held up, the Bear team scratch with their paws. Animal sounds can be used instead of animal movements. Additionally, verbalization of the animal name can be used in conjunction with the stuffed animal or alone. A group challenge may be introduced by telling the group a riddle about one of the animals and have the teams figure out which animal is being described. Examples of riddles include I like to eat carrots, I like to sleep through the winter, and I like to eat honey. As a riddle is read, each team must decide if the riddle is describing their team and pop up, demonstrating their animal behavior or sound. (This game also teaches listening skills, group problem solving, sound discrimination, and visual acuity.)

OUTCOME EVALUATION

Two preliminary outcome studies have been conducted on the effectiveness of the ADHD child group curriculum. The first study examined the effects of a 10-week child training group on children's social behavior at home and school (Reddy et al., 1999). The second study examined the impact of child and parent group training on children's social behavior and parental stress in the home (Files et al., 1999). Children included in both studies were 4.5 to 8 years of age, enrolled at a preschool or elementary school, diagnosed with ADHD by a pediatric neurologist, psychiatrist, and/or psychologist, and met the *DSM-IV* criteria for ADHD (APA, 1994). Training took place at Fairleigh Dickinson University's Child and Adolescent ADHD Clinic.

The first evaluation was conducted with 19 children (10 males, 9 females) with a mean age of 75 months (i.e., 6.3 years). Four children attended preschool, four attended kindergarten, five attended first grade, and six attended second grade. Seventeen of the children were Caucasian and one each was African American and Asian. Parental educational level was as follows: 3 earned high school diplomas, 4 had some college, 17 earned BA/BS, 11 earned MA/MBA, and 3 earned doctoral degrees.

A multimethod multisource assessment approach was used to evaluate the effectiveness of the children's training group. Parents were asked to complete four measures to assess their children's behavior in the home: Child Behavior Checklist (CBCL; Achenbach, 1991a), Conners Parent Rating Scale–Revised (CPRS-R; Conners, Sitarenios, Parker, & Epstein, 1998), Home Situations Questionnaire–Revised (HSQ-R; Barkley, 1998), and the Social Skills Rating System–Parent Form (SSRS; Gresham & Elliot, 1990).

Additionally, parents were asked to complete the Parent Stress Index–III (PSI-III; Abidin, 1990) to evaluate whether the children's training indirectly influenced their stress. Teachers were asked to complete three measures to assess children's classroom behavior: Teacher Report Form (TRF; Achenbach & Edelbrock, 1991b), Conners Teacher Rating Scale–Revised (CTRS-R; Conners, 1989; Conners et al., 1998), and Social Skills Rating System–Teacher Form (SSRS; Gresham & Elliot, 1990). Assessment instruments were administered in the home and school before the start of the program and at program completion.

We evaluated the effectiveness of the two studies by using two approaches. The first approach assessed the statistical or reliable change observed from the start of program to the end of the program. To accomplish this, repeated measures of analyses of variance (ANOVAs) were computed. The second approach assessed the clinically meaningful effects of the child group training in the home and school. D-ratios (i.e., effect size) were computed to determine the practical significance of change observed during the course of treatment. D-ratio values of .20, .50, and .75 indicate that small, medium, and large effects were produced by the training (Cohen, 1988).

Parents that participated in the first study reported that the children's training group produced statistically and clinically significant improvements on children's behavior in the home. For example, parents reported reduced impulsivity, inattention, hyperactivity, anxious/shy behavior, and aggressiveness and improved social skills and concentration in both compliance and leisure situations, as measured by the HSQ-R: Factor 1 and 2, at program completion. Additionally, parents' overall stress (as measured by the PSI-III: Total Stress) and stress related to caring for their child (PSI-III: Child Domain) improved.

Teacher ratings on the three child measures revealed similar behavioral improvements in the school. For example, teachers reported decreased hyperactivity, restlessness, and withdrawn behavior, and increased prosocial behavior and cooperation at program completion.

For the second study, we examined the combined effects of child and parent group training on children's social behavior and parental stress in the home. Eight families (5 fathers, 8 mothers) participated in a child and parent group training program. Parents participated in a 1.5-hour training group for 10 consecutive sessions that ran simultaneously to the child training group. A modified version of Barkley's (1997) Parent Training Curriculum was used. The parent training group had five goals: (1) broaden parents' understanding of their children's disorder; (2) identify their children's strengths and challenges; (3) use behavioral techniques at home and in public places; (4) build healthy family interactions; and (5) improve parental anger/stress management. Weekly homework assignments, which paralleled the skills taught in the child training group, were assigned.

The sample included eight children (6 males, 2 females), with an average age of 68 months (5.7 years). Three children attended preschool, two were in kindergarten, one was in first grade, and two attended second grade. All of the children were Caucasian. Parents' educational level was as follows: one earned a high school diploma, five earned BA/BS, six earned MA/MBA, and one earned a doctoral degree.

The same evaluation approach used in the first study was used in the second investigation. Parent ratings revealed significant improvements in their children's concentration in compliance situations, aggressiveness, oppositional behavior, and internalized distress. Parents also reported significant reductions in their overall stress and stress related to their competence as a parent and ability to manage their child's mood at program completion. In comparison to the first study, the addition of the parent training group produced greater reductions in children's aggressive and disruptive behavior (as measured by the CBCL) and parents' stress (as measured by the PSI-III). These findings are consistent with other investigations (e.g., Pfiffner & McBurnett, 1997; Sheridan, Dee, Morgan, McCormick, & Walker, 1996).

CONCLUSION

Children with ADHD have unique social, behavioral, and cognitive needs that require specially tailored interventions that can be implemented in the home and school. DAGs are potent therapeutic experiences that can be easily designed and transported to the classroom and playground. Group training curriculums that incorporate DAGs with behavioral skill training provide an effective, flexible, and rewarding learning experience for children with special needs.

REFERENCES

Abidin, R.R. (1990). *Parenting Stress Index* (3rd ed.). Charlottesville, VA: Pediatric Psychology Press.

Achenbach, T.M., & Edelbrock, C. (1991a). *Manual for the Child Behavior Checklist/4-18 and revised 1991 Child Behavior profile.* Burlington: University of Vermont, Department of Psychiatry.

Achenbach, T.M., & Edelbrock, C. (1991b). *Manual for the Teacher's Report Form and 1991 profile.* Burlington: University of Vermont, Department of Psychiatry.

American Psychiatric Association. (1994). *Diagnostic and statistical manual of mental disorders* (4th ed.). Washington, DC: Author.

Anastopoulos, A.D., & Barkley, R.A. (1992). Attention deficit-hyperactivity disorder. In C.E. Walker & M.C. Roberts (Eds.), *Handbook of clinical child psychology* (2nd ed., pp. 413–430). New York: Wiley.

Anastopoulos, A.D., Guevremont, D.C., Shelton,T.L., & DuPaul, G.J. (1992). Parenting stress among families of children with attention deficit hyperactivity disorder. *Journal of Abnormal Child Psychology, 20*(5), 503–520.

Bandura, A. (1973). *Aggression: A social learning analysis.* Englewood Cliffs, NJ: Prentice-Hall.

Barkley, R.A. (1990). *Attention deficit hyperactivity disorder: A handbook for diagnosis and treatment.* New York: Guilford Press.

Barkley, R.A. (1997). *ADHD and the nature of self-control.* New York: Guilford Press.

Barkley, R.A. (1998). *Defiant children: A clinician's manual for assessment and parent training.* New York: Guilford Press.

Bay-Hinitz, A., Peterson, R.F., & Quilitch, R.H. (1994). Cooperative games: A way to modify aggressive and cooperative behaviors in young children. *Journal of Applied Behavior Analysis, 27,* 435–446.

Bunker, L.K. (1991). The role of play and motor skill development in building children's self-confidence and self-esteem: Sport and physical education [Special issue]. *Elementary School Journal, 91,* 467–471.

Cohen, J. (1988). *Statistical power analyses for the behavioral sciences* (Rev. ed.). Hillsdale, NJ: Erlbaum.

Conners, C.K., (1989). *Conners Rating Scales manual.* North Tonawanda, NY: Multi-Health Systems.

Conners, C.K., Sitarenios, G., Parker, J.D., & Epstein, J.N. (1998). The revised Conners' Parent Rating Scale (CPRS-R): Factor structure, reliability, and criterion validity. *Journal of Abnormal Child Psychology, 26*(4), 257–268.

Douglas, V.I. (1980). Higher mental processes in hyperactive children: Implications for training. In R. Knights & D. Bakker (Eds.), *Treatment of hyperactive and learning disordered children* (pp. 65–92). Baltimore: University Park Press.

DuPaul, G.J., & Eckert, T.L. (1997). The effects of school-based interventions for attention deficit hyperactivity disorder: A meta-analysis. *School Psychology Review, 26*(1), 5–27.

DuPaul, G.J., Guevremont, D.C., & Barkley, R.A. (1992). Behavioral treatment of attention-deficit hyperactivity disorder in the classroom: The use of the attention training system. *Behavior Modification, 16*(2), 204–225.

DuPaul, G.J., & Stoner, G. (1994). *ADHD in the schools: Assessment and intervention strategies.* New York: Guilford Press.

Ferland, F. (1997). *Play, children with physical disabilities, and occupational therapy.* Ottowa, Canada: University of Ottawa Press.

Files, T.M., Reddy, L.A., Rubel, E., Judd, P., & Spencer, P. (1999, April). *Use of developmentally appropriate low organized games in a child and parent group training program for children with attention deficit hyperactivity disorder: A preliminary investigation.* Poster presented at the Eastern Psychological Association conference, Province, RI.

Garaigordobil, M., & Echbarria, A. (1995). Assessment of peer-helping program on children's development. *Journal of Research in Childhood Education, 10,* 63–70.

Goldstein, A.P. (1988). *The prepare curriculum: Teaching prosocial competencies.* Champaign, IL: Research Press.

Gresham, F.M., & Elliot, S.N. (1990). *Social Skills Rating System: Manual.* Circle Pines, MN: American Guidance Service.

Hand, L. (1986). *Comparison of selected developmentally oriented low organized games and traditional games on the behavior of students with emotional disturbance.* Unpublished master's thesis, Temple University, Philadelphia.

Hoag, M.J., & Burlingame, G.M. (1997). Evaluating the effectiveness of child and adolescent group treatment: A meta-analytic review. *Journal of Clinical Child Psychology, 26*(3), 234–246.

Kendall, P.C. (2000). *Child and adolescent therapy: Cognitive-behavioral procedures.* New York: Guilford Press.

Kendall, P.C., & Braswell, L. (1985). Attention-deficit hyperactivity disorder. In P.C. Kendall (Ed.), *Child and adolescent therapy: Cognitive-behavioral procedures* (pp. 98–128). New York: Guilford Press.

McCain, A.P., & Kelley, M.L. (1993). Managing the classroom behavior of an ADHD preschooler: The efficacy of a school-home note intervention. *Child and Family Behavior Therapy, 15*(3), 33–44.

McGinnis, E., & Goldstein, A.P. (1997). *Skillstreaming the elementary school child: New strategies and perspectives for teaching prosocial skills* (Rev. ed.). Champaign, IL: Research Press.

Pfiffner, L.J. (1996). *All about ADHD: The complete practical guide for classroom teachers.* New York: Scholastic Professional Books.

Pfiffner, L.J., & McBurnett, K. (1997). Social skills training with parent generalization: Treatment effects for children with ADHD. *Journal of Consulting and Clinical Psychology, 65*(5), 749–757.

Pfiffner, L.J., & O'Leary, S.G. (1993). School-based psychological treatments. In J.L. Matson (Ed.), *Handbook of hyperactivity in children* (pp. 234–255). Boston: Allyn & Bacon.

Orlick, T. (1988). Enhancing cooperative skills in games and life. In F.L. Smoll, R. Magill, & M. Ash (Eds.), *Children in sport* (pp. 149–159). Champaign, IL: Human Kinetics.

Reddy, L.A. (2000). *Early Childhood ADHD Child Training Program.* Manuscript in preparation.

Reddy, L.A., & Goldstein, A.P. (in press). Aggressive replacement training: A multimodal intervention for aggressive children. In S.I. Pfeiffer & L.A. Reddy (Eds.), *Innovative mental health prevention programs for children.* New York: Haworth Press.

Reddy, L.A., Hall, T.M., Rubel, E., Porta, N., Isler, L., Zowada, K., Rooney, J., Ricciardelli, D., & Schmelzer, B. (1999, August). *Multimodal treatment study for young children with ADHD.* Poster presented at the American Psychological Association conference, Boston.

Reed, M., Black, T., & Eastman, J. (1978). A new look at perceptual-motor therapy. *Academic Therapy, 14,* 55–65.

Schneider, L.B. (1989). *The effect of selected low organized games on the self-esteem of kindergartners.* Unpublished manuscript, Leonard Gordon Institute for Human Development through Play, Temple University, Philadelphia.

Sheridan, S.M., Dee, C.C., Morgan, J.C., McCormick, M.E., & Walker, D. (1996). A multimodal intervention for social skills deficits in children with ADHD and their parents. *School Psychology Review, 25*(1), 57–76.

Torbert, M. (1994). *Follow me: A handbook of movement activities for children.* New York: Prentice Hall.

Torbert, M., & Schneider, L. (1993). *Follow me too.* Menlo Park, CA: Addison-Wesley.

Part Five

ISSUES AND INNOVATIONS

CHAPTER 15

Primary Mental Health Project: A School-Based Prevention Program

NANCY WOHL and A. DIRK HIGHTOWER

SUCCINCTLY, THE Primary Mental Health Project (PMHP) is a school-based program for the early detection and prevention of school adjustment problems. PMHP strives to find young children in prekindergarten through the primary grades who are experiencing significant life stress and/or are just beginning to show adjustment difficulties in the school setting. Once identified and parental permission is received, children go to a playroom created in the school, either individually or in small groups (2 to 3), for 30- to 40-minute sessions once a week with a carefully selected and trained paraprofessional and a child associate, who is supervised regularly by school-based mental health professionals. The professional–child associate team increases geometrically the number of children who are helped preventively and who otherwise would slip through the cracks in our educational system. While in the playroom, children communicate through

The Primary Mental Health Project is supported in part by the North Tonawanda City School District, the New York State Department of Education, the New York State Office of Mental Health, the Coordinated Care Services of Monroe County, Monroe #1 Board of Cooperative Educational Services, the United Way of Greater Rochester, and other school districts from New York and across the United States. Opinions expressed in this chapter are those of the authors and not necessarily those of the above organizations.

play; develop a strong relationship with the warm, caring, empathic child associate; and develop competencies that help make their stress manageable, enhance their social and emotional functioning, and reduce less desirable behaviors. Ongoing training, program consultations, clinical consultations, and program evaluations help to support the school-based team's effectiveness and the program's integrity.

PMHP's five basic structural components define a PMHP program and have developed systematically since 1957:

A focus on young children.

Early detection and screening of children's early behavioral difficulties.

The use of carefully selected child associates as service providers.

A role change of the school-based mental health professional to that of team coordinator, trainer, supervisor, and mentor.

Ongoing program evaluation.

PMHP began as a small, pilot demonstration project in a single school. It was prompted by two observations that remain valid today: classroom teachers reported that a majority of their time was preempted by the problems of a few (three to four) children, to the detriment of the whole class; and referrals for mental health issues occurred primarily between elementary and high school. However, a review of cumulative school records indicated that many referred children had histories of school adjustment problems that started in kindergarten and the early primary grades. Either helping resources were not available for those students or the significant adults involved had hoped that the troubles would disappear. Far from vanishing, early problems frequently grow and spread to many costly areas, including substance use, delinquency, and serious mental health problems (Cowen, Pedersen, Babigian, Izzo, & Trost, 1973; Ensminger, Kellam, & Rubin, 1983; Hawkins, Jishner, Jenson, & Catalano, 1987; Kellam, Simon, & Ensminger, 1983; Mrazek & Haggerty, 1994).

These observations pointed to the need for an alternative that would provide a prompt, effective, "secondary" preventive intervention or "indicated" prevention program (Durlak, 1997). The goal of PMHP is to find and reduce adjustment difficulties as soon as possible in a youngster's life, so that later, more serious and costly difficulties are prevented. Attending to difficulties early in young, modifiable children is better and more effective than waiting until problems are fully entrenched and the prognosis for change is the poorest.

PMHP is supported by four decades of research demonstrating its effectiveness (Cowen et al., 1975, 1996; Nafpaktitis & Perlmutter, 1998). Reviewers have cited PMHP as an exemplary prevention program (Dwyer & Bernstein, 1998; Elias et al., 1997; Nastasi, 1998; Weissberg, Gulotta, Hampton, Ryan, & Adams, 1997) and PMHP has received a number of awards as an outstanding prevention program: Lela Rowland Award (National Mental Health Association, 1984), Sharing Successful Programs (New York State Education Department, 1988), Model Program in Service Delivery in Child and Family Mental Health (Division of Child Youth and Family Services, American Psychological Association, 1993), and Quality Award for Excellence in Human Service Programming (United Way, 1995).

The five structural elements of PMHP provide its basic framework. The approach allows flexibility and has been used successfully even with substantial variations in its practices. Although the PMHP structural model remains consistent, program implementations have varied in (1) specific measures and processes used in the early detection and screening component; (2) types of child associates (e.g., volunteer versus paid nonprofessionals, students, retired persons, educational levels, gender); (3) types of professional staffing patterns, (4) how child associates actually work with children (e.g., individual versus group, nondirective versus directive, psychodynamic versus behavioral); and (5) the intensity of parent participation.

Successful prevention program implementations must adapt to the realities of each setting, the resources available, the underpinning belief systems, and the prevailing practices (Hightower, Johnson, & Haffey, 1995). PMHP has a track record of demonstrated success in reducing school adjustment difficulties in a variety of settings (Cowen et al., 1983, 1996; Thomas, 1989; Weissberg, Cowen, Lotyczewski, & Gesten, 1983). It is a model that has worked effectively in the states of California, Connecticut, Hawaii, Illinois, Maine, Michigan, New York, Ohio, Oklahoma, and Washington. Similarly, it has been effective in large urban schools such as in New York City and Los Angeles and in small rural schools with a K–12 population of 400 students. Significant improvement has been demonstrated for boys and girls, as well as for African American, Asian American, Caucasian, Hispanic American, and Native American children (Cowen et al., 1996). No single description fully captures how PMHP operates in all schools, but the following provides a reasonable account of the basic program components.

BASIC PROGRAM COMPONENTS

This section is intended to be a summary of PMHP's basic components and how the program works. It begins with a basic sequence of how to set up a PMHP program and the setting where PMHP operates—the playroom and its equipment. Next, it describes PMHP's core defining elements in more detail: the screening and referral processes, the types of children involved, the school staff involved in PMHP and their roles—a typical school-based PMHP team. Special emphasis is given to the characteristics of the child associates, their training, and their supervision. After a case illustration is provided, the structure and functions of PMHP's technical assistance and training centers, Regional Centers, are presented.

PMHP Start-Up: Planning and Preparation

School stakeholders, including the board of education, the superintendent, administrators, mental health professionals, teachers, and parents, need to participate in the planning and start-up steps, both to educate themselves about PMHP and to offer their input in adapting it to a new system. Such involvement increases participants' sense of program ownership, responsibility for the program, and success of the implementation. Program start-up is successful when stakeholders (1) have identified and articulated a need for serving young children's mental health needs early; (2) understand PMHP's rationale and goals and how PMHP works; and (3) have planned how PMHP will be integrated into the school system's continuum of support services that lead to student success. Because schools differ in their readiness and due process decision-making mechanisms, time between initial exposure to PMHP and a program's start may range from six months to 10 years, with an average of two years. A summary of that process is provided here; detailed descriptions of start-up processes are provided in Cowen et al. (1996), Hightower et al. (1995), and Johnson (2000).

First, children's needs must be documented and reported. Suitable methods to garner such information include focus groups with teachers and parents; faculty discussions regarding barriers to learning and pathways to overcome those barriers; a review of school records for children in fourth to eighth grades; and a collection of screening information on the school adjustment and mental health needs of children in grades prekindergarten to third.

After need is established, it is essential for stakeholders to learn enough about PMHP to enable them to form a judgment about its match with their needs and school system. This stage can include presentations from consultants at the school site; viewing available videos; visiting presently functioning programs; attending three-day intensive internships at laboratory demonstration schools; or reading the volumes of PMHP books, program development manuals, and research articles.

Figuring out how PMHP can be integrated into the school system is extremely important. This involves reviews of budgets, personnel and discipline policies, the organizational chart, school schedules, screening and evaluation processes, available program options for young children at risk, staff receptivity, existing staff responsibilities, and communication systems for staff and parents, and available space. In addition, careful planning as to how PMHP will complement existing systems, processes, and programs is necessary. Without such planning, the start-up process will be less than totally successful.

THE PLAYROOM AND ITS EQUIPMENT

Typically, the school principal designates what space will be used by whom in a building. The PMHP playroom should be a safe, comfortable place for children, as well as inviting and welcoming. It is desirable for child associates and children to have individual, semipermanent areas, often partitions in a larger room, they can call their own. Such space offers the privacy needed to work effectively. Empty classrooms can be converted to meet PMHP space needs by using dividers, bookshelves, and storage bins. The goal, in any case, is to carve out an environment that is comfortable and engaging for young children.

Playrooms are like personalities; no two are exactly alike. However, some materials that engage children in play and expressive behavior are found in most playrooms. Examples include a furnished dollhouse with small human figures, puppets, paper, glue, scissors, crayons, paints, paper, clay, dolls, stuffed animals, a sandbox with associated tools, dramatic play materials, and a variety of games. A guiding principle is that the professional and child associate must be comfortable with the materials and organization of the playroom.

SCREENING AND REFERRAL PROCESSES

Early detection, screening, and referral are focal in PMHP; they form the base on which the program's early preventive intervention steps rest. Conceptually, screening in PMHP is an ongoing process. It extends over time, uses multiple methods and sources, and reflects informal as well as formal components.

Personnel in all schools witness children's daily behavior. Typically, when concerns about a child's behavior reach a certain threshold, which can be quite high, the child is referred to a building team or mental health professional. In PMHP schools, a similar informal process occurs, but the acceptable threshold for faculty and staff to seek assistance and consultation is lowered significantly. There is ready access to the PMHP team (e.g., principal, school-based mental health professionals, teacher, and child associates) for raising concerns, discussing them, and getting immediate feedback about next possible steps. Hence, there is continuous informal screening in PMHP schools and a mechanism (i.e., team contact) for addressing concerns that arise spontaneously at any time, in any class.

Screening

PMHP's formal screening process attempts to develop an accurate representation of children's early school adjustment so that appropriate effective services can be provided as early as possible for those children who will benefit the most from PMHP. Additionally, this program structure provides an efficient mechanism by which the school staff, including the PMHP team, can review the early school adjustment of all children targeted (first grade, kindergarten to third grade, etc.). However, not all pertinent emotional and social dimensions can be assessed in an initial screening step. Metaphorically, a series of "snapshots" are taken over time using various techniques, various lenses, and different angles so that a composite description of each child's current adjustment and needs becomes more vivid.

The PMHP screening process begins with the collection of information as soon as school starts. Teachers and other PMHP team members observe students in various school settings (e.g., classrooms, halls, cafeteria, and playground). Child associates often arrange times with teachers to observe children in the classroom. Team members review school records and, when possible, screening information from prior years. Some teams also do structured observations during standardized assessments; others interview parents of selected students.

Many schools use rating scales developed and/or refined by PMHP. For example, the 12-item AML-R Behavior Rating Scale is often completed by the primary grade teacher for each child. This instrument assesses the frequency of acting-out, moodiness and learning problem behaviors (Primary Mental Health Project [PMHP], 1995). Other schools use the slightly longer Teacher–Child Rating Scale that assesses both problem behaviors and competencies (Perkins & Hightower, 2000). For children in second grade and above, the Child Rating Scale, a child self-report measure, can be completed by each child. This measure assesses externalized, internalized, and social behaviors, as well as interest in school (Hightower et al., 1987; PMHP, 1995).

Although many of these informal and formal processes are school or district specific, the overall PMHP screening process strives to be systematic, multidimensional, and outreaching. Its prime goal, at least in a preliminary way, is to identify existing problems and competencies in several relevant domains of school functioning for all children early in their school careers.

Referral

Although the formal screening process identifies most children who are referred to PMHP, referrals are accepted throughout the year. For some children, initial problems that did not meet threshold initially could increase and the teacher might subsequently refer such a child. Other children with behavior problems transfer into a school. Sometimes, children who were doing well initially experience buffetings or life traumas that adversely affect their school adjustment. And, as PMHP becomes better known within a school, parents initiate a number of referrals.

In summary, referrals to PMHP can, and do, come from many sources, and for many reasons; there are multiple routes to services. One of those sources is the formal screening process. Referral, however, is always an open option in a PMHP school; it can come from anyone, for any child, at any time.

CONFERENCE

After initial screening steps are complete, relevant information is brought together at an assignment conference. The PMHP team reviews the assembled information, creates profiles of children's school adjustment, identifies children who are most appropriate for PMHP services, and then seeks written parental consent. If the parent agrees with the referral recommendation, additional data gathering begins and an intervention plan is formulated.

CHILDREN SERVED BY PMHP

PMHP's preventive approach is to intervene effectively with children as soon as problems are identified to optimize children's school functioning. In pursuing this goal, PMHP targets young children with school adjustment problems in the mild to moderate range—not children who need professional help. Children most appropriate for PMHP include those who (1) are shy, withdrawn, not involved, nervous, sad, often fearful in school, or "flat"; (2) become frustrated frequently and act out, lose their tempers easily, fight, seek attention aggressively, or regularly disobey adults; (3) do not get along with peers, are socially isolated, have few friends, or are repeatedly chosen last for games; (4) fail to complete their schoolwork, have limited attention span, are disorganized, routinely need adult attention, or are frequently off-task; or (5) are experiencing life crises such as parental divorce, sickness or trauma of a parent or sibling, or death of a close relative. In summary, PMHP targets and works most effectively with those children who are just starting to show a few of these problems, rather than those with numerous or already serious deeply entrenched difficulties.

SCHOOL-BASED PMHP TEAM

Central to the PMHP team are school-based mental health professionals, such as school psychologists, school social workers, and elementary counselors, both full-time and part-time, and the child associates, who are complemented by the principal and teachers. A principal's positive involvement sets a tone for PMHP to function effectively. Primary grade teachers are central to PMHP; they are the prime source of referrals. Moreover, their efforts, as part of the team and in the classroom, contribute to positive outcomes for children. In some schools, consultants and other school staff (e.g., school nurse, occupational therapist, physical therapist) have important roles to play. The team, in any case, has responsibility for all aspects of a building's PMHP. In that context, teams often hold weekly or biweekly meetings to review program progress and plan for the future.

PROFESSIONAL ROLES AND ACTIVITIES

School-based mental health professionals are intimately involved in the entire program and are usually responsible for overseeing the day-to-day operations. They manage the early detection and screening process; coordinate communication with parents and the public; help select, train, provide clinical oversight to, and supervise child associates; consult with teachers and other school staff; facilitate or conduct the evaluation; assist in preparing project reports; and participate in ongoing staff development. As can be observed, during the time the school-based mental health professionals are involved with PMHP, their roles may differ substantially from the traditional roles. The essence of that difference is that the PMHP professional, rather than doing in-depth diagnostic and therapeutic activities with a few of the school's most troubled children, seeks to promote effective early detection and preventive interventions for many more children than traditional approaches can reach.

THE CHILD ASSOCIATE

Over the long history of PMHP, using paraprofessionals to address the shortage of mental health professionals and to supply direct services to children has proven to be a successful model (Cowen et al., 1996; Durlak,

1979; Hattie, Sharpley, & Rogers, 1984). Key to the success, however, has been the recruitment and selection of persons with "natural talents" who can stimulate a self-healing process in the children selected for this program.

Child associates possess very special qualities that include, but are not limited to, maturity, a history of successful experiences with young children, flexibility, good communication skills, intellectual interest in learning about the field of mental health and child development, responsiveness to the supervision process, good personal adjustment, a sense of humor, and, perhaps most important, strong nurturing and intuitive capabilities.

The above constitutes an impressive list of characteristics. The process of identifying appropriate child associates takes priority over all other considerations, for no training program can compensate for a poor selection at the outset. Insofar as the selection process is critical to the ultimate success of the program, it is strongly recommended that the individuals who will be actively involved in the supervision of child associates be involved in their selection. A rule of thumb is that if any member of the team is uncomfortable with a candidate, the individual should be referred elsewhere for employment.

Training of Child Associates

Training of child associates is a key component in the ongoing delivery of PMHP services. Even associates who have worked for many years in the project require ongoing staff development. Training is generally divided into two broad categories: introductory and continuing. Introductory training includes certain basic components; continuing training should be designed to expose associates to a variety of approaches in the playroom and to refine skills for addressing more specific problem areas.

Introductory training normally involves six to eight training sessions of approximately two hours each. It begins with a review of employment policies, evaluation procedures, and a history and description of the project, its operation, and components. An orientation to the various screening and pre-post measures is undertaken, as associates will be involved in the administration and use of the measures throughout the school year. A significant amount of time is then devoted to confidentiality issues, ethical practice, and child abuse guidelines. The role of mental health services in schools is also covered. School personnel may view project staff in widely discrepant ways: as welcome colleagues, as intruders, even as targets of open hostility. Trainers need to address these concerns with associates and emphasize that PMHP's focus is on the children, their families, and staff who are served by the program, and not on a district's political issues. Last, the role of supervision in PMHP is explained, including the concepts of transference and countertransference. The above topics typically cover three sessions.

Sessions 4 and 5 focus on the child associate's relationship with the child. Core components of relationship building are covered, including unconditional positive regard, reflective listening, and verbal and nonverbal behaviors that enhance trust building. Developmental stages are also outlined, with special attention to the maturational tasks of the elementary school child. Suggested activities for the first session are also presented. It is emphasized that children are not introduced to the program with statements such as "You're here because you have trouble paying attention in class." A number of programs have prepared short coloring books for children that are read in the first sessions and give a child's-eye view of their participation in the playroom. The books focus on what child associates and children will do together, including playing, sharing feelings, and learning new things. Some programs train associates to do kinetic family drawings in the first session, which provide good material for supervision later.

The next two sessions are devoted to what might be termed playroom basics. An understanding of the purpose and value of children's play is provided (Axline, 1947), along with a discussion of what can be gained through play observation. The difference between play content and play process is also taught, as well as the components of age-appropriate or "normal" play. An introduction to child-centered play, its eight principles, introductory and departing messages, and guidelines for setting limits is then undertaken. This session needs to include extensive hands-on practice with the child-centered "stance" and techniques, so a lot of role playing is indicated. Many child associates have commented that this practice is difficult and unfamiliar at first; however, it is our experience that after a time, they become quite natural and expert at it. Having experienced child associates participate with new associates in introductory sessions is extremely useful.

From child-centered play we move into some variations. The work of Joop Hellendoorn (1988) on imaginative play techniques has been incorporated in some training and has provided associates with additional tools. Specifically, she suggests deeper exploration of the child's play, including ways to enhance children's verbalizations via discussion of the play persons, their feelings, and interactions, and how these may relate to the child's life. Discussions at this stage also concern the interpretation of play. Child associates are encouraged to use supervision to prepare for any use of interpretation; whether interpretation will be used depends on the insight and skill of the associate as well as the stage of the relationship and the extent of available knowledge regarding the child's life circumstances.

The final training element in the introductory component deals with termination issues. Termination regularly arouses powerful feelings for both children and associates, so dealing with transference and counter-transference issues is key. Various termination scenarios are role played at this point to prepare associates. Many programs also prescribe a number of specific termination activities; we have successfully used the symbolic bag of items along with a short booklet (i.e., "This star is to remind you to shine and always do your best" . . .) as well as photographs, songs, and termination celebrations, which, in some programs, include parents. Inclusion of parents in a positive, uplifting termination event also serves to underline the legitimacy of the program in the school setting and helps establish support for the program.

Continuing training should serve to expose child associates to what might be called topics in play therapy (Schaefer & O'Connor, 1983), although the term therapy is avoided, as it is not consistent with the preventive nature of the service and also may cause school officials to be worried about program content. Directive techniques begin to be addressed at this stage, with a focus on when and why to introduce directive play. A rule of thumb is that nondirective play is preferable if it appears to be productive, meaning that it is allowing the child to explore personal feelings and themes. Where nondirective play is not deemed helpful in allowing a child to deal with a particular issue/concern or the child is actively avoiding such material, the child associate and supervisor may decide to use directive strategies (Ginott & Lebo, 1961). Directive play may also be indicated if a child needs to address specific skill deficits that can be remedied using prepared materials. In some cases, children may also require specific information that directive materials can provide, as, for example, with family alcoholism or divorce. Continuing training sessions have focused on such areas as game play, use of puppets (particularly with reference to the puppetry work of Elizabeth Irwin), strategies and materials for working with the angry child, storytelling, solution-focused approaches, social problem solving, social skills development, and several common problem areas such as children of divorce and children of substance abusers (Irwin & Shapiro, 1975).

It should be noted that the majority of training for child associates will be delivered by the school mental health professionals responsible for supervising the project. Hence, it becomes imperative for supervisors to undertake their own course of study in play therapy. Many school mental health professionals have found this to be a huge professional and personal bonus of becoming involved in PMHP.

Supervision of Child Associates

In addition to training, child associates are provided with regular, typically weekly, supervision to ensure their growth and development. Also, mental health professionals must assume clinical responsibility for child associates' work, which means ongoing supervision is necessary. Mijangos and Farie (1992) point out, "The supervisory relationship is the vehicle through which professionals and paraprofessionals, together, provide helping services to young children in schools" (p. 2). This relationship is further characterized by an interdependence in which child associates rely on supervisors for expertise, and child associates, in turn, supply special attributes that expand the professionals' reach to many more children. Supervision will vary from program to program, depending on the team's resources, philosophy, and style. Many programs use a combination of individual and group supervision meetings. "As needed" supervision must be anticipated and accommodated; sometimes, this proves to be the most valuable learning time! Supervision may be conducted using case notes, audio or visual materials, and/or by having the supervisor observe sessions with the child.

School mental health professionals vary in their clinical supervision experience; lack of training and/or experience in supervision may result in neglect of the process. In fact, current literature suggests that course work in supervision of work with children is almost nonexistent. Also, when professionals do possess supervisory experience, it has typically been with interns or professionals who lacked experience but had similar educational backgrounds. In contrast, child associates are chosen for their ability to relate to children, not for their professional training. Some professionals may express concerns about the ability of paraprofessionals to be effective; others may romanticize the special attributes of child associates, leading them to expect more than can be delivered. In other cases, supervisors may express ambivalence in this new role (Mijangos & Farie, 1992). It is important for supervisors to discuss their changing role with PMHP program consultants and to obtain ongoing peer support and consultation, which can be provided by PMHP's technical assistance and training centers, the Regional Centers.

In supervising child associates, it is important to remember that the task is not to impart formal theories, but rather to help associates understand young children and relate to and respond to children in ways that are therapeutic. Some supervisors might approach sessions as time to explore ideas; others may translate their own theories into concrete suggestions for words and actions to be tried in the playroom. Ideally, supervisors are flexible in their approach; this is critical in a process whose ultimate goal is often to enhance the child's own flexibility and coping skills.

Although there are many theory bases for mental health work with children, Mijangos and Farie (1992) suggest four frameworks that supervisors need to be versed in: Rogerian theory, cognitive-behavioral theory, systems theory, and psychoanalytic self psychology. Being able to draw from these various approaches will enhance the quality of work that is produced and will offer a range of learning experiences for both associates and professionals. A more detailed discussion of each approach is laid out in the manual, with examples taken from clinical supervision.

In all supervisory work with paraprofessionals, the parallel process will occur. Parallel process is defined as the phenomenon through which supervisees present themselves to their supervisors as their clients present to them. Mijangos and Farie (1992) offer the following illustration of this in supervision of child associates:

> A child associate arrives for supervision unable to begin talking about a child assigned to her. She starts and stops and changes direction with her thoughts and words. Then she tries another tack and begins to ask the supervisor a lot of questions. Confusing as this may seem to the supervisor, supervision has begun. The supervisee is relaying to her supervisor how it looked and felt to be with a child who came into the playroom and didn't know where to begin. . . . In parallel the child associate now looks for help from the supervisor in order to begin. Depending on the supervisor's style and his or her assumptions about what is helpful to people, the response could be as direct as laying out an agenda, or as indirect as saying, "Begin wherever you're comfortable," or could address how it feels to be in a new situation. . . . As the process continues, the supervisor begins to distinguish between the supervisee's words and actions that reflect only the child's words and actions and those that indicate true parallel process in which the supervisee struggles with an issue similar to the child's. (pp. 11–12)

Supervisors must be astute in recognizing their own feelings as the process continues; those feelings and concerns that are introduced into the relationship will also contribute to the direction the supervision takes. For example, if a supervisor is strongly biased toward one approach, this will likely be communicated to the child associate, who will begin to feel there is only one correct way to be helpful.

Conoley and Conoley (1989) suggest that another way of approaching the supervision task is for supervisors to assess their own skills in three areas that define the supervisor role: teaching skills, counseling skills, and consultative skills. Their work defines each skill area operationally and encourages supervisors to identify their preferred style, the areas where they have the least and most experience, their strengths and weaknesses, and important events in their own supervision history.

Additionally, assessment of the supervisee's skill level is critical. The child associate's ability to form a therapeutic relationship, verbal and nonverbal behaviors, willingness to share, willingness to experiment with new strategies, and creativity in selecting playroom activities to meet desired goals all must be considered in the supervision process. Supervisors will also need to evaluate child associates' knowledge level regarding their feelings in relation to the children and their ability to conceptualize. These areas will develop with time; often, we find that experienced child associates become extremely competent, with skill levels equal to those of trained child therapists!

As a program, PMHP has placed great emphasis on the supervisory process and provides specific training sessions on this process for both supervisors and supervisees. With effective supervision, PMHP is a robust and effective program; without effective supervision, PMHP will falter.

CASE ILLUSTRATION

Maggie P. was a second-grade student referred to PMHP by her teacher after the teacher and the school-based mental health professional, in this case a social worker, reviewed the results of the preliminary screening instrument, the AML Behavior Rating Scale. On the AML, Maggie scored in the "at-risk" range for both acting-out and moodiness. Specific items endorsed in the moderately at-risk range included the following: gets into fights or quarrels with classmates, is unhappy, disrupts class discipline, feels hurt when criticized, and is moody. Based on these results, a classroom observation, and her teacher's feeling that she would benefit from the program, a longer scale, the Teacher–Child Rating Scale, was administered. On this measure, Maggie scored with concerns in behavior control, task orientation, and peer social skills. She was noted to be a very bright child who was picking up quickly on classroom skills and who was, in fact, a little too assertive, sometimes bossing other children in the class or complaining against others to the teacher. A self-report measure, the Child Rating Scale, indicated mild concerns under school interest (i.e., being bored, not liking to do school work) and peer social skills (i.e., "other kids are mean to me").

With this information in hand, the social worker contacted the parent to discuss Maggie's participation in PMHP. General information about the nature and intent of the program was offered, along with a brief explanation of some of the presenting concerns in Maggie's case. Maggie's mother indicated that some of these difficulties had been noted at the end of the first grade. She was very welcoming of PMHP services for her daughter. The parent was asked to review an information packet that would be sent home and then to attend the parent orientation meeting in one week. At that time, parental permission could be obtained.

Parental permission was obtained at the meeting. It was agreed that Maggie would begin with the child associate immediately and that a parent conference to set goals and obtain additional background information would be scheduled in three weeks.

Maggie and the child associate, who in this program is referred to as a special friend, began sessions in the playroom. Maggie initially presented herself as quite negative regarding school and other children in particular. She complained that others were routinely mean to her. She liked coming to PMHP and enthusiastically engaged in play activities, but tended to be very bossy and was often critical of her special friend (e.g., "You're not playing with that right. That's not how that piece goes").

This was somewhat difficult for the child associate, who sometimes felt she was being judged by the child and found wanting. It was suggested that she reflect the child's desires back to her, as in "You really want me to get this right," or "You get upset with me if I don't do it the way you want." This established an accepting atmosphere in which the associate could eventually address how other children might respond to such behaviors and also might allow the child to draw her own such conclusions.

Family information was obtained after Maggie had been in the program for three weeks. In this program, parents are met with after approximately three to four sessions. At this conference, we reviewed the selection data and went over the program components again with the parents so they knew what to expect. Pertinent child and family history was obtained and goals were set at the close of the conference. Maggie's mother indicated that rule compliance at home was a problem at times. In addition to Maggie, she has a 3-year-old son, also by Maggie's father, who was noted to have a history of severe respiratory problems, necessitating frequent medical visits. Mrs. P. indicated that she was a single parent, but has recently started dating. She notes that Maggie has been jealous of her dates. Maggie sees her father regularly and the visits were reported to go well. In the mornings she often whines about not wanting to come to school which her mother disallows. Although she is reported to like school more this year than last year, she makes frequent visits to the school nurse asking if she can be sent home. No medical problems were noted and development was within normal limits.

It was suggested that Maggie's mother continue to hold firm about sending her to school. It was further recommended that Mother capitalize on Maggie's many competencies by allowing her opportunities to help with household chores and encourage her to be independent. Three goals were established for Maggie: (1) to increase self-control in the classroom, (2) to demonstrate improved school interest, and (3) to improve peer social skills (i.e., making and keeping friends).

Maggie's special friend used a variety of hands-on materials in the playroom. Initial play materials included Play-Doh, sand, and puppets. She was able to express feelings easily while playing, noting "I don't like to do school work," and expressing concern she might get yelled at by the child associate. A nondirective, child-centered approach worked well here. The only limits that needed to be set related to Maggie's not wanting to leave the playroom. At session 5, the child associate introduced some directive materials, dealing with school adjustment, from a prepared manual. Maggie responded positively to this. During session 7, they agreed together to work on a large body-sized portrait of Maggie that would illustrate all the things she could do herself. In session 8, she commented, "I love coming here. I thought I was going to have to do work, but I get to play." By session 9, Maggie was beginning to demonstrate increased flexibility, was proudly coming to the playroom and returning to class by herself, and was better able to handle limits.

In mid-February, the child associate and social worker conferred with Maggie's teacher, who noted that Maggie was making very good academic progress. She was improving in listening and seemed to be trying. Social skills were a continuing concern; Maggie was bossy, and would then deny or make excuses for her behavior.

Following this conference, the social worker suggested to the child associate during supervision that she introduce additional materials dealing with social skills. These materials included short books, worksheets, and games. Because Maggie engaged freely and imaginatively in puppet play, and her puppet stories often depicted conflicts between characters (e.g., name calling), these scenarios provided rich material for intervention around prosocial versus antisocial behaviors and suggestions on ways to make and keep friends.

Toward termination, some regression was noted. Maggie began to ask many demanding questions and became increasingly bossy and whiny. Once again, a child-centered approach was taken, with limits clearly but unemotionally articulated. During these final sessions, Maggie was given the choice of what to do. She was able to verbalize a lot about her own behavior, stating "I really get angry when I don't get my way. I go in my room and scream." The child associate noted that everyone gets angry and she was already doing something to let her feelings out and not hurt anyone. Again during supervision, it was suggested that the child associate help Maggie with additional anger management techniques, which could be practiced and reinforced in the playroom using games and other manipulatives. Maggie also stated during this time, "I hate my brother sometimes, but I wish he wasn't sick so much." This represented good therapeutic progress and allowed the child associate to acknowledge the child's ambivalent feelings as normal. Maggie was encouraged to share feelings with important adults in her life. By the final session (number 20), Maggie had improved on her social behaviors; she participated cooperatively and was looking forward to the planned social at the end of the year. Termination activities included a small bag of objects symbolizing the relationship, a photograph of the child and her special friend, and a laminated place mat with the handprints of the child associate and the child.

Postdata obtained from the parent indicated that Maggie had improved social skills, was less disruptive at home, and was doing better academically. Mrs. P. had followed through at home with suggestions made, and felt, overall, that Maggie had improved significantly. Maggie's teacher indicated that self-confidence, interest in school, academic performance, and overall school behavior had improved. Visits to the nurse had all but disappeared. Social skills needed to be monitored into the new school year, with a possible referral for a social skills group if needed.

TECHNICAL ASSISTANCE AND TRAINING

Developing, implementing, and maintaining school-based prevention programs require technical assistance and ongoing support (Hightower et al., 1995). PMHP provides technical assistance and training from its home base in Rochester, New York, as well as international on-site consultation and training. In New York and California, where PMHP-initiated programs are more densely located, a system of technical assistance centers or Regional Centers has been developed. Services and materials available worldwide include assistance with all aspects of initial program setup; program development manuals, videos, and resource books; consultation with potential funders; support with the selection and initial training of the PMHP team; help in developing a strong early detection and screening process; ongoing staff development opportunities for school-based mental health professionals and child associates; continuing program consultation; and a full array of evaluation services, including evaluation design, measures, analyses, and reports.

SUMMARY

Few programs of any type can trace their history back four decades. PMHP's success exemplifies how prevention programs can start, evolve, accommodate, and adapt. One reason PMHP has enjoyed success is that its foundation is built on research and program effectiveness data that are sensitive to real-world realities. Second, although the structural elements of the program have remained surprisingly consistent, the structure itself allows for modifications by the people who know the environments into which it is introduced. Third, PMHP is cost-effective. Children receive excellent services from truly exceptional people in an efficient and timely manner. Parents, teachers, administrators, and elected officials can all enjoy benefits of the program that range from changes in children's behavior to a decreased tax burden. Therefore, PMHP, implemented correctly, considering both individual and environmental conditions, not only can survive, but can flourish in times of wealth as well as in times of scarcity.

Professionals with a long-term vision and plan based on solid research and forward thinking create services that people want and need. We believe PMHP is one school-based service that can be implemented successfully and that can create a springboard from which additional prevention efforts will follow.

SOURCE FOR PMHP MATERIALS

Primary Mental Health Project/Community Services
Children's Institute
274 North Goodman, D103
Rochester, NY 14607
Telephone: 877-888-7647 (toll-free)
E-mail: pmhp.org

REFERENCES

Axline, V. (1947). *Play therapy.* Boston: Houghton Mifflin.

Conoley, C.W., & Conoley, J.C. (1989). *Supervision manual.* Lincoln: University of Nebraska.

Cowen, E.L., Hightower, A.D., Pedro-Carroll, J., Work, W.C., Wyman, P.A., & Haffey, W.C. (1996). *School-based prevention for children at-risk: The Primary Mental Health Project.* Washington, DC: American Psychological Association.

Cowen, E.L., Pedersen, A., Babigian, H., Izzo, L.D., & Trost, M.A. (1973). Long-term follow-up of early-detected vulnerable children. *Journal of Consulting and Clinical Psychology, 41,* 438–446.

Cowen, E.L., Trost, M.A., Lorion, R.P., Dorr, D., Izzo, L.D., & Isaacson, R.V. (1975). *New ways in school mental health: Early detection and prevention of school maladaptation.* New York: Human Sciences Press.

Cowen, E.L., Weissberg, R.P., Lotyczewski, B.S., Bromley, M.L., Gilliland-Mallo, G., DeMeis, J.L., Farago, J.P., Grassi, R.J., Haffey, W.G., Weiner, M.J., & Woods, A. (1983). Validity generalization of a school-based preventive mental health program. *Professional Psychology, 14,* 613–623.

Durlak, J.A. (1979). Comparative effectiveness of paraprofessionals and professional helpers. *Psychological Bulletin, 86,* 80–92.

Durlak, J.A. (1997). *Successful prevention programs for children and adolescents.* New York: Plenum Press.

Dwyer, K.P., & Bernstein, R. (1998). Mental health in schools: Linking islands of hope in a sea of despair. *School Psychology Review, 27,* 277–286.

Elias, M.J., Zins, J.E., Weissberg, R.P., Frey, K.S., Greenberg, M.T., Haynes, N.M., Kessler, R., Schwab-Stone, M.E., & Shriver, T.P. (1997). *Promoting social and emotional learning: Guidelines for educators.* Alexandria, VA: Association for Supervision and Curriculum Development.

Ensminger, M.E., Kellam, S.G., & Rubin, R.B. (1983). School and family origins of delinquency: Comparisons by sex. In K.T. VanDusen & S.A. Mednick (Eds.), *Prospective studies of crime and delinquency* (pp. 17–41). Boston: Kluwer Academic.

Ginott, H., & Lebo, D. (1961). Play therapy limits and theoretical orientation. *Journal of Consulting Psychology, 25,* 337–340.

Hattie, J.A., Sharpley, C.F., & Rogers, H.J. (1984). Comparative effectiveness of professional and paraprofessional helpers. *Psychological Bulletin, 95,* 534–541.

Hawkins, J.D., Jishner, D.M., Jenson, J., & Catalano, R.F. (1987). Delinquents and drugs: What evidence suggests about prevention and treatment programming. In B.S. Brown & A.R. Mills (Eds.), *Youth at high risk for substance abuse* (DHHS Publication No. ADM 87-1537, pp. 81–131). Rockville, MD: National Institute on Drug Abuse.

Hellendoorn, J. (1988). Imaginative play techniques in psychotherapy with children. In C.E. Schaefer (Ed.), *Innovative interventions in child and adolescent therapy* (pp. 43–67). New York: Wiley.

Hightower, A.D., Cowen, E.L., Spinell, A.P., Lotyczewski, B.S., Guare, J.C., Rohrbeck, C.A., & Brown, L.P. (1987). The Child Rating Scale: The development and psychometric refinement of a socioemotional self-rating scale for young school children. *School Psychology Review, 16,* 239–255.

Hightower, A.D., Johnson, D.B., & Haffey, W.G. (1995). Best practices in adopting a prevention program. In A. Thomas & J. Grimes (Eds.), *Best practices in school psychology: III* (pp. 311–323). Washington, DC: National Association of School Psychologists.

Irwin, E., & Shapiro, M.I. (1975). Puppetry as a diagnostic and therapeutic technique. In I. Jakab & I. Jacob (Eds.), *Psychiatry and art* (pp. 86–94). Basel, Switzerland: Karger.

Johnson, D.B. (2000). *Primary project program development manual.* Rochester, NY: Children's Institute.

Kellam, S.G., Simon, M.B., & Ensminger, M.E. (1983). Antecedents in first grade of teenage substance use and psychological well-being: A ten-year community-wide prospective study. In D.F. Ricks & B.S. Dohrenwend (Eds.), *Origins of psychopathology: Research and public policy* (pp. 73–97). New York: Cambridge University Press.

Mijangos, L., & Farie, A.M. (1992). *Supervision manual.* Rochester, NY: Primary Mental Health Project.

Mrazek, P.J., & Haggerty, R.J. (Eds.). (1994). *Reducing risks for mental disorders: Frontiers for preventive intervention research.* Washington, DC: National Academy Press.

Nafpaktitis, M., & Perlmutter, B.F. (1998). School-based early mental health intervention with at-risk students. *School Psychology Review, 27,* 420–432.

Nastasi, B. (1998). *Exemplary mental health programs: School psychologists as mental health providers.* Bethesda, MD: National Association of School Psychologists.

Perkins, P.E., & Hightower, A.D. (2000). *Teacher–Child Rating Scale, V21: Technical manual.* Rochester, NY: Children's Institute.

Primary Mental Health Project. (1995). *PMHP screening and evaluation measures.* Rochester, NY: Author.

Schaefer, C.E., & O'Connor, K.J. (Eds.). (1983). *Handbook of play therapy.* New York: Wiley.

Thomas, C.F. (1989). *An evaluation of the effectiveness of the Primary Intervention Program in improving the school and social adjustment of primary grade children: Final report.* Los Alamitos, CA: Southwest Regional Education Laboratory.

Weissberg, R.P., Cowen, E.L., Lotyczewski, B.S., & Gesten, E.L. (1983). Primary Mental Health Project: Seven consecutive years of program outcome research. *Journal of Consulting and Clinical Psychology, 51,* 100–107.

Weissberg, R.P., Gullotta, T.P., Hampton, R.L., Ryan, B.A., & Adams, G.R. (1997). *Establishing preventive services* (Vol. 9). Thousand Oaks, CA: Sage.

CHAPTER 16

Developmental Considerations in Play and Play Therapy with Traumatized Children

ATHENA A. DREWES

PLAY THERAPISTS, school counselors and psychologists, social workers, mental health professionals, child associates, and teachers should have knowledge and an understanding not only of the pathological behaviors of children, but also of normal development. Particular behaviors may be thought to indicate abuse, yet the possibility that the behaviors reflect age-appropriate development may be ignored.

The intent of this chapter is to sensitize and remind the reader of areas of normal play development and behavior. It focuses on various parameters that professionals working with traumatized children come across in their work: play stages and behaviors; the impact of trauma on development; differences in play styles; and special considerations of aggression, language and communication; and sexual behaviors in traumatized and nontraumatized children. Several case examples from the author's experience are given, along with play therapy techniques that may be helpful in working with the traumatized child.

This chapter is a slightly modified version of an article by the same title that originally appeared in the *Journal for the Professional Counselor, 14*(1), Spring 1999, pp. 37–54.

297

When treating children who may have experienced some form of trauma, both experienced and beginning play therapists must consider developmental aspects of children's play and presentation of problems. Knowledge of developmental aspects will help in differentiating normal from maladjusted behaviors. Therapists working with specialized populations in outpatient or residential settings can at times become complacent in assuming that all presenting problems indeed reflect trauma. We may overlook or magnify behaviors that may in fact be normal for the child's age and cognitive or emotional stage. This may be especially true in trying to assess whether sexual behaviors and play are within normal development or reflect some trauma.

Play therapy can be an extremely powerful modality, but it is also a complex, subtle, and sophisticated tool. The play therapist needs an in-depth understanding of how children think, interact, communicate, and change—both normally and when traumatized (Donovan & McIntyre, 1990). It is important to consider the developmental levels of the child when considering what techniques to utilize, what treatment areas will need to wait until later development has occurred, and how best to assess whether there has been progress in treatment. The therapist needs to think not just of symptom reduction when treating a child, but also of improvements in developmental progression. "In direct treatment of the child or in therapeutic work with the child . . . our objective is to bring the child up to the level of development appropriate for his age. . . . This means, further, that a theoretical knowledge of the psychosexual development of children, and the developmental tasks and conflicts which come with each stage, are an indispensable part of the worker's equipment" (Fraiberg, 1951, p. 179). Mordock (1993) also has written that therapists need to evaluate whether the child has reached developmental levels adequate for the child's age, assess the degree to which the child lags behind, and determine whether regression or arrest is responsible for the developmental imbalance. He states that by pinpointing and describing the traumatized child's developmental imbalances, a greater understanding of the child's difficulties is obtained over merely characterizing the child by symptomatology. Thus, he concludes, symptom reduction in traumatized children is not an adequate criterion of therapeutic growth. Rather, the standard of measure should be the child's developmental advancement as compared to developmental mastery for the child's age group.

Trauma can impact all levels of the child's development, including intellectual development, physical health, emotional functioning, academic achievements, and social skills. The development of attachment to caregivers, the way the child regulates affect, the child's sense of self and differentiation, and the use of symbolic and representational thought, as well as peer relations and adaptive school functioning are all affected. Finally, trauma can have different or additional meanings as a child develops. These components may result in significant impact on the child's development and require a return to therapy at a later date. Consequently, a developmentally sequenced approach to treatment needs to be considered (James, 1989).

This chapter outlines three developmental play stages as formulated by Piaget and based on his theory of cognitive development. This chapter also outlines differences in play styles and special areas of consideration, such as aggression, language and communication, and sexual behaviors, as these are manifested by traumatized and nontraumatized children. Case examples with play therapy techniques allow the reader to consider ways of conceptualizing cases along developmental lines.

The work of Piaget (1962) has been used to understand play dynamically. He viewed the development of human intellect as involving two related processes: assimilation and accommodation. In the process of assimilation, individuals abstract information into the organizing schemas representing what they already know. They also modify these organizing schemas when they do not fit adequately with their developing knowledge; this is accommodation. Play, according to Piaget, is a way of abstracting elements from the outside world and manipulating them so they fit the person's organizational schema. As such, play serves a vital function in the child's developing intellect (Bergen, 1988).

PIAGET'S STAGES OF PLAY

Piaget (1962) offers a model of development of play behavior in normal children. He defined three distinct stages in the development of play: sensorimotor play, symbolic play or pretend play, and games that have rules.

STAGE ONE: SENSORIMOTOR STAGE

Nontraumatized Children

Sensorimotor play begins at birth and continues through 18 to 24 months, coinciding with Piaget's sensorimotor stage of cognitive development. In the sensorimotor stage of play, language and symbolic function are absent. The child progresses in a logical order from reflexes through habits and into imitation. Then the child is able to wait before immediately imitating another's action. The primary function at this stage is the assimilation of sensory information into the cognitive processes. Movements attract the child more readily than stationary objects. Play evolves during this stage from a purely reflexive behavior of grasping objects and orienting toward sound and visual stimuli to displaying interest in the self or interest in and conscious control of objects in the external world (Schaefer & O'Connor, 1983). Sensorimotor play is "repetition with deliberate complication" (Rubin, Fein, & Vandenberg, 1983, p. 700), in which adaptive behaviors are consolidated and reorganized. Piaget called sensorimotor play "practice play" because of its repetitive nature (Bergen, 1988).

During the sensorimotor stage, children form object permanence and object constancy. That is, they are able to hold mental representations of people, themselves, and others in a kind of memory system, going from "out of sight, out of mind" to seeking out the missing item (Piaget, 1962). The child comes to know the world on a primitive level (Schaefer & O'Connor, 1983).

By 8 to 12 months, the purpose of play is often to have fun, seek out novel situations, and explore them with interest. Spontaneous play in children at this age is essentially a means of investigation and experimentation with the laws of nature and human relationships (Haworth, 1964). Sensoritactile contact with the world is important. Nontraumatized children continuously test out a new environment to satisfy their curiosity. In turn, they are able to gain familiarity with their surroundings, which contributes to their sense of security. Nontraumatized children will move and discover their body in relation to the space around them. They will test out their energies.

Traumatized Children

In contrast, traumatized children are inhibited in the flexibility, fluidity, and spontaneity typically seen in children during these younger years (Haworth, 1964). With normal development, the child's positive experiences, perceptions, and objects associated with those perceptions are assimilated in a positive way and the child develops trust. When this has not been a positive period, the child is not likely to develop an adequate sense of trust and, in turn, may find the ability to assimilate additional stimuli and experiences inhibited (Schaefer & O'Connor, 1983).

Strong attachment in infancy has been related to later competencies such as empathy, sympathy, problem solving, ego resiliency, high fantasy predisposition, play skills, and sociability (Curry & Bergen, 1988). Children who have suffered from a rejecting or inadequate environment in very early life may grow up with impaired development in self-esteem, unable to experience themselves or the world except as ugly, harsh, cold, painful, and unsafe (Gil, 1991). In later years, they may become needy, demanding, whiny, and constantly searching for support. As a result, transitions are difficult, with the child unable to let go or trust that they will get what they need later when the parent or adult is available. These children may become aggressive and act out, fearing close attachments, which may result in loss. Consequently, they may push people away, distance themselves through withdrawal, have greater difficulty with unfamiliar peer groups, and try to boss and control others (James, 1989).

Play Therapy Techniques

The technique of Theraplay® is useful with children who may have incurred trauma in the sensorimotor stage. Theraplay® focuses on the level of sensorimotor play, helping the child to form a relationship with a safe adult. Theraplay® was developed "to replicate the joyful and adoring features of the parent-infant interaction" (Jernberg, 1983, p. 136). Nurturing activities, imitative of positive parent-infant contact during infancy, may include gentle rocking, soft stroking, singing lullabies, applying powder to the child's back or hand lotion to the hand and arm, and hair combing. The activities allow for a re-creation of this early stage whereby the child can move developmentally forward past the emotional block and come to trust others and the world.

STAGE TWO: SYMBOLIC OR PRETEND PLAY (PREOPERATIONAL STAGE)

Nontraumatized Children

Piaget's (1962) second play stage is based on the child's development of symbolic or pretend play. This is the primary type of play behavior observed in children between 2 and 6 years. This stage coincides with Piaget's preoperational stage of cognitive development whereby the child deals with the world in a more realistic way. Curiosity and excitement are dominant at this stage. Although vocabulary development is rapidly growing, a child still has limited verbal skills during this stage. Thinking tends to be accessible more through nonverbal than verbal means. Thoughts are intuitive, imaginative, characterized by "magical thinking," and unrestrained by adult logical rules. The child begins to have symbolic representation and engages in fantasy activities. For children this age, the world is an alluring place to explore. They want to touch, smell, hear, test things out, and learn through action. They may prefer not to sit and tend to be noisy, having a great deal to say. Their point of reference will be very personal and egocentric, as they want to initiate actions by themselves. Children move from projecting their own wishes and impulses onto the environment; for instance, if a child wants more candy, he or she will state that the stuffed animal wants more candy. Children will also use their own bodies symbolically (e.g., pretending to be a lion or tree). Later, they are able to reproduce both real and fantasized events through dramatic play (Schaefer & O'Connor, 1983). The crucial development in this stage (Nicolich, 1977) is the ability to assume the "as if" position, assimilating enough stimuli and organizing them into perceptions of objects that are consistent enough to allow the child to act as if objects are present when they are not. Later on, actions may be internalized in association with objects, and children can anticipate the consequences of their actions (Schaefer & O'Connor, 1983).

In this second stage, well-functioning children make great strides toward autonomy. They are able to show pleasure in solving a task and remain involved in the face of frustration while examining alternative strategies before giving up efforts in solving the problem (Farber & Egeland, 1987). The preschooler develops self-regulation, impulse control, self-awareness, identity formation, and peer relations. The issue of control (both by the parent and self-control) is particularly critical at this developmental stage; arrests in this area due to trauma can have extreme consequences in later years (Curry & Bergen, 1988).

Gould (1972) points out that children's roles during this stage display primary identification with the nurturant/provider, the aggressor, or the victim. Consistently positive experiences with nurturance result in children's predominant identification with the provider and is evident in their role play; even those roles with highly aggressive content (e.g., Superman, police, doctor) are played with a strongly nurturant and rescuing aspect.

Traumatized Children

Children who have had primarily negative experiences in nurturance portray a prominent identification with either the aggressor or the victim. They will also manifest a rigidity in their defensive depiction of victim or aggressor representations (Gould, 1972). Such children are unable to take distance from themselves in play and tend to become the role, with difficulty distinguishing reality and fantasy. They may also have difficulty engaging successfully in play due to reluctance and limitation in using symbolic play. In addition, motivation to become engaged may come only from extrinsic rewards and requests, and expectations and demands of authority figures may generate frustration and anger. Consequently, disappointment and failed expectations due to undeveloped problem-solving skills, poor abstract cognitive thinking skills, inability to control impulses and emotions, and poor social skill development can result in limited involvement by the child (Curry & Bergen, 1988). New skills and tasks challenge the child's sense of self, and failures associated with new tasks pose a threat. These children feel insecure and untrusting of their own ability and anticipate failure (James, 1989).

A child with impaired abilities to engage in pretend play is at a disadvantage. Pretend play is often assumed to have a strong communication function and therefore is an integral part of the more analytically oriented therapies (Schaefer & O'Connor, 1983).

Play Therapy Techniques

To help stimulate pretend play, one can utilize the sandplay or sand tray technique, whereby the child creates a "picture" in the sand using miniature toys, figures, animals, and materials (Lowenfeld, 1979). Through the sandplay experience and the therapist's understanding of the symbolic meanings of the miniatures selected and arranged, a healing and integrative process occurs for the child. Hand puppets, staged dramas, and charades also help to stimulate the child's fantasies.

STAGE THREE: GAMES AND RULES (CONCRETE OPERATIONAL STAGE)

Nontraumatized Children

Piaget's (1962) final stage of play development deals with the child's participation in games with rules. This stage begins around age 6 and coincides with the concrete operational stage of cognitive development, when the child thinks more concretely and less intuitively than during the previous stage. Children become more rational and more concerned with the categories of objects. Although they are still tied to the "here and now," unable to transcend the concrete and consider different possibilities, they can begin to plan ahead and often will tackle a problem. Their approach can be practical, based on empirical evidence (Phillips, 1969). During the early part of this stage, children enjoy the process of playing, and an interest in cooperative games and eventually competitive games evolves, especially as they enter adolescence. This stage has a strong interpersonal or social component whereby the child learns to cope with constant interpersonal contact (Schaefer & O'Connor, 1983). Although most authors agree with Piaget's delineation of games-with-rules as typifying the play of school-age children, pretend play does continue (Curry & Bergen, 1988). Children are able to use dramatic play to test out many fearful fantasies under the safe guise of play. They can take distance from their frightening fantasies and feel more in control through attempted mastery in staged dramas, both written plays and dramatic play (Arnaud, 1971).

In addition, the child moves from the intrapersonal into the interpersonal level, having to deal more with social contact and group structure. If the child has established secure relationships with others, the child will have the capacity to explore the environment effectively and develop a cooperative relationship with nonfamily members (Bergen, 1988).

Traumatized Children

With impairment in this third play stage, the child's ability to play cooperatively with peers and tolerate losing is handicapped. The feelings aroused by the group situation in peer relationships may serve to escalate the child's emotional state to an uncontrollable level. Competition with rivals for attention and approval can disrupt the sense of cooperation and group cohesion necessary for a stable learning environment. The child may push to maintain a hostile, critical involvement with others (Schaefer & O'Connor, 1983).

Play Therapy Techniques

There are numerous therapeutic board games available, such as The Talking, Feeling and Doing Game by Richard Gardner (1973), that help elicit thematic and emotional material from children. However, the therapist can also be creative in utilizing games such as Checkers and Sorry for diagnostic purposes and to help elicit emotional material (Nickerson & O'Laughlin, 1983). For example, in Checkers, children must answer a question or talk about emotional issues and problems each time they take a checker in a jump, or in Sorry whenever they "bump" a piece when a Sorry card comes up.

IMPACT OF TRAUMA ON DEVELOPMENT

In normal development, the child's capacity for play will progress through developmental stages with little guidance. It is the child who has suffered a trauma, on an acute or chronic level, who can have trouble negotiating through the developmental levels and may become "stuck" at one stage or may regress to earlier infantile levels. When a child has been traumatized by events such as fire, death, divorce of parents, or by abuse, development becomes uneven or injured over many areas of functioning. The different systems (e.g., psychological functioning, physiological, cognitive, social skills and abilities) are interrelated, with advances and lags in one system affecting another (Farber & Egeland, 1987). Given that trauma can cause an arrest in the child's developmental growth process, therapy's goal is to revive this process in an accelerated form (Haworth, 1964). The development of affect regulation and differentiation, attachment to caregivers, sense of self, symbolic/representational thought, peer relations, and adaptive school functioning are all impacted. Therapeutic progress can be measured by the extent to which the child relives and can move beyond each of the earlier phases until the stage appropriate to the child's current maturational level is achieved (Haworth, 1964). The child is able to recapture those phases of former development that have not been fully assimilated into the child's present, incomplete state of maturing.

Assessing Cognitive-Developmental Level

Because emotions enhance, propel, and occasionally impede development, they deserve careful consideration and nurturing on the part of the adults who have chosen to work with children. It is clear that play can be a window to children's emotional lives and that it serves as a diagnostic as well as academic tool. Both the context (i.e., style) and text (i.e., thematic content) of dramatic play can tell us where children are developmentally, what they might be grappling with emotionally, and where there could be emotional interference. These communications can then be used to further children's emotional growth (Curry & Bergen, 1988). Through observation of the child's play, the child play therapist can assess the child's cognitive-developmental level, as well as emotional issues.

Studies have shown that child abuse has severe developmental consequences, regardless of the particular area of development being studied (Farber & Egeland, 1987). Findings across various studies have found that a disproportionately large number of abused children fall below average on measures of intelligence (Morse, Sahler, & Friedman, 1970; Sandgrund, Gaines, & Green, 1974). Further, evidence is increasing that traumatic experience, as well as psychosis, can have powerful, long-lasting, possibly even permanent effects on the developing organism (Van der Kolk, 1987).

DIFFERENCES IN PLAY STYLES

Nontraumatized Children

Children's temperament and personality style need to be taken into consideration along with whether or not they have been traumatized. For example, social orientation exhibited in play is related to cognitive styles (Bergen, 1988). Children who have been identified as field-dependent (i.e., gaining their information from people) or field-independent (i.e., focusing on information in the inanimate world) show differences in play styles. Saracho (1985) suggests that a strong relationship exists between play and cognitive styles, with those children who are field-dependent being more likely to engage in parallel, associative, and cooperative play and those who are field-independent being more likely to prefer solitary play. There are also personality differences in the dimension of "playfulness" (Lieberman, 1965). Intelligence level and characteristics of the home environment also appear to be related to children's playfulness (Barnett & Kleiber, 1984). Gender differences add another dimension, in that activity levels for preschool boys are reported as higher, with girls engaging in more sedentary play (Maccoby & Jacklin, 1974). There are also individual and cultural differences in the way language is used in play. Individual styles of language ability affect levels of pretend play; object-oriented and feeling-oriented speakers show different levels of pretend play, with expressive (feeling) children showing more pretend play. Individual differences in disposition to fantasy play are evident by age 3 or 4 (Singer, 1973). High and low fantasy children do not differ by sex or IQ but do differ on ability to delay gratification and on measures of creativity. In 5-year-olds, high fantasy predisposition is related to originality, spontaneity, verbal fluency, ideational fluency, and flexibility (Pulaski, 1970).

Nontraumatized children will more easily make conversation and tend to discuss their world as it exists for them. They tend to talk more openly, spontaneously, and directly, talking about their friends, teachers, and important aspects of their life, even if shy and needing to "warm up" to the adult. Negative feelings often may be expressed directly, with children playing out in a free and spontaneous way their feelings until relief and satisfaction are achieved (Moustakos, 1959).

TRAUMATIZED CHILDREN

Trauma overwhelms children's usual coping abilities. Often, they cannot play at all, or the play they engage in does not heal them. They may remain silent in their first few sessions, speaking only with great difficulty to the therapist. However, other traumatized children may engage in a nonstop flow of questions and exchanges during their first sessions. They may attack or threaten to attack and may set up barricades, real and emotional, to keep the therapist from coming close to them. They may be cautious and deliberate in their actions, lacking spontaneity (Moustakos, 1959).

SPECIAL AREAS OF CONSIDERATION FOR TRAUMATIZED CHILDREN

AGGRESSION

Aggressive imagery appears in the play of most young preschoolers in unmodulated, barely disguised, and stereotypic depiction of monsters or wild animals, with focus on teeth and claws (Curry & Bergen, 1988). Furthermore, preschoolers and children on into elementary school years engage in rough-and-tumble play similar to that of hostile behavior (e.g., running, chasing, wrestling, jumping, falling, hitting). However, these behaviors are accompanied by signals (e.g., laughter, exaggerated movement, open rather than closed hands and faces) that indicate "this is play" (Bateson, 1956). This type of play is often hard for adults to accept, both because adults are not always able to distinguish it from aggression and also because the increasing levels of arousal that it promotes may cause an escalation that is difficult to control (Aldis, 1975).

Prosocial and aggressive behaviors may go together in some preschoolers (Radke-Yarrow & Zahn-Waxler, 1976). Those children that exhibit the most prosocial behaviors often also show a high level of aggressive behaviors (L.K. Friedrich & Stein, 1973). Children who display both these characteristics are more socially active in general. Four-year-olds with high levels of hostile aggression seem to lack perspective-taking ability, seeing others' actions as hostile to them even when they are not (Curry & Bergen, 1988). Preschoolers who are above average in aggression in play are more likely to be influenced by aggressive television programs (L.K. Friedrich & Stein, 1975).

School-age children will use dramatic play to test out many fearful fantasies under the safe guise of play. Arnaud (1971) notes that normal children will heavily invest in play and role enactment. Their play will usually be "blood and thunder melodramas, dripping with gore, featuring ambush and attack, killing and death" (p. 11). Arnaud further states that the play is often composed of ghosts, statues that come to life, "grisly folk heroes (e.g., Dracula), vampires, and people who turn out to be very different from what they purport to be" (p. 11).

Howe and Silvern (1981) identified differences in play therapy behaviors of aggressive, withdrawn, and well-adjusted children. Aggressive children had frequent play disruptions, conflicted play, self-disclosing statements, high levels of fantasy play, and aggressive behavior toward the therapist and toys. Withdrawn boys were identified by their regression in response to anxiety, bizarre play, rejection of the therapist's intervention, and dysphoric content in play. Well-adjusted children exhibited less emotional discomfort, less social inadequacy, and less fantasy play. However, withdrawn girls could not be differentiated from well-adjusted girls.

LANGUAGE AND COMMUNICATION

Children who have been traumatized may find their feelings generally overflow, and so they need limit setting and calming techniques to help contain these feelings. The children may be unable to talk about things and may be unaware of their difficulty in identifying, containing, and expressing feelings. In addition, other factors may contribute to difficulties in communication, such as parental disinterest or even retaliation if the child openly expresses feelings (James, 1989). Emotional communication may not be valued or encouraged by the family. Personality style or being shy and withdrawn can also be a factor. In the case of the loss of a parent or sibling (by death or divorce) or removal of the child or parent due to sexual or physical abuse, the family environment may not be able to deal with the child's intense feelings or to offer the consistency and reliability that the child needs. The traumatized child may display excessive dependency or become needy, demanding, and/or whiny and constantly search for support from the therapist or teacher (James, 1989).

Children from birth to 2 years of age cannot selectively attend to stimulation; they are more in tune kinesthetically, auditorily, and visually (Athey, 1988). The normally developing child responds to smell, sound, and movement. Once language is acquired, children make a shift in their ability to tune out stimuli. By 5 and 6 years of age, the child is learning more by verbal means than experientially (Athey, 1988).

However, because trauma impacts a child's language and cognitive development, the therapist must focus interactions more in the experiential than verbal sphere (Schaefer & O'Connor, 1983). Nevertheless, language should be used to help children understand their social and emotional functioning. The therapist may need to gear down language by using simpler words and shorter sentences. By pairing language with experiences, the traumatized child may be able to generalize concepts and understanding quickly (Schaefer & O'Connor, 1983).

A child that has difficulty with a concept, such as the death of a parent, may continue to have the same difficulty at each developmental shift as concepts change. However, using language in the beginning of therapy to identify these issues clearly facilitates consistent development and generalization and allows for reprocessing later on, without the need to reexperience the events (Schaefer & O'Connor, 1983). Direct modeling, reinforcement, and teaching of a particular term or concept can help facilitate communication and, in turn, help traumatized children understand feelings (Gil, 1991).

Many children have limited vocabulary to express their feelings or even identify feeling states. There are over 400 affect words, yet many children respond with the words *happy, mad,* and *sad* when asked how they are feeling. The following case example of Maria demonstrates a way to help traumatized children identify and expand their vocabulary of feelings.

CASE EXAMPLES

The following case examples are drawn from the author's personal experience in working with traumatized children.

Maria

Maria was a 5-year-old girl who, when asked how she was feeling, would respond *happy* or *mad*. Her facial expressions were also very limited; she often had one stone-faced expression regardless of the events occurring around her. In therapy, she was introduced to The Feelings Game. Small cards listing over 100 different feeling adjectives were placed into a bag and Maria had to select one of them. She was helped to read and understand the feeling word and encouraged to "try on" the expression on her face, look into a mirror, and either act out or tell a story around the feeling. The therapist and Maria would take turns each session choosing cards and playing out the feelings. Within three months, Maria's affective range and vocabulary had increased dramatically.

It is important to keep in mind that there is a developmental sequence involving children's understanding of feelings. Specifically, the very young child does not realize that feelings can be hidden, whereas latency-age children develop the belief that one can consciously control emotions and actively set aside negative feelings from one's mind. It is not until adolescence that an appreciation for the unconscious emerges (Schaefer & O'Connor, 1983).

There are also developmental differences in children's ability to appreciate that two seemingly contradictory feelings, for example, happy and sad, can coexist simultaneously. Children first deny that such feelings can coexist, then acknowledge that they can occur sequentially, and eventually appreciate the fact that they can simultaneously occur. Children's most difficult conceptual task is to realize that they can have two opposing feelings, say, love and anger, toward the same person at the same time (Schaefer & O'Connor, 1983). Children can learn the concept of ambivalence before they can express it or act it out. Through the use of drawings, they can get the idea that feelings can exist simultaneously, as seen in the next example.

Nick

Nick was a 10-year-old boy who often would walk around with a smile on his face, appearing happy, but at the slightest frustration or teasing by a peer he seethed with anger, ready to fight. In therapy, he often angrily spoke of his longing for his mother to get off drugs and become the nurturing and protective mother of his dreams. When asked to explore his feelings, Nick had difficulty expressing his ambivalence. The Gingerbread Person drawing was helpful for him. A drawing of a gingerbread person shape on paper was given to Nick. He was asked to list several different feelings he might have, and then to put a color that would identify each feeling next to the feeling word. Nick then was asked to think of an experience when he had lots of feelings at once, and to color in on the body of the drawing where each feeling might be. When he finished, Nick was able to quickly see how his ambivalence was felt within himself, and that the smiling face of his drawing masked his emotions of fear, loneliness, and love.

SEXUAL BEHAVIOR

Sexual behavior in children can cause uncertainty in the therapist because of the relationship between sexual abuse and sexual behavior. One of the problems faced by clinicians in assessing children's sexual behaviors is the lack of current normative data on the development of children's sexuality. Sexual behavior in children can be sorted into a number of categories, all of them having an adult behavior correspondence. W.N. Friedrich, Fisher, Broughton, Houston, and Shafran (1998) categorized them as follows: adherence to personal boundaries, exhibitionism, gender role behavior, self-stimulation, sexual anxiety, sexual interest, sexual intrusiveness, sexual knowledge, and voyeuristic behavior. In their study of 1,114 2- to 12-year-old children who were not sexually abused, a broad range of sexual behaviors were exhibited. Sexual behaviors that appear to be the most frequent include self-stimulating behaviors, exhibitionism, and behaviors related to personal boundaries. The researchers found 2-year-olds to be relatively sexual (compared with 10- to 12-year-olds) and noted that children become increasingly sexual up to age 5, when frequency drops. Another drop occurs after age 9, although 11-year-old girls show a slight rise in sexual behavior, primarily coming from an increased interest in the opposite sex. At age 12, boys also show a similar slight increase for the same reasons. Additional findings were noteworthy. The total number of hours in day care per week contributed to a clinically significant increase in reported child sexual behavior in children with no known history of sexual abuse. Also, parents who reported a more relaxed approach to cosleeping, cobathing, family nudity, and opportunities to look at adult movies and witness sexual intercourse reported higher levels of sexual behavior in their 2- to 12-year-old children. Behavior of the children was reflective of the context in which they were raised. W.N. Friedrich et al. (1998) also found that mothers with more years of education and who reported their belief that sexual feelings and behavior in children were normal reported more sexual behavior in their children.

This study is helpful in identifying the normal behaviors across gender and age ranges. It allows therapists, as well as physicians and other practitioners, to be able to inform parents that, for example, simply because a

5-year-old boy touches his genitals occasionally, even after a weekend visit with a noncustodial parent, it does not mean he has been sexually abused. Rather, it is behavior that is seen in almost two-thirds of boys at that age.

Sexually abused children often develop an excessive and abnormal interest in sex, an interest that is frequently expressed in precocious sexual activity (Gil, 1991). Through their work with normal and troubled children, Sgroi, Bunk, and Wabrek (1988) outlined a developmental framework for children's sexuality. Masturbation and looking at others' bodies occurs in children from birth to 5 years. Children ages 6 to 10 will masturbate, look at others' bodies, sexually expose themselves to others, and sexually fondle peers or younger children in play or game-like activities. Children in preadolescence through adolescence (10 to 18 years) will masturbate, sexually expose themselves, be voyeuristic, and engage in open-mouth kissing, sexual fondling, simulated intercourse, and sexual penetration behaviors and intercourse. Adolescents may engage in frequent sexual talk, exposure to others, sexual curiosity, sex play with peers involving genital play and comparison, and early heterosexual interest (Crenshaw, 1993).

Berliner, Manaois, and Monastersky (1986) report that pathological sexual behaviors in children are distinguishable from developmentally appropriate sexual play by examining the dimension of severity. Sexual behaviors considered inappropriate can include persistent, public masturbation that can cause pain or irritation, touching or asking to touch others' genitals, excessive interest in sexual matters (reflected in play, art, or conversation), and sexually stylized behavior imitative of adult sexual relationships. An additional characteristic of many sexualized children is a disinhibition of masturbatory behavior. A child who has not been sexually abused will abruptly stop masturbating when someone enters the room; sexually abused children, possibly having learned the sexual behavior with another person, may continue to masturbate.

Gil (1991) reports that the most severe type of sexualized behavior is coercive, including the use of physical force and resultant injury. Children's sexual behaviors tend to progress over time, with extreme behavior being indicative of psychological disturbance. She further states that premature sexual activity in children suggests two possible stimulants: experience and exposure. In addition, the therapist must keep in mind that the child may have experienced sexual contact with an adult or older child and may be mimicking the learned behavior, or the child may have been overstimulated by exposure to explicit sexual activity and may be acting out this activity.

The therapist should consider a developmentally sequenced type of treatment. Sequenced treatment (James, 1989) is necessary because past traumatic events will have different or additional meaning as the child matures. What was once experienced as generally confusing or uncomfortable may evolve into feeling shameful or exploited at a later time. Children who have been sexually abused may initially experience physical excitement and satisfaction of a reward or heightened stature as a result of sharing the secret of sexual abuse with the adult. However, at a later developmental stage, the child may begin to experience guilt feelings for having enjoyed or at least not resisted the experience. The child may further feel shame and feel responsible for causing the removal of a parent from the home. Fears around sexual identity and worries about becoming a perpetrator may emerge later as the child enters puberty. Consequently, the therapist needs to lay the groundwork that a return to therapy may be needed as additional issues surface during later developmental stages (James, 1989).

SUMMARY

Therapists need to be aware of developmental considerations when working with children in play therapy. At times, therapists can become complacent in assuming the presenting problems of a child reflect trauma when, in fact, they may also indicate normal development. By having a theoretical understanding of development across the dimensions of the stages of play and the differences between traumatized and nontraumatized children in expression of aggression, language and communication, and sexual behavior, the therapist is better able to assess the child's developmental level and lags. Play therapy techniques geared to the child's developmental arrests and regressions can help the child work through the impact of trauma, which leads to developmental advancement.

REFERENCES

Aldis, O. (1975). *Play fighting.* New York: Academic Press.

Arnaud, S.H. (1971). Polish for play's tarnished reputation. In G. Engstrom (Ed.), *Play: The child strives toward self-realization* (pp. 5–12). Washington, DC: National Association for the Education of Young Children.

Athey, I. (1988). The relationship of play to cognitive, language, and moral development. In D. Bergen (Ed.), *Play as a medium for learning and development: A handbook of theory and practice* (pp. 81–101). Portsmouth, NH: Heinemann.

Barnett, L., & Kleiber, D.A. (1984) Playfulness and early play environment. *Journal of Genetic Psychology, 144*(2), 153–164.

Bateson, G. (1956). A theory of play and fantasy. *American Psychiatric Association Research Reports, 2,* 39–51.

Bergen, D. (1988). *Play as a medium for learning and development: A handbook of theory and practice.* Portsmouth, NH: Heinemann.

Berliner, L., Manaois, O., & Monastersky, C. (1986). *Child sexual behavior distur-bance: An assessment and treatment model.* Seattle, WA: Harborview Sexual Assault Center.

Crenshaw, D. (1993). Responding to sexual acting-out. In C.E. Schaefer & A.J. Swanson (Eds.), *Children in residential care: Critical issues in treatment* (pp. 50–76). Northvale, NJ: Aronson.

Curry, N., & Bergen, D. (1988). The relationship of play to emotional, social, and gender/sex role development. In D. Bergen (Ed.), *Play as a medium for learning and development: A handbook of theory and practice* (pp. 107–131). Portsmouth, NH: Heinemann.

Donovan, D.M., & McIntyre, D. (1990). *Healing the hurt child.* New York: Norton.

Drewes, A.A. (1999). Developmental considerations in play and play therapy with traumatized children. *Journal of the Professional Counselor, 14*(1), 37–54.

Farber, E.A., & Egeland, B. (1987). Invulnerability among abused and neglected children. In E.J. Anthony & B.J. Cohler (Eds.), *The invulnerable child* (pp. 253–288). New York: Guilford Press.

Fraiberg, S.H. (1951). Application of psychoanalytic principles in casework prac-tice with children. *Quarterly Journal of Child Behavior, 3,* 175–197, 250–275.

Friedrich, L.K., & Stein, A.H. (1973). Aggressive and prosocial television pro-grams and the natural behavior of preschool children. *Monographs of the Soci-ety for Research in Child Development, 38*(4, Serial No. 151).

Friedrich, L.K., & Stein, A.H. (1975). Prosocial television and young children: The effects of verbal labeling and role playing on learning and behavior. *Child Development, 46,* 27–28.

Friedrich, W.N., Fisher, J., Broughton, D., Houston, M., & Shafran, C. (1998). Normative sexual behavior in children: A contemporary sample [On-line]. *Pediatrics, 101*(4). Available: http://www.pediatrics.org

Gil, E. (1991). *The healing power of play: Working with abused children.* New York: Guilford Press.

Gould, R. (1972). *Child studies through fantasy.* New York: Quadrangle Books.

Haworth, M.R. (1964). *Child psychotherapy: Practice and theory.* Northvale, NJ: Aronson.

Howe, P., & Silvern, L. (1981). Behavioral observation during play therapy: Pre-liminary development of a research instrument. *Journal of Personality Assess-ment, 45,* 168–182.

James, B. (1989). *Treating traumatized children: New insights and creative interven-tions.* Lexington, MA: Lexington Books.

Jernberg, A.M. (1983). Therapeutic use of sensory-motor play. In C.E. Schaefer & K.J. O'Connor (Eds.), *Handbook of play therapy* (pp. 128–147). New York: Wiley.

Landreth, G.L. (1991). *Play therapy: The art of the relationship.* Muncie, IN: Accel-erated Development.

Lieberman, J.N. (1965). Playfulness and divergent thinking: An investigation of their relationship at the kindergarten level. *Journal of Genetic Psychology, 107*(2), 219–224.

Lowenfeld, M. (1979). *The world technique.* London: Allen & Unwin.

Maccoby, E., & Jacklin, C. (1974). *The psychology of sex differences.* Stanford, CA: Stanford University Press.

Mordock, J.B. (1993). Evaluating treatment effectiveness. In C.E. Schaefer & A.J. Swanson (Eds.), *Children in residential care: Critical issues in treatment* (pp. 219–250). Northvale, NJ: Aronson.

Morse, C.W., Sahler, O., & Friedman, S. (1970). A three-year follow-up study of abused and neglected children. *American Journal of Diseases of Children, 120,* 439–446.

Moustakos, C. (1959). *Psychotherapy with children: The living relationship.* New York: Ballantine Books.

Nickerson, E.T., & O'Laughlin, K.S. (1983). The therapeutic use of games. In C.E. Schaefer & K.J. O'Connor (Eds.), *Handbook of play therapy* (pp. 174–187). New York: Wiley.

Nicolich, L.M. (1977). Beyond sensorimotor intelligence: Assessment of symbolic maturity through analysis of pretend play. *Merrill-Palmer Quarterly, 23*(2), 89–99.

Phillips, J.L. (1969). *The origins of intellect: Piaget's theory.* San Francisco: Freeman.

Piaget, J. (1962). *Play, dreams and imitation in childhood.* New York: Norton.

Pulaski, M. (1970). Play as a function of toy structure and fantasy disposition. *Child Development, 41,* 531–537.

Radke-Yarrow, M.R., & Zahn-Waxler, C. (1976). Dimensions and correlates of prosocial behaviors in young children. *Child Development, 47,* 118–125.

Rubin, K.N., Fein, G.G., & Vandenberg, B. (1983). Play. In P.H. Mussen (Series Ed.) & E.M. Hetherington (Vol. Ed.), *Handbook of child psychology: Socialization, personality, and social development* (Vol. 4, pp. 698–774). New York: Wiley.

Sandgrund, A., Gaines, R., & Green, A. (1974). Child abuse and mental retardation: A problem of cause and effect. *American Journal of Mental Deficiency, 79,* 327–330.

Saracho, O.N. (1985). Young children's play behaviors and cognitive styles. *Early Child Development and Care, 22*(1), 1–18.

Schaefer, C.E., & O'Connor, K.J. (Eds.). (1983). *Handbook of play therapy.* New York: Wiley.

Sgroi, S.M., Bunk, B.S., & Wabrek, C.J. (1988). A clinical approach to adult survivors of child sexual abuse. In S.M. Sgroi (Ed.), *Vulnerable population* (pp. 137–186). Lexington, MA: Lexington Books.

Singer, J.L. (1973). *The child's world of make-believe: Experimental studies of imaginative play.* New York: Academic Press.

Van der Kolk, B.A. (1987). *Psychological trauma.* Washington, DC: American Psychiatric Press.

CHAPTER 17

An Integrative Play Therapy Approach to Working with Children

MARIJANE FALL

MR. BROWN, a fifth-grade teacher, corners the school counselor in the lounge with concerns about Adam. Although Adam is not a behavior problem in the classroom, he is not paying attention in class, appears to be "in a fog" most of the time, is very slow to do his work, does work of very low quality, and has no close friends in the classroom. Two particular occurrences have concerned Mr. Brown. Testing by school personnel has revealed no identifying reasons for the classroom inattentiveness and problems completing assignments. Adam is of average intelligence and there are no great discrepancies in his scores on standardized measures. Second, Mr. Brown has detected an odor that appears to be coming from Adam at times. He suspects that the odor is feces. Because Adam is always immaculately clean as far as his outer appearance, Mr. Brown is confused about this odor. He notices that classmates are also reacting to the smell. "Straighten him out!" says Mr. Brown. "I'm not having that type of thing in my classroom. This is the fifth grade!"

School counselors are asked to "fix" all types of learning and behavior problems with children in a school, even problems with odor. Yet, there is no formula for a quick remedy. How should the counselor work with Adam? Question him as to the odor and tell him what to do to keep clean? Speak to the nurse about the odor? Discuss strategies for paying attention in class? Listen to him, reflect his expressed meanings and feelings, and allow him to move through his issues when he is ready? Support him with warm fuzzies and a neat pencil that says "I feel good about myself"? Ask him about his life at home and at school and attempt to figure out the problem? All of these questions have probably been asked by most of us at times. Sometimes one solution has worked, sometimes another. Sometimes no solution has worked.

This chapter presents one way for school counselors to decide how to work with a student. It is an integrative approach with the child's needs and problems directing which theory to use to assist the child with academic, personal, and social success in school. In turn, each theory has corresponding techniques. The integrative approach is presented here with three theories of play therapy. It is the expressed belief of many authors that play allows a child to communicate when no other form of communication is possible (Hughes, 1999) and that most children express themselves best through play (Henniger, 1995). Research corroborates that belief and shows differing play therapy interventions to be useful in assisting children (Landreth, Homeyer, Glover, & Sweeney, 1996). For these reasons, only play therapy theories will be described. Case examples are presented so that the reader can understand the application of theories of play in the school setting. The integrative approach utilizing the three theories follows these descriptions.

CHILD-CENTERED THEORY

Child-centered theory advocates that children will strive for self-actualization, for personal growth, given certain conditions in a relationship with the counselor (Axline, 1969; Landreth, 1991). The counselor should exhibit the qualities of caring, warmth, genuineness, and nonjudgmental acceptance of the individual exactly as he or she is (Landreth, 1991). Eventually, within this safe relationship and atmosphere, the child will not need the defense of behaviors that are currently working against learning, desirable classroom behaviors, and acceptable interpersonal social behaviors. The child will become free to change. This change may mean lowering the threshold of defensive behaviors and choosing behaviors that assist the child's natural inclinations toward growth.

The school counselor who is operating from this theoretical base will be helping the child feel safe enough through the relationship to lower his or her defenses. This is accomplished by accepting the child just as he or she is, by responding to actions or words in nonjudgmental ways, by consistently setting appropriate limits, and by being genuine in the relationship. It will not matter if the child is speaking or playing: the child's issue will be expressed in the playroom. The counselor will be responding in an empathic manner, reflecting actions, meaning, and feelings associated with the child's play and words. This response to children is what helps them feel accepted, and feeling accepted, children can begin to accept themselves and move forward in self-growth.

School counselors utilizing child-centered play therapy follow the child's lead at all times. One way to picture this relationship is to picture the child leading, pulling a rope with the counselor at the end, following along behind. The counselor reflects the child's feelings or the meaning or action of the child's words or play. The counselor does not ask questions, as that would be jumping ahead of the child and taking the lead.

Child-centered play therapy theory is a nondirective approach, but limits are an integral part of work in the playroom. However, limits are not set by telling the child not to do something; instead, as described by Landreth (1991), there are three steps to setting limits: acknowledge the feelings, state the limit, and redirect the child. Two examples of limit setting using this approach follow.

EXAMPLE 1

The child is about to stomp on the crayons.

COUNSELOR: You're mad at me and you'd like to smash those. The crayons aren't for smashing. You may punch the punching bag.

EXAMPLE 2

A child with sexualized behaviors starts to stroke the counselor's leg.

COUNSELOR: You're feeling close to me right now. My body (leg) is not for rubbing. You may sit here right beside me.

This formula for limit setting easily brings a behavior change because the limit is not about the child; the child is not being bad. The limit is about something or someone else and behaviors associated with it. Children's feelings are validated: It is OK to be who you are.

A therapist using child-centered theory might believe that Adam is somewhat defenseless in a powerful world, and assuming no physical problem with his bowels, is exhibiting encopresis as a result of this tension. He may be unable to form relationships due to shutting out the world, because the world is not a safe place to be in, a defense that has helped him cope. Although the defense may work for him in lowering his tension, it is working against him in the school learning situation and in social situations with peers. The school counselor will work with Adam in ways similar to the examples below, reflecting feelings, meaning, and actions. The counselor will allow the issues to emerge rather than questioning Adam. Examples 3 and 4 illustrate how this theory might work with two children in a school.

EXAMPLE 3

Yolanda, a first-grade student, comes into the school counselor's office with a pouty face, doesn't speak, and goes over to the toy shelves and dumps three things off. She then looks over to the counselor with a defiant look on her face.

COUNSELOR: Looks like you're feeling pretty angry today and wondering what I'm going to do about the dumping. In here, children may use the toys in most any way they choose.

YOLANDA: (Knocks two more toys on the floor and looks again at the counselor.)

COUNSELOR: Still feeling that way.

YOLANDA: (Kicks the beanbag, then pushes it away from its current place.)

COUNSELOR: Kicking that, feeling like you're the one in control, you're the one deciding things in here.

YOLANDA: (Looks at the counselor, goes to kick the counselor.)

COUNSELOR: You're still feeling angry. I'm not for kicking. You can kick the beanbag.

YOLANDA: I'm not going to stay after school even if the principal tries to make me!

COUNSELOR: You're serious about this—you won't do it.

YOLANDA: He can't make me.

COUNSELOR: You're tired of people telling you what to do.

In this dialogue, it doesn't make any difference if Yolanda speaks through her words or through her actions. The school counselor reflects her meaning, feelings, and actions. The child-centered approach results in Yolanda's experiencing the school counselor as someone who sees everything she does and still accepts her without judgment. This allows Yolanda to put her own judgment on her behaviors and, eventually, to give up the defensive behaviors that she presently uses.

EXAMPLE 4

Greely, a third-grade student, has come to see the school counselor because of a playground fight.

GREELY: It isn't fair. He always gets away with it. I always get caught.
COUNSELOR: You wish he would get caught sometimes.
GREELY: Yeah. He causes it, and I have to stay after school.
COUNSELOR: It's just not fair.
GREELY: I hate him. I really hate him. Everyone thinks he's so special, wants to be his friend.
COUNSELOR: You wish they'd notice you. You'd like to be friends.
GREELY: Well, not with everybody, but with Robbie and Steve. They think he's so-o-o great.
COUNSELOR: You get left out.
GREELY: My mother says to ignore them, but I'd like to play, too. How do you think I feel not being allowed to play?
COUNSELOR: You wish they'd play with you instead of him.

Again, the school counselor is not telling Greely that what he is doing is wrong. There is no judgment. Instead, the counselor is listening carefully for the meaning behind his words, reflecting that, and letting him know that he is heard and accepted exactly as he is. In time, Greely may be able to let go of his protective defenses and change his behaviors in order to have friends.

ADLERIAN THEORY

Adlerian theory posits recognizing children as social beings who are goal-driven and who become discouraged when their needs aren't met (Dreikurs & Soltz, 1964; Kottman, 1995). Children may then try to get needs met through goals of misbehavior such as attention, power, revenge, and inadequacy. Goal-driven behaviors of children tend to bring about corresponding emotional reactions in adults. Adults can learn to identify the child's goal through recognition of the adult feeling. Changing the adult reaction will bring about a corresponding change in the child's behaviors. This knowledge is especially useful for teachers and other adults in schools in interactions with students.

Adlerian play therapy has four phases or stages: establishing a relationship, determining the lifestyle, generating tentative hypotheses, and reorienting and educating (Kottman, 1995). The first stage is very similar to the relationship component of child-centered theory. The school counselor establishes an egalitarian relationship of equal respect and minimized power differential with the student. This is accomplished by, for instance, demystifying the counseling process, tracking behaviors, reflecting feelings, restating content, answering questions, asking questions, interacting with the child, and cleaning the playroom together. The "we" of the relationship is encouraged, in contrast to the emphasis on the "you" in the child-centered relationship. In the second stage, the lifestyle analysis, the counselor concentrates on finding out, from the child's perspective, how the child sees the world. The counselor also is interested in the views of the parents and teacher but does not debate the child's view; the child's perspective is accepted. As the counselor gains in understanding of the child's beliefs about the world and self, the counselor explores this with the child in the third stage by generating tentative hypotheses. "Could it be that . . ." or "I'm wondering if . . ." are phrases frequently used with the student to check out perceptions. If the student agrees with the statement, the school counselor may ask if the child would like to learn some new ways to deal with that hypothesis. If the child agrees, the two move into the fourth phase of finding new behaviors and trying them out in small steps. These four phases may take place over time or may be contained in a single session. An advantage of counseling in the schools is that less counseling time is necessary, as school counselors already have a relationship with most children and some information concerning the child's lifestyle.

Many interactive techniques are commonly used in Adlerian play therapy. School counselors may play games, suggest activities, or engage in bibliotherapy with the child. The game interaction often leads to hypotheses about the child's interactions with peers, reactions to stress, risk-taking behaviors, ability to make choices, and reactions to the introduction to new materials. These are all characteristic patterns that are influential in the learning process. Activities such as exploration of family constellations, birth order, three wishes, and early recollections all bring valuable information to the school counselor while assisting the child in feeling recognized as worthy and accepted without judgment.

The Adlerian play therapist frequently uses art media such as clay, painting, or drawing. A frequent assignment is "Draw a picture of your family with everyone doing something." Another tool is to use the play media to illustrate problems, for example, "Show me with the clay balls what happens to you on the playground. You are the red ball and you go out to play. What happens next?" The counselor uses the same reflective techniques utilized by the child-centered therapist and adds some perspective-taking questions and measures. The counselor tries to understand how the student functions in relationships when in the classroom, family, and social settings. Most important, how does the student perceive the interactions? This lifestyle analysis comes through the medium of the egalitarian relationship between the counselor and the student. The counselor then is able to form tentative hypotheses and assist the student in movement toward new behaviors. The example of Adam is used below.

EXAMPLE 5

COUNSELOR: Adam, Mr. Brown thought that it might be good for us to get together. He said it looked like you were having a hard time with friends in the classroom and on the playground. What's been happening?

ADAM: Nothin.

COUNSELOR: I noticed you out at recess yesterday. You were just walking around by yourself.

ADAM: No one wants to play with me.

COUNSELOR: That sounds pretty lonely.

ADAM: It's okay. My dad says to just ignore em.

COUNSELOR: Is it like you're trying to ignore them but you're still lonely?

ADAM: Yeah.

COUNSELOR: So at school it's pretty lonely. What's it like at home Adam?

ADAM: It's okay. Well, I guess it's the same. I live with my mom during the week, but she works a lot. I go to Dad's house on the weekend. They're busy, though, cause the baby cries and everything. I'm not sposed to make a mess. I try to be careful. I don't want to cause any trouble.

COUNSELOR: You try to do the right thing but it doesn't work sometimes. I wonder if you could draw a picture of your family with everyone doing something. There are some markers and paper over there.

In this session, the counselor is trying to assess Adam's perception of his world. The counselor uses a combination of dialogue and expressive media to aid in clarity and expression. How does Adam operate within that world? The counselor makes an assessment and works toward a point where tentative hypotheses can be shared with the student. If agreement can be reached, a goal is determined and small steps designed to reach that goal. The counselor recognizes that Adam cannot learn at his highest potential if his social needs are not met.

The school counselor has quickly determined that Adam is having a pretty lonely time and needs some help, but the smell of feces has not been addressed. The counselor will talk with the parent and/or school nurse and share the concerns of the teacher. A medical appointment for a check-up may be recommended to help determine the cause of the odor. If the problem is poor hygiene, the school nurse can assist the family in cleaning routines. If the problem is encopresis, the next step is determining if the cause is medical or psychological and planning treatment accordingly. This is an example of the school counselor also serving as consultant to others in contact with the child.

A second example of dialogue in Adlerian play therapy is illustrated next.

EXAMPLE 6

A 5-year-old boy has classroom and playground problems of getting along with others.

DOMINIC: OK. We're going to play house. You be the maid and I'll be the man who goes to work.

COUNSELOR: (whispering) What should I do?

DOMINIC: You do everything I tell you to and you say "Yes sir" and "No sir" to me.

COUNSELOR: Yes sir.

DOMINIC: Now go clean everything up. Get my lunch. Hurry up or you'll be fired. I've got to go to work.

COUNSELOR: (getting lunch) I'm getting everything for you. You're the boss of me.

DOMINIC: Yes. And you're not even getting paid because that's not a good lunch. And you didn't hurry enough. I'll be late. Get my hat. Now!

COUNSELOR: Nothing I do is right.

DOMINIC: Not that hat, dummy, my fireman's hat.

COUNSELOR: It's so confusing. You're letting me know that I'm always wrong.

This example shows how the simple play of a child can illustrate the child's world far better than words. In the role of the maid, the counselor is probably experiencing what it feels like to be the child. For the child, this experience of being accepted as a person with feelings of confusion and a lack of power and control, and having a chance to act out this role, begin the process of change. The counselor's acceptance and tentative hypotheses are validating ("I'm wondering if you feel like the maid sometimes. Everyone tells you what to do but it's never right."). If the child agrees, the school counselor may suggest, "Let's think of some ways you can get unconfused when Mom and Dad are both telling you different things."

COGNITIVE-BEHAVIORAL PLAY THERAPY

Cognitive-behavioral play therapy utilizes many of the techniques of expressive media from Adlerian play therapy (Knell, 1995). However, a principal difference lies in the role of feelings. Whereas Adlerian theory promotes the expression and recognition of feelings as essential to change, the cognitive behaviorist believes that if thinking or behavior changes, the feelings will change in turn. Thus, there is no emphasis on feelings; they are essentially ignored. The school counselor needs to figure out the puzzle and decide on a solution. The counselor then designs small steps that will aid the student in building the necessary skills or producing the helpful thought changes. Sometimes, the school counselor simply uses the play media to illustrate a point or to assist in the problem definition. Sometimes, the play media are used for a directive intervention. The counselor decides. In the example below, the school counselor works to aid Adam with his social skills.

EXAMPLE 7

COUNSELOR: Pretend your doll is you out on the playground and my doll is John. What usually happens when John walks by? (Counselor walks the John doll by the Adam doll.)

ADAM: Nothin. Well, I might turn around so I couldn't see John and he wouldn't see me.

COUNSELOR: OK, so turn your doll around backwards like you do. What would my doll think if you turn away? (Moves the John doll behind the Adam doll and has the doll act confused and then move along.)

ADAM: I don't know. I guess he would think I'm busy or I didn't see him.

COUNSELOR: Yeah. He might not have any idea that you would like to play with him. Let's have the dolls do that again, only this time see if you can find a way to let John know that you'd like to play with him. (Walks the John doll around a bit and then walks the doll near the Adam doll.)

ADAM: What am I supposed to do?

COUNSELOR: What do you think you could do that would at least let John know you'd like to play with him someday? (Continues to walk the John doll around in the vicinity of the Adam doll.)

ADAM: This is stupid.

COUNSELOR: (smiles) It might seem dumb to play this way, but you want a friend. Let's see what we can come up with, Adam. This may help us come up with some ideas.

ADAM: Okay. I guess I could say "Hi."

COUNSELOR: You're getting it. That's one thing you could do. Show me with the doll.

ADAM: "Hi."

COUNSELOR: (with doll) "Hi." OK. That is one way you've come up with. What might be another thing that your doll could do to let John know that you'd like to play with him?

The counselor is working to get Adam involved in the generation of possible responses in a similar situation. Although it may be a slow start, because Adam may feel a bit uneasy, acting out the scenario with dolls then possibly using a role play could be of great benefit to Adam. The small steps may enable him to get necessary support as he tries new behaviors and cognitions.

AN INTEGRATIVE APPROACH TO WORKING WITH CHILDREN

Theory is important for school counselors. It can be a guide for ways to assist a student in getting to another point emotionally, in thoughts, or in behaviors. Many school counselors believe in and utilize one theoretical approach for all children with all problems; the integrative approach advocates using multiple theories of play therapy based on the particular needs of the child at any particular time. Research shows that play therapy works (Landreth et al., 1996). This integrative approach works especially well in schools, where the purpose of school counseling is to assist children with problems and issues that interfere with reaching their learning potential (Baker, 2000). Some problems are very small; cognitive-behavioral theory is helpful to the school counselor designing an intervention in problem solving. Some problems concern ways to get along in families, with friends, or in the school classroom; Adlerian play therapy theory is helpful to the school counselor consulting with parents and teachers or working with the child. Some problems concern a child's sense of self or emotionality; child-centered play therapy can address such issues. The integrative approach to working with a child is simple: Let the child's problem be the guide! Table 17.1 suggests a few common problems for which children are frequently referred to the school counselor by self or others. Although it may appear that only one theory will

Table 17.1
Common Problems in a School

Child-centered play theory for
- Children with diffuse anger, sadness.
- Children with a lack of a sense of self.
- Children with deep scars or hurts.
- Children without language skills.
- Children who appear unsafe and afraid of conversation.

Adlerian play theory for
- Children with social problems.
- Children with family issues.
- Children who exhibit goals of misbehavior such as power, attention, revenge, inadequacy.

Cognitive-behavioral play theory for
- Children with attentional issues who need to learn how to focus.
- Children needing social skills.
- Children who lack study skills.
- Children who are depressed.
- Children who wish to learn specific behaviors.
- Children involved in special education.

work with a particular problem, that is not the case; the list shows one classification only.

The child's problem is also the guide for the time needed for the play intervention. School counselors often express that there is little time for individual counseling when they are responsible for hundreds of students. However, because research has shown that counseling interventions in schools make a difference in children's learning (Borders & Drury, 1992; Fall, Balvanz, Johnson, & Nelson, 1999) and because individual counseling is one of the roles of a school counselor (Campbell & Dahir, 1997), it is important to maximize the effect of the time spent on this function. Osterweil (1986) stresses that the counselor should tell the child how many sessions there will be and how much time will be spent in those sessions. The student adjusts more easily to termination under these conditions.

The integrative play therapy approach is both proactive and reactive, two components of a school counselor's job description (Baker, 2000; Campbell & Dahir, 1997). For example, school counselors treat angry students. Safe expression of the anger may require the student to learn new behaviors (reactive). The anger itself may need to be examined and dealt with as a symptom (proactive). In this example, the reactive component may best use a cognitive-behavioral play treatment; the proactive component may best use an Adlerian or child-centered approach. The theory itself helps to guide the school counselor to best assist the student with facilitative techniques.

An example of the proactive and reactive components is demonstrated below by a child needing social skills to gain friends and needing assistance with a great deal of sadness at the same time. Using the integrative approach, the counselor may work to establish a relationship that is characterized by nonjudgmental acceptance, warmth, and caring, and may work in an Adlerian play therapy mode to begin to allow the sadness to be expressed. At the same time, the school counselor may also work on some small steps for the student to gain friends in social situations, using cognitive-behavioral play techniques. Handling these two theories may be clearly marked, as in example 8 below, or may be a fluid transition, as in example 9.

EXAMPLE 8

COUNSELOR: Joey, it sounds like you have two things you needed to see me about. You seem pretty sad and you may want to come here and use the toys or talk with me for a few times while that gets better. Is that right?

JOEY: Yeah. I'd like to.

COUNSELOR: The other thing is, it sounds like you've been needing a friend. I'm wondering if you would like us to work together to see if you could get one. Would that be another thing you would like?

JOEY: I'd really like a friend . . . especially on the bus . . . and at recess.

COUNSELOR: So we've got a deal. We're going to work on two things. I've got an idea. How about if you come and play or talk on Tuesdays for a half hour for, maybe, four weeks. And then we'll get together on each Monday for 10 minutes and make plans for getting friends. Would that be a plan that would work for you?

JOEY: Yeah. I want a friend, and maybe I won't be sad after my grandpa gets home from the hospital. But my mom says he is probably going to die. He's just my best friend ever since he came to live with us when I was a baby. He always took care of me.

EXAMPLE 9

COUNSELOR: (working from goals) Joey, it sounds like you would like to make a change as far as friends, and also you would like to not be sad all the time. I'm wondering if you would like to come in every week on Mondays at 10 for six weeks and we will work together to help you make those changes. Would that be OK with you?

In these examples, school counselors request different numbers of sessions to work with students on particular problems. Two principal reasons for the session differential are the nature of the issues and the amount of time available to school counselor. Many issues need only one session to assist the student with some new ideas for handling situations; other issues cannot be solved quickly. A school counselor can suggest outside counseling and then serve as the school liaison between that therapist and the teachers. For some students, outside counseling is not possible due to family circumstances; a school counselor may decide to see those students for more sessions to have an impact on learning. In general, with many young students, four to six sessions can have an effect that will be reflected in the classroom (Fall et al., 1999).

SUMMARY AND CONCLUSION

School counselors see many students for individual counseling in an elementary school. The students are most often referred to the counselor by teachers and parents who wish for changed behaviors in the child. An integrated theoretical approach to working with these students allows the school counselor to have an expanded "bag of tricks" while still remaining within the framework of theoretical guidelines. The child's problem or problems become the selection point of one or more theories and the corresponding techniques. In this day of accountability, the school counselor can operate within theoretical boundaries and let theory determine techniques. Treatment planning is still necessary within the school walls, but the best solutions come from the powerful combination of directions from theory, research, and practice.

REFERENCES

Axline, V. (1969). *Play therapy* (Rev. ed.). New York: Ballantine Books.

Baker, S. (2000). *School counseling for the twenty-first century* (3rd ed.). Upper Saddle River, NJ: Merrill.

Borders, D., & Drury, S. (1992). Comprehensive school counseling programs: A review for policymakers and practitioners. *Journal of Counseling and Development, 70*, 487–498.

Campbell, C., & Dahir, C. (1997). *The national standards for school counseling programs.* Alexandria, VA: American School Counselor Association.

Dreikurs, R., & Soltz, V. (1964). *Children: The challenge.* New York: Hawthorn/Dutton.

Fall, M., Balvanz, J., Johnson, L., & Nelson, L. (1999). The relationship of a play therapy intervention to self-efficacy and classroom learning. *Professional School Counseling, 2,* 194–204.

Henniger, M. (1995). Play: Antidote for childhood stress. *Early Child Development and Care, 105,* 7–12.

Hughes, F. (1999). *Children, play, and development* (3rd ed.). Boston: Allyn & Bacon.

Knell, S. (1995). *Cognitive-behavioral play therapy.* Northvale, NJ: Aronson.

Kottman, T. (1995). *Partners in play: An Adlerian approach to play therapy.* Alexandria, VA: American Counseling Association.

Landreth, G.L. (1987). Play therapy: Facilitative use of child's play in elementary school counseling. *Elementary School Guidance and Counseling, 21,* 253–261.

Landreth, G.L. (1991). *Play therapy: The art of the relationship.* Muncie, IN: Accelerated Development.

Landreth, G., Homeyer, L., Glover, G., & Sweeney, D. (1996). *Play therapy interventions with children's problems.* Northvale, NJ: Aronson.

Osterweil, Z. (1986). Time-limited play therapy. *School Psychology International, 7,* 224–230.

CHAPTER 18

Group Sandplay in Elementary Schools

THERESA KESTLY

"YOU MEAN you're just going to let us play?" asks a fifth-grade boy who is just beginning his first session in a sand tray friendship group at school. He and five other boys are going to play together for an hour using small trays of sand and miniature figurines. They will meet for the next 12 weeks to create scenes in their sand trays and then tell stories about their worlds if they choose. It is hard for the boys to believe they are actually going to play during school time.

Unless it is recess time, the idea of play with other children during school hours is a surprise for many children and for adults as well. Why and how these sand tray friendship groups work is the focus of this chapter.

DESCRIPTION OF SAND TRAY FRIENDSHIP GROUP

In schools where opportunities for sand tray group counseling occur, children meet regularly, usually every week, for group sand tray sessions. Calling these *sand tray friendship groups* gives children a natural frame and a focus for the group process, and it helps to reduce the stigma often associated with a trip to the school counselor's office.

Sand tray friendship groups utilize both parallel and joint play with elementary school children, with the school counselor acting as a witness

329

and a facilitator for the group process (the term *counselor* is used throughout the chapter to denote school counselor, school social worker, and other mental health workers). Drawing from the ideas of Margaret Lowenfeld (1979/1993) and Dora Kalff (1980), the counselor creates a protected space where children are free to play and create stories relevant to their lives. The amount of time for the play and the storytelling depends on the age of the children; usually, the groups meet weekly for 10 to 20 sessions.

To begin, each child has an individual sand tray; if the budget permits, a large group tray for joint play is available when the desire and need for community play arises. From a collection of hundreds of miniature figurines, children may select the things they need to build their worldviews in the sand. Although children may tell stories about the worlds they create, they are free to participate in the process without using any words. For nonverbal children or children with limited language proficiency, this choice is very freeing. Through symbolic thinking processes, these children sometimes learn how to establish communication, enabling them to use words more effectively.

The counselor creates a *free and protected space* (Kalff, 1980) where children may deal with issues by playing out situations personally relevant to them. The protected play space provides children with the safety and freedom they need to play at the growing edges of their development. The counselor acts as a psychological container for the play and for the peer interactions that arise from it.

RATIONALE FOR GROUP SANDPLAY IN THE SCHOOL SETTING

Sand tray group play seems to be a good fit for elementary school children. There is growing evidence that it influences behavior changes in a positive direction, is developmentally appropriate for the age group, and is efficient in terms of the counselor's limited time for in-depth work with children. In addition, it capitalizes on children's needs for friendship through playing with peers, and it offers a unique format for addressing social-emotional needs by engaging both right and left brain thinking processes.

BEHAVIOR CHANGE

Several months after one sand tray friendship group ended, the school principal noticed that the boys from the group had not been referred to her office since they participated. She was surprised. This group of fifth-grade boys, referred primarily for fighting on the playground and disruptive behavior in the classroom, had been frequent visitors to her office before they started the sand tray group play. Even more surprising was their ability to maintain their behavior changes several months after the group ended. Although not every child experiences such noticeable behavior shifts, the following school year this same principal noted again a dramatic decrease in referrals to her office of other children who participated in the sand tray groups.

Teachers often report calm behavior when children return to class after participating in sand tray counseling. One teacher said her students could do academic group work better after participating in a sand tray group; she felt their group play helped them cooperate more effectively in the academic setting. Academic and behavioral improvements seem to occur in many cases. One special education boy observed his own improved behavior. Without any solicitation from the counselor, he volunteered, "Since I have been in this group, I haven't been in any more trouble." Not long after he made this comment, his teacher reported that he had caught up on all his academic work. Research currently is in process in the Albuquerque Public Schools in New Mexico to explore and document these kinds of changes in a more systematic way.

DEVELOPMENTAL APPROPRIATENESS

From a developmental perspective, group sand tray counseling is a natural context in which children can work on issues relevant to their age group. The development of friendships is paramount for elementary school children. A great deal of social and emotional development occurs between the ages of 6 and 12, and much of it occurs within peer groups. Rules of social behavior, ideas about caring for others, and a sense of justice and self-esteem are some of the things children learn from peers firsthand. Whereas families and other significant adults are essential for teaching social and moral values, it is with peers that children learn how to negotiate and practice these skills. The equality children feel with their peers, unlike the inherently unequal relationships they have with adults, allows them freedom to try out social behaviors. The word *peer* means "equal standing." This equality gives children a level playing field where they may explore how to live in the world without the fear of negative consequences if their attempts do not succeed the first time around. They have opportunities to learn about fair play, to regulate aggression, to practice reciprocity and equality, and to develop empathy for others.

Because children have implicit understanding of their *equality among peers* and because they understand that *play is just for fun,* play serves another very important developmental function. It allows children to work on developmental tasks in whatever stage they are in without fear of ridicule from others. For instance, a fifth-grade girl pretending that a baby is throwing a temper tantrum in a sand tray world finds acceptance from her peers because it is *just play*, and yet it can satisfy and be very relevant to her if she has unresolved early developmental tasks around this issue.

According to Erikson (1963, 1968), children between the ages of 6 and 12 typically are dealing with developmental tasks related to industry versus inferiority (social interaction with peers and academic performance). Children referred for counseling services, however, often are dealing with earlier stages: basic trust versus mistrust, autonomy versus shame and doubt, and initiative versus guilt. These earlier developmental tasks may be worked on at any age in group sandplay. The fifth-grade girl cited above may still be working on very early issues around autonomy, but because it is *just play*, her peers accept her playing out the early tantrum behavior. Children play at their own growing edges, and so facilitators have many opportunities to support children exactly where they are.

Efficiency and Effectiveness of Sandplay Group Process

One impetus for the development of the group sandplay process in schools is the need to see many children in a short time. Although sand tray play requires cleanup time, it is still more efficient in terms of doing in-depth work with a number of children. For example, Table 18.1 shows

Table 18.1
Group Efficiency and Effectiveness for 4 or 6 Children

	Time Needed			Quality Enhancement
	Session Hours	Cleanup Hours	Total Hours	1. Peer motivation for change.
4 individual children	4	1	5	2. Positive adult attention by trained counselors.
4 children in group	1	1	2	3. Prevention through containment.
6 individual children	6	1.5	7.5	4. Enhancement of brain functioning.
6 children in group	1	1.5	2.5	5. Simultaneous participant-observer capability.

how much time it takes to work with individuals versus with groups of children. Seeing six children individually in counseling takes 7.5 hours (including 15 minutes for cleanup for each individual session). Seeing those same six children in a group takes 2.5 hours.

In addition to saving time, in many instances the group process is more productive because it (1) involves peer motivation for change, (2) provides positive adult attention that is nonintrusive, (3) serves to prevent later, more chronic problem behaviors, (4) enhances brain functioning, and (5) allows the child to be participant and observer simultaneously. In the sand tray friendship groups, specially trained counselors capitalize on the intrinsic motivation of peers to develop relationships through play. They help children apply and consolidate school and family values by setting kind but firm limits around negative interpersonal communications while simultaneously containing the potential of the group for positive and productive interpersonal relationships. Specific training enables the counselor to contain the group members in this protected social-emotional space without intruding on the peer play. The counselor refrains from either positive or negative reinforcement of children or from solving problems for the group. Once children know how to obtain what they need in socially appropriate ways, they are very willing to do so. The development of effective social skills early in life helps to prevent many chronic problems that can emerge in later life due to unmet social-emotional needs.

Although brain processing involves a complicated integration of the left and right hemispheres, in most people the right brain specializes in certain tasks such as spatial thinking, artistic and nonverbal processing, and emotional awareness. It sees the world in an all-at-once fashion. When children use the sand tray modality, they engage the right brain through symbolic thinking, often bypassing cognitive awareness when they first begin to play. They choose miniature figurines and play activities, however, that are central to the developmental tasks they need to accomplish. Because their abstract reasoning and language proficiency are not yet fully developed, they rely more heavily than adults on their symbolic, right brain thinking processes, and they use experiential learning to deal with issues that are important to them. For example, children with posttraumatic stress play out the trauma event repeatedly to gain mastery over the situation. They replay so they can reexperience it until the pieces fit together in some satisfactory way.

Because experience is multidimensional in nature, it is necessary, as Lowenfeld (1979/1993) postulated, to provide children with an apparatus that is conducive to expressing simultaneously the various dimensions of experience, including color, form, movement, relationships among things and activities, and so on. Language, due to its linear nature, is inadequate for children who need to communicate their complicated inner experiences. Because of its miniaturization, the sand tray is an expansive language providing children with a large vocabulary of miniature images for expressing their elaborate inner worlds.

The participant-observer phenomenon is another unique and important aspect of the sand tray modality. With the sand tray, children are both participants and observers. They are the directors of their "plays" and the actors as well. Unlike conventional play therapy where the child is immersed in the play, the miniature sand tray allows the child to be *in* the play and *apart* from the play at the same time. This dual role allows children simultaneously to observe in concrete form their own inner worlds and to re-create them before their own eyes. Children project their worldviews into a miniature container, where it is held physically by the boundaries of the tray and psychologically by the trained counselor. Within this container, children see and feel and play their experiences in objective form. Words alone are not adequate for accomplishing this task, especially while children are still in the process of developing their capacities for verbal abstract reasoning.

ORGANIZING GROUP SANDPLAY IN THE SCHOOL SETTING

The success of sand tray friendship groups is greatly improved with good preparation and organization. Adequate space, the collection of miniatures, composition of groups, and preparing children for group play, are important for success.

CREATING AN APPROPRIATE SPACE

Available space for counseling services in schools varies widely, from large, attractive rooms to small, closetlike spaces that are dimly lit with no windows. It is difficult to work with sand tray groups in cramped quarters or in public spaces where children do not have a sense of privacy and safety. A sand tray group is at least two children and may be six or more, depending on the number of facilitators and the type of children in the group. At a minimum, there needs to be enough space for at least one miniature sand tray for each child, a small shelf or table for a collection of miniatures, and space for the counselor to sit nearby. In a space the size of a classroom, it is possible to accommodate two groups at the same time if there are two counselors and if there is some kind of physical divider to create a sense of a protected space for each group. If funds are available, it is helpful to have enough floor space for a large group tray (about 4 to 5 feet in diameter, or 5 feet square).

In addition to adequate physical space, it is important to create an attractive display that invites children to use their imaginations and creativity for building miniature worlds. Even in a small room with no windows it is possible to arrange the miniatures and the sand trays in a way that stimulates delight when entering the room. Even teachers and parents notice when the environment is inviting; the room simply has an atmosphere that communicates *This is a good place to play.* Often, even adults say "I want to build a world." The space is inviting, and it speaks for itself. It clearly is designed with children in mind, and most children know exactly what to do when they enter it.

PREPARING CHILDREN FOR GROUP EXPERIENCE

It is important to introduce the sand tray friendship group to children without stigmatizing them for being in it. It is sufficient to tell them that they will have a chance to be in a sand tray friendship group where they will play with others because that is the way most children make and develop friendships. Children usually do not know the reason for referral unless the parent or someone other than the counselor tells them. The counselor can avoid this problem by instructing the referring person about the nature of the sand tray process. Whatever the counselor does to decrease stigma for the children will increase the safety and protection that is so essential to sand tray play. If the child does need to know about the referral situation, the counselor can discuss it apart from the sand tray so the child does not confuse the nonjudgmental nature of the sand tray play with the referral problem, which is often perceived as negative. It is essential to communicate to the children the special safety and protection that surrounds the sand tray play.

Permission forms are sent to parents depending on school policy about group counseling. The permission form contains a description about the process and includes goals and purposes of the friendship group.

OBTAINING SAND TRAYS AND A MINIATURE COLLECTION FOR SCHOOL SETTINGS

The cost of sand trays varies from about $5 for a plastic storage container to $200 for a beautifully crafted, wooden, water-resistant tray. Therapists who follow the Kalff tradition use sand trays with a standard inside dimension of 28.5 inches wide by 19.5 inches tall by 3 inches deep (Mitchell & Friedman, 1994). For very active children, more depth (4 or 5 inches) is desirable to contain the sand within the tray during active and dynamic play. Although wooden trays are aesthetically pleasing, most schools cannot afford the number needed for group play. Children do appreciate aesthetically pleasing sand trays, but they are quite happy to play in the inexpensive plastic storage trays (approximately 15 by 21 by 6 inches). Although the storage trays are a little small in terms of surface area, having a chance to play in a plastic tray is far better than not being able to play at all. It is important, however, to provide trays with blue bottoms to simulate water.

Typically, miniature collections for schools contain a wide variety of small objects that children encounter in their daily lives. The cost of a collection for group use ranges from about $500 to $2,000. In general, it is important to collect miniatures and to organize them in ways that reduce the need for limit setting while children are creating their worlds. If the counselor does not have to worry about objects that might break or get ruined if they get wet, it is easier to relax and focus on the crucial task of witnessing the children's worlds. Although limit setting is necessary and appropriate in therapy sessions with children, the aim of sand tray play is to provide as much freedom as possible within the constraints of the container and the miniature collection. This freedom encourages children to use imagination and creativity to play out their difficult situations.

Building an appropriate collection for children is a topic in numerous sand tray books and articles. Many catalogues exist specifically with sandplay therapists in mind, and most teachers who provide sand tray training include these kinds of resource lists in their training sessions.

The appropriate size of a miniature collection is sometimes debated. Some therapists worry that a large collection will overwhelm children, yet others believe children can work comfortably and intelligently with large collections similar to ones used by adults. If the collection is too small, it will be difficult for children to express themselves. Lowenfeld (1979/1993), originator of the sand tray modality, used a cabinet with labeled drawers to prevent children from being overwhelmed. Baskets are useful for organizing miniatures by categories to help children stay focused and to help counselors with reshelving. A combination of open shelves and baskets is good for creating an attractive collection that is also well organized. If children become chaotic with a large collection, it is usually a therapeutic issue. (See the section on limit setting for further discussion of large collections and chaotic behavior.)

COMPOSITION OF GROUPS

The effectiveness of group sandplay depends to a great extent on the composition of group members. For example, a group of three or four attention-deficit-type children is very difficult and often not very productive; having too many shy children in a group is equally unproductive. It helps to balance a shy child with an extroverted child, if possible;

they will teach each other alternative behaviors when they play together, and sometimes they mirror each other in terms of the kinds of objects they use. For instance, after about four weeks in a sand tray group, a very shy child began selecting a large striped tiger that was a favorite of an extroverted child in the same group. Soon after, the classroom teacher described the shy child as much less intimidated with his peers, and for the first time he was willing to go out with the other children at recess time.

Ginott (1961) recommends the following strategies for composing groups: (1) combining dissimilar personality syndromes, (2) using mixed-gender groups for young children and same-gender groups for older children, (3) selecting children by age within a range of 12 months, (4) not having more than five children in a group, (5) not combining siblings and classmates in the same group, and (6) not allowing antisocial children to be dominant in a group. Ginott also says children should be in a group where they will not reexperience the devastating influences of their outside lives. For instance, a submissive boy may not do well in a group where others dominate, prolonging the circumstance that makes it difficult for him to assert himself. Ginott's chapter on group composition in *Group Psychotherapy with Children* offers detailed discussion of these and other important considerations for organizing play groups (pp. 29–36). Most of his ideas apply to sand tray group counseling.

Preliminary screening for the group, including a play interview with the child and standard referral information from teachers, parents, and other involved adults, is worthwhile. Fortunately, in the school setting there is flexibility for moving children from one group to another or even into individual counseling if, despite preliminary screening, a situation arises in which the child clearly cannot function in a way that is beneficial to self and others. If the need arises to transfer a child out of a group, it is essential to communicate this move to the child in a way that supports continued growth and will not be seen as a punishment for not being able to function with a particular group of children.

MANAGING GROUP ACTIVITIES

Group counseling requires a structure and management style different from working with individual children. There is more planning and organization before the group begins, and it is necessary to balance limit setting with the permissiveness that is needed for creative imagination to develop among the children. The counselor's attitude is central for effective sandplay groups, and the practical elements of structuring the group time, cleaning up, and protecting confidentiality all make a difference in how well the group process works.

COUNSELOR'S ROLE VERSUS TEACHER'S ROLE IN THE SCHOOL SETTING

It is sometimes difficult for school counselors to maintain a therapeutic stance when so often they have to serve in other roles, such as playground duty person, disciplinarian, guidance teacher, and sometimes even administrative assistant to the principal. If counselors cannot avoid these multiple roles, it is very important to communicate when and where the children may be in relationship to the counselor as a counselor. Children need to know that in a sand tray play group the counselor will not issue discipline slips, share confidential information with their teachers or parents, give them grades, direct their play, or judge them as good or bad for the things they create in their worlds. Children need to know they are free to create.

LIMIT SETTING THAT MAXIMIZES GROUP CREATIVITY

As the number of children increases in a counseling situation, the need for structuring also increases. Even so, the structuring can be done in nonjudgmental ways. At the beginning of group sand tray play, it is important to eliminate as many rules as possible so that children's creative energy has a chance to express itself early in the group. Subsequently, the counselor can create rules as needed. For instance, if a child spills sand outside the tray, the counselor can say, "In here, the sand has to stay in the tray." With some groups there is never a need for this rule. Some children play very well together with almost no explicit rules. Too many rules at the beginning may thwart creativity and imagination.

Helping Children Respect Boundaries

One rule that seems to support the creative process at the beginning is asking children not to touch the worlds of other children and not to allow others to touch their own worlds. In this way, children know they have a space, a physical container, of their very own. It provides them with concrete boundaries that often are lacking for children who come into counseling. Later, if children elect to play in a large group tray, these boundaries may be renegotiated, but it helps children at the beginning to see and feel and work within the bounds of their own protected space.

Flooding with Water and/or Figurines

Occasionally, children decide to use a lot of miniatures in a very chaotic and disorganized manner. They use their arms to sweep entire shelves into their baskets or shirts and then dump them into their trays until the tray is full. This event is usually distressing for the counselor because of cleanup. When this happens, although it rarely does, it is usually an important therapeutic issue. One way to handle this situation is to encourage children to use as many things as they want. The counselor can say things like "Oh, you need all of the cars today," or "I see you need a lot of things," or "Do you need some more?" From these kinds of statements, the children know the counselor is "containing" their chaotic energy psychologically but without any judgment. It may be the first time they have not heard someone say "Stop it. That's enough." Some children truly feel there is never enough of anything they need, so it surprises them when an adult asks them if they need more, and it helps them to shift their point of view. If there is time to allow children this kind of disorganized play, they will often learn, from their own inner core, how to organize things by their own volition. One second-grader who flooded his tray with figurines for four sessions in a row finally pulled out of the chaotic play by himself. Once he achieved organization in his tray, he never went back to chaotic play, and his classroom teacher reported that he improved greatly in his ability to organize his academic classroom activities. He learned "order" at the core of his being, where real behavioral changes occur.

If children have opportunities to use as much water as they want, they often will flood their tray with water. This kind of flooding is very therapeutic, but in schools where there are time pressures for seeing a lot of children, it is difficult to allow this process on a frequent basis. Children who really need to use a lot of water for therapeutic reasons will wash items over and over again with spray bottles, or they will ask repeatedly for more water even after they know they have exceeded the limit on how much they may have. For these children, it is usually beneficial to schedule one or two individual sessions when they may use as much water as they wish. Children love to pour water into the sand trays, but it is not necessary to allow this if there are time pressures. Although it is traditional to have both wet and dry sand available, it is better to use only dry sand than to offer no sand at all.

Breaking Miniatures on Purpose

Most of the time, children break miniatures accidentally, but occasionally a child demonstrates clearly that he or she intended to break an object. This intentional breaking calls for a limit or a shift in activity. The counselor might say in a neutral voice without any blame or negativity, "The toys here are not for breaking." Children appreciate receiving these limits in clear, neutral tones because then they know where the boundaries are and they feel safe when they know where and how they are being held psychologically.

Supporting Collaboration and Community Building

If there is a large community tray in the sand tray room, children will usually notice it somewhere between week four and week eight. They will begin to ask what it is for and whether they may use it. This curiosity is usually a good indication that they are ready for the pleasures and challenges of community play. It helps to have divider sticks available to mark off space in the large tray. If these are not available or the children decide not to use them, the counselor simply asks "How do you want to share this space?" The counselor helps the group negotiate rules for playing in the communal space both explicitly and implicitly. This is a perfect place for children to see firsthand what it means to share space, to live in the world together, to wage war, to deal with conflict, to negotiate, to make peace—while exploring the values their families and school have taught. What does it all mean? From peer play, they get a chance to see it in action.

Community play is very powerful for children. Although it presents additional challenges for the counselor, it is an important avenue of actual experience for children to learn how to negotiate with one another. Teachers sometimes notice the increased ability of children to cooperate more effectively with academic tasks after they have had a chance to play together. De Domenico (1999) provides a discussion on other aspects of community sand tray play, and some of her suggestions are helpful for sand tray group counseling in the schools.

Stealing

In individual sand tray counseling, stealing is not usually an issue, but it often comes up in the group counseling situation where it is much easier to conceal miniatures when leaving the play area. Limits need to be set around this issue to protect the integrity and safety of the sand tray environment. Several factors to consider are the age of the child, the intention, and therapeutic issues. If children are very young, the counselor can simply ask "You know the little red car you were using today? We are missing it and wonder if you could help us find it?" Most often, they will soon "find" it on the playground and return it. Children learn that the counselor values the integrity of the collection and that there are expectations for how they behave in relation to objects they desire that do not belong to them.

With older children who take things intentionally in a provocative manner, it is important to confront them. One group of fifth-grade boys left a sand tray room, pulling objects out of their pockets and claiming they brought them from home. After several special items disappeared from the collection, the counselor told the boys that things were missing from the collection and that it would not be possible to continue with the sand tray group until everything was returned. They expressed unhappiness and anger about not getting to come for their group time. The counselor gave them suggestions for how to return the figurines anonymously so they could maintain their privacy around the issue, but she held firm. After about three weeks and several meetings to discuss the problem, the boys finally returned everything. In a very open and honest conversation, they told the counselor they had been stealing all over their neighborhood and no one had even noticed. This group of boys had to problem-solve together to figure out how to resume their sand tray group. It was an important step for them, and it helped them establish a very productive working relationship with the counselor for the remainder of the year.

Disrupting the Group Process

Some children try to be the center of attention in the group through negative behavior, and this usually creates disruption for the group process. If this happens even after careful screening and careful group composition planning, the counselor will need to set clear limits. For instance, one boy continued to make loud vehicle noises and insisted on returning to the shelves for more miniatures after the beginning of stories, when selecting time was over. Another boy in the group was telling his story, and clearly he wanted his peers to listen. After the counselor reminded the disruptive boy about playing quietly beside his tray during story time and he still continued his disruptive behavior, the counselor said, "Michael, making loud noises and going to the shelves during story time is not allowed here in this group because we want to listen to Daniel's story. If you continue, I'll take it to mean that you are deciding to end your playtime here with us today to go back to class. It is fine for you to play quietly by your tray while we listen." This is just one example of a clearly stated limit delivered with no blame. The statement includes what the child is doing that is not acceptable, what will happen if the behavior continues, and what the alternative acceptable behaviors are.

Skills in limit setting are essential for the success of sand tray group counseling. Many play therapy texts, play therapy videos, and training workshops provide opportunities for counselor skill development in this area. Without these skills, it is difficult to create the free and protected space necessary for sand tray group counseling.

Structuring Group Time for Sand Tray Play and Storytelling

The number of sessions for a sand tray group varies depending on the goals, therapeutic issues, and other constraining factors. It is difficult to observe measurable changes with fewer than 8 or 10 sessions. For children with severe emotional issues, 10 sessions are usually inadequate. For non-clinical populations, even one session is a treat. Most often, a group usually meets for 10 to 12 weekly sessions.

Although sandplay therapy is essentially a nonverbal process, words often help children gain insight into their creative process, and words help them claim their experiences at a conscious level. Older children usually meet for one hour for the sandplay group; younger children, in kindergarten and first grade, usually meet for about 45 minutes. The last 15 or 20 minutes are for story time. Table 18.2 shows examples of how to structure the session time.

When storytelling time is near, children get a five-minute notice from the counselor—"You have five more minutes for building"—and then again at one minute before story time. When the time is up for building, children may no longer go to the miniature collection to select figurines. They may, however, continue to play quietly in their trays while other children tell their stories. It is almost impossible for children not to play in their own trays while listening to other children. Children may not want to talk about their worlds, although usually, after the first two or three weeks, children want to tell stories and usually want a second or third turn to talk. Sometimes it is necessary to limit each child to the amount of time he or she may have for stories. It is very important to allow children to choose not to talk at story time, even if they choose to pass every session throughout the entire group process; this choice to talk or not talk is one of the defining features of the free and protected space.

It takes several sessions for children to catch on to being good listeners during story time. The most important way children learn to listen to others is through the modeling of their counselor, who demonstrates clear interest and good reflective listening skills during story time. The

Table 18.2
Structuring Time for the Group Process

	One-Hour Group, Grades 2–6	45-Minute Group, Grades K–1
Building time	1:00 P.M.	1:00 P.M.
5-minute notice for ending building	1:35 P.M.	1:25 P.M.
1-minute notice for ending building	1:39 P.M.	1:29 P.M.
Story time	1:40 P.M.	1:30 P.M.
End session	2:00 P.M.	1:45 P.M.

counselor can enhance the idea of holding a free and protected space by avoiding intrusive questions, by expressing interest in the stories, by inviting elaboration through reflective listening, and sometimes by just saying "I see it," "I hear it," or "I feel it." To the extent possible, it is important for the counselor to give total attention to the children's building process and the story process. This is challenging, but children feel the difference when the counselor is paying full attention or is distracted by telephones, deskwork, other school personnel intruding during sessions, and so on. Children really appreciate it when others, both counselors and peers, listen to their stories. When others listen, it gives them a chance to express what is really important in their inner worlds.

CLEANUP ISSUES

Cleanup can make or break a good sand tray group process. It is essential for the counselor to schedule adequate time for cleanup between groups and to remember that it is more efficient to work with groups of children than individuals, even when cleanup time is added to the process. If there is not enough time for cleanup after the group leaves, it is very difficult to hold the space for children as a free and protected container.

Having adequate supplies for cleanup helps. The following items are useful: (1) sieves for sifting debris out of sand and clearing glass stones and treasures from the tray, (2) water container for children to rinse hands before washing their hands where plumbing might get clogged with sand, (3) strainers for drying out objects that are dipped in water for cleaning, (4) containers to hold the strainer as water drains off the objects, (5) paper or cotton towels, (6) several small brush and dustpan sets, (7) combs for raking and smoothing sand, and (8) small tarps to protect carpeted areas or to contain sand spills.

In general, children do not clear their own trays. There is some controversy surrounding this issue, however. In individual sandplay according to the Kalffian tradition, the therapist always clears the tray. On the other hand, De Domenico (1999) notes that there are times when it is appropriate for clients to clear their own trays, but that it should be done with care and perhaps with a sense of ritual or ceremony. Tibetan monks have special ceremonies for clearing and releasing the intricate sand mandalas they create over many hours and days as a reminder of the impermanence of life; Navajo Indians also have a ritual when clearing sand paintings used in healing ceremonies. If children help to clear their own trays, they should do it with respect and care under the supervision of the counselor.

Some counselors believe it is important for children to leave the session with their sand tray images intact. Children do think about their trays and plan from week to week what they will do next. It may be important for them to leave knowing the counselor will contain and then take care of the world they created.

Protecting Confidentiality of Group Members in the School Context

Children need to know the policy on confidentiality regarding what they say or create in the counselor's office. Generally, their play and verbal expression are confidential, with the exception of legal limits of confidentiality. The counselor needs to explain the policy in clear, developmentally appropriate language. If the counselor intends to share information with the teacher or a parent, the child needs to know beforehand. If the counselor tells children that the counseling is confidential within stated limits, then the sand tray worlds also are confidential, even if children use no words to describe them.

PLANNING FOR EVALUATION OUTCOMES

Teachers, principals, and parents do not always understand how sand tray play therapy works. Although Lowenfeld (1979/1993) believed that normal development was not possible in the absence of play, society often regards play as a waste of time for children, or at best an unimportant use of time. So the counselor faces many challenges in terms of articulating why play is essential for children's development, especially for children with social-emotional problems. Funding sources usually ask, "What is the science base of this program?" School mental health workers can help to build the science base of sand tray play by planning for outcome evaluation at the beginning of the process. Even the simplest measures, such as teacher rating scales, contribute to the body of data that help to explain the crucial necessity of play in childhood. The focus of this section is on collecting data to assess outcomes.

Need for Research

Historically, there is a dearth of empirical studies related to sandplay therapy. Mitchell and Friedman (1994) provide a good summary of the current state of research in sandplay therapy. They report a long period of sandplay development by Kalff and her followers without any quantitative or controlled methods of research. More recently, however, there is growing interest in research related to traditional sandplay therapy and also to sand tray group counseling in the schools. Although not directly related to sand tray play, research studies from the Primary Mental Health Project (PMHP; Cowen et al., 1996) provide impressive and significant data from large-scale, small-scale, long- and short-term evaluation studies to support the efficacy of play therapy in school settings. These studies provide the beginnings of a science base for including play modalities in the schools. It is essential, however, to collect evaluation data in the specific context of sand tray group counseling. Using varied research methods will help build the science base of sand tray counseling and provide direction for responsible program development. This movement toward more data collection is crucial if mental health workers want to include play modalities in school settings, where there is a great deal of competition for limited funding sources.

QUALITATIVE DATA

Sand tray photographs are good sources of qualitative data. A photograph of each tray for each child on a weekly basis helps track individual and group progress for qualitative analysis. Many times, the counselor notices, via a series of photographs, progress that was not apparent during the actual building and storytelling process. Over time, the photographs often reveal consistent emerging themes. Digital cameras and computer printouts, after the initial investment, are an inexpensive way to track individual and group gains. Name tags and dates of sessions in all the photographs will help with the management of photographic data. It is helpful to record teacher and parent comments and observations regarding a child's progress during and after the sand tray counseling sessions. Informal anecdotal reports and clinical observations are important also; they provide the basis for exploring more formally the efficacy of sand tray group counseling. When sufficient in number, they become the basis of research questions and strategies for collecting more formal quantitative data.

QUANTITATIVE DATA

Obtaining quantitative data for experimental studies is difficult in the school setting because educational goals and protection of privacy are paramount. Teacher rating scales are fairly acceptable, however, and some provide good standardized data with national norms for comparison. The PMHP (Cowen et al., 1996) and the Behavior Assessment System for Children (BASC; Reynolds & Kamphaus, 1998) both offer a variety of rating scales with national norms (see reference list for information). The BASC has both clinical and adaptive scales to track children's progress in terms of teachers' perceptions. Both the PMHP and the BASC rating forms may be used as pre- and posttest measures.

HOLDING THE SPACE FOR GROUP EXPERIENCE: THE SCHOOL MENTAL HEALTH WORKER'S CHALLENGE

The most challenging part of the group sandplay process is learning how to hold the space for group experience. It is relatively easy to learn most of the organizational and management techniques that help groups run smoothly. Holding space for group experience, however, requires the counselor to use a focused, nonintrusive stance and to deal with transference issues that sometimes get stirred up more deeply because of the visual processing required by sand tray play. It also requires the counselor to track group process while letting go of many of the details of individual play, which can induce worries about not knowing what the children are doing when they play together.

TRACKING BOTH THE GROUP PROCESS AND THE INDIVIDUAL MEMBERS OF THE GROUP

Clinicians who follow the Kalffian tradition of sandplay therapy express caution regarding sandplay in the group context, concerned that group interaction of the clients will take precedence over the expression of the individual psyche (Mitchell & Friedman, 1994). De Domenico (1999), however, contends that there are appropriate times to work with the communal psyche as well as the individual psyche. Furthermore, she does not think the individual process is muted when clients work together in a sand tray process. Based on the developmental appropriateness of sand tray play for latency-age children discussed earlier in this chapter, there is a possibility that the group process actually enhances the potential for individual psychological growth as a child plays with peers.

Nevertheless, tracking the group process is a major challenge for most school mental health workers. One loses individual details in the service of holding the entire group process. It comes as a surprise to some that children still develop in positive directions even though the witness-observer misses many of the details. Children's resiliency comes through even in the group process, perhaps especially in the free and protected process of group play. The counselor must know how to extend the creation of the protected space to the group process as a whole. Experience, training, and good supervision are all helpful as the counselor develops this ability to hold group space.

The Role of the Counselor as a Witness

One of the greatest challenges of sand tray group play is the counselor's need to take a nonintrusive stance while concentrating on the group dynamic and the activities of individual children. The counselor, as witness, needs to be willing to maintain focused attention without knowing exactly what will emerge. This is difficult for many counselors, yet it is this very sense of *not knowing* that allows children the freedom to move with their own creative energies. There is no need for interpreting worlds for children. Children need no direction on how to build their worlds. The mental health worker has to use all of his or her energy to hold the process as it emerges, rather than using energy to direct and manage the process. This means the counselor needs to organize the environment so that it is conducive to creativity and imagination and reduces the need for unnecessary limit setting. For instance, one counselor included a beautiful sailing ship in her collection; it was made of wood and had a fragile paper sail. When a child reached for it to put it in her tray of wet sand, the counselor said, "You can't use that one in the wet sand." This is an example of an unnecessary limit. If the counselor gives children wet sand or spray bottles to use in building their worlds, it is important not to have anything in the collection that cannot be in contact with water. This way, the counselor can concentrate on paying attention to the children's worlds and not on setting unnecessary limits.

Countertransference is another important challenge. In many instances, witnessing visual images is more potent than verbal therapy because, like the children, the counselor's own symbolic thinking processes become active. The children's trays can be deeply moving for the counselor. The counselor's capacity to join with children at the experiencing level is critical because it allows children to derive maximum benefit from their trays. When this joining happens, however, the counselor has to deal with countertransference issues that arise inevitably in response to the children's images and stories. Otherwise, it is difficult to hold the group space so that children can open up more deeply to their own experiences that need to be played out. Witnessing children who are playing out painful experiences in the concentrated form of a miniature world is indeed very potent. Specific training for the role of witness is essential.

Recommended Training and Experience

Following are some recommendations for preparation and training for using sand tray group counseling in the schools:

1. Do your own sand tray building process with a competent therapist so you know what it is like to use images that lead you into experiential processing.
2. Do your own sand tray group process to learn what it is like to share and process images at the community level.
3. Attend training seminars and workshops in both individual sandplay therapy and sandplay group counseling.
4. Attend training workshops that provide live presentations.
5. Review developmental needs of elementary school children.
6. Before starting sand tray groups, practice sandplay counseling with many individual clients until you are very comfortable with the process.
7. Organize your first group with just two children, and then increase the size of your next group to fit your level of comfort and training.
8. Obtain supervision from qualified persons who have used the group process, particularly the sand tray group counseling process.
9. Try to conduct your first groups with a trained colleague to help with postsession processing.
10. Read books and articles related to sandplay therapy and study relevant cases.

Group sandplay is relatively new, so it takes some effort to find good training opportunities. Training for individual sand tray therapy is available in many regions of the country, and, although less available, there are some training situations for sand tray group work. Training for individual work is an important first step. Although general play therapy training benefits the sand tray group counselor, there are some elements of practice that are specific to sandplay therapy. Good preparation will help the counselor avoid a number of pitfalls that can easily occur with sand tray group counseling. When it goes well, however, it is a process like no other. It is a special gift for children when they can belong to a safe group where they can utilize symbolic language to deal with their innermost problems. They open up very quickly, and when they contact their own creative energies, they are astounding. Children are resilient; in the free and protected space their resiliency comes through, and they leap at the chance to develop themselves more fully.

REFERENCES

Cowen, E.L., Hightower, A.D., Pedro-Carroll, J.L., Work, W.C., Wyman, P.A., & Haffey, W.G. (1996). *School-based prevention for children at risk: The Primary Mental Health Project.* Washington, DC: American Psychological Association.

De Domenico, G. (1999). Group sandtray-worldplay: New dimensions in sandplay therapy. In D. Sweeney & L. Homeyer (Eds.), *The handbook of group play therapy: How to do it, how it works, whom it's best for* (pp. 215–233). San Francisco: Jossey-Bass.

Erikson, E. (1963). *Childhood and society.* New York: Norton.

Erikson, E. (1968). *Identity, youth and crisis.* New York: Norton.

Ginott, H. (1961). *Group psychotherapy with children.* Northvale, NJ: Aronson.

Kalff, D. (1980). *Sandplay: A psychotherapeutic approach to the psyche.* Boston: Sigo Press.

Lowenfeld, M. (1993). *Understanding children's sandplay.* London: Margaret Lowenfeld Trust. (Original work published 1979)

Mitchell, R.R., & Friedman, H.S. (1994). *Sandplay: Past, present, and future.* New York: Routledge.

Reynolds, C., & Kamphaus, R. (1998). *Behavior assessment system for children: Manual.* Circle Pines, MN: American Guidance Service.

CHAPTER 19

Innovative Applications of Play Therapy in School Settings

CYNTHIA REYNOLDS and CAROL STANLEY

PLAY THERAPY is defined by the Association for Play Therapy (2000, p. 1) as "the systematic use of a theoretical model to establish an interpersonal process wherein trained play therapists use the therapeutic powers of play to help clients prevent or resolve psychosocial difficulties and achieve optimal growth and development." Play therapy is based on the rationale that play is a naturally occurring phenomenon in children. Because children under 10 have less well-developed expressive language, they are more accustomed to using toys and play to communicate (Kottman, 1995). Play has the power not only to facilitate normal child development, but also to alleviate abnormal behavior (Schaefer, 1993). Play can help overcome resistance; build competence; enhance self-expression, problem solving, role taking, and creativity; and provide an opportunity for abreaction, catharsis, attachment formation, and alleviation of fears (Schaefer, 1993). In addition, the positive emotions that occur during play can help to build resiliency in children.

There are many different theories of play therapy. Each approach has its own unique beliefs regarding the nature of human beings, the conceptualization of people and personality, the definition of the role of the counselor, and the interaction with clients and their parents. It is up to the counselor to discover which theory of play therapy works best with his or her own personality and beliefs about people (Kottman, 1995).

Most counselors choose an integrative approach and select from several theories to find what best matches the needs of the individual client. Specific theories range from therapist-directed to child-directed process and from structured to unstructured materials. It is the task of the individual counselor to do the personal work necessary to feel comfortable and competent to use play therapy with children.

INTRODUCING PLAY THERAPY

It is important for elementary school counselors to build a base of support from which to operate when beginning to implement play therapy techniques. Some counselors find that the use of the term "therapy" is especially hard to sell in a school setting because therapy is generally believed to be beyond the scope of practice of the school counselor and beyond the role of the school. These counselors have chosen to use terms such as "play counseling" or "counseling with toys" to circumvent potential objections. Changing the name, however, does not alter the healing properties associated with play, nor build trust with those who are being deceived. With an appropriate explanation of the background, rationale, developmental relevance, and benefits of play therapy, there is usually less resistance regarding the name. School counselors will need to assess the sociocultural environment to determine the best course of action in their school district.

Most school administrators are delighted to have an elementary counselor who is able to utilize new or innovative ways to reach children and will offer their support immediately. One issue that must be addressed with administration, however, is the difference between play therapy and "playing around." Many school officials do not take kindly to the idea of paying employees to play around. They need to be convinced that the outcomes of play therapy are in line with the mission/purpose of the school district. Because the major objective of elementary schools is to assist in the intellectual, physical, and social development of children by providing adequate learning opportunities, play therapy can be utilized to help get children ready to profit from the learning experiences offered (Landreth, 1983). It is helpful to provide videotapes of experts, books, relevant research, guest speakers, play therapy Web site addresses, and so on to support the argument for the use of play therapy in the school. Case examples can also be persuasive in helping school administrators understand the benefits of the use of play therapy to help children. The most powerful selling point, however, comes from witnessing the actual improvement in a child's behavioral or academic performance as a result of play therapy interventions.

Teachers are generally pleased to have enlisted the school counselor's help with children who are struggling academically, emotionally, or socially in their classroom. Often, much pressure is put on the school counselor to "fix" the child. Play does not outwardly appear to belong in the "fix this child quick" equation.

CASE EXAMPLE

Mr. Jacobs was concerned about Haley, a girl in his fourth-grade class. She had been caught stealing from other children in his classroom three times during the year. Mr. Jacobs (with parents' permission) referred Haley to the school counselor for help in dealing with her problem. After her second visit with the counselor, Mr. Jacobs asked Haley if the counseling was helping her with the stealing. Haley replied, "We have had a lot of fun playing." Mr. Jacobs felt that the school counselor was not doing her job, and that play was definitely not the answer for an offense as serious as stealing. He did not encourage other children to seek help from the counselor, and began "forgetting" to send Haley to the counselor's office at the designated time.

School counselors need to be proactive with school staff in providing the rationale, benefits, contraindications, and appropriate expectations for play therapy. Understanding the training and education needed to become a play therapist may also help teachers appreciate the depth of skills needed to reach children using these techniques. A presentation at a beginning-of-the-year staff meeting will help to alleviate the quite natural misunderstandings that may occur in schools.

Parents who are eagerly seeking help for their child's issues will welcome the idea of play therapy being offered at the school. The parents may have been struggling with their child's problems for months or years and have tried many remedies to little or no avail. Parents can appreciate that talking to a child and telling him or her to straighten up may not produce the desired outcome. Parents realize that play may help to reduce their child's anxieties about going to the counselor. On the other hand, a few parents may resent sending their child for play therapy because they view it as a reward for bad behavior. Educating these parents about play therapy may convince them to give it a try or may confirm their decision to seek another kind of help.

Presentations about play therapy at parent meetings or parent-teacher organizations can be an essential component of building support for integrating play therapy into an elementary counseling program. Creating a brochure describing play therapy or submitting articles to the school newsletter may also help to spread the word about how the school counselor utilizes play therapy.

ETHICAL ISSUES

The American School Counselor Association's "Ethical Standards for School Counselors" (1992) states, "Each person has the right to privacy and thereby the right to expect the counselor-client relationship will comply with all laws, policies, and ethical standards pertaining to confidentiality." Confidentiality refers to an individual's right to privacy that is inherent in counseling relationships. In fact, confidentiality is the heart of the counseling relationship, as children are more willing to trust and disclose if they believe what they say (and play) will be kept private. Confidentiality is established in an agreement between the school counselor and the child when they begin a helping relationship. The exceptions can be discussed at the outset. The counselor could say, "I am the school counselor. My job is to be a friendly helper to children, and to help them cope with stress or uncomfortable feelings, or to help them deal with things that are bothering them. We will talk and play when we meet. What you say and do in here is just between us, except the times when you are getting hurt, hurting others, or hurting yourself. In those cases, I must, by law, make sure that your parents or other helping people know what is happening so that the hurting can be stopped."

Privileged communication refers to the client's right to be protected from having confidential information revealed in a public hearing or court of law. In 1987, only 20 states granted some form of privileged communication rights to students in school counseling relationships (Sheeley & Herlihy, 1988). Many times, in cases of minor children, the parent/guardian is the holder of the privilege. Therefore, the school counselor must face the daunting task of balancing the parent's or guardians' right to know what is going on in counseling with the child's need for privacy. The counselor could say, "There may be times when your parent/guardian would like to know what we are working on because he/she is responsible for you and cares about you. I will always check out with you first what I want to talk to your parent about. We can decide together what to say to your parent/guardian, if you would like me to talk to him/her by myself, if you would like to talk to him/her by yourself, or if we should do it together. I wouldn't tell your parent/guardian if you hated his/her new haircut, but if you were really worried or scared about something that your parent/guardian could help you with, I would ask you if it is okay for us to discuss it with him/her."

School counselors often function as members of intervention assistance teams, which devise strategies to help students who are not meeting their academic potential. Information related to the student's performance is often shared at these meetings or with the principal, speech therapist, school psychologist, special education teacher, reading specialist, tutor, or classroom teacher. The student's confidentiality is of utmost importance, and the school counselor must find a balance of contributing helpful ideas to the team without revealing confidential information. Again, seeking the child's and/or parent's/guardian's permission regarding what to share with the team or the teacher is crucial. The counselor could say, "There is a group of teachers who are very concerned about you. They want you to do the best you can in school. We are meeting next week to come up with ideas that could be helpful to you. Is there anything that you would like me to share with the group? It seems like it might be useful for them to know how scared you are about _____. Would it be okay if I mentioned that to them? Is there anything that we've talked about or done together that you do not want me to share with them?"

The issue of confidentiality becomes even more complex in small group and classroom guidance activities, as it is impossible for the counselor to guarantee that students will respect each other's privacy. In these cases, confidentiality can be described and the hurtful consequences of not respecting confidentiality can be discussed. Young children especially may need to be guided about what is appropriate to share in a group setting and what may be more appropriate in a one-to-one situation. They should be cautioned that confidentiality cannot be absolutely guaranteed. The counselor could say, "What we talk about in group should stay in here. You would not want what you say or do in here to be gossiped about to others. You are free to talk about what you said or did in group if you like, but you shouldn't talk about what other children in the group did or said. If you are not sure about what you want to share with the group, you can always ask me privately about it. You could also ask another friend or parent/guardian what they think. You might also want to wait and see how you feel about the group after a few weeks, before deciding how much you want to share."

Generally, we think of confidentiality as referring to what is said in a counseling session. In play therapy, confidentiality should also protect the play and/or artwork. Very sensitive material can be expressed in play and artwork. There always exists the potential for harm to the client if that play or artwork is misunderstood, misrepresented, or misused by others.

CASE EXAMPLE

The school counselor was concerned about the personal nature of several drawings done by a child in play therapy. Rather than send the picture back to the classroom with the child after the session, the counselor kept the picture in an envelope to be picked up at the end of the day. The counselor also called the parent to let him/her know what to expect and gave suggestions regarding the best way to react to the drawing. In this case, the school counselor was sensitive to the potential harm that could result if the child inadvertently divulged the artwork to classmates or teachers. The call to the parent was made with the child's permission, and the parent was coached on how to respond appropriately.

CASE EXAMPLE

Jeff's father, Bill, had a history of violence and trouble with the law. Jeff was not able to express angry feelings at home because of how his father might react. Bill killed someone, was found guilty of murder, and was sentenced to prison for life. Several months after his father was sent away, Jeff drew a picture in play therapy at school that demonstrated angry feelings toward his father. The school counselor called Jeff's mother to report the breakthrough and provide support for Jeff's expression of feelings. Several months later, the school counselor received an angry letter from Bill in prison, accusing her of turning his son against him. When the counselor talked to Jeff's mother, she admitted that she had taken the picture (without Jeff's knowing) to Bill during a visit to explain why Jeff did not want to come to visit Bill in prison. This is an excellent example of how confidential art material was misunderstood and misused to the child's detriment.

Another ethical responsibility of the school counselor that falls under the American School Counselor Association's (1992) Responsibilities to Students involves adequately preparing the student to transition from the play therapy session back to the classroom. Children may need coaching on understanding how the limits during play therapy/counseling differ from those of the classroom and those at home. Children may need assistance on how to come down from a particularly emotional or expressive session, to become centered, and to reenter the classroom. Children are able to understand that there are different rules for different places, but it is the counselor's responsibility to educate them about how to negotiate those differences. By allowing a few minutes between appointments, the counselor can avoid the negative consequences of "dumping" the child back in the classroom without adequate time to compose himself or herself.

TRAINING AND SUPERVISION

The Association for Play Therapy is dedicated to promoting play therapy and addressing members' professional needs to better help children and others in need (APT, 2000). APT lists specific academic and clinical criteria needed to become a Registered Play Therapist. Despite this, some counselors believe that playing is a natural talent and that they don't need specialized training to do play therapy with children.

The American School Counselor Association's Ethical Standards (1992) specifically address this issue under Responsibilities to Self: "The school counselor functions within the boundaries of the individual professional competence and accepts responsibility for the consequences of his or her actions." Because APT has clearly defined competence in terms of practicing play therapists, it can be concluded that it is unethical to practice play therapy without appropriate training. The guideline states that the school counselor "strives through personal initiatives to maintain professional competence and keep abreast of innovations and trends in the profession. Professional and personal growth is continuous and ongoing throughout the counselor's career." This brings additional support for the obligation of the school counselor to devote the necessary time and resources to stay up-to-date on advances in the field.

Historically, school counselors have received administrative supervision, but clinical supervision has been a rare occurrence. Elementary school counselors, in particular, have one of the loneliest positions, as they usually are the only one in a small district, and in a larger district may travel to several buildings and have no opportunity to cross paths with other counselors. Meeting the criteria to become a Registered Play Therapist will provide the school counselor with supervision. School counselors may also find peer supervision groups useful and supportive.

INTEGRATING PLAY THERAPY INTO ELEMENTARY COUNSELING PROGRAMS

SETTINGS

Many elementary school counselors have set up shop in rooms where the word "storage" has been pried off the door. Some have had the luxury of a whole classroom as an office. Others have traveled to three or more buildings and have no assigned room. Despite the specifics of the setting, it is possible for the school counselor to implement some form of play therapy.

One Building (Play Therapy Stations)

The school counselor attended several play therapy conferences and wanted to implement play therapy into her program, but she was uncomfortable with the structure of the traditional play therapy room. She modeled her office (which was the size of half of a regular classroom) after a concept she had been familiar with as a teacher: learning centers. She created seven different play therapy stations: a nurturing station with baby dolls, stuffed animals, cradle, blankets, rocking chair, dishes and play food, dollhouse with people, and baby bottle; a safety and protection station with Bobo, handcuffs, pounding bench, foam bats, plastic shield and armor, hardhat, rope; an art station containing paper, crayons, markers, pastels, easel, paint, strips of cloth, pipe cleaners, glue, scissors, magazines; a sand tray station; a games station with both therapeutic and other games; a puppet station; and a clay station with clay, mats, hammer, garlic press, potato peeler, butter knife, rolling pin. When she first began implementing play therapy, she gave children the choice of playing at two or three stations during a 20-minute session. She was concerned that giving children free rein would create too much chaos and that she would spend too much time cleaning up the room after each child's session. After a few weeks following this model, she realized that her restrictions were artificial and limiting to the child's expression. She continued to use the play therapy stations, but allowed the children the freedom to choose whatever they wanted during the session.

Another school counselor worked in a building in which there had been a drop in enrollment. She was assigned an entire classroom to use as her office. She divided the room into four quadrants, with a section for the actual office, a section for group work, a section for parent conferences, and a section for play therapy. She was delighted to have so much room, but at times felt the room was almost too big, as voices would echo and children sometimes seemed more inhibited. She really liked having the sink available for cleanup and water play. She realized that there are both advantages and disadvantages to large rooms.

Two Buildings

Another school counselor traveled between two buildings and shared rooms with the speech therapist, school psychologist, and reading tutor. He got tired of carrying materials between buildings, but found that when he left material in one office, it was not there when he returned. He worked with the principals on funding for two large lockable cabinets, one for each building. He was able to place all play therapy equipment in the cabinets and keep them locked when he was not present in the building.

Multiple Buildings

Another counselor was hired to develop a counseling program in a school district with five elementary buildings. She wanted to integrate play therapy into the program, so she purchased a large tote bag and stocked it with essential play therapy items. Although her toys were limited, she felt that she was able to use play therapy to produce positive outcomes for her students. The district was so impressed they hired an additional elementary counselor within two years.

EQUIPMENT

The selection of toys to be used in play therapy deserves careful consideration, as toys are considered to be vehicles of communication. Different play therapy theorists recommend general categories of toys as essential; among these are aggressive, nurturing, creative, expressive, fantasy, and real-life toys (Axline, 1947, Ginott, 1961; Guerney, 1983; Kottman, 1995; Landreth, 1991; Oaklander, 1978; O'Connor, 1991). School counselors need to familiarize themselves with this literature and make toy selections that are congruent with their theoretical orientation.

Landreth (1991) suggested that play therapists evaluate toys for use in the playroom based on the following criteria. According to him, toys and materials should

1. Facilitate a broad range of creative and emotional expression.
2. Be interesting to children.
3. Allow for verbal and nonverbal exploration and expression in the play room.
4. Provide experiences for children in which they can feel successful, without having to follow certain preordained procedures.
5. Be well made and durable.

It is important for school counselors to avoid toys that they feel uncomfortable about, as children will pick up on the counselor's nonverbal communication, and this may create an unnecessary dynamic. No toys should be selected that cannot be replaced.

Recent episodes of school violence have resulted in school districts establishing zero tolerance policies: students with any weapon, real or toy, are suspended from school. In light of these developments, the school counselor is faced with the dilemma of whether to include toys that have traditionally been used for fantasy aggression, such as rubber knives, dart guns, and handcuffs. Thinking on this matter appears to be at polar extremes. On one side, if toys are words and play is language, children are robbed of their ability to communicate about angry/aggressive feelings by not including aggressive toys in the playroom; the use of aggressive toys provides an avenue for children to have a healthy release of anger and may actually decrease aggressive acts in daily life. On the other side, if promoting a peaceful society is desired, children's exposure to the tools of violence should be eliminated—including allowing guns in the playroom or allowing toy guns at school socializes children that violence is an acceptable alternative. Wherever the school counselor stands on this issue, it is important to develop a sound rationale to gain support from the administration and parents, so that all are aware of what is available in the playroom and the purposes for which the toys are being used. It is possible that politics around this issue will determine the future of an elementary counseling program.

CASE EXAMPLE

An elementary counselor had been using play therapy for several years. She had the typical aggressive play equipment: dart gun, rubber knife, rope, bop bag, batacas, and handcuffs. After the shootings at Jonesboro, her district adopted the zero tolerance policy. One day, a first-grader commented on leaving the play therapy session, "Miss A, you could get kicked out of school for having that gun and knife." Miss A rethought the need for the rubber knife and gun and put them away. However, she kept the other aggressive toys and included miniature toy soldiers in the sand tray collection.

Financing the cost of play materials can be expensive, and few elementary counselors have budgets. The counselor can make a wish list as part of presentations for parent organizations. Many PTOs give classroom teachers a yearly budget for items, and the school counselor can ask to be included in that budget. Grant money designated for violence or drug prevention can be used for elementary counseling materials. Working cooperatively with other grant writers from the district may lead to funds for a play therapy room. Finally, soliciting donations from teachers, parents, or local community businesses can be helpful. Distributing a list of needed items eliminates sorting through bags of junk. It is possible even with limited funds to build up a well-equipped play therapy room in a few years.

CASE EXAMPLE

An elementary counselor went to a conference on the use of sand trays with children. She also attended workshops to become competent in this area. She wanted to purchase sand tray equipment to use in her school but had no funds. She first went to the PTO and they agreed to purchase the sand tray. A friend of the family donated items from a miniature train collection. The counselor's daughter was getting rid of old shelves and the counselor repainted them. She collected seashells, rocks, and pinecones while on vacation. Teachers donated a number of items. To round out her collection, she spent a total of $50 at the dollar store and garage sales. Within a few months, her dream was realized.

After investing much time, energy, and funds for play therapy equipment, school counselors will want to keep it protected. This may require locking cabinets and doors. Students will expect certain items to be available and can be extremely disappointed when an item is missing. Locking also prevents students from being tempted to steal and prevents colleagues from dropping in to borrow items when the counselor is not there. At some level, using play therapy materials for others to "play around with" compromises the therapeutic effectiveness of the materials.

CASE EXAMPLE

The special education teacher, Mr. B, was impressed with how the sand tray sessions helped Jose calm down when he was having a bad day. One day, when Jose was particularly distraught, Mr. B. took Jose to the counselor's office. The counselor was in a classroom teaching a third-grade guidance lesson. Mr. B decided to let Jose play in the sand tray for a while. When the counselor returned, she found Mr. B standing over Jose and speaking sternly, "I don't know why you picked that item to put in the sand. That wasn't a good idea." The counselor had to educate Mr. B about the sacredness of sandplay and the training criteria. The counselor had to deal with the setback to therapeutic progress that occurred when Mr. B criticized Jose. The counselor began to lock her office door when gone for any lengthy period of time.

Techniques

There are hundreds of play therapy interventions and techniques (Kaduson & Schaefer, 1997; Kottman, 1995; Kottman & Schaefer, 1993; Landreth, Homeyer, Glover, & Sweeney, 1996; Oaklander, 1978; O'Connor, 1991; Schaefer & Cangelosi, 1977; Schaefer & O'Connor, 1983). For the purposes of this chapter, four techniques are discussed and specific examples of successful integration into an elementary counseling program are described.

Puppets

Puppets are one of the most useful tools in play therapy because they are naturally attractive and fun. Puppets can be used with a variety of theoretical approaches along the continuum of directive to nondirective. Barnes (1996) describes four functions that puppets can serve: regression, projection, modeling boundaries, and as a step toward increased verbal communication.

Regression.   Puppets have the potential to take children back to an earlier developmental stage in a socially acceptable fashion. Even upper elementary students, who reject most things "babyish," may enjoy creating dramas with puppets. It is part of the process of honoring and respecting children to allow them to play or not play with the puppets. Forcing a child who does not want to use them is countertherapeutic.

Projection.   It can be terrifying for a child to express feelings or disclose personal issues/problems to an adult who is in a position of power. Puppets provide an avenue that is far less threatening. Both real and fantasy thoughts/feelings can be expressed through the puppet character without fear of judgment; therefore, it is crucial to not jump to conclusions regarding specific material presented. When the child engages the school counselor in puppet play, the use of the whisper technique ("What would you like me to do or say?"; Landreth, 1991) can be especially effective in encouraging the unfolding of the child's issues.

Modeling.   Puppets can be used to model desired behaviors. Many children seem much more inclined to listen to and take suggestions from a puppet rather than an adult. It is important when modeling with puppets to never use them in a way that is critical or negative to the child.

Increased Verbal Communication.   For children who are reluctant or afraid to speak to adults, the puppets can offer a possibility for communication that can be a first step to more direct communication.

When beginning a puppet collection, it is important to represent the polarities of both good and bad. Suggestions include family figures; cute and cuddly figures, such as dog, kitten, rabbit, lamb; aggressive figures such as shark, wolf, alligator, dinosaur; king, queen, prince, and princess; witch and wizard; angel and devil; police officer, rescue worker, judge; owl, clam, and turtle.

CASE EXAMPLE

Mrs. C, an elementary school counselor, won a large puppet at a local amusement park that was fuzzy and could be worn with its legs and arms wrapped around her body. She wore "Fergie" on the first day of school and walked up and down the primary hallway greeting students as they entered the buildings looking for their classrooms. Mrs. C and Fergie discovered "lost" students and escorted them to the appropriate classrooms. Later that day, Mrs. C and Fergie visited the first- and second-grade classrooms to talk about what it was like for Fergie to be new to the school and what the students could do to help him and other new students feel comfortable.

CASE EXAMPLE

In a first-grade social skills group, the school counselor was teaching about "I care" language. She selected certain puppets to demonstrate examples of people using "I care" language. Each student was allowed to select a puppet, then were asked to create skits in which the puppets used "I care" language. The students were animated and involved. They were asked to use "I care" language at home and at school at least three times before the next group session.

CASE EXAMPLE

Joshua was a fourth-grade boy referred for counseling because he had witnessed his father's death due to a heart attack at home but refused to discuss the event with anyone. Joshua seemed restless and agitated at home and withdrawn at school. His favorite puppet was a black-and-white-spotted Dalmatian firedog that represented the symbol for rescue to Joshua. Each week during play therapy, he would create dramas in which other puppets became caught up in life-threatening situations and Firedog would come to the rescue, saving them in the nick of time. After many such rescues, the school counselor asked Joshua if he ever wished he could be like Firedog. Joshua burst into tears and talked about his father's death and how bad he felt that he could do nothing to save his father. After this session, Joshua showed a marked improvement both at school and home.

CASE EXAMPLE

The counselor asked fifth-grade students to create a puppet play to demonstrate the schoolwide character trait of the month, which was responsibility. A videotape was made of the play and was used at the Board of Education and PTO meetings to demonstrate the newly implemented Character Education Program.

Creative Movement

Children are often expected to sit still behind desks and passively absorb educational information; this process robs children of their natural energies and zest for life. Instead, this inherent desire to move can be used to enrich and enhance learning rather than inhibit it (Benzwie, 1987). The use of creative movement by counselors can facilitate children's problem solving, self-esteem, and cooperation.

CASE EXAMPLE

Louis was a 9-year-old boy who refused to talk at school even though he spoke regularly at home. There were no medical or cultural explanations for his lack of speech at school. The school counselor and physical education teacher met to discuss options because Louis's mother stated that P.E. was his favorite class. The P.E. teacher noticed that Louis was particularly gifted in movement activities. The counselor and the P.E. teacher scheduled joint movement sessions for Louis and three other friends. During the first few weeks, no speech was necessary to participate. The sessions were structured so that more cooperative play was needed each week. Before long, Louis was whispering to both the friends and the counselor at school. Within several months, he was speaking in class as well.

CASE EXAMPLE

In sixth grade, guidance lessons focused on awareness, identification, and appropriate expression of feelings. One game called Feelings Charades was popular with the students. The counselor made a list of 30 different feelings, and then put them on individual index cards. A student designated as "it" drew an index card and was required to act out the feeling without words. The rest of the class had three tries to guess what the feeling was. If the feeling was not guessed, the person who was "it" gave a hint until it was guessed. After the feeling was guessed, "it" shared a time he or she felt that way. The person who guessed correctly was the next "it." A follow-up lesson included role-playing appropriate expression of feelings. The sixth-graders stated that they learned they had many feelings similar to others in their class. Some were surprised to learn that other students had feelings they did not expect. Other students realized that people vary in the degree to which they express feelings verbally and nonverbally. The Feelings Charades game opened up levels of discussion that had not been possible before.

Clay

Clay is a medium with naturally healing properties that make it ideal to use with children. Its flexibility and elasticity is a great deterrent to the perfectionism of some children, in that mistakes can be corrected with ease. Clay is much cleaner than many of the synthetic doughs and modeling clays; it cleans up with a sponge when wet, and can be brushed off clothing and other surfaces when dried. It is no coincidence that spas offer high-priced clay facial masques and mud baths for wealthy clientele; for it is both soothing and cooling. Most children love to get their hands messy, but occasionally a child may find the regressive nature of clay too uncomfortable. The counselor should honor the child's reluctance or refusal to use this medium.

CASE EXAMPLE

The school counselor developed two different classroom guidance lessons (one for third grade and one for sixth grade) that involved the use of clay. Third-graders used the clay during a lesson on anger management that focused on the "turtle technique" (retreating into your shell to gain time to control angry feelings). Students made clay turtles and practiced going into the shells to count to 10 and breathe before reacting to anger. The sixth-graders used clay to create their own angry monster. They presented their angry monster to the class and discussed how it interfered with their lives. Students then destroyed their angry monsters and created another clay figure to replace it.

CASE EXAMPLE

Lori was a new third-grade student whom the teachers were extremely worried about. She seemed to live in her own world. She never made any sense when she talked, as she constantly contradicted herself. She was beginning to develop a reputation for being a liar with the other children. The counselor found when using most of the other play therapy media, Lori could be elusive, evasive, and unengaged. After four or five visits using clay, the counselor felt that Lori was beginning to feel grounded and safe enough to allow her real self to be known.

Sandplay

Sandplay is one of the most important tools available for psychological healing. It involves the use of a small tray of sand and numerous small figurines to create worlds, scenes, or stories. Through this process, which actually reflects the child's emotional world, the child faces many conflicts and problems and learns to resolve issues that had previously blocked his or her growth and development. When a child participates, he or she enters a realm of healing that operates on a very deep level. Ideally, the sandplay itself provides what Kalff (1980) calls a "free and protected space" catalytic to the healing process. Pioneers in the field of sandplay include the Navajo Indians (Weinrib, 1983), Margaret Lowenfeld (1979), and Dora Kalff (1971). The school counselor who is interested in using this form of therapy should read extensively (Carey, 1999; De Domenico, 1988; Mitchell & Friedman, 1994; Weinrib, 1983), seek adequate training, receive supervised experience, and complete personal sandplay therapy

(Sweeney, 1999). The following examples are offered to demonstrate the power of sandplay therapy. Readers are cautioned to gain the necessary preparation before implementing these interventions.

CASE EXAMPLE

The building principal asked the school counselor to develop a program to deal with a group of at-risk fifth-grade boys. The counselor attended training on how to implement group sandplay in the schools. She was especially eager to see how a more culturally sensitive approach might work with the boys. Before each session, she led the boys in a centering activity and helped to remind them of the guidelines. Then, each boy would create a world in the sand. When finished, the group would witness each other's worlds. Within several months, the counselor received notes and calls from both parents and teachers inquiring as to what she was doing with the boys. It seemed the group was making a significant impact on their acting-out behavior. Both parents and teachers remarked that when group was cancelled, the boys were very upset. By the end of the year, the boys experienced significant improvement in behavior in school.

CASE EXAMPLE

Barry, age 8, was referred to the school counselor because of his emotional distress following his parents' bitter divorce. Despite the fact that their continuous litigation was creating significant stress for him, they refused to alter their behaviors. The school counselor stated that she would work with Barry if the parents agreed to allow Barry complete confidentiality and to not use the counseling as evidence in litigation. Barry was drawn to the sand tray when he first walked into the counselor's office. He wanted to spend his time making battle scenes. Each week he would create the scenes and say nothing until he was ready to leave. As he went out the door, he would say, "I feel much better." After five or six sessions, the counselor and Barry agreed that he could decide when he needed to come and make a scene again. He returned every several weeks for the rest of the semester and was reported to be doing better in school. The counselor and Barry never discussed the divorce.

CONCLUSIONS AND RECOMMENDATIONS

Play therapy can be integrated into existing elementary counseling programs, as it is an appropriate tool to facilitate children's ability to effectively utilize education interventions. Play therapy is the most developmentally appropriate counseling approach available to use with elementary school children. As school districts move toward implementing the National Standards for School Counseling (Dahir, Sheldon, & Valiga, 1997), elementary counselors can demonstrate how play therapy can help meet both Standard A in Academic Development, "Students will acquire the attitudes, knowledge, and skills that contribute to effective learning in school and across the life span" (p. 6), and Standard B in Personal Social Development, "Students will acquire the attitudes, knowledge, and interpersonal skills to help them understand and respect self and others" (p. 6). With appropriate training and experience, elementary school counselors can take school counseling to the place it ought to be: centered on helping children.

REFERENCES

American School Counselor Association. (1992). Ethical standards for school counselors. Alexandria, VA: Author.

Association for Play Therapy. (2000). *Newsletter, 19*(2).

Axline, V. (1947). *Play therapy.* Boston: Houghton Mifflin.

Barnes, M.A. (1996). *The healing path with children: An exploration for parents and professionals.* Clayton, NY: Victoria, Fermoyle and Berrigan.

Benzwie, T. (1987). *A moving experience: Dance for lovers of children and the child within.* Tucson, AZ: Zephyr Press.

Carey, L. (1999). *Sandplay with children and families.* Northvale, NJ: Aronson.

Dahir, C.A., Sheldon, C.B., & Valiga, M.J. (1997). *Sharing the vision: The national standards for school counseling programs.* Alexandria, VA: American Counseling Association.

De Domenico, G. (1988). *Sandtray worldplay: A comprehensive guide to the use of the sandtray in psychotherapeutic and transformational settings.* Oakland, CA: Author.

Ginott, H.G. (1961). *Group psychotherapy with children.* New York: McGraw-Hill.

Guerney, L. (1983). Client-centered (nondirective) play therapy. In C.E. Schaefer & K.J. O'Connor (Eds.), *Handbook of play therapy.* New York: Wiley.

Kaduson, H., & Schaefer, C. (Eds.). (1997). *101 favorite play therapy techniques.* Northvale, NJ: Aronson.

Kalff, D. (1971). *Sandplay: Mirror of the child's psyche.* San Francisco: Browser.

Kalff, D. (1980). *Sandplay* (2nd ed.). Santa Monica, CA: Sigo Press.

Kottman, T. (1995). *Partners in play: An Adlerian approach to play therapy.* Alexandria, VA: American Counseling Association.

Kottman, T., & Schaefer, C. (Eds.). (1993). *Play therapy in action: A casebook for practitioners.* Northvale, NJ: Aronson.

Landreth, G.L. (1983). Play therapy in elementary school settings. In C.E. Schaefer & K.J. O'Connor (Eds.), *Handbook of play therapy* (pp. 200–212). New York: Wiley.

Landreth, G.L. (1991). Play therapy: The art of the relationship. Muncie, IN: Accelerated Development.

Landreth, G.L., Homeyer, L.E., Glover, G., & Sweeney, D.S. (1996). *Play therapy interventions with children's problems.* Northvale, NJ: Aronson.

Lowenfeld, M. (1979). *The world technique.* London: Allen & Unwin.

Mitchell, R., & Friedman, H. (1994). *Sandplay: Past, present, and future.* New York: Routledge.

Oaklander, V. (1978). *Windows to our children.* Moab, UT: Real People Press.

O'Connor, K.J. (1991). *The play therapy primer: An integration of theories and techniques.* New York: Wiley.

Schaefer, C. (1993). *The therapeutic powers of play.* Northvale, NJ: Aronson.

Schaefer, C., & Cangelosi, D. (Eds.). (1997). *Play therapy techniques.* Northvale, NJ: Aronson.

Schaefer, C., & O'Connor, K. (Eds.). (1983). *Handbook of play therapy.* New York: Wiley.

Sheeley, V.L., & Herlihy, B. (1988). Privileged communication in schools and counseling: Status update. In W.C. Huey & T.P. Remley, Jr. (Eds.), *Ethical and legal issues in school counseling* (pp. 85–92). Alexandria, VA: American Association for Counseling and Development.

Sweeney, D. (1999). Foreword. In L. Carey (Ed.), *Sandplay therapy with children and families.* Northvale, NJ: Aronson.

Weinrib, E. (1983). *Images of the self.* Boston: Sigo Press.

CHAPTER 20

Counselors Coaching Teachers to Use Play Therapy in Classrooms: The Play and Language to Succeed (PALS) Early, School-Based Intervention for Behaviorally At-Risk Children

W. BARRY CHALONER

TEACHERS AND school counselors are increasingly being asked to handle violent children often without the time, resources, or skills to intervene successfully (National Association for the Education of Young Children [NAEYC], 1996, Carlsson-Paige & Levin, 1992). The incidence of violence in schools has increased significantly over the past 30 years, as has the severity of the incidents (Children's Defense Fund [CDF], 2000; NAEYC, 1996; Walker, Severson, & Feil, 1995). This trend may be due primarily to impaired caregiver-child attachments (Perry, 1996). The NAEYC *Position Statement on Violence in the Lives of American Children* (1996) documents that 25% of children age 6 and under are living in high-risk environments known to produce behavioral disorders, impaired attachments, and later violence. Numerous researchers across disciplines have documented that to be successful, intervention needs to begin early (Shore, 1997). The mental health system is failing to meet this challenge. Vernon (1998) noted that although 43 million Americans experience some form of mental or emotional problem, only 7 million can be effectively served with our current system of service delivery.

Although many of these at-risk children never reach the mental health system, most go to elementary or preschool, making early, school-based services critical (Goleman, 1995). When a child has a behavior problem in school, teachers or principals typically refer the child to the school counselor for individual or group services. School counselors and principals are becoming overwhelmed with counseling and discipline referrals as increasing numbers of behaviorally challenging children enter their schools. Research indicating that counseling alone in schools yields poor results (Sprague & Walker, 2000) as well as the sheer numbers of at-risk children dictate that we expand our methods of service delivery beyond traditional "pull-out" counseling. Feeling this burden, many school counselors, play therapists, and other practitioners are looking for ways to maximize the number of challenging children they can effectively reach in schools. An alternative is to train teachers to act, in certain cases, as the primary interventionists and school counselors and play therapists to act as their coaches within a broader intervention system that includes play therapy. This chapter describes the Play And Language to Succeed™ (PALS) early intervention model. PALS trains teachers, counselors, play therapists, and administrators to work collaboratively to intervene as part of a comprehensive, school-based intervention program to reduce counseling and discipline referrals and prevent violence.

REVIEW OF EARLY, SCHOOL-BASED INTERVENTION RESEARCH

Attachment, emotional intelligence, and resilience are key concepts to understanding the rationale for early, school-based intervention. James (1994, p. 2) defines attachment as "A reciprocal, enduring, emotional, and physical affiliation between a child and caregivers" that "provides the base from which a child learns to explore his or her world." Goleman (1995) defines emotional intelligence (EQ) as the ability to be emotionally self-aware, control impulses, delay gratification, read social-emotional cues, be empathic, and know the difference between feelings and actions. Werner and Smith (1992) define resilience as the ability to rise above and thrive despite life's adversities. EQ and resilience are dependent on attachment and are necessary for healthy social-emotional functioning throughout life (Shore, 1997).

Research across disciplines has shown that the quality of adult-child attachments in the early years is a critical factor in the development of social bonding, resilience, emotional intelligence, and many aspects of brain development as well as the prevention of later violence (Egeland, 1996; Egeland, Carlson, & Sroufe, 1993; Hawkins, Catalano, & Miller, 1992; Perry, 1996; Renken, Egeland, Marvinney, Mangelsdorf, & Sroufe, 1989; Schaps & Battistich, 1991; Shore 1997; Werner & Smith, 1982, 1992). Perry (1996) points out that an individual's tendency toward violence is the result of caregiver neglect (cognitive and emotional) and traumatic stress resulting in impaired attachment. When these two factors persist, certain areas of the brain related to survival, fight, and flight become overdeveloped while areas related to empathy and impulse control remain underdeveloped. He argues that this leaves an individual less neurologically responsive to later intervention. Violent trauma is not always the primary factor in impaired attachment. Longitudinal research (Renken, et al., 1989) has shown that children whose caregivers were emotionally unavailable in the early years exhibited more aggression and conduct problems in adolescence. Renken also noted that anxious-avoidant attachment resulting from unresponsive caregiving appeared to predispose children to be violent across all cultures where attachment has been studied. Other researchers (Hawkins et al., 1992; Werner, 1987; Werner & Smith, 1982, 1992) point to the critical role a positive adult-child attachment in the early years plays in the development of resilience. In their longitudinal study, Egeland et al. (1993) found that children from poor, high-risk environments who thrived and demonstrated resilient traits had secure attachments with their caregivers. None of the children in this study whose attachments were impaired, due to chaotic homes or abusive caregivers, thrived socially or academically. Shore (1997) has reviewed and summarized recent findings in brain and attachment research across disciplines. Her research strongly suggests that the prime time for the neurological development of social-emotional capacities is from birth to age 8. Furthermore, research clearly suggests that having a secure attachment with a teacher can partially compensate for an insecure one with a parent (Elicker & Fortner-Wood, 1995; Greenberg, 1997; Oppenheim, Sagi, & Lamb, 1988; Shore, 1997).

There are numerous intervention programs for high-risk children (Barton, Hopkins, McElhaney, Heigel, & Salassi, 1995; Goleman, 1995; Yale Child Study Center, 1996), but many do not begin early enough in the child's developmental process to prevent behavioral problems (Chaloner, 1996; Goleman, 1995; NAEYC, 1996; Ramey & Ramey, 1998; Schaps & Battistich, 1991; Shore, 1997) or facilitate the neurological development of emotional intelligence and resilience (Shore, 1997). Programs that do begin before age 8 often do not employ principles and practices known to be developmentally appropriate for social skill acquisition at Piaget's pre-operational stage of cognitive development (age 2 to 7) (Bredekamp, 1993; Chaloner, 1996; Cowen, Hightower, Pedro, Carroll, Work, & Wyman, 1996; Elkind, 1986, 1988; Forman & Kuschner, 1983; Piaget, 1950; Scherer, 1996; Shore, 1997). Children in the preoperational stage are highly concrete, very egocentric, have a short attention span, and usually remember and respond to only what is immediately and emotionally meaningful. They need interventions and instructional strategies that are emotionally meaningful, immediate, and concrete enough for them to learn and apply what is being taught. They also have not reached the cognitive stage where they are able to independently and reliably use cause-effect thinking to solve problems (Bredekamp, 1993). But many early interventions, including social-emotional curricula, conflict resolution models, discipline strategies, and information-oriented approaches, often require cause-effect thinking for success. Research also indicates that children age 2 to 7 primarily learn and develop social-emotional skills in the context of an adult-child attachment relationship (Bredekamp, 1993). Therefore, any attempt to intervene and teach young children social skills must occur in a safe environment with a caring adult, use a medium that is emotionally meaningful such as play, and provide immediate, concrete feedback.

At-risk children often do not reach mental health clinics or private practitioners soon enough, if at all in many cases, but most at-risk children attend elementary or preschool programs at the onset (CDF, 2000; Goleman, 1995; Shore, 1997). Research indicates that children are hard-wired to make multiple attachments by age 2, that attachments with parents and teachers can function independently, and that a secure teacher-child attachment can partially compensate for an insecure one with the caregiver (Elicker & Fortner-Wood, 1995; Greenberg, 1997; NAEYC, 1996; Shore, 1997), thereby reducing risk. Teachers in preschool and the primary grades (Pre-K–2), due to their consistent and frequent contact, may be better positioned than most professionals to intervene early, when this prime window of opportunity is open between age 2 and 8. For these reasons, programs targeting this behaviorally at-risk population early should be largely school-based (Chaloner, 1996; Goleman, 1995; Schaps & Battistich, 1991; Shore, 1997). In summary, interventions for at-risk children should ideally begin by age 7, utilize developmentally appropriate methods including play, address attachment needs, and be, at least in part, school-based.

THE POWER OF PLAY, PLAY THERAPY, AND PLAY-BASED INTERVENTIONS

Play is perhaps the most developmentally appropriate and powerful medium for young children to build adult-child relationships, develop cause-effect thinking critical to impulse control, process stressful experiences, and learn social skills (Bredekamp, 1993; Chaloner, 1996; Fein & Rivkin, 1986; Landreth, 1991; Rogers & Sawyers, 1988). Ray's (1998) review of outcome studies on play therapy indicates ample evidence that play therapy is an effective treatment for a variety of childhood social-emotional disorders. Child therapists have been using this medium successfully for over 70 years (Landreth, 1991). Nondirective toddler play therapy has been shown to be an effective treatment with attachment disordered toddlers and their mothers (Cohen et al., 1999). The Primary Mental Health Project (PMHP), a school-based Pre-K–3 intervention program, uses trained and supervised laypersons called "special friends" to provide regular, 20-minute individual child-centered play sessions as a key intervention ingredient. PMHP has over 20 years of research demonstrating the model's success as an early intervention as well as the efficacy of laypersons using play at the Pre-K–3 level to intervene (Cowen et al., 1996). Bernard Guerney's (1964) work in training parents to use methods derived from child-centered play therapy with their children (Filial Therapy) has been shown to significantly improve children's behavior, parental acceptance, and parental behavior (Oxman, 1971). It has also demonstrated that parents can be trained to use play therapeutically (Oxman, 1971; Stover & Guerney, 1967). Coufal and Brock (1979) looked at three interventions with parents (parent skills training, parent skills and play, and no treatment) and found that parents in the skills and play group showed significant differences in improved parental behavior and acceptance. Louise Guerney's Foster Parent Skills (Guerney & Wolfgang, 1981) and her subsequent Parenting Skills (Guerney, 1992) Training Programs have proven effective in increasing parental acceptance, developing positive parenting skills, and decreasing negative parenting behaviors (Guerney & Wolfgang, 1981). Her parent program adapts and applies aspects of therapeutic limit setting used by play therapists. One of the central strategies is to teach parents to give language first by reflecting the feeling the child is expressing back to the child before setting limits. B. Guerney and Flumen (1970) demonstrated the successful application of Filial Therapy to train elementary teachers to act as therapeutic agents with withdrawn children. The pioneering work of the Guerneys, PMHP, and, most recently, researchers studying attachment, brain development, and developmentally appropriate practices provides a rationale and template for training teachers to use play and language as part of an early intervention system. This body of research and work has proven that play-based, early intervention is an effective practice. Furthermore, it demonstrates that laypersons and teachers can be successful therapeutic agents in schools with young, at-risk children. The PALS model builds on this pioneering work to create a new rationale and set of practices for an inclusive, classroom-based framework that trains teachers to use play and language to create positive teacher-child attachments as the central component of a broader early intervention strategy.

OVERVIEW OF THE PLAY AND LANGUAGE TO SUCCEED™ (PALS) MODEL

The Play And Language to Succeed (PALS) early intervention model trains school counselors and play therapists to act as PALS partners (coaches) for teachers, who, in turn, are trained to act as the primary interventionists with at-risk children age 3 to 8. In this training, Pre-K–2 teachers and support staff learn to identify at-risk children and use various developmentally appropriate practices, including play, to build secure teacher-child attachments. A small number of in-house staff are selected and certified to take over PALS training, program coordination, and ongoing implementation for their organization, school, district, or region, thus eliminating the need for outside trainers. In addition, school counselors and other behavior staff are trained (if needed) to provide play therapy for those children who either do not respond to the bonding part of the teacher's intervention. This approach is referred to as *relationship-based* versus *curriculum-* or *behavior-based* early intervention because the central intervention strategy focuses on social bonding as well as problem behavior.

BONDING, BOUNDARIES, AND LANGUAGE

Building secure adult-child attachments requires a balance of three key elements: bonding, boundaries, and language. It is their combined effect that facilitates both the establishment of an adult-child attachment and the resulting positive change in behavior. All three elements must be part of the intervention and applied equally to ensure the greatest chance for success.

Teachers then identify and give language to the drivers of misbehavior and the themes expressed in play. In PALS, themes are defined as the feelings, needs, and beliefs children have about themselves, their learning, and their world that are expressed symbolically during play with miniatures or in pretend play. Drivers are defined as the feelings, needs, and beliefs children have that determine the form and function of their behavior and learning problems. This breakdown of themes and drivers into feelings, needs, and beliefs is one of the innovations of the PALS model.

Bonding is achieved when Pre-K–2 teachers use play and learning activities to develop warm, caring relationships with identified at-risk children. Building a warm, personal relationship while giving language to themes during play and learning meets the child's emotional and neurological need to belong. Bonding and language alone reduce many problem behaviors driven by this need. Attending and giving language to themes during play, in particular, helps children communicate about, process, and release stress caused by impaired attachments with caregivers because toys are words and play is language. It also helps them feel understood by at least one caring adult, which has been shown to be critical to the development of resilience (Shore, 1997). Teachers can briefly give language to play while roaming among the various centers or activity areas where play has been established as an option. They begin by leveling, that is, kneeling or sitting in the center near the child. For example, while leveling with a child playing with dinosaur miniatures, the teacher would give language to the themes being expressed: "The dinosaurs are fighting" (tracking), followed by a thematic statement like "The T-rex is angry" or "The momma long neck is scared the T-rex might hurt her or her babies!" (feeling themes). At this point, the child is likely to provide a verbal or nonverbal response. The teacher acknowledges the response and adds "You can keep playing and I'll be back in a little bit to see what you're doing." Then she gets up and roams to another area or briefly attends to another child's play in that same area. After making the rounds, she returns to attend and give language to the first child's play again. This might occur three to six times with each at-risk child over a 30-minute period. Classroom play periods are scheduled 2 to 5 times per week depending on the grade level, teaching style, routine, and academic constraints. As an alternative, when teachers cannot provide play in the classroom, counselors can substitute weekly, 30-minute individual play therapy sessions as the bonding and stress reduction part of the intervention plan.

Boundaries are established when teachers create meaningful rewards and consequences and consistent, developmentally appropriate rules, instructions, and expectations. Play and giving language also provide a developmentally appropriate medium and method for establishing boundaries and teaching social skills in the classroom. As the teacher roams, she watches for any behavior problems so she can respond proactively and teach social skills. For example, the teacher observes a child playing with miniature dinosaurs who begins yelling at another child to give him back a dinosaur. On her way to the center, she asks herself what the child feels, needs, or believes that's driving this behavior. Once at the center, she levels, gets the child's attention, and gives language to one feeling, need, or belief driver before stating the rule or consequence or offering alternatives. Feeling driver: "You're mad that Tim won't give you that dinosaur back." Need driver: "You want that dinosaur back so much you're yelling at Tim to get it." Belief driver: "You think that if you yell at Tim he will give you that dinosaur back." Then the teacher pauses briefly to observe the child's verbal and nonverbal response to confirm if she identified the correct driver. If she has, she employs standard strategies, such as teaching a substitute skill, stating a rule, or reminding the child of the consequence if the behavior persists. It is critical, though, that the teacher offer specific substitute skills and even models them in the moment so they are tied to the language she gave, the child's emotions, and the immediate event. This is an example of a developmentally appropriate educational practice for the preoperational stage because it is immediate, meaningful, and concrete and models cause-effect thinking. It also builds connections between the feeling and thinking centers of the brain critical to impulse control and the development of EQ. She would also address Tim's behavior by giving language to the driver of his misbehavior. For instance: "You wanted that dinosaur so much you took it" (need driver). She briefly pauses again to observe the child to confirm if she identified the correct driver. Then she continues by teaching an alternative skill along with whatever strategies she otherwise uses.

This developmentally appropriate practice of giving language first to the drivers of behavior and learning problems coupled with teaching substitute social skills can be spontaneously applied and sandwiched into most teacher's instructional practices and routines, not just during play time. When teachers give language to play themes, learning themes, and behavioral drivers, they are loaning their brain's language and cause-effect thinking centers to the child, bridging the gap between the child's concrete experience and symbolic thought. Adults talk to themselves or others (symbolic thought) about what they feel, need, or believe as well as think of alternatives and consequences (cause-effect thinking) to control their impulses and self-regulate their behavior. Teachers model this process when they give language. Because this process is developmentally appropriate to the preoperational stage (i.e., is child-centered, concrete, meaningful, and immediate), teachers are better able to help young children more rapidly understand their behavior and control their impulses without complex, time-consuming behavior plans, conflict resolution models, or another curriculum. This has not only reduced the problem behaviors of specific at-risk children and their need for counseling services and discipline referrals, but has decreased teacher, counselor, and principal stress. It has also enhanced overall EQ in the classroom. Counselors and PALS partners help teachers integrate this process into the classroom as the boundaries part of the intervention. Bonding, boundaries, and language can be easily and spontaneously integrated into most teachers' instructional practices and routines.

PALS COMPONENTS AND IMPLEMENTATION

As the PALS model developed and has been implemented at various sites over the past seven years, the primary focus has become school-based services for at-risk children versus their families. Currently, the necessary components for successful implementation of PALS are (1) inclusive, classroom-based interventions by teachers; (2) individual and small group play therapy; (3) initial and ongoing districtwide staff development and support; (4) ongoing administrative and staff collaboration regarding program planning, funding, policies, procedures, and staff development; and (5) early, proactive behavioral screening, rating, and assessment.

Using Toys and Play in Pre-K–2 Classrooms versus Traditional Playrooms

Using toys and having symbolic play centers in Pre-K–2 classrooms versus a traditional playroom requires different strategies to be successful. Most Pre-K–2 teachers use some form of educational center time or free choice time as part of their teaching strategy and routine. Center time is an ideal place in the routine to set up two to three separate play centers or areas designed to allow children access to toys. Teachers can usually be free during this time to roam from center to center working with multiple small groups while managing their class. In today's schools with overcrowded classrooms, lack of funds for substitute teachers and aids, and increasing academic pressures, teachers cannot easily take a child to a playroom and most districts cannot afford to hire additional staff to do so. This often makes programs that require additional staff or time out of classrooms by teachers impractical. In the classroom, they can, at most, make three to six brief contacts per at-risk child, giving language to play during a 30-minute center time 2 to 5 times per week. Experience over the past seven years and PALS outcome data indicate that these brief but frequent contacts (bonding on the run) are very effective. Even in the grade 1 and 2 classrooms, where play is used only a few times per week, it still appears to have a positive effect. In these circumstances, Mondays and Fridays are recommended, as play appears to help the child process stress from the weekend and reconnect with the teacher on Monday (often making the whole week go better); on Friday, play helps prepare the child for a stressful weekend. One 30-minute (not including pickup time) and one 5-to-10-minute free choice or center periods with play per day are recommended for full-day programs and one 30-minute for half-day programs. All day programs benefit from placing the longer play period at the end of the morning session and the shorter one at the end of the afternoon session. They not only are used to build bonds and help the child process stress but provide the teacher with a wonderful medium to teach social skills and reward appropriate behavior. A little later in the year, after secure teacher-child bonds are built, the 30-minute periods become very powerful and meaningful rewards children can work toward or lose (part of) depending on their behavior. Care must be taken not to abuse this. Counselors and PALS partners use these 30-minute play periods to coach and assist teachers and to work with multiple children in the classroom versus individually in the playroom.

Certain traditional playroom toys work well in classrooms and others do not. Such toys as guns, foam swords, Big Wheels trucks, military vehicles, toys with violent TV or movie themes, and action figures including soldiers tend to overexcite some at-risk children, predispose others to conflict, and make certain teachers anxious or even unwilling to use play in the classroom. Miniature toys versus pretend play items such as baby dolls are also easier for some teachers to display, store, and manage, especially in grade 1 and 2 classrooms. A kit for Pre-K–2 classrooms consists primarily of miniature families (farm, dinosaur, zoo, and human), career figures (doctor, police, etc.), vehicles (police, passenger, school bus, ambulance, and fire), and a few pretend play items (baby doll, bottle, etc.). Two identical sets of miniatures, each in their own plastic box (with a lid), are recommended so they can be quickly moved to separate areas of the classroom to create instant play centers and stored easily on shelves or in cupboards when not in use. Having two identical sets also reduces conflicts over popular items.

Rules that need to be established first before using play centers in classrooms include the following:

1. "Symbolic" expression of aggression through play is acceptable, but no one is for hurting and the toys are not for taking or breaking. Teachers and children are taught to distinguish the difference between the symbolic expression of aggression during symbolic play versus real violence during play. This is emphasized to prevent them from becoming anxious or confused about what is appropriate in play or even stop using play. It is important to note that it is simply not true that appropriate symbolic expression of aggression leads to actual aggression. When adults state that they are angry, they are symbolically (with words) expressing aggression. Young

children simply use and prefer play to express some feelings symbolically, hence symbolic play. As children develop, they gradually replace symbolic play with symbolic verbal expression.

2. Limit both the area in which play can occur in each center and the number of children who can be at any given center at the same time.

3. Keep an eye on the play centers while roaming to make sure play does not escalate into inappropriate behaviors as well as watching for opportunities to teach social skills.

4. Give language to play while roaming versus using it as time to catch up on paperwork.

5. Note shifts in play over time.

6. Use loss of time in play centers as the most meaningful and immediate consequence for breaking center rules.

Triage in School Settings: Teacher- versus Counselor-Based Interventions

Various sources (Beland, 1997; Cowen et al., 1996; Dwyer & Osher, 2000; NAEYC, 1996) indicate that 13% to 30% of students today require some form of behavioral intervention at one of two levels: focused or intermediate. When teachers are successfully applying intervention strategies in the classroom, triage priorities often change from the traditional "worst case first" to "worst case in the highest-risk classroom first." Anyone who has worked very long in the school system knows that a certain percentage of teachers may not use play or the other methods described here despite training and coaching. This means that about 3% of students, usually in the highest-risk classrooms, are served with a "focused" intervention such as play therapy first. In these cases the counselor can provide the bonding part of the intervention plan through individual play therapy. This facilitates the needed adult-child bond and gives the child a regular opportunity to process emotional stress. To be effective however weekly, 30-minute individual sessions are needed throughout the school year. The boundaries part of the plan would be facilitated by the counselor or PALS partner through helping the teacher establish developmentally appropriate rules, instructions, rewards, and consequences. Approximately 22% of students can be served solely by coaching the remaining teachers to use the intermediate, inclusive interventions of bonding, boundaries, and language described above in their classrooms. The remaining 75% of students can be served by developmentally appropriate methods of teaching social skills and having positive, well-designed, school- or districtwide discipline procedures in place: the foundation. This system requires counselors to schedule and use their time somewhat differently: roughly two days per week providing focused interventions (play therapy, etc.), two days providing assistance with intermediate, inclusive interventions (classroom coaching, etc.), and one day for the foundation (assisting with positive discipline, early identification, team meetings, and teaching social skills). Administrators are encouraged to include rating teacher-student interaction skills as part of all teachers' performance assessments when they work with young children. Unfortunately, because of the impact teachers can have on young children's brain development and related capacities, there is no middle ground in early childhood education: adults either help or hurt at this stage of child development.

Initial and Ongoing Staff Development and Support at All Levels

Teachers need about 24 hours of training split into at least two events about a month apart. This is because (1) the concepts of using play and giving language to the drivers of misbehavior are foreign to most educators; (2) they need time to practice and be coached in the classroom to learn the skills; (3) they need to see the model work to accept it; and (4) too little training has been found to be counterproductive. School counselors and other behavior support staff receive an additional 18 to 24 hours of training to learn to act as PALS partners (coaches) in classrooms and two additional days, if needed, in child-centered play therapy.

Teachers need ongoing support and training to sustain their skills. No more teachers are trained than there are PALS partners available to support them. Peer support is provided at 30-minute focus groups facilitated by a PALS partner and usually held after school every other week. PALS partners also visit classrooms on a regular basis to observe, model, and record observations or suggestions for later discussion with teachers. Partners meet monthly at a districtwide focus and support group facilitated by the district's PALS coordinator(s). The PALS coordinator also facilitates three administrator meetings annually to ensure continued support and collaboration. Annual one-day refresher training is provided to all PALS veteran staff at the beginning of each school year. It is strongly recommended that pre- and posttest data on at-risk students and teacher surveys be collected and compiled into an annual report by the PALS coordinator and presented to the school board and administrators.

District- or Regionwide Collaboration

The most critical component to success is collaboration among all staff at all levels. Initially, it was thought that developing an inclusive, teacher-friendly, early intervention model based on the research was a prescription for success. However, experience has shown that without collaboration among staff at all levels regarding implementation, any program, no matter how effective, will eventually fail. To build collaboration within the school system on issues such as discipline, evaluation, and service delivery policies and procedures, implementation planning, funding, and staff development coordination, PALS begins with a two-day training for administrators, school counselors, psychologists, social workers, and key teachers. Ideally, this takes place no later than early spring prior to fall implementation. The training reviews what works and does not work in school-based interventions, overviews the PALS program, and sets a three-year minimum time line for full implementation. Participants identify and assess existing intervention efforts in their district or region, assess and define intervention needs and obstacles, and decide whether to commit to implementation. This process helps circumvent problems created by administrative changes, political shifts, funding issues, lack of leadership, disagreement among staff, new or competing programs, and shortsighted planning. The training concludes with all staff signing collaboration agreements that spell out their responsibilities prior to implementation. A recommendation is made to propose to the school board to put the program into the district's five-year school improvement and staff development plans.

DISCIPLINE, ASSESSMENT, AND SERVICE DELIVERY POLICIES AND PROCEDURES

Another common issue is the absence of clear Pre-K–2 discipline and violence intervention policies and procedures. This issue stems from the fact that, in the past, preschool and elementary programs did not have the discipline and violence problems they experience today. Research is clear on this point that well-designed, consistent school- or districtwide discipline policies and procedures that are positive and proactive, not just focused on punishment, are necessary to build a successful intervention program for at-risk children (Sprague & Walker, 2000).

PROACTIVE BEHAVIORAL SCREENING, RATING, AND ASSESSMENT

Many early childhood educators are reluctant to identify these children as at-risk for fear of stigmatizing them later. But research is clear: children who demonstrate antisocial behaviors early are often antisocial later and so early, proactive identification is critical (Sprague & Walker, 2000). Districts are encouraged to adopt one set of procedures and tools for initial screening, rating, and gathering of data that meets the legal requirements laid out by the Individuals with Disabilities Education Act (IDEA). Educators are inundated with repetitive paperwork of all kinds. Discipline referrals to the principal require one process, referrals to the counselor another, referrals to the student assistance team (SAT) still another, and referrals to Special Education (Sp. Ed.) for school psychological evaluations and functional behavioral assessments (FBA) yet another. Adding another process for play-based, early intervention is usually met with resistance by staff. In addition, regular education and Special Education tend to operate autonomously, further complicating the process. As a result, PALS encourages districts to view the process of intervening with behaviorally challenging children on a continuum rather than as a set of separate processes. This continuum ranges from the teacher's first attempt to intervene in the classroom with PALS, to Sp. Ed. evaluations and placements. At the two-day training, staff develop a plan to collaborate to integrate, consolidate, and simplify the various policies, procedures, and forms into one workable set. A four-tiered set of procedures is recommended that span from teachers and peers to the counselor or PALS partner to SAT to Special Education. This same set serves all levels of the existing intervention process including PALS. No matter who initiates the procedure, all staff start by having the classroom teacher fill out a one-page behavior worksheet that identifies environmental triggers and behavioral drivers and a one-page intervention plan that includes bonding as well as boundaries. Both are designed for use by the teacher or any of the specialists on the continuum. These forms assist teachers in designing their own PALS intervention strategy (including using play) or getting assistance from peers, their PALS partner or the counselor, and SAT. As part of the second intervention procedure, teachers are also trained to complete a behavior rating scale. Counselors and behavior support staff are taught to interpret the rating scale for screening risk levels, writing SAT or individual education plan (IEP) behavioral goals, and documenting behavioral change. The Conners (1989) Teacher Rating Scale (CTRS-39) is recommended. These procedures give the counselor, SAT team, and school psychologist the initial documentation and information needed to proceed and assess outcomes without asking the teacher to use another set of procedures and tools. The same forms can also be used to make SAT, Special Education, or discipline referrals.

PALS FIVE-YEAR CASE STUDY

The following case illustrates how potent a collaborative relationship among play therapists, counselors, and teachers can be in facilitating change with severely at-risk children while maximizing service delivery.

Four-year-old Joey was in preschool and his teacher was PALS-trained. Both his teacher and her PALS partner (the author) observed Joey's behavior to be extremely demanding, impulsive, sullen, emotional, indulgent, quarrelsome, moody, unpredictable, violent, and defiant. This is the kind of behavior pattern that often results in preschool expulsion. Joey was rated using the CTRS-39. He scored clinically significant in three of the five scales that measure social-emotional behavior (conduct problem, indulgent-emotional, asocial). Joey received initial play-based assessment sessions with the author in which possible sexual abuse was detected and confirmed by the mother. Once it was reported to social services, however, the mother denied it, nothing was done by social services, and permission to do further individual play therapy at school with Joey was withdrawn.

An alternative was to coach the teacher to intervene in the classroom as part of her normal classroom duties related to discipline and teaching social skills. First a Bonding Plan was devised consisting of where, when, and how frequently the teacher would have symbolic play centers. She planned specifically what she might do and say while roaming to these centers, including sample statements she could make during Joey's play. One difference between PALS and Filial Therapy is that the teacher cannot spend more than a few minutes at a time giving language to themes during play, as she must roam from center to center as well as manage the classroom.

Joey, like most at-risk children, usually chose either the blocks with miniatures or housekeeping centers versus art or science centers. Observing Joey's play in the classroom, the teacher and her PALS partner identified various themes, including perpetrator, victim, fear, anger, protection, safety, empowerment, and punishment. He often selected aggressive toys to attack mother, child, or baby symbols as well as protector symbols. When at a play center with Joey, his teacher was coached by her PALS partner to enter the interaction by leveling (sitting, kneeling, etc. at the child's level) and making a tracking statement: "The shark is trying to hurt the baby dolphin." Then, pausing to observe his reaction, she was coached to ask herself silently "What do the shark and the dolphin each feel, need, or believe?" and then to make one or two thematic statements: "The baby dolphin is scared of the shark." Again pausing to observe, she followed this with another statement: "The shark is angry and thinks it's okay to hurt the dolphin." She was then coached to say "You can keep playing and I'll be back in a little bit to see what you're doing." She would then roam to art and other centers, then back to Joey, attending and giving language to his play again. This usually occurred three to six times during a daily 30-minute period called Plan, Do and Review. Her PALS partner shadowed her, gave suggestions and praise, and in some cases modeled the skills. Within a few weeks, the teacher built a strong bond with Joey, reduced some of his problem behaviors, and greatly increased her skills at identifying themes in play and giving language to them.

A Boundaries Plan was developed by the teacher with the PALS partner's help. It consisted of identifying when and where problem behaviors occurred, possible triggers and drivers, sample driver statements, substitute skills, and meaningful rewards and consequences. Joey lived in a dysfunctional family where limit setting ranged from being very harsh to nonexistent. The teacher and PALS partner reasoned that one belief driver was "If I'm angry, it's okay to hurt others or destroy objects." Many of Joey's aggressive and destructive behaviors occurred when he became frustrated during center play time and transitions. When the teacher saw that Joey was acting out aggressively, she was coached to (1) intervene and make the classroom safe; (2) ask herself silently what Joey feels, needs, or believes that is driving his behavior; (3) take a deep breath; (4) level and get his attention by making eye contact; and (5) state in a calm voice "Somewhere it's okay to hit when you're angry" (belief driver). She was then coached to observe if the driver was correct and say "You can take a deep breath (modeling) or tell someone you're angry (substitute behavior)." Again, she was coached to pause to allow Joey to comprehend the alternatives, then state "But at school people are not for hurting when you're angry (rule). When you hurt someone at a center you have to leave that center for a little while (meaningful consequence). You can go to art or science now and I'll come and get you when it's time to come back here." In the case where he had not hit or hurt someone or something yet, but was very close, the teacher was coached to level and say "I'm worried you may hurt Tim because you're so angry" (anger driver). She was coached to then pause for observation and comprehension and say "You can use your words and say to Tim 'I'm angry.'" After a brief pause she stated "Tim, I'm mad that you took my dinosaur. Please give it back. Or you can go to the feelings center and come back and say it" (proactive substitute skills). If Joey didn't cooperate, the teacher was coached to say "I'd be sad if you had to leave this center for hurting Tim and I know you wouldn't like that either" (cause-effect reminder). Then she might roam, keeping an eye on Joey. She was also coached to protect herself and the other child if necessary.

Another feeling theme that emerged was Joey's explosive anger about his abuse experience. Part of the Boundaries Plan was to coach the teacher to anticipate a violent outburst by giving language to his anger and redirecting him to acceptable substitute skills. For instance, when his teacher saw an explosion building, she was coached to safely get close, level, make eye contact, and say "You're so angry today you feel like hitting if you don't like what someone does (anger driver). You can go to the feelings center, take a deep breath, or tell someone if you're angry. You decide (proactive substitute skills). It's okay here to be mad but not okay to hurt someone (rule and separating feelings from actions). I'll come back in a little while to see how you're doing." The teacher then roamed to other centers, keeping an eye on Joey. Joey got angry but went to the feelings center, expressed his anger appropriately, and returned to the block center. The teacher was coached to approach Joey and say "Even though you got mad at Tim you didn't hurt him" (Joey smiles at his teacher). She then said, "It makes you feel good when you can be the boss of your anger" (encouragement). She also could have said, "You worked hard to control your anger" (encouragement). Each of the boundary-building scenarios described above took only several minutes. There will always be times in the school environment when such interventions would not be possible or even safe, so teachers are trained to build this into their expectations, trying to sandwich this type of intervention in as much as is humanly possible.

By midyear, Joey's aggressive behavior had been reduced, but his play scenarios still contained themes of anger and protection. He also began to engage in a wider range of classroom activities that gave the teacher another medium to extend their bond. For instance, the teacher was coached to sandwich encouraging statements into her instruction, such as "You want me to see how hard you worked on your picture today" or "You finished cutting that out even though it was hard!" Joey finished the year a happier child, more interested in learning, and better able to control his anger. His Conners posttest showed a significant reduction in risk in two of the three scales that were clinically elevated (indulgent-emotional and asocial); he also showed a moderate reduction in risk on the third elevated scale (conduct problem). Although still aggressive, he was rarely physically violent.

Joey's kindergarten teacher and her aide were also PALS-trained, but neither ever became comfortable giving language during play. The teacher really did not bond well with Joey either, but the aide was more positive and seemed to develop a better relationship. Fortunately, they both gave language during limit setting to the drivers of misbehavior, generally used the PALS' Boundary Plan that was developed, and allowed symbolic play on a daily basis. The author or another PALS partner gave language during play and limit setting with Joey and several other at-risk children in the classroom for about 30 minutes each week. Joey sustained the gains he made in preschool through the end of his kindergarten year despite his teacher's limitations.

Joey's first-grade teacher was PALS-trained and very skillful at building bonds and boundaries, but play periods were not part of her routine. So, in addition to the Boundary Plan, we developed a Bonding Plan where the teacher was coached to use her contact during learning activities to build a bond, enhance learner self-image, and encourage mastery. For instance, while the teacher was roaming helping students with math, she was coached to level and sandwich in language regarding Joey's learner themes, such as "You're not sure how to start" or "You're thinking hard about that problem." Then she would proceed to teach Joey as she normally would. She was then coached to encourage Joey with statements like "It makes you feel good when you try and get the right answer." By the end of his first-grade year, Joey showed a significant reduction in risk in all three elevated scales, an absence of aggressive behavior, and was working at grade level academically.

In his second-grade year, he regressed somewhat (as compared to first grade) in both the conduct problem scale related to aggression and the asocial scale related to social skills. His teacher was not PALS-trained, nor did she receive any coaching. Though a warm and caring person, she was very inconsistent and chaotic in her setting of boundaries. Joey's temporary regression appeared to be due in part to academic stress that often accompanies the transition from first to second grade and in part to the chaotic classroom environment. Joey's third-grade teacher was not PALS-trained either, received no coaching, and was not particularly warm with students. But she did set limits adequately in a more traditional manner. Joey's regression completely reversed in third grade in all scales and was his best year yet, both academically and behaviorally. One possible reason for this is that his teacher's classroom boundaries may have been more important at this developmental stage than bonding (within reason), because Joey had experienced two previous positive teacher attachments and was more interested in peer relations.

The research indicates that if a child exhibits antisocial behavior early on, he or she will continue to be antisocial unless there is a successful intervention (Conners, 1989; Sprague & Walker, 2000). If a child finishes grade 3 without showing signs of an emotional or behavioral disorder, one is much less likely to develop later. Joey has completed grade 3 successfully with all his Conners scales in the normal range for his age and gender. His academic performance is above grade level in math and at grade level in reading, and his prognosis is good despite living in an extended family environment with multiple risk factors, including poverty and substance abuse. Joey's case is not an isolated one, as posttests on 68% of 36 other very at-risk children being followed showed and sustained a significant reduction in risk.

The PALS partner's role over the course of the first three years was that of a coach versus a traditional counselor. Because Joey's teachers in second and third grade were not PALS-trained, no coaching occurred after first grade. This illustrates how potent Joey's Pre-K–1 teachers were as change agents. It is important to note that the PALS coaching was critical to the ongoing success of the teachers' interventions and it is unlikely that most teachers would be as successful without that ongoing support.

BRIEF OVERVIEW OF FIVE YEARS OF PALS OUTCOME DATA

Five years of outcome data have been collected on 13 children judged to be extremely high-risk by the Conners Rating Scale (two or more of the five scales related to social-emotional problems had to be at 65 T or above). They all received PALS intervention services at the Pre-K–2 level. Although these results are only preliminary, they are very promising. The study appears to indicate (comparing pretests from the fall of 1995 to posttests from the spring of 2000) that 77% of the 13 at-risk children showed a significant reduction in risk. Risk was measured by the 39-item Conners Teacher Rating Scale (CTRS-39), which has been shown to be a valid screener for children's behavioral disorders (Conners, 1989). Specifically, 10 of the 13 subjects (77%) dropped in two or more of the elevated pretest scales one standard deviation or more (2-point code) without any of the original pretest scales that were below 65 T rising above 65 T (the level indicating clinical significance) on the posttests. In addition to the original group of 13 above, another 24 children are being followed with two to four years of posttest data. Looking at the entire group of 37 participants, 68% showed a significant reduction in risk. A comparison group is planned to start in fall of 2001.

Positive anecdotal evidence has been surfacing as well. Teachers and principals are reporting fewer behavior problems than before with children who have received PALS early intervention services, despite the fact that the number of at-risk children in these school districts appears unchanged. It also appears (at the Pre-K–3 level) that fewer referrals are being seen for Special Education, discipline, and counseling. One district reported a 57% reduction in discipline referrals to the principal after one year at the K–2 level and an overall improvement in conflict resolution districtwide at the Pre-K–3 level.

SUMMARY

The incidence and severity of violence in schools has increased significantly over the past 30 years. Research indicates that impaired caregiver-child attachment is a primary risk factor for violence. Brain, attachment, and child development research indicate that to be successful, intervention must begin early and be developmentally appropriate for young children. The mental health system in agencies and schools is overloaded and many programs that do exist do not begin early enough or do not utilize developmentally appropriate strategies when they do. Pre-K–2 teachers, due to their consistent and frequent contact with at-risk children, may be better positioned than most professionals to intervene early. Research shows that a secure teacher-child attachment can partially compensate for an insecure one with a caregiver, thereby reducing risk.

Play is one of the most developmentally appropriate mediums to reach and socialize children. The Play And Language to Succeed™ Model (PALS) trains school counselors, play therapists, and Pre-K–2 teachers to intervene early, using the three key elements of bonding, boundaries, and language to form positive attachments and teach social skills via play and other developmentally appropriate practices. The components that are necessary for successful implementation of PALS are (1) inclusive, classroom-based interventions by teachers; (2) individual and small group play therapy; (3) initial and ongoing districtwide staff development and support; (4) ongoing administrative and staff collaboration regarding program implementation; and (5) early, proactive behavioral screening, rating, and assessment. The rationale and framework for the PALS model were derived from B. Guerney's work in Filial-Play Therapy (1964) and Louise Guerney's work in parenting skills (1981/1992), the application of Piaget's child development theories as described by Bredekamp (1993), and the brain and attachment research described by Shore (1997). The case study in this chapter illustrated how potent a collaborative relationship among play therapists, counselors, and teachers can be in facilitating change with severely at-risk children while maximizing service delivery. Five years of outcome data appear to demonstrate the model's effectiveness.

Interventions for at-risk children ideally should begin by age 7, utilize developmentally appropriate methods including play, address attachment needs, and be, at least in part, school-based. The author can be reached at pals@frontier.net, 800-960-PALS, or www.pals4schools.com.

REFERENCES

Barton, H.A., Hopkins, K.N., McElhaney, S.J., Heigel, J., & Salassi, A. (1995). *Getting started: The NMHA directory of model programs to prevent mental disorders and promote mental health.* Alexandria, VA: National Mental Health Association.

Beland, K. (1997). *Second step: A violence prevention curriculum teacher's guide-grades 1–3* (2nd ed., p. 1). Seattle, WA: Committee for Children

Bredekamp, S. (Ed.). (1993). *Developmentally appropriate practice in early childhood programs serving children from birth through age eight.* Washington, DC: National Association for the Education of Young Children.

Carlsson-Paige, N., & Levin, D.E. (1992, November). Making peace in violent times: A constructivist approach to conflict resolution. *Young Children,* 4–13.

Chaloner, W.B. (1996). *The language of challenging children: A guide to changing problem behavior in Pre-K-2 classrooms.* Durango, CO: BCA Publishing.

Chaloner, W.B. (1998, July 9). *Building teacher-child attachments as the central early intervention strategy with behaviorally at-risk Pre K-2 children.* Unpublished research paper presented at Head Start's fourth annual research conference, Washington, DC.

Children's Defense Fund. (2000). *Yearbook 2000: The state of America's children.* Washington, DC: Author.

Cohen, N.J., Muir, E., Lojkasek, M., Muir, R., Parker, C., Barwick, M., & Brown, M. (1999). Watch, wait, and wonder: Testing the effectiveness of a new approach to mother-infant psychotherapy. *Infant Mental Health Journal, 20*(4), 429–451.

Conners, C.K. (1989). *Manual for Conners' Rating Scales.* New York: Multi-Health Systems.

Coufal, J.D., & Brock, G.W. (1979). Parent-child relationship enhancement: A skills training approach. In N. Stinnett, B. Chesser, & J. DeFrain (Eds.), *Building family strengths: Blueprints for action* (Vol. 1, pp. 196–221). Lincoln: University of Nebraska Press.

Cowen, E.L., Hightower, A.D., Pedro-Carroll, J.L., Work, W.C., Wyman, P.A., & Haffey, W.G. (1996). *School-based prevention for children at risk: The Primary Mental Health Project.* Washington, DC: American Psychological Association.

Dwyer, K., & Osher, D. (2000). *Safeguarding our children: An action guide.* Washington, DC: U.S. Departments of Education and Justice, American Institutes for Research.

Egeland, B. (1996). Mediators of the effects of child maltreatment on developmental adaptation in adolescence. In D. Cicchetti & S.L. Toth (Eds.), *Rochester Symposium on Developmental Psychopathology: The effects of trauma on the developmental process* (Vol. 8). Rochester, NY: University of Rochester Press.

Egeland, B., Carlson, B.E., & Sroufe, L.A. (1993). Resilience as process. In *Development and psychopathology* (p. 520). New York: Cambridge University Press.

Elicker, J., & Fortner-Wood, C. (1995, November). Adult-child relationships in early childhood programs. *Young Children, 51*(1), 69–78.

Elkind, D. (1986, May). Formal education and early childhood education: An essential difference. *Phi Delta Kappan,* 631–636.

Elkind, D. (1988). The resistance to developmentally appropriate educational practice with young children: The real issue. In C. Warger (Ed.), *Public school early child programs.* Alexandria, VA: Association for Supervision and Curriculum Development.

Fein, G., & Rivkin, M. (1986). *The young child at play: Reviews of research* (Vol. 4). Washington, DC: National Association for the Education of Young Children.

Forman, G., & Kuschner, D. (1983). *The child's construction of knowledge: Piaget for teaching children.* Washington, DC: National Association for the Education of Young Children.

Goleman, D. (1995). *Emotional intelligence: Why it can matter more than IQ.* New York: Bantam Books.

Greenberg, S.H. (1997, Spring/Summer). The loving ties that bond. *Newsweek: Your child from birth to three* [Special issue]. 68–72.

Guerney, B. (1964). Filial Therapy: Description and rationale. *Journal of Consulting Psychology, 28,* 304–310.

Guerney, B., & Flumen, A.B. (1970). Teachers as psychotherapeutic agents for withdrawn children. *Journal of School Psychology, 8,* 107–113.

Guerney, L.F. (1992). *Parenting: A skills training manual.* State College, PA: Institute for the Development of Emotional and Life Skills.

Guerney, L.F., & Wolfgang, G. (1981, Spring). Long-range evaluation of effects on foster parents of a foster parent skills training program. *Journal of Clinical Child Psychology,* 33–37.

Hawkins, J.D., Catalano, R.F., & Miller, J.Y. (1992). Risk and protective factors for alcohol and other drug problems. *Psychological Bulletin, 112*(1), 64–105.

James, B. (1994). Human attachments and trauma. In B. James (Ed.), *Handbook for treatment of attachment-trauma problems in children* (p. 2). New York: Free Press.

Landreth, G.L. (1991). *Play therapy: The art of the relationship.* Muncie, IN: Accelerated Development.

National Association for the Education of Young Children. (1996). *National Association for the Education of Young Children's position statement on violence in the lives of children.* Washington, DC: Author.

Oppenheim, D., Sagi, A., & Lamb, M.E. (1988). Infant-attachments on the kibbutz and their relation to socioemotional development four years later. *Developmental Psychology 24,* 427–433.

Oxman, L. (1971). *The effectiveness of Filial Therapy: A controlled study.* Unpublished doctoral dissertation, Rutgers University, New Brunswick, NJ.

Perry, B.D. (1996). Incubated in terror: Neurodevelopmental factors in the cycle of violence. In J.D. Osofsky (Ed.), *Children, youth and violence: Searching for solutions.* New York: Guilford Press.

Piaget, J. (1950). *The psychology of intelligence.* London: Routledge & Kegan Paul.

Ramey, C.T., & Ramey, S.L. (1998). Early intervention and early experience. *American Psychologist, 53*(2), 109–120.

Ray, D. (1998, October). *What the research shows about play therapy.* Paper presented at the International Play Therapy conference, Phoenix, AZ.

Renken, B., Egeland, B., Marvinney, D., Mangelsdorf, S., & Sroufe, L.A. (1989). Early childhood antecedents of aggression and passive-withdrawal in early elementary school. *Journal of Personality, 57*(2), 257–281.

Rogers, C.S., & Sawyers, J.K. (1988). *Play in the lives of children.* Washington, DC: National Association for the Education of Young Children.

Schaps, E., & Battistich, V. (1991). Promoting health development through school-based prevention: New approaches. In E.N. Goplerud (Ed.), *Office for Substance Abuse Prevention Monograph 8,* 127–181.

Scherer, M. (1996). On our changing family values: A conversation with David Elkind. In M. Scherer (Ed.), *The best of educational leadership* (pp. 13–17). Alexandria, VA: Association for Supervision and Curriculum Development.

Shore, R. (1997). *Rethinking the brain: New insights into early development.* New York: Families and Work Institute.

Sprague, J., & Walker, H. (2000). Early identification and intervention for youth with antisocial and violent behavior. *Exceptional Children, 66*(3), 367–379.

Stover, L., & Guerney, B.G. (1967). The efficacy of training procedures from others in Filial Therapy. *Psychotherapy: Theory, Research and Practice, 4,* 110–115.

Vernon, A. (1998). Promoting prevention: Applications of rational emotive behavior therapy. *Beyond Behavior, Council for Children with Behavioral Disorders, 9*(2), 14.

Walker, H.M., Severson, H.H., & Feil, E.G. (1995). *Early screening project: A proven child-find process.* Longmont, CO: Sopris West.

Werner, E.E. (1987). Vulnerability and resilience in children at risk for delinquency: A longitudinal study from birth to young adulthood. In J. Bouchard & S.N. Bouchard (Eds.), *Prevention of delinquent behavior.* Beverly Hills, CA: Sage.

Werner, E.E., & Smith, R.S. (1982). *Vulnerable but invincible: A longitudinal study of resilient children and youth.* New York: McGraw-Hill.

Werner, E.E., & Smith, R.S. (1992). *Overcoming the odds: High risk children from birth to adulthood.* Ithaca, NY: Cornell University Press.

Yale Child Study Center. (1996). *Collaborative for the advancement of social and emotional learning* (Casel directory). New Haven, CT: Author.

Index